Law and Bioethics: The Beginning of Life in China

Chinese and Comparative Law Series

VOLUME 14

The titles published in this series are listed at brill.com/ccls

To my grandfather Luciano, who taught me the value of education,
And to my friend Claudio, who keeps teaching me that knowledge is never enough

A journey of a thousand *li* starts beneath one foot

DAO DE JING, Chapter 64

Contents

Abbreviations

ART	Assisted Reproductive Technology
BSHSB	Basic Standards for Human Sperm Bank (2003)
CC	Civil Code (PRC, 2020)
CPC	Communist Party of China
CdlSP	Code de la Santé Publique
CJO	China Judgments Online
CL	Criminal Law (PRC)
DoH	Department of Health (Taiwan)
ECtHR	European Court of Human Rights
EPIHART	Ethical Principles for Implementation of HART (2001)
EPIHARTSB	Ethical Principles for Implementation of HART and Sperm Bank (2003)
ESchG	Embryonenschutzgesetz (German Embryo Protection Law)
FP	Fertility Preservation
GEPL	German Embryo Protection Law (1990)
GMC	Guomindang (国民党, Nationalist Party)
GPCL	General Principles of Civil Law (1986)
HART	Human Assisted Reproduction Technology
IVF	In Vitro Fertilisation
MAHART	Measures on Administration of HART (2001)
MIHCL	Maternal and Infant Health Care Law (1994)
ML	Marriage Law
MoH	Ministry of Health (1954–2013)
MPL	Minors Protection Law
NHC	National Health Commission (2018–)
NHFPC	National Health and Family Planning Commission (2013–2018)
NPC	National People's Congress
PAR	Posthumous Assisted Reproduction
PFPL	Population and Family Planning Law (2001)
PRC	People's Republic of China
PWRIL	Protection of Women's Rights and Interests Law (1992)
RIVF	Reciprocal In Vitro Fertilisation
RoC	Republic of China (Taiwan)
SB	Sperm Bank
SPC	Supreme People's Court
TCM	Traditional Chinese Medicine

TSHART	Technical Specifications for HART (2003)
TSHSB	Technical Specifications for Human Sperm Bank (2003)
UNESCO	United Nations Educational, Scientific and Cultural Organization
UNCRC	United Nations Convention on the Rights of the Child
WLT	Western Legal Tradition

INTRODUCTION

Bioethics and the Law: Why China?

A researcher makes genome-edited babies;[1] hospitals offer unproven cell therapies to local and international patients;[2] a scientist and a surgeon plan to transplant the head of a person paralysed neck-down onto the body of a deceased donor;[3] parents get the chance to use sperm extracted from their own son's corpse to produce a male heir.[4] Although featuring different biotechnological achievements, the news stories above share many common themes, most obviously their ability to blur the boundaries between life and death. Thus, each of them has sparked a heated debate on whether ethics and morals should set new limits on human actions and, if so, how the law should reflect these limits when science has reached so far beyond the boundaries of what was once considered 'natural.' Yet, these cases share another, less evident characteristic: They all took place in the People's Republic of China (hereafter: PRC) and/or had as their main protagonists people of Chinese origin.

This is not surprising, since bioscience is playing a major role in PRC's global competitiveness. China's 13th Five-Year Plan (2016–2020) named biomedicine, synthetic biology, and regenerative medicine as strategic fields and industries.[5] As a result, already in 2016 China was highlighted as a 'rising

---

1 Wang Jianing 王佳宁, 'Jiyin bianji ying'aer an yishen xuanpan Hejiankui deng san beigao ren bei zhuijiu xingshi zeren ' 基因编辑婴儿"案一审宣判 贺建奎等三被告人被追究刑事责任 (He Jiankui and Other Three Defendants Prosecuted for Criminal liability)' 新华网 (*Xinhuanet*) (30 December 2019) <http://www.xinhuanet.com/legal/2019-12/30/c_1125403802.htm> accessed 13 December 2021; Dennis Normile, 'Chinese Scientist Who Produced Genetically Altered Babies Sentenced to 3 Years in Jail' <https://www.science.org/content/article/chinese-scientist-who-produced-genetically-altered-babies-sentenced-3-years-jail> accessed 13 December 2021.

2 David Cyranoski, 'China Urged to Abandon Plan to Sell Unproven Cell Therapies' [2019] Nature <https://www.nature.com/articles/d41586-019-01725-2> accessed 13 December 2021.

3 Grigorios Gkasdaris and Theodossios Birbilis 'First Human Head Transplantation: Surgically Challenging, Ethically Controversial and Historically Tempting – an Experimental Endeavor or a Scientific Landmark?' (2019) 14 Mædica 5 <https://www.ncbi.nlm.nih.gov/pmc/articles/PMC6511668/> accessed 13 December 2021.

4 'Parents given Chance to Use Sperm from Deceased Son to Produce Male Heir Raises Ethical Concerns | National Post' <https://nationalpost.com/health/posthumous-parenthood-parents-to-use-sperm-from-deceased-son> accessed 13 December 2021.

5 'Engineering a Biomedical Revolution in China – Scientific American' <https://www.scientificamerican.com/article/engineering-a-biomedical-revolution-in-china/> accessed 13 December 2021.

 | DOI:10.1163/9789004754300_002

star' in Nature Index, an open database of author affiliations and institutional relationships, with many Chinese Institutions showing rapid improvement in their research output and ranking.[6] In 2022, China overtook the US in natural science for the first time,[7] and in 2024 China moved from the second place to the first for its overall contribution to research in the four natural science categories covered by Nature Index: physical sciences, chemistry, biological sciences and Earth and environmental sciences.[8] These results have been achieved despite the fact that worsening US-China trade relations and greater restrictions imposed by Western countries on collaboration with Chinese scientists in sensitive research areas have slowed the PRC's growth in scientific publications[9] and shifted the country's focus toward self-sufficiency.[10] In particular, China's 14th Five-Year Plan (2021–2026, hereafter: the Plan), approved on 11 March 2021, clearly reflects the latter intent. The Plan pushes for self-reliance, aiming to build closer ties between academia and industry for the purpose of creating a 'strategic research force for the nation,' especially in areas like brain science, artificial intelligence, quantum information, genomics, clinical medicine, and deep-sea and deep-space exploration.[11]

The emphasis on industrial collaboration and the reduction of international cooperation shifted the system of academic evaluation and promotion from a method based on the number of publications to one that measures the impact of researchers' works on the real world. However, this certainly did not set China back in the race for scientific and technological primacy, as shown by the Nature Index's rankings mentioned above. This is also confirmed by statistics on the country's spending on research and development

---

6 'China Becomes Brightest Nature Index 2016 Rising Star | Study In China' <https://www.studyinchina.com.my/web/page/china-brightest-nature-index-2016-rising-star/> accessed 4 August 2025.

7 Chris Woolston, 'Nature Index Annual Tables 2023: China Tops Natural-Science Table' [2023] Nature <https://www.nature.com/articles/d41586-023-01868-3> accessed 28 February 2024.

8 'Nature Index 2025 Research Leaders: United States Losing Ground as China's Lead Expands Rapidly' (*Nature Index*, 11 June 2025) <https://www.nature.com/nature-index/news/nature-index-research-leaders-united-states-losing-ground-china-lead-expands-rapidly> accessed 4 August 2025.

9 Catherine Armitage, 'Fresh Twists in China's Bid for Research Dominance' (2021) 593 Nature S1 <https://www.nature.com/articles/d41586-021-01401-4> accessed 13 December 2021.

10 Smriti Mallapaty, 'China's Five-Year Plan Focuses on Scientific Self-Reliance' (2021) 591 Nature 353 <https://www.nature.com/articles/d41586-021-00638-3> accessed 13 December 2021.

11 Ibid.

(hereafter R&D). For example, according to 'PRC's Statistical Report on National Economic and Social Development in 2020' (*Zhongghua renmin gongheguo 2020 nian guomin jingji he shehui fazhang tongji gongbao* 中华人民共和国 2020 年国民经济和社会发展统计公报)[12] released on 28 February 2021 by the National Bureau of Statistics (*Guojia tongji ju* 国家统计局), in 2020, China spent 2,4426 trillion Renminbi (approx. 378 billion USD) on R&D, corresponds to 2.4% of its gross domestic product (hereafter: GDP), a growth of 10.3% compared to 2019.[13] Even though this marked was the slowest annual percentage increase in the past five years, down from the annualised 12.5% rise in 2019,[14] the total outlay set a new record for China[15] and a great achievement, in particular considering the overall global decline in R&D spending due to the Covid-2019 pandemic crisis.[16]

The political and economic reasons behind China's determination to emerge as a global biotech powerhouse are clear and known. Indeed, many European, American, and Chinese authors highlight the strategic importance of biotechnological development for a populous and rapidly aging country like the PRC.[17] As a matter of fact, biotech innovation can give new impetus to China's economic development, which has slowed since the early 2010s, and, at the same time, improve the quality of life and healthy life expectancy for millions of Chinese citizens. Hence, biotechnology could help the PRC become a 'great modern socialist country' with a moderately prosperous society, and help secure its sizable international prestige and power – a goal that its leaders have promised and since 2018 is even stated in the Preamble of its Constitution.[18]

---

12 Zhonghua renmin gongheguo 2020 nian guomin jingji he shejui fazhang tongji gongbao '中华人民共和国 2020 年国民经济和社会发展统计公报' <http://www.stats.gov.cn/tjsj/zxfb/202102/t20210227_1814154.html> accessed 13 December 2021. In the following pages, the pinyin system will be used to transcribe Chinese names and terms, and the Hepburn system will be used to transcribe Japanese names and terms. Proper names will be transcribed according to Chinese and Japanese usage, with the surname always preceding the given name.

13 Ibid.

14 Armitage (2*n*9).

15 Sam Shead, 'China's Spending on Research and Development Hits a Record $378 Billion' (*CNBC*, 1 March 2021) <https://www.cnbc.com/2021/03/01/chinas-spending-on-rd-hits-a-record-378-billion.html> accessed 13 December 2021.

16 'How Will COVID-19 Reshape Science, Technology and Innovation?' (*OECD*) <https://www.oecd.org/coronavirus/policy-responses/how-will-covid-19-reshape-science-technology-and-innovation-2332334d/> accessed 13 December 2021.

17 Ibid.

18 Constitution of the People's Republic of China 2018, Preamble, paragraph 7.

The international community follows China's growing pursuit of technological proficiency with a mixture of admiration and concern, with the latter usually prevailing. Articles in international publications describing China's accomplishments frequently also voice worries that China could use its technical monopoly to impose its authoritarian political model on the rest of the globe.[19] In addition, many foreign observers depict the PRC as the 'Wild East' of biomedical research,[20] pointing to the country's 'lax ethical environment' and lack of proper legislation as the main reasons behind its rise in medicine.[21]

It seems incredible that not even twenty years have elapsed since the creation of the world's first human-rabbit embryos (2001) or the outbreak of SARS (2003),[22] when – acknowledging the lack of a sound bioethical framework in China on the one hand, and the pressure of biomedical market on the other – Chinese commentators wondered how to protect their fellow citizens from reckless researchers' miscues and prevent foreign biotech powers[23] from exploiting their country's biological resources and knowledge. At the time, the concern was that scientists from developed countries could take advantage of their experience in international trade and laws, making 'use of the ignorance and willingness of their colleagues in developing countries to carry out experiments banned in their own countries.'[24]

It was in consideration of this risk that China started to enact national regulations and enforce international standards in biosciences. It is worth remembering that, since its first formulation in 1984, the Patent Law of the PRC (*Zhongguo renmin gongheguo zhuanli fa* 中华人民共和国专利法) established in Article 5 a moral exclusion for any 'invention-creation that is contrary to social morality or the laws of the State or that is detrimental to the

---

19 'Biotechnologies in China: A State of Play' (*Fondapol*) <https://www.fondapol.org/en/study/biotechnologies-in-china-a-state-of-play/> accessed 13 December 2021.

20 Didi Kirsten Tatlow, 'A Scientific Ethical Divide Between China and West' *The New York Times* (29 June 2015) <https://www.nytimes.com/2015/06/30/science/a-scientific-ethical-divide-between-china-and-west.html> accessed 21 December 2021.

21 'China Will Always Be Bad at Bioethics – Foreign Policy' <https://foreignpolicy.com/2018/04/13/china-will-always-be-bad-at-bioethics/> accessed 20 December 2021.

22 'Engineering a Biomedical Revolution in China – Scientific American' (1*n*5).

23 Ole Doring, 'Chinese Researchers Promote Biomedical Regulations: What Are the Motives of the Biopolitical Dawn in China and Where Are They Heading?' (2004) 14 Kennedy Institute of Ethics Journal 39, 40.

24 Wolfgang Hennig, 'Bioethics in China: Although National Guidelines Are in Place, Their Implementation Remains Difficult' (2006) 7 EMBO Reports 850 <https://www.ncbi.nlm.nih.gov/pmc/articles/PMC1559670/> accessed 20 December 2021; Doring (4*n*23).

public interest.'[25] Even though it did not originally refer to the biosciences, this provision became useful in the field, starting in the first decade of the twenty-first century. Accordingly, in 2003, the Ministry of Science and Technology and, at the time, the Ministry of Health (MoH) had already issued the 'Guiding Principles on Human Embryonic Stem Cell Research Ethics' (*Ren peitai ganxibao yanjiu lunli zhidao yuanze* 人胚胎干细胞研究伦理指导原则).[26] Then, between 2009 and 2013 the MoH introduced administrative measures and regulations to govern the clinical application of medical technology and stem cells, while a national standard for laboratory animal institutes came into effect in 2014.[27] More recently, on 28 May 2019, the State Council of the PRC approved the 'Regulation of the People's Republic of China on the Administration of Human Genetic Resources' (*Zhongguo renmin gongheguo renlei yichuan ziyuan guanli tiaoli* 中华人民共和国人类遗传资源管理条例)[28] and, on 17 October 2020, the Standing Committee of the PRC National People's Congress passed the 'Biosecurity Law of the People's Republic of China' (*Zhonghua renmin gongheguo shengwu anquan fa* 中华人民共和国生物安全法, hereafter: BL).

The BL, in force since 15 April 2021, is China's first national law dedicated to biosecurity and biosafety. In formulating it, Chinese legislators considered both the concerns underlying the regulatory evolution described above and the rising aspirations of the PRC to position itself as a new leader in biotechnologies. Therefore, the BL not only aims at 'maintaining national security, preventing and responding to biosecurity hazards, safeguarding the lives and health of the people, protecting biological resources and the environment.'[29] At the same time, it promotes 'the sound development of biotechnology,' and aims to boost 'the construction of a community with a shared future for mankind' and 'the harmonious coexistence of man and nature.'[30] To reach these

25 Zhongguo renmin gongheguo zuali fa 中华人民共和国专利法 [Patent Law of the PRC] 1984 [Order No.11 of the President of the People's Republic of China].

26 Ren peitai ganxibao yanjia lunli zhidao yuanze 人胚胎干细胞研究伦理指导原则 [Guiding Principles on Human Embryonic Stem Cell Research Ethics] 2003.

27 Smriti Mallapaty, 'Engineering a Biomedical Revolution' (2018) 564 Nature S66 <https://www.nature.com/articles/d41586-018-07692-4> accessed 27 December 2021.

28 Zhonghua renmin gongheguo renlei yichuan ziyuan guanli tiaoli 中华人民共和国人类遗传资源管理条例 [Guidelines on Human Embryonic Stem Cell Research Ethics of the People's Republic of China] 2019 [Guo ling di 717 hao 国令第 717 号 (State decree n. 717)].

29 Zhonghua renmin gongheguo shengwu anquan fa 中华人民共和国生物安全法 (Biosecurity Law of the People's Republic of China) 2020 [Order No. 56 of the President of the People's Republic of China] para 1.

30 Ibid.

ambitious goals, the State will 'perform the obligations provided for by any international treaty concluded or acceded to by the PRC,'[31] and it will 'actively participate in the study and formulation of international rules on biosecurity,'[32] promoting the improvement of global security governance.[33] Furthermore, the BL acknowledges that, in order to avoid risks and overcome ignorance and suspicion of advanced biomedicine,[34] rules are not sufficient, as they should also be known and disseminated. Thus, the BL establishes that relevant institutions must transpose biosecurity laws, regulations, and knowledge into educational and training programmes to raise the awareness of students and professionals on biosecurity and ethics.[35] This should help ensure that those engaged in research, development, and application of biotechnologies conform to ethical principles, as provided for by article 34.[36] Finally, and to further protect human beings' rights and welfare from abuses, Article 40 of the BL states that clinical research on new biomedical technologies must pass an ethical review and be conducted in a medical institution with corresponding conditions.[37]

As I have pointed out above, notwithstanding such evolution and even if in the last two decades China's bioethics landscape has completely changed, ethical standards and laws continue to be at the centre of the debate, at least according to some observers. Yet, the roles of the actors involved have been swapped. The PRC now seems to pose a threat, endangering the entire planet, along (once again) with the most vulnerable Chinese citizens. Both the former and the latter risk succumbing to an almighty state riven by widespread corruption[38] that usually overlooks safety in the name of economic achievements,[39] historically/systematically placing power before ethics, and the benefit of society as a whole before the individual good;[40] a state where laws (when

31 Ibid 6.

32 Ibid.

33 Ibid.

34 Leifan Wang, Fangzhong Wang and Weiwen Zhang, 'Bioethics in China's Biosecurity Law: Forms, Effects, and Unsettled Issues' (2021) 8 Journal of Law and the Biosciences lsab019, 4 <https://doi.org/10.1093/jlb/lsab019> accessed 13 December 2021.

35 Zhonghua renmin gongheguo shengwu anquan fa 中华人民共和国生物安全法 (Biosecurity Law of the People's Republic of China) (5*n*29) para 7.2.

36 Ibid 34.2.

37 Ibid 40.

38 Hennig (4*n*24).

39 'China Will Always Be Bad at Bioethics – Foreign Policy' (4*n*21).

40 Hongqi Wang and Xin Wang, 'Medical Ethics Education in China' (2014) 4 Bioethics Education in a Global Perspective 81 <https://www.ncbi.nlm.nih.gov/pmc/articles/PMC7123482/> accessed 27 December 2021.

they exist) exist only on paper,[41] and human dignity, as well as the boundaries set by nature, have only a relative value.

In 1934, Marcel Granet described to the Western public the essence of Chinese customs as having 'neither God, nor Law.'[42] Should we conclude that they have no ethics, especially bioethics, either?

At least from the point of view of PRC's written laws, this does not seem to be the case. Alongside the law and regulations on biotechnology mentioned above, many new or recently amended Chinese statutes contain references to ethics, morality, or related principles, in particular when scientific research or medical practice is at stake. We can take as an example Article 1009 of the PRC Civil Code (民法典 *Minfadian*, 2020): 'Medical and scientific research activities concerning human genes and human embryos, among others, shall be carried out in accordance with the laws, administrative regulations and relevant provisions issued by the state, without endangering human health, *violating moral principles* or damaging public interests';[43] Article 32 of the Law of the People's Republic of China on the Promotion of Basic Medical and Health Care (*Jiben yiliao weisheng yu jiankang cujin fa* 基本医疗卫生与健康促进法, 2019): 'Clinical experiments and other medical research of drugs and medical devices shall *comply with the medical ethics* and specifications, *pass ethical review* according to the law, and obtain informed consent';[44] Article 20 of the Medicinal Product Administration Law of the People's Republic of China (*Yaoping guanli fa* 药品管理法, adopted in 1984, revised in 2001; 2013; 2015; and 2019): 'Pharmaceutical clinical trials shall be conducted *in conformity with ethical principles*, and clinical trial protocols shall be developed, subject to the *review and consent of the ethics committee*';[45] Article 51 of the Scientific and Technological Progress Law of the People's Republic of China (*Kexue jishu jinbu fa* 科学技术进步法, adopted in 1993 and revised in 2007 and 2021): 'Scientific and technological research and development institutions shall formulate their bylaws/internal regulations in accordance with the law, and conduct scientific and technological research and development activities in accordance with the functional positioning and business scope stipulated therein; they shall strengthen the improvement of conduct in scientific research and studies, establish and *improve scientific research integrity and scientific and technological ethics management systems*, and comply with *good scientific*

41 Mallapaty (5*n*27).

42 Marcel Granet, *La pensée chinoise* (3rd edn, Albin Michel 1934) 476.

43 Italics added.

44 Italics added.

45 Italics added.

research practices; they shall not organise, participate in, or support superstitious activities.'[46]

All these rules establish a duty for researchers and research institutes to comply with ethical standards and implement control mechanisms to be carried out by review/supervisory committees. The importance attached to ethics in the current Chinese context led the legislature in 2023 to include a reference to it in the Law on Legislation (立法法 *Li fa fa*), Article 8 of which now reads: 'Legislation shall [...] adhere to the combination of the rule of law and the rule of virtue, forge a strong sense of community of the Chinese nation, and promote socialist cultural-ethical progress.' Hence, why so much suspicion about China's ethical conception and the importance it attributes to it? Is it only a problem of application/ineffectiveness of these provisions, or is there something intrinsically wrong with Chinese ethics?

Thanks to the development of comparative sciences since Granet's famous assertion, increasingly, the international community has become more aware of the plurality of experiences in different cultures and better understands the need to take into account a variety of values. Regarding bioethics, the most important international conventions and declarations, such as the 'Universal Declaration on Bioethics and Human Rights' (hereafter: Declaration 2005), adopted by UNESCO's General Conference on 19 October 2005,[47] now incorporate this 'pluralistic' principle. The Declaration 2005 defines bioethics as 'ethical issues related to medicine, life sciences and associated technologies as applied to human beings, considering their social, legal and environmental dimensions' (Article 1). Article 12 remarks on 'the importance of cultural diversity and pluralism,' to which 'it should be given due regard,' unless it infringes upon 'human dignity, human rights and fundamental freedoms,' or breaches the principles set in the Declaration or limits their scope.

Does Chinese cultural diversity fall within the latter part of Article 12 of the Declaration? Are Chinese people, or China's culture, truly insensitive to ethical issues and unwilling to discuss ethical standards – as pointed out by distinguished scholars[48] – or are they rather implementing an 'ethics with Chinese characteristics' that differs from the Western concept of ethics but is equally worthy of respect? If so, what does it consist of? Is it compatible with, or antithetical to, current international standards? How could it influence legal regulation on biotechnologies, within and beyond the PRC?

46 Italics added.

47 Universal Declaration on Bioethics and Human Rights 2005.

48 Doring (4*n*23) 45.

The need to answer these questions is becoming urgent. After all, perhaps the twenty-first century will not be 'China's century,' as some experts have argued,[49] and it is probably too early to say that the 'tables have turned on the power balance between Chinese and Western culture.'[50] However, the PRC has already transformed itself from an outsider to a participant in, and even an architect of, the international system and is now in a position to bring its own interests and standards into the global arena. The idea of a strong and prosperous China 'that not only restores its own status, but also takes on a large responsibility for the world,' as advocated by Sun Yatsen at the beginning of the twentieth century[51] and revived by Xi Jinping a hundred years later as part of his 'Chinese dream of the great rejuvenation of the Chinese nation' (*Zhonghua minzu weida fuxin de zhongguo meng* 中华民族伟大复兴的中国梦), is turning into reality. Thus, being familiar with the interplay among ethics, law, and new technologies in the Chinese context will be crucial to predict and understand developments in the regulation of new technologies at the global level.

Surprisingly, however, it is very difficult to find Chinese or English book-length publications inspired by an interdisciplinary approach to the topic.

This is not to say that PRC scholars or politicians ignore the issue or underestimate its importance. During the fourth and fifth Plenary Session of the 19th Communist Party of China Central Committee (hereafter CPCCC) Chinese leaders called for improved governance of science and technology ethics.[52] The goal was then included in the CPCCC's 'Decision on Upholding and Perfecting Socialism with Chinese Characteristics and Advancing the Modernisation of the Governance System and Governance Ability' (2019) and in the 'Long-Range Objectives Throughout Year 2035' (2020). Those documents considered the strengthening of ethical supervision, the enhancement of relevant laws and regulations, and regulation of scientific activities all indispensable to

49 Honghua Men, 'China's Position in the World and Orientation of Its Grand Strategy' in Steve Tsang and Honghua Men (eds), *China in the Xi Jinping Era* (Springer International Publishing 2016) 210 <https://doi.org/10.1007/978-3-319-29549-7_12> accessed 6 January 2022.

50 Yingchun Sun, 'Tradition, Cultural Modernization, and Soft Power' in Steve Tsang and Honghua Men (eds), *China in the Xi Jinping Era* (Springer International Publishing 2016) 164 <https://doi.org/10.1007/978-3-319-29549-7_9> accessed 6 January 2022.

51 Sun Zhongshan 孙中山, 'Sun Zhongshan Xuanji 孙中山选集 [Selected Works of Sun Zhongshan]' (百度百科) <https://baike.baidu.com/item/%E5%AD%99%E4%B8%AD%E5%B1%B1%E9%80%89%E9%9B%86/2051325> accessed 19 January 2022.

52 Zhao Peng 赵鹏, Shengwu yixue yanjiu lunli guizhi de fazhi hua '生物医学研究伦理规制的法治化 [The Legalization of Ethical Regulation in Biomedical Research]' [2019] Zhongguo fafa 中国法法 25, 25.

the construction of the rule of law in Mainland China.[53] Moreover, a webinar entitled 'Bioethics and law' recently discussed the need to promote dialogue at an academic level among all the parties involved.[54] The conference, held on 29 October 2021, was organised by some of the most prestigious Chinese research centres and universities, such as the Centre for Civil and Commercial Legal Science, the Research Group on Human Embryonic Gene Editing Legislation, the Institute of Bioethics of the Centre for Ethics and Moral Construction Research of the Renmin University of China, and the Centre for Bioethics Research of Central China University of Science and Technology.[55] It was attended by more than two hundred legal scholars, ethicists, scientists and representatives of biotech industry, and it focused on the necessity to institutionalise bioethics and transform research results into laws and regulation.[56]

Scholars who have dealt with the subject, while still few in number, feel the same need, often raising the topic in the wake of sensationalist events, such as genetically altered babies mentioned above, to show how the lack of systematic analyses of the legislative role in promoting ethical governance of science and technology has social repercussion, and to call for the adoption of an interdisciplinary approach in research.[57]

Nevertheless, the trend is only just beginning. At the time of starting the project for this book (February 2022) a search on academic articles, titles or abstracts containing the terms 'bioethics' (*shenming lunli xue* 生命伦理学, or *shengwu lunli xue* 生物伦理学), 'law' (法律 *falü*), and 'China' (*Zhongguo* 中国) as keywords, in China's most comprehensive database, CNKI (China National Knowledge Infrastructure, 中国知网)[58] retrieved just 31 results between Chinese and international publications (respectively: 15 articles in Chinese and 16 in other languages). Although CNKI collects works from 1915 onwards, the old-

53 Ibid.

54 Shengming lunlixue yu falü "'生命伦理学与法律" 跨学科研讨会成功举办 ("Bioethics and Law" Interdisciplinary Symposium Successfully Held) 告|实录 – 学术公 – 中国民商法网' (中国民商法网, 21 October 2021) <https://www.civillaw.com.cn/gg/t/?id=38097> accessed 20 January 2022.

55 Ibid.

56 Ibid.

57 Zhao Peng 赵 鹏, 'Shengwu yixue yanjiu lunli guizhi de fazhihua 生物医学研究伦理规制的法治化 [The Legalization of Ethical Regulation in Biomedical Research]' [2019] *Zhongguo fafa* 中国法法 25; Zheng Ge 郑戈, 'Mai xiang shengming xian zhi – Falü ruhe huiying jiyin bianji jishu yingyong de fengxian 迈向生命宪制 -法律如何回应基因编辑技术应用中的风险 [Moving Towards Bioconstitutionalism: How Should Law Respond to the Risks Brought by Genome Editing Technologies]' (2019) 190 *Fashan yanjiu* 法 商 研 究 3.

58 'CNKI' <https://oversea-cnki-net.bibliopass.unito.it/index/> accessed 9 February 2022.

est of the articles retrieved dated from 1997 and were solely concerned with ethical problems surrounding treatments for AIDS,[59] while as few as four articles (all written in English for international journals) were published in 2021.[60]

The results of the database do not change much when replacing the term 'bioethics' with the expression considered as its old designation:[61] i.e.: 'medical ethics' (*yixue lunlixue* 医学伦理学). This trick makes it possible to retrieve articles that are about a decade older[62] and it expands the number of topics covered, allowing the inclusion of entries about, for example, moral issues related to euthanasia,[63] or the removal of organs from inmates on death row.[64] However – and despite the fact that Xi'an (Shaanxi Province) Jiatong University established the Chinese Society of Medical Ethics in 1988 and started publishing a journal entitled 'Chinese medical ethics' (*Zhongguo yixue lunlinxue* 中国医学伦理学)[65] – this change in keywords retrieved just 51 articles, only slightly more than the previous search parameters. But, by

59 Yan-Guang Wang, 'AIDS, Policy and Bioethics: Ethical Dilemmas Facing China in HIV Prevention: A Report from China' (1997) 11 Bioethics 323.

60 Hui Zhang and others, 'Patient Privacy and Autonomy: A Comparative Analysis of Cases of Ethical Dilemmas in China and the United States' (2021) 22 BMC Medical Ethics 8 <https://doi.org/10.1186/s12910-021-00579-6> accessed 2 February 2022; Lingqiao Song and Yann Joly, 'After He Jianku: China's Biotechnology Regulation Reforms' (2021) 21 Medical Law International 174 <https://doi.org/10.1177/0968533221993504> accessed 2 February 2022; Wang, Wang and Zhang (n 33); Valeria Piersanti and others, 'Surrogacy and "Procreative Tourism". What Does the Future Hold from the Ethical and Legal Perspectives?' (2021) 57 Medicina (Kaunas, Lithuania) 47.

61 Nie Jing-Bao, *Medical Ethics in China: A Transcultural Interpretation*, p 3 <https://www.routledge.com/Medical-Ethics-in-China-A-Transcultural-Interpretation/Nie/p/book/9780415724562> accessed 9 February 2022.

62 Hu Wenhao 胡文浩, 'Anlesi zhiyi 安乐死质疑 [Euthanasia Challenges]' [1988] Shije zi yixueyuan bao 石河子医学院学报 137.

63 Ibid; Wang Hongling 王鸿麟, 'Wo guo shou li anlesi anjian pagjue – Hanzhongshi fayuan xuangao liang beigao wu zui 我国首例安乐死案件判决——汉中市法院宣告两被告无罪 [Verdict in China's first euthanasia case – Hanzhong City Court acquits two defendants]' [1991] Zhongguo yinxue lunli 中国医学伦理学 27.

64 Norbert W Paul and others, 'Human Rights Violations in Organ Procurement Practice in China' (2017) 18 BMC Medical Ethics 11; Kirk C Allison and others, 'Historical Development and Current Status of Organ Procurement from Death-Row Prisoners in China' (2015) 16 BMC Medical Ethics 85; Liu Changqiu, 'Definition of Life Law and the Situation with Problems of China's Life Jurisprudence' (2008) 19 Journal International De Bioethique = International Journal of Bioethics 33.

65 'Zhongguo Yixue Lunlixue 中国医学伦理学 [Chinese Medical Ethics]' <https://oversea-cnki-net.bibliopass.unito.it/KNavi/JournalDetail?pcode=CJFD&pykm=XNLX&Year=&Issue=> accessed 9 February 2022.

simply excluding the term 'law,' CNKI retrieved 572 articles for 'bioethics' as 生命伦理学 *shenming lunli xue* and 'China,' 199 articles for 'bioethics' as *shengwu lunli xue* 生物伦理学 and 'China,' and as many as 938 articles for 'medical ethics' and 'China.' It is also noteworthy that at the conclusion of the research in summer 2025, a subsequent database search using identical parameters yielded no results. Notably, 47 publications were identified through a broader search strategy that incorporated the words 'Title, keyword, and abstract', which, it should be noted, encompasses articles on medical ethics. Nevertheless, this observation does not impact the following conclusions.

Two aspects are particularly worth mentioning. First, despite the growing number of journal articles on the issue and the increasing interest shown by Chinese political leaders, academics and the general public, legal analyses on the topic remain infrequent. In China and elsewhere, bioethics researchers may abound in medicine, philosophy or sociology, even more so now than ten years ago, but few focus on the law.[66] Moreover, the authors prefer to deal with the subject in (relatively) short reports, articles, or essays. English-language books on law and bioethics/medical ethics in Mainland China remain extremely rare, and usually focus on the legal aspects of some specific bioethical issue, for example, Li Jiang's comparative study on the patentability of human embryonic stem cells and morality in China, the United States, and Europe.[67] The few Chinese-language legal books on bioethics generally focus on criminal law and/or come at the subject from the perspective of the laws that should be enacted (*de iure condendo*) rather than discussing existing regulation (*de iure condito*). Furthermore, they usually take for granted the universality of (bio)ethics, without considering the possibility of a China-specific path. To illustrate this trend, I can cite the two works on bioethics and legal issues in medical technology, published in 2002 and 2021, by Professor Guo Zili, director of the Criminal Law Department of Beijing University Law School,[68] as well as Xu Ming's 2016 book on the legal regulation of biotechnology.[69]

---

66 Li En-Chang, 'Bioethics in China' (2008) 22 Bioethics 448, 448.

67 Li Jiang, *Regulating Human Embryonic Stem Cell in China. A Comparative Study on Human Embryonic Stem Cell's Patentability and Morality in US and EU* (Springer 2016).

68 Guo Zili 郭自力, *Xiandai yiliao jishu zhong de sheng ming lunli he falü wenti yanjiu* 现代医疗技术中的生命伦理和法律问题研究 [*Research on Bioethics and Legal Issues in Modern Medical Technology*] (Zhongguo shehui kexue chubanshe 中国社会科学出版社 2021); Guo Zili 郭自力, *Shengwu yixue de falü he lunli wenti* 生物医学的法律和伦理问题 [*The Legal and Ethical Issues on Biomedicine*] (Beijing daxue chubanshe 北京大学出版社 2002).

69 Xu Ming 徐明, *Shengming keji wenti de falü guizhi yanjiu* 生命科技问题的法律规制研究 [*Research on the legal regulation of biotechnology*] (Beijing Book Co Inc 2016).

Finding English publications on bioethics in the PRC is still difficult, even considering works not specifically dedicated to law. On the other hand, Chinese books on non-legal aspects of bioethics in Mainland China have proliferated, in particular after the publication of 'Bioethics' (生命伦理学 *Shenming lunlixue*)[70] by Professor Qiu Renzong, a researcher at the Institute of Philosophy at the Chinese Academy of Social Sciences (*shehui kexue yuan* 中国社会科学院 hereafter: CASS). Published in Shanghai in 1987, and reprinted in 1988 with a slightly different title in Hong Kong and Taiwan,[71] that book represents the first systematic study on bioethics in China, Asia and 'developing countries,'[72] and the earliest attempt at portraying the full scope of bioethics for Chinese people.[73] Since its publication, many authors have started analysing Chinese bioethics from the different viewpoints of history, tradition, philosophy, and so on.[74] However, none of these books, not even Professor Qiu's, has been translated into English.

Indeed, foreign (non-Chinese) researchers and publishers seem to be more interested in medical ethics in China. Take, for example, Paul Unshuld's book on professional ethics in imperial China, published as early as 1979,[75] or the works on ethical governance of biomedical research and practice in China edited by Professor Ole Döring.[76] Several books in English have focused on

---

70 Qiu Renzong 邱仁宗, *Shengming lunli xue* 生命伦理学 [*Bioethics*] (1st edition, Zhongguo renmin daxue chubanshe 中国人民大学出版社 2020).

71 Qiu Renzong 邱仁宗, *Shengsi zhi jian – daode nanti yu shengming lunli* 生死之间 ——— 道德难题与生命伦理 [*Between Life and Death – Moral Difficulties and Bioethics*] (Zhonghua shuju 中华书局 1988).

72 Qiu Renzong 邱仁宗, *Shengming lunli xue* 生命伦理学 [*Bioethics*] (13*n*70) 23.

73 Li En-Chang (12*n*66) 449.

74 Li Hongwen 李红文, *Daojia Wenming Lunli de Chuantong Shiyu Yu Xiandai Zhuanxing* 道家生命伦理的传统视域与现代转型 [*Taoist Bioethics: Traditional Perspectives and Modern Transformation*] (Zhongguo shehui kexue chubanshe 中国社会科学出版社 2020) <https://item.jd.com/12662791.html> accessed 15 February 2022; 黄进兴 Huang JInxing, *Cong lunxue dao lunli xue: Qing mo Min chu daode yishi de zhuanhua* 从理学到伦理学:清末民初道德意识的转化 (*From Science to Ethics: The Transformation of Moral Consciousness in the Late Qing and Early Republican Periods*) (中华书局 2014) <https://item.jd.com/11436389.html> accessed 15 February 2022.

75 Paul U Unschuld, *Medical Ethics in Imperial China. A Study in Historical Anthropology* (University of California Press 1979).

76 Ole Döring (ed), *Chinese Scientists and Responsibility: Ethical Issues of Human Genetics in Chinese and International Contexts* (Institut für Asienkunde 1999); Ole Döring (ed), *BIONET-Textbook "Life Sciences in Translation – A Sino-European Dialogue on Ethical Governance of the Life Sciences* (2009) <https://www.lse.ac.uk/researchAndExpertise/units/BIONET/pdfs/BIONET%20Textbook%20-%202nd%20Edition%20-%20Dec%2009.pdf>.

the relationship between ethics and the human body from the point of view of Chinese philosophical traditions like Confucianism, Daoism, and Mohism,[77] while others explore particular topics related to medical ethics, such as nursing ethics[78] or abortion, both in Mainland China[79] and in Taiwan.[80] Among these publications, Nie Jingbao's 2013 book[81] is particularly noteworthy. Taking advantage of being simultaneously an insider and an outsider, with respect to bioethics and culture in China and in the West,[82] Prof Nie successfully investigates medical ethics from a Chinese-Western perspective, trying to formulate a 'transcultural bioethics' (i.e.: 'an ethics that is rooted in particular cultural experiences but seeks to transcend their limitations by following ethical ideals and moral imperatives').[83] His analysis is extremely interesting and thorough. However, his book, like all those mentioned above, deals only marginally with the legal aspects of the issue.

My work aims to fill the void, using the tools of comparative law to: (1) understand whether a Chinese approach to bioethical issues exists and, if it does, what it comprises; (2) assess if and how such an approach influenced the formation of legal rules 'with Chinese characteristics' on the subject; and (3) to what extent Chinese values and legal norms are consistent with, or contradict, Western counterparts, whether they are accepted in international legislation or in force in individual European legal systems or in the United States.

To facilitate a deeper analysis, the present volume will concentrate on the relationship between ethics and the law in the realm of biotechnologies related to the formation and birth of the human being, with particular reference to the

77 Mark Csikszentmihalyi, *Material Virtue: Ethics and the Body in Early China* (Brill 2021) <https://brill.com/view/title/11174> accessed 6 January 2022; Fan Ruipinp, *Confucian Bioethics* (2002nd edn, Springer); Chris Fraser, Dan Robins and Timothy O'Leary (eds), *Ethics in Early China: An Anthology* (Hong Kong University Press 2011) <https://hongkong.universitypressscholarship.com/10.5790/hongkong/9789888028931.001.0001/upso-9789888028931> accessed 6 January 2022; May Sim, *Remastering Morals with Aristotle and Confucius* (Cambridge University Press 2007) <https://www.cambridge.org/core/books/remastering-morals-with-aristotle-and-confucius/E6E818D81A1815878D3D3DC88DCD676B> accessed 6 January 2022.

78 Samantha Mei-che Pang, *Nursing Ethics in Modern China: Conflicting Values and Competing Role Requirements* (Brill 2021) <https://brill.com/view/title/31161> accessed 8 March 2022.

79 Nie Jing-Bao, *Behind the Silence: Chinese Voices on Abortion* (Rowman & Littlefield Pub Inc 2005).

80 Marc L Moskowitz, *The Haunting Fetus: Abortion, Sexuality, and the Spirit World in Taiwan* (University of Hawaii Press, 2001).

81 Nie Jing-Bao (11*n*61).

82 Ibid Prologue, XVIII.

83 Ibid Prologue, XVI.

intersection of clinical practices with population policy and quality of life issues. I will explore this relationship from both a diachronic and a synchronic perspective, to elucidate the evolution of the contemporary approach to specific clinical practices and associated ethical issues within the Chinese context, from the vantage point of legal and cultural history. The research will start from the definitions of bioethics in the European-American and Chinese contexts, focusing on the (different?) reasons that led to the birth and development of this science in the Western world and in China. The purpose is to understand if, and to what extent, the philosophies, ideologies, and religions (both native and of 'foreign' origin) that have become part of Mainland China's cultural substratum (Confucianism, Daoism, Mohism, Buddhism, and Marxism) have affected the current Chinese concept of the human body and the events related to a human being's inception in the world. Is China completely unfamiliar with those ethical constraints (especially of a religious origin) that in many countries influence regulations on abortion and assisted reproduction? Are there 'Chinese characteristics' in the approach to science and technology, and if so, what limits (if any) do they place on the development of knowledge? What are the principles underlying Chinese bioethics? Do these principles find expression in current regulations on biotechnologies, and/or could they influence future development?

The underlying assumption of this study is that the identification of the characteristics and relationship between biotechnology, ethics, and law in a context traditionally perceived as 'distant' and 'different' from that of Europe and North America can facilitate a more profound comprehension of the dynamics and principles traditionally employed by WLT legal systems to interpret and regulate these phenomena. This, in turn, is expected to engender transnational dialogue and cooperation in solving problems that are by their nature universal.

PART 1

Law, Ethics, and Bioethics in the Euro-American and Chinese Context: Approaches and Definitions

CHAPTER 1

Law and Morality: A 'Natural' Relationship (with 'Chinese Characteristics?')

1 Introduction

On the 10th of December 2016, while chairing the 37th Collective Study Session of the Political Bureau of the 18th CPC Central Committee, President Xi Jinping described the relationship between law (*fa* 法) and 'morality'[1] (*daode* 道德), as follows:

> Law is written morality and morality is inner law (*falü shi chengwen de daode, daode shi nexin de falü* 法律是成文的道德, 道德是内心的法律). Both law and morality have the role of regulating social behaviour, regulating social relations and maintaining social order, and both have their place and function in national governance. Law secures the world, and morality enriches people's hearts. Effective implementation of the law depends on moral support, moral practice is inseparable from legal constraints. The rule of law and moral governance cannot be separated and cannot be neglected, and national governance requires the synergistic efforts of law and morality.[2]

In the following years, the content of this speech has been echoed in numerous venues, academic and elsewhere, to show not only the 'natural' relationship between morality (or ethics) and law in a modern socialist rule of law with Chinese characteristics, but also its roots in traditional Chinese culture and values. Even if the emphasis on the relationship between law and morality seems relatively new in the Chinese context, this duality has been a standard topic in Western legal philosophy.[3] The Euro-American perspective generally accepts that the two share important characteristics and have many principles

1 The Chinese expression could also be translated as 'ethics,' or 'virtue'.

2 The full speech can be found online (in Chinese) at: http://zw.china.com.cn/2016-12/12/content_39893931.htm> accessed 2 May 2022.

3 Wibren van der Burg, 'Law and Ethics: The Twin Disciplines' (2020) 10–02 Erasmus Working Paper Series on Jurisprudence and Socio-Legal Studies 2 <https://www.academia.edu/32618045/Law_and_Ethics_The_Twin_Disciplines> accessed 2 May 2022.

 | DOI:10.1163/9789004754300_003

in common,[4] as both morality (or ethics) and the law are hermeneutic, normative, argumentative, and interdisciplinary, and are based on concepts such as justice, freedom, and rights.[5] The two domains are so close that some authors even define them as 'twin disciplines,'[6] the link particularly strong in certain fields, most notably biomedicine.[7]

The latter statement is not surprising, considering that, since the second half of the twentieth century, advancements in biomedical sciences and clinical medicine have transformed previously perceived natural and unavoidable events into choices. These technological developments created unfamiliar moral dilemmas, necessitating cooperation between ethicists and jurists in Western countries. It was not the first encounter between ethics and medicine in history. From the time of Hippocrates (fifth to fourth centuries BC), Europe began shaping ethical reflection on medical practice. Referred to as medical ethics, for centuries this discipline mainly focused on the relationship between doctors and their patients, exploring the qualities that good doctors should possess and their conduct towards their peers. In China, bioethics is also placed within the domain of medical ethics, being considered as a branch[8] or, as Qiu Renzong wrote back in 1987, 'an extension of medical ethics.'[9] It is worth remarking that the expression 'medical ethics' was understood slightly differently in the European and Asian traditional contexts. In particular, while Hippocrates emphasised rules of behaviour and focused on individual patients, considered autonomous in decision making, the symbol of traditional medical ethics in China, Sun Simiao (581–682), in his book *On the Absolute Sincerity of the Great Physician*, emphasised relationships and trust, with the commitment to family and filial piety at the centre.[10] Thus, from its outset Chinese medical morality implied the duty to treat patients as if there were members of one's own family; to treat each person equally,

---

4 Ibid 1.

5 Ibid 2.

6 Burg (19*n*3).

7 Wibren van der Burg, 'Law and Bioethics', *A Companion to Bioethics* (John Wiley & Sons, Ltd 2009) 56 <https://onlinelibrary.wiley.com/doi/abs/10.1002/9781444307818.ch6> accessed 2 May 2022.

8 Cong Yali, 'Bioethics in China', *Annals of Bioethics: Regional Perspectives in Bioethics* (Taylor & Francis 2003) 239.

9 Qiu Renzong 邱仁宗, *Shengming lunli xue* 生命伦理学(增订版)(精)/当代中国人文大系 [*Bioethics*] (Zhongguo renmin daxue chuban she 中国人民大学出版社 2020) 6.

10 Nie Jing-Bao (11*n*61) 246; Paul U Unschuld, *Medical Ethics in Imperial China: A Study in Historical Anthropology* (1979).

even if the relationship between different people is not equal; to attend to patients' emotional side, and not simply their rational side; to maintain a harmonious relationship not only with the patients but also with their family, whose interest was seen as aligned with the patient.[11]

Since the 1960s, the availability of new medical technologies, the need to limit the power of doctors and scientists after discovering the horrors of Nazi experiments,[12] and the important social and cultural changes taking place in Europe and in the U.S. dramatically changed the scenario in those countries. This not only forced the ethical disciplines pertaining to health (with the more recent nursing ethics flanking medical ethics)[13] to move from a 'doctor-cantered approach' to an attitude that puts patients and their rights at the centre, recognising 'care' as an ethical duty.[14] It also elicited questions about the body, the way it is used, and the right to make decisions about it that, until then, no one had even thought of asking.

In a context of limited resources, what criteria should health professionals follow to choose which seriously ill patients will get access to biotech innovations – a dialysis machine, in the case of the Seattle "God Committee" in 1962,[15] or a respirator, as we witnessed during the more recent 2020 pandemic[16] – and thus stand a better chance to survive, and who will die?[17] Who has the right to decide whether to maintain on life support for a patient who will never regain consciousness, a question submitted to the New Jersey Supreme Court in 1976 in the case of Karen Ann Quinlan?[18] Are there limits to scientific research, or does progress justify any choice, including injecting active cancer cells into patients hospitalised for chronic diseases, as occurred

11 Cong Yali (20*n*8) 240.

12 Wibren Van Der Burg, 'Bioethics and Law: A Developmental Perspective' (1997) 11 Bioethics 91, 98.

13 Helga Kuhse and Peter Singer, 'What Is Bioethics? A Historical Introduction', *A Companion to Bioethics* (John Wiley & Sons, Ltd 2009) 6 <https://onlinelibrary.wiley.com/doi/abs/10.1002/9781444307818.ch1> accessed 3 May 2022.

14 Ibid 6–7.

15 Ibid 8; Albert R Jonsen, 'The God Squad and the Origins of Transplantation Ethics and Policy' (2007) 35 The Journal of Law, Medicine & Ethics: A Journal of the American Society of Law, Medicine & Ethics 238.

16 Amelia Hill, 'Favouring Young over Old in Covid-19 Treatment Justifiable, Says Ethicist' *The Guardian* (22 April 2020) <https://www.theguardian.com/world/2020/apr/22/favouring-young-over-old-in-covid-19-treatment-justifiable-says-ethicist> accessed 25 May 2022.

17 Jonsen (21*n*15).

18 Kuhse and Singer (21*n*13) 9.

at the Jewish Chronic Disease Hospital in Brooklyn,[19] or the spread of the hepatitis virus among mentally disabled children between 1965 and 1970 at Willowbrook State Hospital in New York,[20] or withholding treatment for black men infected with syphilis in order to maintain continuity in the study of the disease's evolution, a study that ran from 1932 until the early 1970s in Tuskegee, Alabama?[21] Do patients (any patient, especially those considered 'expendable' like the aforementioned) have the right to participate actively in choices concerning their health and physical integrity? Where to draw the line between what is acceptable to do with one's own body and that of another, and what is not? Does a frozen embryo have personal interests and rights? Can a child born years after the death of one or both of its parents claim rights as their descendant? Who is the mother of a child born to a woman with whom it has no genetic link?

These inquiries evidently pertain to a much broader field than traditional medical ethics.[22] Their answers not only imply, or are limited to, the creation of codes of conduct for doctors, but also entail a profound exploration and understanding of the issue that opens up further considerations, which include the analysis of fundamental matters, such as the meaning and value of life, the moment in which a group of cells starts or stops being a person, and even the significance of the term 'human'. The above examples also raise moral issues beyond the merely theoretical. Despite their speculative importance, they require practical answers, which cross the boundaries of philosophy and theology to encompass medicine, nursing, economics, and even public policy. Still, for what interests us the most here, they need to be incorporated into the law and enforced by judges. A new branch of science – characterised since the beginning by its strong interdisciplinary approach – was born, which in the U.S. has been referred to as bioethics since the late 1960s.

At that time, the PRC was too busy with the Great Cultural Revolution (*Wenhua da geming* 文化大革命) and too isolated from the rest of the world to bother with this debate. Another 20 years – and the launch of the reform

19 Ruth R Faden and Tom L Beauchamp, *A History and Theory of Informed Consent* (Oxford University Press 1986) 161; Paul Murray McNeill, *The Ethics and Politics of Human Experimentation* (CUP Archive 1993) 57; Jonathan D Moreno, *Undue Risk: Secret State Experiments on Humans* (Routledge 2013) 246–248.

20 Kuhse and Singer (21*n*13) 9.

21 Susan M Reverby, *Examining Tuskegee: The Infamous Syphilis Study and Its Legacy* (Univ of North Carolina Press 2009).

22 Alexander Morgan Capron and Vicki Michel, 'Law and Bioethics' 27 Loyola of Los Angeles Law Review 25, 27.

and opening-up (*gaige kaifang* 改革开放) policies inaugurated by Deng Xiaoping in 1978 – would elapse before social, ethical, and legal issues related to the application of advanced technology in biomedicine and health care began emerging in Mainland China.[23]

To better understand how the matter has been received and elaborated in the PRC, it is crucial to acknowledge the main ethical theories underpinning what is generally regarded as international bioethics and, on the other hand, the Chinese traditional approach towards virtue, the body, and the events related to it. This chapter briefly describes these issues, and how they may have influenced the conception, and regulation, of bioethics in relevant settings. First, we must clarify the definition of 'law' and 'legal system' adopted for the purposes of the research, and to which 'China' the research will refer to. These topics which will be covered in the following sections.

2 What Is 'Law' in China? Or: Is 'Chinese Law' an Oxymoron?

In the introduction of his seminal work on 'Legal Orientalism. China, the United States, and Modern Law,'[24] Teemu Ruskola describes the law as the 'key aspect of the political ontology of the modern world.'[25] According to the author, not only would it be extremely difficult to conceive of politics outside of a state's framework and, likewise, conceive of a state outside the framework of the law,[26] it would also be impossible to fully understand the current global situation without taking into consideration China's stance.[27] The problem arises when trying to pair the concept of law with China.[28] In fact, one of the crucial cultural and political features of China is its alleged lawlessness.[29] I have already quoted Marcel Granet's renowned formula on the fundamental nature of Chinese culture: 'ni Dieu, ni Loi.'[30] In the same chapter of 'La pensée

23 Qiu Renzong, 'Medical Ethics in China', *Chinese Scientists and Responsibility. Ethical Issues of Human Genetics in Chinese and International Context* (Institut für Asienkunde 1999) 24.

24 Teemu Ruskola, *Legal Orientalism. China, the United States, and Modern Law* (Harvard University Press 2013).

25 Ibid 1.

26 Ibid.

27 Teemu Ruskola, 'Legal Orientalism' 101 Michigan Law Review 57, 1.

28 Ruskola, *Legal Orientalism. China, the United States, and Modern Law* (23*n*24).

29 Ibid 4.

30 Marcel Granet, *La pensée chinoise* (3rd edn, Albin Michel 1934) 476.

chinoise,' Granet explained the second part of this phrase by affirming that 'the Chinese notion of order excludes, in all its aspects, the idea of Law.'[31]

Almost a century has passed since Granet's manuscript was first published. In the meantime, China has undergone various political and legislative changes, including more than forty years of Western-style legal reforms. However, the common perception of the Chinese legal system has not changed much, either among ordinary people or academics. There is no need to cite newspaper articles or statements by political leaders. Like many other Chinese law scholars, I have lost track of how many times – after mentioning my field of expertise – I have been asked the same questions: 'Do they really have law in China?' or even 'Chinese Law is an oxymoron, isn't it?' This happens even when the interlocutor is a legal comparatist or a sinologist. Indeed, comparative law scholars specialising in Chinese law are too often considered by their colleagues to have limited scientific interests, no matter how many different areas of Chinese Law they have researched and written about. The root of this attitude can partly be traced back to Granet's prejudice regarding China's lack of law: at the end of the day, what could be more academically limited (and, therefore, insignificant) than studying a non-existent legal system?

Such misbelief is deeply ingrained and globally widespread. In fact, comments on the non-existence of Chinese law prompted Ruskola to investigate the origins of such misconception and why it easily gains traction with so many people.[32] Eventually, he formulated the notion of 'legal Orientalism,'[33] defined as 'a set of interlocking narratives about what is and what is not law, and who are and who are not its proper subjects.'[34]

The concept of 'legal orientalism' echoes Edward Said's renowned monograph on 'Orientalism.'[35] Said, in this work and others published under a similar title,[36] used the term to indicate the discourses structuring the Western understanding of the East,[37] which in the first half of the nineteenth century were used by Europeans to transform the Orient into a 'passive object,' to be handled and shaped in all its aspects.[38] This process entails projecting onto

31 Ibid 479.

32 Ruskola, *Legal Orientalism. China, the United States, and Modern Law* (23*n*24) 4.

33 Teemu Ruskola, 'Law Without Law, or Is "Chinese Law" an Oxymoron?' [2003] SSRN Electronic Journal <http://www.ssrn.com/abstract=412380> accessed 1 July 2022.

34 Ruskola, *Legal Orientalism. China, the United States, and Modern Law* (23*n*24) 5.

35 Edward W Said, *Orientalism* (Pantheon Books 1978).

36 Edward W Said, 'Orientalism Reconsidered' [1985] Cultural Critique 89; Edward W Said, 'Orientalism: An Afterword' (1995) 3 Raritan 32.

37 Ruskola, *Legal Orientalism. China, the United States, and Modern Law* (23*n*24) 4.

38 Said, *Orientalism* (24*n*35) 3.

the 'Oriental Other' all of various things that 'we' (the West) are not,[39] thus defining the East and the West as opposites: passive vs. active; emotional vs. rational; despotic vs. democratic; collectivist vs. individualistic, etc.[40] Said's works focus on the Middle East. In the past three decades, however, an anti-orientalist approach has been successfully used to analyse the West's representations of East Asia, especially China. Once again, through these depictions, the West expresses a judgement on itself: China was what the West was not (again: 'non-Europe') in a positive or in a negative way, depending on historical moments and authors. For example, during the seventeenth and the eighteenth centuries, Europeans admired China and generally considered it superior to the other (i.e. European) countries in administration, politics, and order.[41] At a time when religious wars ravaged Europe, Jesuits like Matteo Ricci and thinkers like Voltaire praised Chinese stability and religious tolerance, and extolled its government, run in accordance with Confucian principles, with only the most educated and virtuous men eligible for state office.[42] Even the Chinese language was greatly appreciated. Famous, in this regard, is the opinion of Leibniz, who saw the Chinese script as the (albeit only partial) realisation of his ideal of a universal language. Leibniz regarded Chinese characters as pure elements of meaning, devoid of any phonetic value, akin to algebraic signs, and thus immediately comprehensible to anyone who had learnt them, regardless of the idiom spoken.[43] His appreciation, however, was limited to this aspect, as he believed that his universal writing plan would surpass Chinese characters by far. While Chinese is extremely complicated and challenging to memorise, due to the infinite number of characters required to convey countless concepts, Leibniz's system could be learned in a matter of weeks thanks to symbols perfectly related to the order and connection of things.[44] It is worth noting that the awkwardness of the Chinese language was one of the first barriers that Westerners had to overcome and, therefore, acknowledge as such in their encounter-clash with China. Moreover, the reference to the perceived 'lack of rationality,' and the inability to create organic and functional taxonomies would become a classic *topos* in judging Chinese culture. However, at the beginning of the nineteenth

39 Ruskola, 'Legal Orientalism' (23*n*27) 209.

40 Donald C Clarke, 'Anti Anti-Orientalism, or is Chinese Law Different?' (2020) 68(1) *American Journal of Comparative Law* 55, 60.

41 Ruskola, 'Legal Orientalism' (23*n*27) 209.

42 Paul Bailey, 'Voltaire and Confucius: French Attitudes towards China in the Early Twentieth Century' (1992) 14 History of European Ideas 817.

43 Olivier Roy, *Leibniz et la Chine* (Librairie Philosophique J Vrin 1972) 135.

44 Jacques Derrida, *Of Grammatology* (4th edn, John Hopkins University Press 2016) 86.

century, the European situation changed and, with it, Europeans' attitude towards China also changed. China's extraordinary stability and immobility, hitherto considered strengths, became its main flaws. Among the most striking and most cited examples of this paradigm shift surely is Hegel's 'Philosophy of History,' in which the German philosopher stated that: 'The History of the World travels from East to West, for Europe is absolutely the end of History, Asia the beginning.'[45] In his view: 'Freedom is the sole truth of Spirit'[46] and '[T]he History of the world is none other than the progress of the consciousness of Freedom.'[47] China's main characteristics are durability and stability: for China "every change is excluded.'[48] Therefore, it lies outside History,[49] in a sort of 'unhistorical History,'[50] which represents 'the childhood' of human historical development.[51] Furthermore, it belongs to 'mere space, as distinguished from Time.'[52] In Hegel description, China is no longer a country ruled by the wisest, as it had been during the Enlightenment. In contrast, it becomes the paradigmatic example of 'Oriental Despotism.'[53] 'Its Monarch is Chief as Patriarch,'[54] while its citizenry lack the very concept of self-consciousness, and are unable to distinguish between morality and law.[55] They obey rules as children obey their parents, without will or insight of their own.[56] Like children, for the Chinese, for whom the sense of honour has not yet developed, the only restrain is the fear of punishment, not the awareness of any wrongdoing.[57] This is in sharp contrast – 'an anti-model,' in Ruskola's words[58] – with Hegel's idea of the West, which exists in the form of time, and whose Spirit (especially in its German appearance) aims at the realisation of absolute Truth as the unlimited self-determination of Freedom.[59] Similar criticism of China and of the immutability and stability of its culture and institutions, especially when compared with the West's attitude to movement and development, can be found in the writ-

45 Georg Wilhelm Friedrich Hegel, *The Philosophy of History* (Batoche Books 2001) 121.
46 Ibid 31.
47 Ibid.
48 Ibid 133.
49 Ibid.
50 Ibid 123.
51 Ibid 122.
52 Ibid 123.
53 Ibid 133.
54 Ibid 129.
55 Ibid.
56 Ibid 122.
57 Ibid 145.
58 Ruskola, 'Legal Orientalism' (23*n*27) 215.
59 Hegel (26*n*45) 358.

ings of Marx and Weber. Marx's description of China as 'vegetating in the teeth of time'[60] is well-known, as it is Weber's opinion on the static nature of Chinese intellectual life, to which he attributed its failure to develop modern capitalism.[61] In sum, throughout European history, China was used as a mirror, capable of reflecting the image that European thinkers wished belonged, or did not belong, to the West, or (more frequently) showing how far more advanced European culture was. In this sense, as stated by Derrida with reference to the Chinese system of writing, the image of China was a sort of European 'hallucination,' which 'translated less an ignorance than a misunderstanding.'[62]

Anti-Orientalism aims to correct such misconceptions by looking at the Oriental-Other with an attitude as unbiased as possible from the contingent categories of modern Western culture. With reference to law – but, *mutatis mutandis*, also to ethics, as we will better see in few pages – it means breaking down the assumption that only Western law is true law and only Westerners can define the contents of true law. This has as its basis the contention that legal categories, even when they seem 'natural' and 'innate,' are nothing more than the product of the cultural environment that shaped them.[63]

Since Said's publication, anti-Orientalism has grown into a mainstream approach,[64] with scholars using the term 'Orientalism' sometimes as a sort of academic weapon to discredit those who disagree with them.[65]

However, the discussion on these issues has never completely died down. With regard to legal Orientalism in general and legal Orientalism towards China in particular, the debate has gained new vigour after the publication in 2020 of an article by Donald Clarke, provocatively entitled 'Anti anti-Orientalism or is Chinese Law different?'[66] In a nutshell, Clarke argues that we should be open to the idea that what we usually call Chinese legal institutions little resemble what we call legal institutions in the West. Although he seeks to avoid taking a position or providing any general definition of law, in the end, his approach is to consider those institutions as part of an 'order

---

60 Karl Marx, '(Trade or Opium?)' *New York Daily Tribune* (New York, 20 September 1858) <https://moodle2.units.it/pluginfile.php/101065/mod_resource/content/2/Marx_Writings_on_China_NYDT_1853–60.pdf>.

61 Max Weber, *The Religion of China: Confucianism and Taoism* (The Free Press 1968) 55.

62 Derrida (25*n*44) 86.

63 Ruskola, 'Legal Orientalism' (23*n*27) 234.

64 Clarke (25*n*40) 64.

65 Ibid 56.

66 Clarke (25*n*40).

system' vs. a 'legal' one.[67] According to Clarke, examining Chinese institutions using legal (Western) terms is not only a linguistic mistake – akin to calling 'basketball' 'hockey,' or confusing 'a wedding with a criminal trial'[68] – it would also prevent us from understanding their real nature, like using the same criteria to study 'a fish with an impaired gill function and a human being trying to breathe underwater.'[69]

Professor Clarke has raised an issue too often taken for granted. His opinion deserves special consideration in these times, not only because of the economic and political power acquired by China, but also because, after decades of decidedly Western-style legal transplants, the Chinese (legal?) system has matured enough to try new paths, perhaps different from those familiar to, and favoured by, Western countries, the U.S. in particular. Furthermore, his inquiries are the very core of comparative method. The problem is to understand: 1) when two things are the same,[70] and 2) to what extent it is possible to translate a concept into a language that belongs to a culture that ignores its existence, or in which that concept, when it does exist, refers to a different taxonomy, or recalls a different system of values. It is worth noticing that, with reference to law, these issues have been thoroughly discussed by legal anthropology, linguistics, and comparative law since the second half of the twentieth century.[71]

The discussion of conceptual denotations of law transcends the scope of this study. Nevertheless, in the light of Clarke's reflection, it seems appropriate to recall in what sense the word 'law' can be used according to the most authoritative exponents of legal anthropology, linguistics, and comparative law. Furthermore, I need to specify in what sense I intend to use it in the following pages.

In his book on legal anthropology, Rodolfo Sacco claims that anthropologists (and legal comparatists, given their partial overlap in research areas) consider 'law' to be 'every rule imposed by a generic social pressure.'[72] They

67 Thomas B Stephens, *Order and Discipline in China* (University of Washington Press 1992) <https://uwapress.uw.edu/book/9780295971230/order-and-discipline-in-china> accessed 25 July 2022.

68 Clarke (25*n*40) 59.

69 Ibid 87.

70 Paul Bohannan, 'Ethnography and Comparison in Legal Anthropology' in Laura Nader (ed), *Law in Culture and Society* (1969th edn, University of California Press 1997) 408 <https://www.degruyter.com/document/doi/10.1525/9780520341807-023/html> accessed 25 July 2022.

71 Domenico Jervolino, 'Translation as Paradig for Hermeneutics and Its Implication for an Ethics of Hospitality' in Giuseppe Zaccaria (ed), *Translation in Law* (LIT Verlag Münster 2000) 57.

72 Rodolfo Sacco, *Antropologia giuridica* (Il Mulino 2007) 18; Rodolfo Sacco, *Anthropologie juridique: Apport à une macro-histoire du droit* (Editions Dalloz 2008).

count as legal any rule, even when they do not like its content, or even abhor its consequences, as in the case of Roman slavery, Stalin's purges, or the Nuremberg laws.[73] They cannot take as reference their culture to delimit the contents of law, since 'Law' as a concept, or 'container,' has no precise correspondence across all cultures.[74] Undoubtedly, Islamic shari'a, the 'fa' of the Chinese tradition, the Indian 'dharma' do not perfectly translate the Western meaning of 'law.'[75] However, they have something in common, like Venn Diagram circles that intersect with one another, but do not fully overlap. Here we touch on the issue raised by Clarke who, by using the same metaphor, was in the position to ask how we can be sure that they are all circles, that we are not trying to match circles with squares, or even teapots. My personal answer: We cannot be completely sure. Although, I believe that, if we reason in this way, it would be very difficult to say anything about any aspect of any other culture. As an example, outside the legal field, let's consider John 1.1.: 'In the beginning was the Word.'[76] The English term 'Word' is the translation of the Greek 'logos' (λόγος).[77] Even if we can reasonably doubt the perfect overlap of the two phrases, nevertheless, we accept this version, since, among its many meanings, 'logos' also means 'word, speech.' In fact, that is the way in which, in the same context (but not in other ones),[78] it is rendered also in Latin and in many modern European languages. From this point of view, the Chinese translation of this very verse can be problematic, because the Chinese translate 'logos' as 'dao' (道).[79] Now, it is evident that 'logos,' 'Word' and 'dao' in their respective culture of origin refer to completely different semantic areas. Yet the translations in English and Chinese somehow convey, partially, the original Greek meaning.[80]

All translators, in any language and in any field, are very familiar with this problem, which Umberto Eco effectively called 'to say almost the same

73 Sacco, *Antropologia giuridica* (28*n*72) 18.

74 Ibid 19.

75 Ibid.

76 'John 1:1 In the Beginning Was the Word, and the Word Was with God, and the Word Was God.' <https://biblehub.com/john/1-1.htm> accessed 29 July 2022.

77 'Bibbia NT Greco | Nuovo Testamento | Vangeli | Giovanni | 1' <https://www.bibbiaedu.it/GRECO_NT/nt/Gv/1/> accessed 29 July 2022.

78 'Logos | Definition, History, & Facts | Britannica' <https://www.britannica.com/topic/logos> accessed 2 August 2022.

79 'Bible Gateway Passage: 約 翰 福 音 1 – Chinese Union Version (Traditional)' (*Bible Gateway*) <https://www.biblegateway.com/passage/?search=%E7%B4%84%20%E7%BF%B0%20%E7%A6%8F%20%E9%9F%B3%201&version=CUV> accessed 29 July 2022.

80 On the issue of the translation of ancient Greek into English, see Virginia Woolf and Elena Gualtieri, *On Not Knowing Greek* (Hesperus Pr 2008).

thing.'[81] In legal translations, this means abandoning the illusion of literal correspondence between terms and supporting the appraisal of texts with legal comparison.[82] Finally, we do it every time when we use Common Law terms to describe in English legal institutions developed in Civil Law countries. Without legal comparison, it would be impossible to understand the meaning of the most common legal words. Take the use of the words 'contract/contratto' in the English and Italian legal systems as an example. Despite the linguistic assonance of the two terms, and the cultural proximity even from a juridical perspective, we cannot say that an English 'contract' and an Italian 'contratto' are the same thing. Anyone who believes this would erroneously think that the Italian contract requires consideration, and therefore would not understand why a donation in Italy is a 'contratto.'[83] Similarly, in one of Clarke's examples, Chinese people reading the Chinese translation of the U.S. Department of State, *Guowuyuan* 国务院, might naturally take for granted that its competencies match those of the PRC's State Council, which bares the same name (*Guowuyuan* 国务院), even though the former better resembles the functions of China's Foreign Ministry, while the latter is the administrative arm of the Chinese state.[84] Sometimes, the terms are so culturally specific that translating them can be misleading. In these cases, there are two course of action: do not translate the word, as in the case of terms like 'soviet' or 'mafia,' or rely instead on a neologism.[85] The latter choice is rarer, but happens in China because many Western legal terms – the typical example is 'rights,' which is translated as *quanli* 权利 – put forward concepts that do not exist in traditional Chinese law.[86] I note briefly that translators of the early Confucian lexicon faced, and still face, similar problems, since the Confucian concept-cluster great differs from the philosophical concept-cluster of Western ethics.[87] In fact, the latter is

---

81 Umberto Eco, *Dire quasi la stessa cosa: Esperienze di traduzione* (Bompiani 2013).

82 Gianmaria Ajani, Domenico Francavilla and Barbara Pasa, *Diritto comparato. Lezioni e materiali* (Giappichelli 2018) 80.

83 Rodolfo Sacco, 'Il Contratto in Prospettiva Comparatistica' [2001] Europa e diritto privato 479; E Ioriatti Ferrari, *La traduzione del diritto comunitario ed europeo: riflessioni metodologiche. Atti del Convegno* (Università degli Studi di Trento 2007); Ajani, Francavilla and Pasa (30*n*82) 69–70.

84 Clarke (25*n*40) 58.

85 Ajani, Francavilla and Pasa (30*n*82) 80.

86 Deborah Cao, *Chinese Law: A Language Perspective* (1° edizione, Routledge 2017) ch 5.

87 Henry Rosemont, 'Rights-Bearing Individuals and Role-Bearing Persons,' *Confucian Role Ethics: A Moral Vision for the 21st Century?* (V&R unipress) 45. For the definition of concept-cluster, see *infra*, Chapter three.

based on the concept of 'moral,'[88] which does not directly correspond to any concept in the traditional Chinese mindset, and therefore has no single lexical equivalent in the classical Chinese language.[89] Coming back to the Chinese legal terms, a more recent example of a neologism is the expression 'Social Credit System,' created as the English-language equivalent of the new (and in many aspects characteristically Chinese) PRC initiative to rank the reputation of its citizens, the *Shehui xinyong tixi* 社会信用体系.[90] Indeed, and to sum up, the work of translation – or rather, of transposition of concepts born and developed in one context into a language different from the one spoken in the original context – is always practicable. As with interpretation, and many other aspects of human thought, we should not expect to find a translation that is incontrovertibly 'true.' Instead, and as the philosophy of language has demonstrated, we should be aware that the various possible translations are all subject to pragmatic restrictions of meaningfulness and credibility.[91]

My methodology draws inspiration from Rodolfo Sacco's theory of legal formants,[92] according to which 'it is possible to speak of law with reference to all human societies, and whoever wants to (the choice is subjective) can do so with reference to many evolved animal societies.'[93] According to Sacco, we cannot speak of law, or of a legal system, only in three cases: 1) when there is no perception on the part of the subjects of what the law provides in that concrete case; 2) where the subjects do not choose their behaviour, but are dominated by instincts; 3) where the deviation of the subject from the rule does not imply any reaction within the community.[94]

I believe the latter criteria do not apply to China, either to imperial or modern China and, therefore, we can speak about 'law' with reference to it. Nevertheless, the question of whether Chinese law is true law is different and, in my opinion, finds its roots in cultural relativism. It is the same attitude that

---

88 Henry Rosemont and Roger Ames, 'On Translation & Interpretation (With Special Reference to Classical Chinese),' *Confucian Role Ethics* (V&R unipress GmbH 2016) 22.

89 Ibid.

90 It is worth noting that the English neologism does not literally translate the Chinese original, whose characters rather mean 'social trust system.'

91 Alan Durant and Janny HC Leung, 'Pragmatics in Legal Interpretation' in Anne Barron, Yueguo Gu and Gerard Steen (eds), *The Routledge Handbook of Pragmatics* (1st edn, Routledge 2017) 535 <https://www.taylorfrancis.com/books/9781317362579/chapters/10.4324/9781315668925-38> accessed 29 July 2022.

92 Rodolfo Sacco, 'Legal Formants: A Dynamic Approach to Comparative Law (Installment I of II)' (1991) 39 The American Journal of Comparative Law 1.

93 Sacco, *Antropologia giuridica* (28n72) 19.

94 Ibid.

previously allowed dominant societies to declare that some other peoples lacked a true language. If the ancient Greek example of what they considered 'barbarians' seems too distant in time, we need only think back to National Socialist Germany, when someone started to say that the only true language was German.[95] Similarly, I find extremely objectionable the assertion that Chinese law is not 'real' law, an unfortunate attitude that is increasingly popular among many legal scholars (especially U.S. scholars, as Clarke's paper demonstrates) who more or less explicitly identify 'true' law with the law of their own country. From a scientific point of view, this represents a setback rather than progress, and an obstacle rather than an incentive to achieve a better understanding of the Chinese system. Moreover, it stands in stark contrast to the most recent trends in comparative law,[96] and does not consider the results obtained by critical comparison in appreciating what legal scholars, practitioners and ordinary people living in another cultural context think, when they think about 'the law.'

Finally, this approach contrasts with the interpretation of the purpose of comparative law, according to which:

> [...] Comparing the laws of different peoples and states means cooperation and peace: understanding each other [...] is a step [...] always necessary for cooperation and peace. Breaking out of the enclosure of one's own legal system means broadening one's horizon and experience [...] realising one's own limitations in a spirit of modesty which, in turn, entails tolerance and freedom.[97]

Tolerance, freedom, cooperation, and peace are words increasingly needed in the current historical period. It is with this in mind that I will examine Chinese biotechnology regulation: to increase mutual understanding and reciprocal learning among different traditions and legal cultures. In doing so, the legal comparative method has to be complemented by other disciplines, such as language studies and philosophy, ethics and bioethics, in particular, taking into account perspectives and diverging voices internal and external to the

---

95 Ibid 20.

96 Werner F Menski, *Comparative Law in a Global Context: The Legal Systems of Asia and Africa* (2nd edn, Cambridge University Press 2006) <https://www.cambridge.org/core/books/comparative-law-in-a-global-context/4705C7C2B21A97742DA59ED690FD9534> accessed 2 August 2022; H Patrick Glenn, *Legal Traditions of the World: Sustainable Diversity in Law* (Oxford University Press 2014).

97 Tullio Ascarelli, *Studi di diritto comparato e in tema di interpretazione* (Giuffrè 1952) 43; Vittoria Barsotti and Vincenzo Varano, *La tradizione giuridica occidentale: Testo e materiali per un confronto civil law common law. Quinta edizione* (G Giappichelli Editore 2014) 15.

system in question. Before starting our analysis, a description of these fields of research in the Euro-American and Chinese contexts is therefore inescapable. However: which 'Chinese' context will be referred to?

3 Which China?

What is commonly considered as China, i.e.: the People's Republic of China, is defined in art. 1 of its 2018 Constitution as 'a socialist state under the people's democratic dictatorship led by the working class and based on the alliance of workers and peasants' (art. 1 (1)) in which 'The leadership of the Communist Party of China is the defining feature of socialism with Chinese characteristics (art. 1 (2)). This constitutional framework underpins the governance of the world's largest country by land area, encompassing one-fourteenth of the Earth's terrestrial surface. China exhibits extraordinary geographic and climatic diversity, ranging from Mount Everest on the Nepal-Tibet border to the Turfan Depression in the Xinjiang Autonomous Region, and from the arid, desert-like conditions of the northwest to the tropical monsoon climate of the southeast. This geographic span creates the world's greatest temperature contrast between northern and southern borders within a single nation. Demographically, whilst China ranks as the world's second most populous country after India, it comprises fifty-six ethnic minorities alongside the dominant Han nationality, which constitutes approximately 92% of the population and represents the majority in all provinces and autonomous regions except Tibet and Xinjiang.[98]

Despite this remarkable diversity, Chinese leadership has historically pursued the concept of a 'one China', consistently striving for national reunification even during periods of territorial fragmentation. This historical aspiration, now frequently used with refence to the international relationship, in particular towards Taiwan,[99] informed the post-revolutionary rejection of Soviet-style federalism in favour of a centralised system that nonetheless incorporates degrees of regional autonomy. The PRC's contemporary adminis-

---

98 Brian E McKnite and Denis C Twitchett, 'China | Events, People, Dates, Flag, Map, & Facts | Britannica', *Encyclopedia Britannica,* (2025) <https://www.britannica.com/place/China> accessed 5 August 2025.

99 Global Taiwan Institute, 'The "One-China Principle": China's "Norm" versus Global Realities' (*Global Taiwan Institute*, 21 February 2024) <https://globaltaiwan.org/2024/02/the-one-china-principle-chinas-norm-versus-global-realities/> accessed 5 August 2025.

trative framework operates through a hierarchical structure comprising the national government in Beijing and 33 provincial-level units: four directly administered municipalities, five autonomous regions, two special administrative regions (Hong Kong and Macau), and 22 provinces (excluding Taiwan, which remains under the governance of the Republic of China). These entities collectively form part of the informal concept of 'Greater China,' which encompasses Mainland China, Hong Kong, Macau, and Taiwan. This provincial tier subdivides into approximately 330 prefectural bodies, over 2,850 county-level entities, and numerous cities, towns, and townships, with larger cities further divided into urban wards and counties. This territorial organisation serves to coordinate and implement the diverse policies emanating from the central government. More specifically, Chinese governance exemplifies what Xu Chenggang terms 'regionally decentralised authoritarianism'[100] – a distinctive synthesis of political centralisation with economic and administrative decentralisation. Under this system, the central government establishes broad policy frameworks whilst provincial authorities develop specific local implementation measures, often initially on an experimental basis.[101] Furthermore, the centre may strategically select particular localities based on their economic or social characteristics to pilot new policies before national implementation, as exemplified by the 'two-child policy', which underwent experimental implementation in Yicheng county, Shanxi Province, for thirty years (1985–2015).[102]

This complex institutional architecture requires a nuanced analytical approach that recognises regional differences in enforcement incentives, institutional capacity and policy implementation. Such an approach reveals the layered, multifaceted nature of Chinese governance, challenging simplistic characterisations of the country as monolithic and highlighting the sophisticated interplay between unity and diversity that defines the political and administrative landscape of contemporary China.

It is this 'China' that I will refer to in the following chapters.

---

100 Xu Chenggang, 'The Fundamental Institutions of China's Reforms and Development' (2011) 49 Journal of Economic Literature 1076.

101 Pranab Bardhan, 'The Chinese Governance System: Its Strengths and Weaknesses in a Comparative Development Perspective' (2020) 61 China Economic Review 101430.

102 Qin Yu and Wang Fei, 'Too Early or Too Late: What Have We Learned from the 30-Year Two-Child Policy Experiment in Yicheng, China?' (2017) 37 Demographic Research 929.

CHAPTER 2

Morality, Ethics, and Bioethics in the Euro-American ('Western') Context

1 Morality, Ethics, and the Birth of Bioethics

Joseph Fletcher's *Moral and Medicine. The Moral Problems of the Patient's Right to Know the Truth, Contraception, Artificial Insemination, Sterilization, Euthanasia,*[1] published in 1954, is generally considered the first modern work on bioethics.[2] However, it was only in the 1960s that this new field of study started taking shape, due to a combination of social changes and advancements in biotechnology. At the beginning, though, it was not called 'bioethics.' That name was used for the first time in 1970 by Van Rensselaer Potter to indicate a discipline that he described as a 'science of survival.'[3] This science would bring together ethical values and biological facts, leading to a 'knowledge of how to use knowledge for the social good,' which would ensure the survival of the biosphere as a whole and improve the quality of human life.[4] Potter was an oncologist, and through this interdisciplinary scientific approach, he wanted to prevent human beings from becoming to the Earth what cancer is to the human body, in the mistaken belief that 'science could produce "more and better" of everything that man needed and that progress could be equated with growthmanship.'[5] His statement now sounds sadly prophetic and has in fact recently been adopted by several scholars,[6] becoming a truly

1 Joseph F Fletcher, *Morals and Medicine: The Moral Problems of the Patient's Right to Know the Truth, Contraception, Artificial Insemination, Sterilization, Euthanasia* (Princeton University Press 2015) <https://www.degruyter.com/document/doi/10.1515/9781400868377/html> accessed 7 August 2022.

2 Albert R Jonsen, *The Birth of Bioethics* (Oxford University Press 2003) 45; Robert M Veatch, *The Basics of Bioethics* (3rd edn, Routledge 2016); H Tristram Engelhardt, *Bioethics and Secular Humanism: The Search for a Common Morality* (Wipf and Stock Publishers 2011) 56; Kuhse and Singer (21*n*13) 7.

3 Van Rensselaer Potter, 'Bioethics, the Science of Survival' (1970) 14 Perspectives in Biology and Medicine 127, 127; Qiu Renzong 邱仁宗, *Shengming lunli xue* 生命伦理学(增订版)(精)/当代中国人文大系 [*Bioethics*] (2019) 1.

4 Potter (35*n*3) 129.

5 Ibid.

6 Lisa M Lee, 'A Bridge Back to the Future: Public Health Ethics, Bioethics, and Environmental Ethics' (2017) 17 The American Journal of Bioethics 5; Cheryl Macpherson, 'Global Bioethics:

 | DOI:10.1163/9789004754300_004

global feature since 2005, with the publication of the Universal Declaration on Bioethics and Human Rights (DUBDH) by Unesco.[7] At the time, however, the significance of 'bioethics' as a 'bridge between present and future [...] and finally between humankind and nature'[8] had little success.[9] On the contrary, the term was increasingly used in a narrow sense, to indicate the growing interest in ethical issues related to the relationships among the individual, health-care, and biomedical sciences[10] It was in this 'reductionist version'[11] that bioethics entered the academic sphere, and expanded from the United States to other countries.[12] This was also due to the student protests during those years, which demanded, among other things, reforms of Euro-American university courses to include the most topical and socially interesting issues.[13] The change involved the practice of philosophy, as well: indeed, in the 1960s the prevailing orthodoxy, especially among English-speaking moral philosophers, was that philosophy should focus on the analysis of moral terms rather than on practical issues.[14] Since the 1970s, however, the need to address practical ethical problems such as abortion, euthanasia, the allocation of scarce medical resources, and animal rights led to a renewed interest in normative and applied ethics.[15] But what is it all about? What is the difference between morality and ethics? Do ethical theory and bioethics have any kind of relationship? What does it look like?

1.1 *Definitions and Theories*

The *Encyclopedia Britannica* defines ethics as 'the discipline concerned with what is morally good and bad and morally right and wrong,'[16] and considers it

---

It's Past and Future' (2022) 33 Global Bioethics 45; Peter J Whitehouse, 'The Rebirth of Bioethics: A Tribute to Van Rensselaer Potter' (2001) 14 Global Bioethics 37; Henk ten Have, 'The Universal Declaration on Bioethics and Human Rights as a Landmark in the Development of Global Bioethics,' *International Biolaw and Shared Ethical Principles* (Routledge 2018) 32.

7 Universal Declaration on Bioethics and Human Rights 2005.

8 Henk AMJ ten Have, 'Potter's Notion of Bioethics' (2012) 22 Kennedy Institute of Ethics Journal 59, 59.

9 Thiago Cunha and Cláudio Lorenzo, 'Global Bioethics from the Perspective of Critical' 'Global bioethics from the perspective of critical bioethics' (2014) 22(1) *Revista Bioética* 116, 117.

10 Kuhse and Singer (21*n*13) 3.

11 Cunha and Lorenzo (36*n*9) 117.

12 Ibid.

13 Kuhse and Singer (21*n*13) 7.

14 Ibid.

15 Ibid.

16 'Ethics | Definition, History, Examples, Types, Philosophy, & Facts | Britannica' <https://www.britannica.com/topic/ethics-philosophy> accessed 7 August 2022.

a synonym for moral philosophy,[17] a feature that is very deep-rooted. In fact, it is linked to the very etymology of the word 'moral,' created by Cicero as a neologism to translate the Greek term *ethos* (ἦθος).[18] As the author explained in the first paragraph of the 'De Fato,' *ethos* referred to the part of philosophy 'related to manners,' which in Latin at that time was called 'philosophy concerned with manners.'[19] To enrich and elevate the Latin language, Cicero proposed a new adjective formed from the Latin word *mos, moris* (like the Greek *ethos*, meaning custom, manners), and called it 'moral' philosophy.[20] In his words: '[…] *quia pertinet ad mores, quod ἦϑος illi vocant, nos eam partem philosophiae de moribus appellare solemus, sed decet augentem linguam Latinam nominare moralem.*'[21]

Cicero's suggestion was later taken up by other Latin authors, like Seneca[22] and Quintiliano,[23] leading to the consolidation of the use of the word in this sense. Essentially, 'morality' is the Latin translation of the Greek word for 'ethics'; any difference between the two concepts boils down to the difference between Latin and Greek. Again, and as we have seen with reference to the translation of legal terms, the two words meant 'almost the same thing,' but with a different emphasis: while *mos* means 'manners' with a nuance closer to that of social expectation, the meaning of the Greek *ethos* is closer to 'manners' in the sense of individual character.[24] Later on, however, the two terms would sometimes be construed as referring to separate and contrasting fields of inquiry.[25] In particular, the word 'morality' evolved from its original meaning, shifting toward what Elizabeth Anscombe defined as 'a law notion of eth-

17 Ibid.

18 Bernard Williams, *Ethics and the Limits of Philosophy* (2015) 6.

19 'M. Tullius Cicero, De Fato, Section 1' <http://www.perseus.tufts.edu/hopper/text?doc=Cic.%20Fat.%201.1&lang=original> accessed 8 August 2022.

20 'Ethics | Definition, History, Examples, Types, Philosophy, & Facts | Britannica' (n 201).

21 'M. Tullius Cicero, De Fato, Section 1' (37*n*19).

22 'Seneca, Ad Lucilium Epistulae Morales, Seneca Lucilio Suo Salutem, Section 9' <http://www.perseus.tufts.edu/hopper/text?doc=Sen.%20Ep.%2089.9&lang=original> accessed 8 August 2022.

23 'Quintilian, Institutio Oratoria, Book 6, Chapter 2, Section 8' <http://www.perseus.tufts.edu/hopper/text?doc=Quint.%20Inst.%206.2.8&lang=original> accessed 8 August 2022; 'Quintilian, Institutio Oratoria, Book 12, Chapter 2, Section 10' <http://www.perseus.tufts.edu/hopper/text?doc=Quint.%20Inst.%2012.2.10&lang=original> accessed 8 August 2022.

24 Williams (37*n*18) act 6; Sarah J Harper, 'Ethics versus Morality: A Problematic Divide' (2009) 35 Philosophy & Social Criticism 1063, act 1064.

25 Harper (37*n*24) 1064.

ics.'[26] Anscombe attributes this change to the emergence of Christianity, which derived its ethical concepts from the Torah. Therefore, due to Christianity's emphasis on God's law, starting from the Middle Ages, the expressions 'should,' 'needs,' 'ought', and 'must,' once related to what is good or bad, became the equivalent of 'is obliged to,' or 'is bound to,' or 'is required to,' in the sense that one can be obliged or bound by law.[27] Even after Protestants gave up their belief in divine law at the time of the Reformation, 'the notion "obligation" survived, and the notion "ought" was invested with that peculiar force having which it is said to be used in a "moral" sense.'[28] Hume posited the endurance of a concept outside the framework that made it intelligible,[29] and Anscombe compares that to a situation where the term 'criminal' somehow survives the abolishment and erasure of criminal law and courts.[30] Hume concluded that there was a special sentiment, inherent in the word 'moral,' which alone gave the word its sense. Anscombe, followed by other British philosophers, such as Bernard Williams,[31] went a step forward. Since no content can be found in the notion of 'morally ought,' she proposed discarding the concepts of 'moral obligation' and 'moral duty.' In her view, they are only 'survivals, or derivatives of survivals, from a notion of ethics which no longer generally survives, and can only be dangerous without it.'[32] Modern philosophers, therefore, 'should be better off without it.'[33] Notwithstanding, contemporary moral philosophy still frequently draws a distinction between ethics and morality. Sara Harper attributes this to two reasons. First, a view exists of the history of philosophy in which separates ancient morality from modern. Philosophers like Henry Sidgwick, who follow this interpretation,[34] consider the former to be rooted in the desire of every individual for the good and motivated by an attraction to the good, referring to it as 'ethics,' while they call the latter, which is rooted in reason and restrictive rather than attractive, 'morality.'[35] The second reason is practical: Many philosophers find it useful to

26 Gertrude Elizabeth Margareth Anscombe, 'Modern Moral Philosophy' (1958) 33 Philosophy 1, 5.
27 Ibid.
28 Ibid 6.
29 Ibid.
30 Ibid.
31 Williams (37*n*18).
32 Anscombe (38*n*26) 1.
33 Williams (37*n*18) 174.
34 Henry Sidgwick, *Methods of Ethics* (7° edizione, Hackett Pub Co Inc 1981).
35 Ibid 105; Harper (37*n*24) 1065.

separate ethics from morality, based on their objectives.[36] Harper cites as examples the anti-moralist followers of Freud, Nietzsche, and Marx. In fact, maintaining the distinction between ethics and morality allow them to generically criticise moral principles while, at the same time, keep and spread certain moral ideas, such as what constitutes a good/bad life and what is good/bad for people. To do this, they use the term 'morality' in a narrower sense to refer to principles of action, and the term 'ethics' in a broader sense to indicate a certain range of moral phenomena. Even defenders of neutralist liberalism have made use of the distinction between ethics and morality, but for different purposes. They use the word 'moral' to talk about questions of rights that they consider as social and distinguished from personal questions of preference and lifestyle, which they regard as ethical. For them, the latter should be immune to social critique, except when it interferes with rights. Other philosophers, such as Williams, Avishai Margalit, and Ronald Dworkin, use the difference between ethics and morality to separate the 'self-regarding' nature of ethics, which pertains to convictions about what kind of lives are good or bad for a person (specifically myself and those to whom I am close) to lead, from the 'other-regarding' nature of morality.[37] Thus, morality regulates our 'thin relationship' with the stranger and the remote[38] and tells us how we should treat them,[39] encompassing principles of action that are alien to ethics.[40] These are only a few examples of how modern moral philosophers have interpreted the dichotomy between ethics and morality. They include, but are not limited to, the differences between 'the right and the good, duty and virtue, principles and convictions, actions and lives, thick and thin relations, non-scalar and scalar evaluations, other-regarding and self-regarding, modern and ancient.'[41] According to Harper, the distinction has been employed in so many different ways and to achieve so many different purposes that we should question whether it has any real meaning at all. Furthermore, it has proven theoretically problematic in its failure to meet certain standards of coherence.[42] On this basis, she proposes to approach moral phenomena through a role-cantered moral theory. Since social roles do not fit neatly either into eth-

---

36 Harper (37*n*24) 1065.

37 Williams (n 203) 14; Avishai Margalit, *The Ethics of Memory* (Harvard Univ Pr 2004) acts 7–8; Ronald Dworkin, *Sovereign Virtue: The Theory and Practice of Equality* (Harvard Univ Pr 2002) act 485 n. I.

38 Margalit (39*n*37) 7–8.

39 Dworkin (39*n*37) 145.

40 Harper (37*n*24) 1068.

41 Ibid 1071.

42 Ibid.

ics or morality, a moral theory inspired by them can resist the kind of 'moral bifurcation' expressed in the divide discussed above, lending some coherence in this group of contrasts.[43] I will come back to this theory in a few lines, with reference to care ethics. For now, I will just point out that most ethicists nowadays consider the two terms interchangeable.[44] Furthermore, the word 'ethics' is sometimes used in a broader sense than in its original/etymological meaning – which, as noted, is that of moral philosophy, as a systematic reflection on morality. In fact, it can also indicate a sub-discipline of theology (theological ethics, or moral theology) and some forms of descriptive ethics[45] that do not belong to philosophy but to other sciences, such as sociology or psychology.[46] In addition, the term is also used to refer to the deontological duties of certain professions. The expression 'law and ethics,' for instance, is often used to indicate ethical standards for legal practitioners, particularly, though not limited to, lawyers. In this book, the phrase is used to indicate the relationship between law (particularly Chinese law, as understood in the previous section) and the philosophical discipline that studies morality, which I am going to briefly address in the next section.

2 Western Ethics' Subdisciplines: Normative and Nonnormative Ethics

In their influential book on *Principles of Biomedical Ethics*,[47] Tom Beauchamp and James Childress split the approach to ethics into two groups: normative and nonnormative,[48] according to their purposes. While normative ethics aims to establish what should be ethically acceptable, or what is ethically valuable, the nonnormative approach strives to define the factual or conceptual nature of ethics.[49] Both, in turn, comprise two subdisciplines. In particular:

---

43 Ibid.

44 'What's the Difference Between Morality and Ethics? | Britannica' <https://www.britannica.com/story/whats-the-difference-between-morality-and-ethics> accessed 15 August 2022; Tom L Beauchamp and James F Childress, *Principles of Biomedical Ethics* (Oxford University Press 2009) 333; van der Burg (19*n*3) 53, 56.

45 See below, next paragraph.

46 Wibren van der Burg, 'Law and Ethics: The Twin Disciplines' (14 July 2010) 5 <https://papers.ssrn.com/abstract=1631720> accessed 15 August 2022.

47 Beauchamp and Childress (40*n*44).

48 Ibid 1.

49 Ibid 2.

a) Normative ethics encompasses general normative ethics and practical ethics. General normative ethics, commonly considered ethics' core subdiscipline,[50] aims to identify and justify moral norms (often called principles),[51] values and virtues. However, not even the best general theory can adequately answer all the practical questions arising in real life. Therefore, it is necessary for general rules to be interpreted in the specific context of a problem. That is precisely the intent of the second normative approach to ethics, known as applied ethics, or practical ethics. This approach sees general norms only as starting points to decide the 'practical' norms of conduct that should be followed in professions, institutions, and government.[52]

b) Nonnormative ethics includes descriptive ethics and metaethics. The first, defined as 'the factual investigation of moral belief and conduct,' is used more often by scientists than philosophers (e.g. anthropologists, sociologists, psychologists, historians) and employs the scientific method to study how people reason and act, trying to determine which moral norms and attitude are expressed, for example, in professional codes, or in public policies. Metaethics, on the hand, involves the analysis of certain aspects of normative ethics, such as language, concepts, and methods of reasoning. For example, the meaning of terms such as 'rights,' 'virtue,' 'morality,' and the nature of 'moral truth' are some of the topics in metaethics.[53]

Qiu Renzong used a similar taxonomy in his 1987 book, and it has since been recognized and accepted by Chinese bioethicists.[54] In this work, I will apply descriptive ethics to identify the ethical principles that inspire Chinese regulation of biotechnology. My aim, however, is to analyse the value of these principles and the practical norms derived from them in light of the moral theories they rely on. Since the latter is a normative issue, a brief recap of the most significant Western normative theories in the field of bioethics will precede my investigation of the Chinese context.

---

50 van der Burg (19*n*3) 5; Qiu Renzong 邱仁宗, *Shengming lunli xue* 生命伦理学(增订版)(精)/当代中国人文大系 [*Bioethics*] (20*n*9) 8.

51 Beauchamp and Childress (40*n*44) 1.

52 Ibid 2.

53 Ibid.

54 Qiu Renzong 邱仁宗, *Shengming lunli xue* 生命伦理学 [*Bioethics*] (13*n*70) 20.

2.1 *Normative Theories*

In the great variety of moral theories discussed by the authors who have dealt with bioethics, the distinction between consequentialist and deontological/nonconsequentalist theories deserves a special place. This is also true in China: Even if you cannot find dominant bioethical theories that are explicitly labelled as 'deontology' or 'utilitarianism,' Chinese manuals on bioethics rely on and discuss both these principles.[55] Therefore, I will summarize their main contents below.

2.1.1 Consequentialist Theories: Utilitarianism

Theories that assess the morality of an action based on its consequences are considered to belong to consequentialism.[56] In practice, consequentialism judges an act as right or wrong depending on whether it produces the best possible result according to the relevant theory of value.[57] The main consequentialist theory is utilitarianism, which places the principle of utility at the core of ethical evaluation. This principle is often understood as the requirement to do the greatest good in the sense of well-being for the greatest number of individuals, to be determined by assigning equal weight to the legitimate interests of each party concerned.[58] The main representatives of this theory are Jeremy Bentham (1748–1832) and John Stuart Mill (1806–1873),[59] who evaluate utility/well-being in terms of happiness and pleasure, to be regarded as synonyms for these purposes.[60] Although all utilitarians agree that human actions should be evaluated on the basis of their capacity to maximise a value, they nevertheless differ as to which value should be maximized.[61] For instance, some philosophers have recently questioned whether happiness can actually lead to well-being, noting the role played by other values, such as knowledge, health, and success, in pursuit of it.[62] The values considered fundamental by

55 Cong Yali (2018) 248.

56 Qiu Renzong 邱仁宗, *Shengming lunli xue* 生命伦理学(增订版)(精)/当代中国人文大系 [*Bioethics*] (2019) 12.

57 Beauchamp and Childress (40n44) 336.

58 Ibid 337.

59 Qiu Renzong 邱仁宗, *Shengming lunli xue* 生命伦理学(增订版)(精)/当代中国人文大系 [*Bioethics*] (2019) 12.

60 Jeremy Bentham, *An Introduction to the Principles of Morals and Legislation* (Dover Publications 2007); John Stuart Mill, *Utilitarianism* (CDED 2018) ch 2.

61 Beauchamp and Childress (40n44) 337.

62 James Griffin, *Well-Being: Its Meaning, Measurement and Moral Importance* (1988) <https://academic.oup.com/book/3189> accessed 18 August 2022.

these thinkers for the achievement of well-being are different; they do, however, share the view that an action should be evaluated on the basis of the total intrinsic value it produces. Other utilitarians, on the contrary, value the greatest good with reference to an individual's preference. In their view, what we should maximise is the overall degree of satisfaction of the preferences of the greatest number of individuals.[63] Another controversial issue within utilitarianism concerns whether utility should be evaluated over particular acts performed in particular situations (act utilitarianism), or to general rules that establish which behaviour is right or wrong, regardless of the context (rule utilitarianism).[64] As an example of the latter position, Beauchamp and Childress mention Worthington Hooker,[65] a prominent American physician who in the first half of the nineteenth century published a book on *Physician and Patient; Or, A Practical View of the Mutual Duties, Relations and Interests of the Medical Profession and the Community*.[66] According to Dr Hooker, doctors must always tell their patients the truth, without exception. While allowing that in some cases a white lie can give hope to the terminally ill and therefore 'maximise' their good, Dr Hooker held that any good obtained in such cases is nothing compared to 'the evil which would result from a general adoption of a system of deception.'[67] This example gives us the opportunity to comment on the contrasting approach to truth-telling in medical ethics between Western and Asian, especially Chinese, perspectives, particularly concerning terminally ill patients. The prevalent view suggests that while open and direct disclosure is considered the Western norm, Chinese culture and traditional medical ethics (*yi de* 医德)[68] lean towards nondisclosure or indirect communication via family members.[69] The literature on the subject is extensive and, in general, confirms this stereotype.[70] In recent years, however, some scholars have begun to

63 Beauchamp and Childress (40*n*44) 337.

64 Ibid 339.

65 Ibid 340.

66 Worthington Hooker, *Physician and Patient; Or, A Practical View of the Mutual Duties, Relations and Interests of the Medical Profession and the Community* (Baker and Scribner 1849).

67 Ibid 378.

68 On the difference between traditional medical ethics (*yide* 医德) and 'modern' medical ethics (*yixue lunli* 医学伦理) see Qiu Renzong 邱仁宗, *Shengming lunli xue* 生命伦理学 [*Bioethics*] (13*n*70) 13.

69 Nie Jing-Bao (11*n*61) 98; Cong Yali (20*n*8) 242–243.

70 Phyllis N Butow, Martin HN Tattersall and David Goldstein, 'Communication with Cancer Patients in Culturally Diverse Societies' (1997) 809 Annals of the New York Academy of Sciences 317; Arthur Kleinman, *The Illness Narratives: Suffering, Healing, And The Human Condition* (New edizione, Basic Books 2020); Yuxiu Liu and others, 'Disclosure

question its validity, demonstrating, through documentary evidence, that revealing the truth about the patient's state of health was traditionally a duty for Chinese physicians, whereas in the West, this practice has only recently become the standard.[71] Without taking a position on the topic, and returning to our discourse on utilitarianism, I simply point out that the rule-utilitarian approach followed by Dr Hooker is not the only one contemplated by this Western doctrine. In fact, according to act utilitarianism, a physician should decide on a case-by-case basis whether telling a terminally ill patient the truth would maximize the good. When informing the patient on his or her diagnosis and prognosis is harmful, the doctor should outright lie, without weakening or threatening the general value of respect for moral rules.[72] Thus, and at least concerning utilitarian philosophy, a physician's obligation to truth-telling appears far from being an absolute duty, even within the Western framework.

As this overview of utilitarian doctrine concludes, it's worth highlighting the general appreciation among Chinese bioethicists for act utilitarianism's emphasis on the contextual nature of norms. Even scholars who argue that mainland China, due to its traditions, might never fully adopt utilitarian theories, acknowledge their influence on Chinese legislators' decisions in the realm of bioethics.[73] Qiu Renzong himself suggests that these principles adhere to criteria that are more easily identifiable compared to those underlying deontological theories, notably Kantianism,[74] or natural law theory, of

---

of Cancer Diagnosis in China: The Incidence, Patients’ Situation, and Different Preferences between Patients and Their Family Members and Related Influence Factors' (2018) 10 Cancer Management and Research 2173; MC Pang, 'Protective Truthfulness: The Chinese Way of Safeguarding Patients in Informed Treatment Decisions' (1999) 25 Journal of Medical Ethics 247; Hongchun Wang and others, 'To Tell or Not: The Chinese Doctors' Dilemma on Disclosure of a Cancer Diagnosis to the Patient' (2018) 47 Iranian Journal of Public Health 1773; Zanhua Zhang and Xiaoyan Min, 'The Ethical Dilemma of Truth-Telling in Healthcare in China' (2020) 17 Journal of Bioethical Inquiry 337; Siew Tzuh Tang and Shiu-Yu C Lee, 'Cancer Diagnosis and Prognosis in Taiwan: Patient Preferences versus Experiences' (2004) 13 Psycho-Oncology 1; Siew Tzuh Tang and others, 'Patient Awareness of Prognosis, Patient-Family Caregiver Congruence on the Preferred Place of Death, and Caregiving Burden of Families Contribute to the Quality of Life for Terminally Ill Cancer Patients in Taiwan' (2008) 17 Psycho-Oncology 1202; Ruiping Fan and Benfu Li, 'Truth Telling in Medicine: The Confucian View' (2004) 29 The Journal of Medicine and Philosophy 179.

71 Nie Jing-Bao (11*n*61) 98–115.

72 Beauchamp and Childress (40*n*44) 340.

73 Cong Yali (20*n*8) 249.

74 Qiu Renzong 邱仁宗, *Shengming lunli xue* 生命伦理学 [*Bioethics*] (13*n*70) 24.

which he regarded Thomas Aquinas as the foremost exponent.[75] However, the mention of the latter seems more linked to the political challenges faced by China in the 1980s, particularly the one-child policy, rather than the relevance of naturalism from a bioethical perspective. In his 1987 publication, Qiu briefly describes it only to point out the difficulty in employing this theory to make 'reasonable' decisions regarding population policy and contraception, since its principles do not clarify whether it is 'naturally moral' to exclusively aim sex at reproduction.[76] Therefore, I will refrain from exploring natural law theory and solely focus on the other group of deontological theories highlighted by the Chinese author.

2.1.2 Deontological Theories: Kantianism

Deontological, or nonconsequentialist, theories assess the correctness of an action beyond only its consequences.[77] The most influential of these philosophies is Kantianism.[78] The ethics of Immanuel Kant (1724–1804) has so profoundly influenced this current of thought that deontological theories are sometimes even referred to as Kantian.[79] Kant, who considered morality to be grounded in reason[80] held that any action should be evaluated on what he called the 'Categorical imperative': 'Act so that the maxim of thy will can always at the same time hold good as a principle of universal legislation.'[81] This criterion is the basis for judging the moral acceptability of the maxims that lead to action: a rule is moral only if it can be consistently universalized. We can find different formulations of the categorical imperative even in Kant's works. In the 'Groundwork on the Metaphysics of Morals,' for example, he sets another equally important version, which he defined as the categorical imperative regarding human will.[82] The ground rule of this principle is: 'a rational nature exists as an end in itself,'[83] so the practical imperative sounds like: '[...] act that you use humanity, in your own person as well as in the

75 Ibid 24–25.

76 Ibid 25.

77 Beauchamp and Childress (40*n*44) 343.

78 van der Burg (19*n*3) 6; Qiu Renzong 邱仁宗, *Shengming lunli xue* 生命伦理学 [*Bioethics*] (13*n*70) 14.

79 Beauchamp and Childress (40*n*44) 343.

80 Immanuel Kant, *Critique of Practical Reason* (Thomas Kingsmill Abbott tr, DigiCat 2022) 36.

81 Ibid 35.

82 Christine M Korsgaard, Mary Gregor and Jens Timmermann, *Kant: Groundwork of the Metaphysics of Morals* (2° edizione, Cambridge University Press 2012) 41.

83 Ibid.

person of any other, always at the same time as an end, never merely as a means.'[84] This imperative has become particularly important in bioethics, especially with reference to the inderogability of voluntary consent in human experimentation, set forth in 1947 in the 'Nuremberg Code.'[85] The modern concept of respect for autonomy inherent in the previously mentioned principle of medical ethics should not confuse us. For Kant, autonomy means acting consciously according to moral principles which have been verified in the light of the categorical imperative. He contrasts moral autonomy in this sense with the heteronomy of those who regulate their actions based on motives other than moral principles, such as desire, ambition, or self-interest.[86] Many contemporary philosophers have developed Kantian moral theories, with particular reference to the second categorical imperative. Among them, we can mention Bernard Williams and Thomas Nagel, who developed their doctrine of 'deontological constraints' starting from Kant's conception of never using another person as a means;[87] Aland Donagan, who found in Kant's conception of persons in themselves as an end the 'philosophical core' of Hebrew-Christian morality;[88] and even John Rawls, who drew inspiration for his theory of justice from Kant's idea of morality as stemming from pure rationality.[89]

2.1.2.1 *The Union of Consequentialist and Deontological Approaches: The Four Principles of Beauchamp and Childress*

Kantian thought has been enormously influential on modern moral theories, especially biomedical ethics.[90] However, various deontological and consequentialist moral principles appear in bioethical debate, often mixed together.[91] For example, and as noted by Childress in 2009, most moral justifications of research involving human beings invoke deontological principles

84 Ibid.

85 'Nuremberg Code' (*United States Holocaust Memorial Museum*) <https://www.ushmm.org/information/exhibitions/online-exhibitions/special-focus/doctors-trial/nuremberg-code#Permissible> accessed 22 August 2022.

86 Korsgaard, Gregor and Timmermann (45*n*82) 62.

87 Williams (37*n*18); Thomas Nagel, 'Personal Rights and Public Space' (1995) 24 Philosophy <html_ent glyph="@amp;" ascii="&"/> Public Affairs 83.

88 Alan Donagan, *The Theory of Morality* (New edizione, University of Chicago Press 1979).

89 John Rawls, *A Theory of Justice: Revised Edition* (Revised edizione, Belknap Pr 1999).

90 Beauchamp and Childress (40*n*44) 349.

91 James F Childress, 'A Principle-Based Approach,' *A Companion to Bioethics* (John Wiley & Sons, Ltd 2009) 68 <https://onlinelibrary.wiley.com/doi/abs/10.1002/9781444307818.ch7> accessed 22 August 2022.

along with consequentialist considerations.[92] Moreover, some bioethicists have tried to unite consequentialist and deontological principles. This is precisely the position of Beauchamp and Childress who propose a group of moral principles as a general guide for the formulation of more specific rules,[93] specifically: (1) respect for autonomy, (2) nonmaleficence; (3) beneficence (included utility);[94] (4) justice. According to the two authors, these primary or fundamental principles 'express the general norms of the common morality that are a suitable starting point for bioethics.'[95] From them, a series of 'derivatives rules' stem, such as 'telling the truth' and 'keeping promises.[96] The idea of a 'common morality,' which is 'a universal shared product,' because it is 'shared by all persons committed to morality'[97] is extremely interesting for our purpose. Beauchamp and Childress provide examples of the standards of action found in it, such as 'do not kill,' 'do not cause pain or suffering to the others,' 'prevent evil or harm from occurring,' 'rescue person in danger,' 'tell the truth,' 'nurture the young and dependent,' 'keep your promise,' 'do not steal,' 'do not punish the innocent,' and 'obey the law.'[98] Furthermore, they list moral traits, or virtues, recognised in common morality: 'nonmalevolence,' honesty, integrity, conscientiousness, trustworthiness, fidelity, gratitude, truthfulness, lovingness, and kindness.[99]

In 1987, Qiu Renzong introduced the four principles of Beauchamp and Childress into China, which were swiftly embraced by medical ethicists and integrated into medical school curricula.[100] However, their interpretation was influenced by socialist principles that had shaped medical ethics in mainland China since the establishment of the PRC. These socialist principles encompassed the 'spirit of self-sacrifice, self-cultivation, a high sense of responsibility, modesty, self-control, and devotion.'[101] Additionally, they included the notions of the sanctity of life, a duty-based ethics of medicine, and the overarching belief that public benefit should take precedence over individual

92 Ibid.

93 Beauchamp and Childress (40*n*44).

94 Childress (47*n*91) 68.

95 Beauchamp and Childress (40*n*44) 3.

96 Ibid 13.

97 Ibid 3.

98 Ibid.

99 Ibid.

100 Cong Yali (20*n*8) 248–249.

101 Nie Jingbao, 'The Plurality of Chinese and American Medical Moralities: Toward an Interpretive Cross-Cultural Bioethics' (2000) 10 Kennedy Institute of Ethics Journal 239, 240.

benefit in cases of conflict.[102] As highlighted by Fan Ruipin in 1997, pre-existing Chinese values did not lead to the rejection of the new Western principles, but rather reordered their hierarchy, relative to the original model. Thus, while in the American context, autonomy held the greatest significance, in the Chinese context, the principle of beneficence took precedence.[103]

Interestingly, the inclination to emphasise context and interpersonal relations in ethical discourse, traditionally acknowledged as a Chinese characteristic, has now evolved into a global trend within normative ethics. In particular, abstract theories have been criticised because they mainly focus on the way we treat the others, paying little, if any, attention to the special attachment we experience in our moral life towards family and friends.[104] Furthermore, feminist philosophers have highlighted the aptitude of traditional normative theories to concentrate on abstract, gender-neutral, and therefore non-existent, persons. They advocate, on the contrary, for the need for ethics, especially bioethics, to deal with actual men and women, placed in their context, and to take into account their histories and the caring relationships they have with their loved ones.[105] Neo-Aristotelian philosophers, who emphasise the importance of personal character, hold a similar position, and propose virtue ethics as an alternative to both deontology and consequentialism. These two approaches are particularly interesting compared with the Chinese attitude towards ethics. I will therefore conclude this section on Western normative theories with a short description of them.

2.1.3 Virtue Ethics

The renewed interest in the ancient notion of virtue can be traced back to a 1958 article by Elizabeth Anscombe on 'Modern Moral Philosophy.' However, it was only from the 1980s onwards that the virtue-based approach to ethics really began to take hold, thanks to thinkers such as, among others, the already mentioned Bernard Williams, and Alasdair McIntyre,[106] who deserves our special attention because his philosophy has been explored in relation to

---

102 Wu Zhaohua, 'Conflicts between Chinese Traditional Ethics and Bioethics' (1994) 3 Cambridge Quarterly of Healthcare Ethics 367, 370; Cong Yali (2*n*8) 248.

103 Fan Ruiping, 'Three Levels of Problems in Cross-Cultural Explorations of Bioethics: A Methodological Approach' in Hoshino Kazumasa (ed), *Japanese and Western Bioethics: Studies in Moral Diversity* (Springer Netherlands 1997) 196–197 <https://doi.org/10.1007/978-94-015-8895-9_17> accessed 4 January 2024.

104 van der Burg (40*n*46) 7.

105 Ibid.

106 Alasdair MacIntyre, *After Virtue: A Study in Moral Theory, Third Edition* (3° edizione, New Publisher 2021).

Confucianism.[107] Indeed, over the course of the twenty-first century, the development and refinement of virtue ethics have made it a credible alternative to the consequentialist and deontological approaches, from which it differs already from its starting point. Whereas traditional normative theories focus on moral behaviours, asking what we should do, virtue ethics is cantered on moral agents, wondering what kind of person we should be and what kind of life we should lead. In this way, it succeeds in making up for the excessive abstraction found in consequentialism and Kantianism, sometimes deemed incapable of guiding action in concrete circumstances.[108] In fact, while consequentialism and Kantianism can only judge an action as right or wrong, mandatory or permitted, virtue ethics is founded on human virtues, which are more nuanced and thus can enrich the range of choice for a moral act.[109] The virtue approach also elevates the importance of context and interpersonal relations.[110] These aspects are particularly important in bioethics, especially when it comes to the care of patients, where an approach focused on the character and virtue of the health professional can be particularly fruitful. Indeed, the criterion used as the basis to develop most virtue approaches to bioethics can be summarised as follows: 'an action is right if and only if it is what an agent with a virtuous character would do in the circumstances.'[111] Most virtue ethicists believe that this criterion not only refers to the outward appearance of behaviour, but also to the motivation and disposition of mind that a virtuous agent should possess in that given situation.[112] This interpretation is in line with Aristotle's description of virtue in the Nicomachean Ethics, according to which '[...]it is not merely the state in accordance with the right rule, but the state that implies the presence of the right rule, that is virtue (*ἀρετή*).'[113] Virtues are not just agent-cantered: according to many contemporary virtue ethicists, virtues are also 'intrinsic goods that are plural,'[114] and therefore cannot be reduced to a single underlying value, such as utility, as in the case of utilitarianism.[115] Contemporary virtue ethicists' approach can be

107 Sim (14*n*77).

108 Justin Oakley, 'A Virtue Ethics Approach,' *A Companion to Bioethics: Second Edition* (2010) 92.

109 Ibid 95.

110 Ibid 92.

111 Ibid 93.

112 Ibid.

113 'Nicomachean Ethics: Text – IntraText CT' pt VI,13 <http://www.intratext.com/IXT/ENG2244/_P1V.HTM> accessed 24 August 2022.

114 Oakley (49*n*108) 95.

115 Ibid.

split into two types. The first approach sticks to Aristotle's idea of *eudaimonia* (*εὐδαιμονία*: happiness, flourishing) as a human being's supreme goal, or *telos* (*τέλος*). This view defines virtues as the character traits we need to reach *eudaimonia*, i.e. to live humanely flourishing lives. The second approach rejects this interpretation, as in the thought of Michael Slote, who derives virtues from our common-sense ideas about what character traits we find estimable, regardless of whether those traits help an individual flourish.[116]

Indeed, virtue ethics gives new perspectives on many issues in bioethics, with particular reference to the topics we will discuss in the following chapters of this book. Furthermore, being goal-cantered and recognising role-differentiation, virtue ethics provides a useful basis to develop a set of principles for various professional roles, such as health professions, legal practice, and business.[117]

2.1.4 Care Ethics

Like virtue ethics, care ethics also has only recently emerged as a systematic normative theory. Indeed, historical antecedents to this approach are often traced back to philosophers such as David Hume and even Adam Smith, for their belief that we should generalise behaviour from our relationships with our loved ones.[118] However, Nel Noddings's 1984 book *Caring: A feminine Approach to Ethics and Moral Education* is considered the first contemporary work on care as a moral compass.[119] Other thinkers, such as Sara Ruddick,[120] Rita Manning,[121] Annette Baier,[122] and especially Virginia Held, later developed and expanded this perspective.[123] According to Rita Manning, 'care involves a basic human capacity to recognize and respond to the needs of others, and to moderate our behaviour in light of the good of harm it might

116 Michael Slote, *Morals from Motives* (Oxford University Press 2003).

117 Oakley/Cocking, *Virtue Ethics and Professional Roles* (1° edizione, Cambridge University Press 2008).

118 Rita C Manning, 'A Care Approach,' *A Companion to Bioethics* (John Wiley & Sons, Ltd 2009) 105 <http://onlinelibrary.wiley.com/doi/abs/10.1002/9781444307818.ch11> accessed 25 August 2022.

119 Nel Noddings, *Caring: A Feminine Approach to Ethics and Moral Education* (2° edizione, Univ of California Pr 2003).

120 Sara Ruddick, *Maternal Thinking: Toward a Politics of Peace* (Reprint edizione, Beacon Press 1995).

121 Rita C Manning, *Speaking from the Heart: A Feminist Perspective on Ethics* (Rowman & Littlefield Pub Inc 1992).

122 Annette C Baier, *Moral Prejudices: Essays on Ethics* (Harvard University Press 1995).

123 Manning (50*n*118) 106–107.

cause to others.'[124] The foundation of this approach lies in the recognition of empathy as an innate feature of human beings, and in the urge to help and care as a natural human reaction to the suffering of a fellow human being. In particular, we feel such a drive towards our loved ones. The essential idea is that we must understand the values and practices underlying people's caring behaviour towards their loved ones and apply these same values to our relationships with strangers. Manning identifies four central processes in an ethics of care: 'moral attention,' 'sympathetic understanding' (also known as 'maternalism'), 'relationship awareness,' and 'harmony and accommodation.'[125] To these, Michael Slote adds 'benevolence' as a characteristic of ideal agents.[126] We will see in the next section how familiar all these principles may sound to Chinese ethicists. For now, let's look at how care ethics can prove valuable in several areas of bioethics. The most obvious may be in the clinical setting, since it is commonly acknowledged that care and concern for the well-being of patients are important aspects of the doctor/nurse-to-patient relationship. However, it is precisely in that context, with particular reference to nursing ethics, that some authors have criticised the view of the ethics of care as a 'female' approach to ethics. Helga Kuhse has argued against Nel Noddings[127] and Carol Gilligan's[128] interpretation of a 'female ethics of care' as opposed to a 'male ethics of justice.'[129] According to the author, this view merely re-proposes and corroborates the thesis that women 'lack a head for abstract principles and especially a sense of justice,'[130] a claim that runs through the history of philosophy among prominent thinkers such as Aristotle, Rousseau, Schopenhauer, and Freud.[131] Therefore, while maintaining that 'care' is necessary for good patient care, Kuhse opposes using the idea as an adequate foundational concept for nursing (and women's) ethics.[132] The research setting and the setting of resource allocation are other fields in which care approach, in particular Slote's theory of balancing and his ideal benevolent agent, can be useful. Indeed, acknowledging that even people far

124 Manning (50*n*118) 105.

125 Ibid 106–107.

126 Slote (50*n*116) 63.

127 Noddings (50*n*119).

128 Carol Gilligan, *In a Different Voice: Psychological Theory and Women's Development* (Reprint edizione, Harvard Univ Pr 2016).

129 Helga Kuhse, 'Clinical Ethics and Nursing: "Yes" to Caring, but "No" to a Female Ethics of Care' (1995) 9 Bioethics 207.

130 Ibid 108.

131 Ibid 207–208, 219.

132 Ibid 219.

away from us have the same wishes, hopes and needs as our own kin can help researchers and politicians make moral choices in situations where different interests are at stake.[133]

But is that really the case? Do people far away from us, such as the Chinese, have the same wishes, hopes and needs as us? Even if they do, what principles and doctrines, if any, do their politicians use to make moral choices? Are there other 'morals,' different from those we are used to? Let's start by looking at the meaning of the word 'ethics' in Chinese.

---

133 Manning (50*n*118) 114–115.

CHAPTER 3

Morality, Ethics, and Bioethics in the Chinese Context

1 Introduction

The theories discussed so far have shaped the overall approach to bioethics and serve as reference points in the development of a regulatory framework. Not surprisingly, even Chinese bioethicists like Qiu Renzong routinely refer to such theories,[1] even though they were formulated and developed in Europe and North America. Therefore, it is fair to ask whether the Chinese approach to bioethics merely reflects these foreign theories or includes other latent principles so ingrained in their own culture that Chinese authors take them for granted, as if they were some kind of 'moral cryptotypes.' Is there bioethics 'with Chinese characteristics?' If so, what are its philosophical references? Even more basic: What is the meaning of 'ethics' in the Chinese context? Has a Chinese ethics – in its original Greek-Roman sense of moral philosophy – ever existed?

These are not idle questions. Like Western legal concepts and norms, Western philosophical notions have only been introduced in China since the late nineteenth century, when they were translated into Chinese, thus transforming (and in turn being transformed by) the indigenous Chinese categories. This process, much studied by comparatists from a legal transplant perspective, is not as common in philosophy and similar subjects. Yet it cannot be ignored in research investigating the relationship between regulations and moral principles in the field of bioethics.

This chapter provides a brief account of the complexity of rendering foreign philosophical terms into Chinese and vice-versa, followed by a description of the key aspects of the doctrines that have influenced the Chinese conception of the physical body and any relevant issues. Particular attention will be dedicated to Confucianism, predominant in the imperial era, which in recent years has been rediscovered by Chinese leaders as the cornerstone of 'typically Chinese' values to be promoted within society. Besides Confucianism, I will also describe the basic features of Daoism, Mohism, Buddhism, and Marxism,

1 Qiu Renzong 邱仁宗, *Shengming lunli xue* 生命伦理学(增订版)(精)/当代中国人文大系 [*Bioethics*] (2019) 8–15.

 | DOI:10.1163/9789004754300_005

all of which have helped shaped Chinese culture and society, and further analyse their respective approaches to the beginning of life in the second part of this book, where I will examine their possible impact on current Chinese bioethical regulations.

2 Chinese Ethics: Another Oxymoron?

To understand whether a Chinese approach to bioethics exists, we must first define Chinese ethics. This philosophical and linguistic challenge faces further complication from the fact that ancient Chinese lacks any single lexical equivalent for the English word 'moral.'[2] This aspect is little known and even neglected by translators, who have often stretched the meaning of various characters to make them somehow match the Western concept, altering not only the genuine meaning of notions from the Chinese tradition, but also causing Western philosophers to look down on Chinese thinkers.[3] Indeed, in standard translations, Confucian philosophical terms are rendered by using values typical of the Judeo-Christian tradition.[4] Thus, *Tian* 天 becomes Heaven, *li* 礼 ritual, *yi* 义 justice, *ren* 仁 benevolence, *de* 德 virtue, and so.[5] Rather than making ancient Chinese writers more immediately comprehensible to a Western audience, these simplistic translations have in fact led many to judge Confucius's thought as a watered-down, less incisive version of Christianity.[6] Meanwhile, attempts to overcome such linguistic barriers by using terms less related to the Abrahamic religions have also fallen short, either turning Confucianism into a sort of secular humanism, deprived of its own deep religious dimension, or misrepresenting its holistic worldview by likening it to mysticism and occultism.[7] Even today, philosophy departments in European and North American universities rarely include the study of ancient Chinese thought in their programmes, instead, relegating them to the sphere of religious or regional studies.[8]

A similar process happens in with law. Firstly, Western categories are applied to the Chinese context. Then, the Chinese context is found to be 'lack-

2 Henry Rosemont, 'Against Relativism' in Eliot Deutsch and Gerald James Larson (eds), *Interpreting Across Boundaries: New Essays in Comparative Philosophy* (Princeton University Press 1988) 61; Rosemont and Ames (31*n*88) 21–22.

3 Rosemont and Ames (31*n*88) 20–21.

4 Ibid 24.

5 Ibid 23–24.

6 Ibid 24.

7 Ibid.

8 Ibid.

ing' some typical aspect of the Western experience. Finally, the Western experience postulated as the standard in that given field, China is considered not only 'lacking' something compared to the West, but in an absolute sense. From there, it's a short step to concluding that China has never had law, philosophy, or morality.

To overcome this problem, at least in the philosophical sphere, Ames and Rosemont recommend *not* translating Chinese terms into European languages, but to leave them in characters or use the characters' transliteration to express them. In practice, a similar circumstance and technique applies to legal terms when their peculiar semantic value cannot be rendered in the target idiom without generating misunderstandings. For the same reason, they suggest taking into account both the peculiarities of the Chinese language and the cluster of concepts that accompany Chinese philosophical notions when approaching ancient Chinese texts.[9] Before explaining these solutions, we must recognize that Chinese academics do not unanimously accept the Ames and Rosemont approach. Prof Zhang Longxi, a leading scholar in cross-cultural studies, is one such prominent critic. Once again, the contrast between (supposedly) universalist and relativist positions lies at the heart of the issue. Universalists hold that cultures, while different, have matching equivalents that always make them mutually intelligible, while relativists believe that irreconcilable dissimilarities render another culture difficult, at times even impossible, to fully understand. While Professor Zhang would place himself in the first group, Ames and Rosemont, in the footsteps of Confucian philosopher Qian Mu (1895–1990), would belong to the second. The debate somehow replicates the controversy on the translatability of legal concepts, not least due to mutual accusations of ethnocentrism and orientalism.[10] Without going into details, the disagreement mainly comes down to methodology. In my opinion, Qian Mu's claim that, 'with sufficient explanation, the Confucian world can be appreciated in important degrees by those from without'[11] is not substantially different from Zhang Longxi's recent statement that 'translation means not only a one-to-one equivalence, but involves annotation, explanation, and interpretation; it requires tireless efforts to make communication possible.'[12] While I agree with Profs Sacco and Zhang that translation is always possible, I also consider Ames and Rose-

9 Ibid 23.

10 Ibid 25–28; Zhang Longxi, 'Cross-Cultural Translatability: Challenges and Prospects' (2015) 23 European Review 369, 374–376.

11 Rosemont and Ames (31*n*88) 24.

12 Zhang Longxi (55*n*10) 377.

mont's pluralist and openly generativist position[13] very useful to fully understand Chinese ethics and bioethics, particularly regarding their focus on language.

In fact, Classical Chinese differs from all other languages, particularly Indo-European ones, for being an 'event'-based language rather than a 'thing'-based language.[14] Each character can function as a noun, verb, and often as an adjective or adverb, depending on its position in the sentence. Classical Chinese terms do not have a precise grammar function separate from their context.[15] Moreover, it brings linguistic dynamism and a de-emphasis on nouns,[16] two aspects that proved crucial in shaping early Chinese metaphysics.[17]

In particular, the lesser importance given to nouns would explain the absence of the concept of 'substance' or 'essence' in ancient Chinese thought, while the focus of the language on events might have led to putting the person in its relational dimension, rather than as an individual self, at the centre of ethical reflections.[18] This might also be the reason for favouring nuance and ambiguity over precision, typical not just of Chinese art[19] but also (as far as we are concerned here) of the legislative style of the PRC.

Understanding the structure of language can shed light on the Chinese philosophical perspective, but not enough to make the message of Chinese thinkers intelligible to modern readers. To achieve this without altering the original message, we must translate the terms contained in ancient Chinese texts, using Ames and Rosemont's notion of a concept-cluster, or the overall vocabulary used in a given context to assess human behaviour.[20]

This approach seems to suit our purposes very well. In fact, through the lens of our twenty-first-century Western culture, we cannot speak about moral issues without using concepts such as liberty, freedom, self-determination, rationality, objective, subjective, choice, dilemma, duty, and rights.[21] All these terms and concepts specify and delimitate our idea of what is 'moral,' or – using Ames and Rosemont's words – of what constitute the concept-cluster revolving around the notion of morals in our contemporary context. The point is that none of these terms/concepts (including, it is worth repeating, 'morals' itself)

13 Rosemont and Ames (31*n*88) 21.
14 Ibid 20.
15 Ibid.
16 Ibid 21.
17 Ibid 20.
18 Ibid 21.
19 Ibid.
20 Ibid 22.
21 Rosemont (54*n*2) 60.

has a lexical equivalent in classical Chinese. What is more, when, at the end of the Qing era (1644–1912), Western scholars tried to introduce these concepts and terms into China, it took countless attempts to find ways of conveying them into characters that would make their meaning at least partially understandable to the Chinese. Even then, the meaning of such neologisms often had negative overtones not inherent to the original words. Take, for instance, the word 'liberty.' In early English-Chinese dictionaries, published mostly by English missionaries in the first half of the nineteenth century, liberty is either translated as *zizhu zhili* 自主之理 (literally: principle of self-determination), *zicao zhiquan* 自操之权 (right of self-government), or *ziyou* 自由 (unrestrained).[22] While all these expressions closely reflect the meaning of the English term[23] none actually describes a status or a type of behaviour that a Chinese person of the late Qing era would consider ethically sound or even remotely desirable. In fact, for millennia, the conduct of the members of Chinese society had been assessed following entirely different criteria deriving from Confucian thought. They were centred on the concept/character of *ren* 仁, together with notions such as *xin* 心, *xiao* 孝, de 德, xin 信, *junzi* 君子, *zhi* 知, *xiaoren* 小人, *yi* 义, *cheng* 诚, and *li* 礼.

We will see what these concepts/characters consist of later on. For the time being, it is worth pointing out the traditional Chinese vision differs from the Western one, not just for its reference to different principles, or for its emphasis on the relationships among things rather than on the things in themselves. A third aspect concerns more specifically the way of conceiving life, the cosmos, and man's role. Once again, it is language that exemplifies these differences in the clearest way.

Consider, for example, the dualism between body and mind, typical of classical Western philosophical thought. The concepts behind such dualities are perceived as distinct and antithetical, and for this reason European languages use separate words to refer to them. In the Chinese view, however, mind and body are not separate entities, but intertwined aspects of existence, involved in a continuous relationship of mutual exchange. For this reason, Chinese often combines them in a single disyllabic word: *shenxin* 身心 (literally: body-heart, body-mind), which describes human essence as a whole, conceiving it as a binary entity, without distinctions or hierarchies, in a constant state of

---

22 Xiong Yuezhi, '"Liberty", "Democracy", "President": The Translation and Usage of Some Political Terms in Late Qing China', *NewNew Terms for New Ideas: Western Knowledge and Lexical Change in Late Imperial China* (Brill 2001) 69 <https://brill.com/view/book/edcoll/9789004501669/B9789004501669_s008.xml> accessed 3 November 2022.

23 Xiong Yuezhi (57*n*22).

flow and becoming. Like any other aspect of experience, *shenxin* takes shape and functions (again: two separate concepts in Western languages, expressed in Chinese by just one disyllabic word: *tiyong* 体用), and perpetually oscillates between transience and persistence (another disyllabic word: *biantong* 变通).[24] The same reasoning applies to another couple of concepts that are extremely important for ethics, in general, and bioethics, in particular. I am referring to the Western dualism between theory and practice, which the Chinese language expresses with a single word that combines the two meanings: *zhixing* 知行.[25] This aspect recalls the 'unity of theory and practice' in which Marxism has recognised itself since its origins,[26] which might partly explain why such ideology has been so successful in China; certainly, it must not have been difficult for Chairman Mao to adopt the concept by defining theory as 'practice-oriented knowledge.'[27]

Many foreign observers have long attributed this complementary view of extremes, which ignores the supposed supremacy of spirit over matter, to the Chinese propensity for avoiding abstraction. In the previous section I mentioned Liebniz's opinion regarding the tendency of the Chinese language to focus on concrete descriptions and details, thus, fail to grasp essence. Similarly, Western thinkers considered Chinese thought incapable of generalisation and, therefore, 'unable to rise above the ground of materiality and literality toward any spiritual height.'[28]

Until very recently, many authors agreed with this idea. For example, Fox and Swazey, among the first American bioethicists to conduct a field study in China, expressed views about Chinese doctors and nurses' perceived lack of inclination towards theoretical speculation.[29] In their article 'Medical Bioethics Is Not Bioethics,' the two authors pointed out that they felt closer to the humanistic approach to ethics typical of Chinese health professionals than to

24 Rosemont and Ames (31*n*88) 28.

25 Ibid.

26 Frederic L Bender, 'Marxism East and West: Lenin's Revisions of Orthodox Marxism and Their Significance for Non-Western Revolution' (1973) 23 Philosophy East and West 299, 299.

27 Donald M Lowe, *The Function of China in Marx, Lenin, and Mao* (First Edition, Berkeley, University Of California Press 1966) 117.

28 Zhang Longxi, 'Translating Cultures: China and the West' in Karl-Heinz Pohl (ed), *Chinese Thought in a Global Context: A Dialogue Between Chinese and Western Philosophical Approaches* (Brill 1999) 45 <https://brill.com/display/book/edcoll/9789004501676/B9789004501676_s005.xml> accessed 20 November 2022.

29 Renée C Fox and Judith P Swazey, 'Medical Morality Is Not Bioethics Medical Ethics in China and the United States' (1984) 27 Perspectives in Biology and Medicine 336.

their American colleagues' ethnocentric definition of bioethics.[30] In the meantime, however, Fox and Swazey found that Chinese doctors and nurses were not at all interested in purely abstract speculation about social and moral issues, or what Chinese scholars historically have called 'playing with emptiness.'[31]

The article was written in the early 1980s, at a time when new biomedical technologies, inherent ethical problems and even the very concept of bioethics were absent from everyday practice in China's hospitals. Even then, however, '"work ethics," "civic virtues" and their relationship to the integrity and development of society as a whole'[32] seemed to be 'constantly stressed, ideologically and politically, in every sphere of Chinese life,'[33] medical practice included. Indeed, for Fox and Swazey, ethics was 'the centre of the Chinese worldview – its very core and essence in Chinese society today as it has been for thousands of years.'[34] In particular, the authors were struck by the 'Chinese-ness' of Chinese medical morality, which they saw as a synthesis and harmonisation of the ideas of Marxism, Confucianism, Daoism, and Buddhism.[35]

At this point, a brief analysis of these philosophies will help us better perceive the 'Chinese characteristics' in the approach to bioethical issues within the PRC and what they consist of. Let us start with the ideology that has had the greatest influence, not only in Mainland China's culture, but also in Korea, Japan, Hong Kong, and Taiwan: Confucianism.[36]

2.1 *Confucianism*

Many authors acknowledge the relevance of Confucianism on the everyday lives of people in East Asia. Many articles and books have been written about its impact on bioethics in the region, suggesting ways in which the Confucian approach can be useful in addressing new bioethical challenges at a global level. Not surprisingly, the entry 'Confucianism' has been included in recent editions of encyclopaedias on bioethics.[37] However, the abundance of studies does not make it any easier to summarise its ethical approach. First of

30 Ibid 337,339.

31 Ibid 339.

32 Ibid 340.

33 Ibid.

34 Ibid 339.

35 Ibid 347.

36 Ruiping Fan, 'Introduction: Towards a Confucian Bioethics', *Confucian Bioethics: 61* (1999th edition, Springer 1999).

37 Stephen Garrard Post, *Encyclopedia of Bioethics*, vol 1 (Macmillan Reference USA 2004) 508.

all, Confucianism has never been monolithic, nor has it ever existed in conceptual isolation. Depending on the historical moments, and with regard to both the theory of its thinkers and practice in everyday lives, it was influenced by other doctrines, such as Daoism, Mahayana Buddhism, and even local folk religions. It subsequently evolved and changed significantly over the millennia that separate the Spring and Autumn period – the time when Master Kong (*Kong fuzi* 孔夫子, Latinised into 'Confucius' by the first missionaries, 551–479 BC) lived – to the twenty-first-century declinations of his thought.

During the same period, the core principles and overarching objectives of this philosophy significantly shaped medical ethics and the training of physicians. It is widely acknowledged that in Imperial times, aspiring medical practitioners were expected to have studied the Confucian canon. Particularly during Song dynasty (920–1279) and Ming dynasty (1368–1644), numerous Confucian scholars ventured into the field of medicine, establishing a distinct practice known as Confucian medicine.[38] Some scholars argue that the influence of Confucianism, especially concerning the nexus between ethics and politics, has long been ingrained in the Chinese medical profession.[39] This imprint continues to shape the approach of Chinese doctors towards contemporary bioethical issues, such as abortion and euthanasia.[40] To grasp the essence of this approach, an examination of Confucianism's fundamental concepts is therefore imperative. For simplicity, I will primarily delve into these concepts as originally formulated in the oldest collection of Master Kong's teachings, the Lunyu 论语, commonly referred to as the Analects.

The Analects is a selection of sayings and brief anecdotes attributed to Confucius and some of his disciples. Two of its most important concepts are *Dao* 道, usually translated as 'the Way,' and *de* 德, 'potency,' also translated as 'virtue.'[41] The two concepts are interdependent: a person's *de* is his or her potential to act according to the *Dao,* here understood as the proper course of human conduct and of the organisation of the government.[42] In an ideal world, the ruler should not have to do anything at all (*wu wei* 无为): He should simply trust *de*, the potency he radiates which is powerful enough to guide others to the Way.[43] Note that the Analects mentions the concept of *wuwei*

38 Cong Yali (2018) 241.

39 Ibid.

40 Ibid.

41 AC Graham, *Disputers of the Tao: Philosophical Argument in Ancient China* (First Edition, Open Court 1989) 9.

42 Ibid 13.

43 Ibid 14.

just once.[44] However, its presence together with the notions of *Dao* and *de* illustrates the extreme permeability of ancient Chinese philosophical ideas, since these three concepts, albeit with slightly different meanings, later play a crucial role in Daoism.[45]

The most important Confucian virtue is *ren* 仁, often translated into English as 'benevolence,' yet in its original Confucian context seems closer to the concept of 'noble' or 'human' in a social and 'moral'[46] sense. *Ren* is the virtue that distinguishes the gentleman (*junzi* 君子), the exemplary person, from commoners (*xiao ren* 小人). In the Analects, Confucius explains what kind of behaviour constitutes *ren*:

> When you go abroad, to behave to every one as if you were receiving a great guest; to employ the people as if you were assisting at a great sacrifice; not to do to others as you would not wish done to yourself; to have no murmuring against you in the country, and none in the family.[47]

As it is often the case in the Analects, the quote above juxtaposes the concept of *ren* with that of *li* 礼 (ceremonial propriety), another key notion of Confucianism that indicates a body of concrete guidelines for action in various contexts. Ceremonial propriety, however, cannot exhaust the behavioural content of *ren*. Not only is there a great deal of human interaction outside the scope of rites, but the demands of propriety often conflict with one another. Perhaps for these reasons, Confucius here associates *ren* with a universal norm, i.e.: not to do to others as you would not wish done to yourself. This expression, which Graham defines as 'the negative form of the Golden Rule at the heart of ethics,'[48] can be found several times in the Analects. In some cases, it is summarised in a single word: *shu* 恕,[49] which is formed by *ru* 如 'be like,' a basis of analogical thinking in Chinese, and the 'heart' radical (*xin* 心), which often marks verbs of thinking and feeling. The resulting character means 'thinking of [self and others] as alike'[50] and indicates the disinterested concern for the

---

44 Confucius and DC Lau, *The Analects* (James Legge tr, 1° edizione, Penguin Classics 1979) ch 15.5 Wei Ling Gong-卫灵公.

45 Graham (60*n*41) 13, 14.

46 I use this term with the *caveat* I have expressed *supra*, in this section.

47 Confucius and Lau (61*n*44) ch 12.2 Yan Yuan-颜渊.

48 Graham (60*n*41) 20.

49 Confucius and Lau (61*n*44) ch 15.24 Wei Ling Gong-卫灵公.

50 Graham (60*n*41) 20.

other person,'[51] the feeling that, according to Confucius, should guide a man's actions throughout his life.

Inevitably, the Confucian emphasis on concepts such as *ren* and *de* led modern bioethicists to make comparisons with the role of virtues in Aristotelian ethics,[52] and some scholars have even referred to Confucianism as a form of virtue ethics.[53] While admitting that the typical moral vision of virtue ethics is closer to Confucian than Kantian or utilitarian ethical theories, many sinologists have contested this association of philosophies, arguing that juxtaposing Confucianism with the most modern versions of virtue ethics, such as care ethics, would be to cage Confucian thought in Western categories and miss out on its originality, thereby disqualifying it from consideration as a valid alternative to conventional (and Western) ethical and bioethical approaches.[54] The same authors notice, instead, that Confucianism represents a specific way of looking at human beings as relational persons defined by the roles they play in society rather than as individuals. Moreover, Confucianism expresses a specific vision of moral life that considers family feelings as the starting point to developing perfect 'moral' competence.[55] They argue, therefore, that Confucianism should be seen as a form of role ethics.[56] This interpretation is particularly persuasive to me because it is closer to the original source and it better clarifies the distinctive aspects of Confucian thought. Thus, unless otherwise stated, the following description of Confucian ethics derives from the works of scholars who interpret it as a form of role ethics.

Undoubtedly, the character *ren* 仁 itself expresses the centrality of relationships in the Confucian path to 'moral' perfection, being composed from the radical of man 人, and the number two 二. The resulting ideogram shows that one cannot be noble, or even human, when alone or isolated from the rest of

51 Ibid 18.

52 Sim (14*n*77); Jiyuan Yu, *The Ethics of Confucius and Aristotle: Mirrors of Virtue* (1st edition, Routledge 2007).

53 Li Yuan, Robert Chia and Jonathan Gosling, 'Confucian Virtue Ethics and Ethical Leadership in Modern China' (2023) 182 Journal of Business Ethics 119; Stephen Angle and Michael Slote (eds), *Virtue Ethics and Confucianism* (1st edition, Routledge 2015); Csikszentmihalyi (14*n*77) 7.

54 Roger T Ames and Jr Henry Rosemont, 'Were the Early Confucians Virtuous?' in Chris Fraser, Dan Robins and Timothy O'Leary (eds), *Ethics in Early China: An Anthology* (Hong Kong University Press 2011) 17 <https://doi.org/10.5790/hongkong/9789888028931.003.0002> accessed 15 May 2023.

55 Ibid.

56 Ibid; Zhu Qin, 'Ethics, Society, and Technology: A Confucian Role Ethics Perspective' (2020) 63 Technology in Society 101424, 1; Roger T Ames, *Confucian Role Ethics: A Vocabulary* (Chinese University Press 2011).

mankind. *Ren* cannot be cultivated in solitude: Becoming *ren* 'is something we either do together, or not at all.'[57] As the Master reminds us, *ren* is 'to love all men' (*ai ren* 爱人),[58] the highest standard in dealing with human relationships and the relationship between the individual and society. This also clarifies the significance of ritual performance to the ethical cultivation of character. Rituals (*li* 礼) are not an external restriction on the self, as it is the case for the law (*fa* 法). *Li* is the outward expression of the *ren*'s moral sensibility. In this sense, both *li* and *ren* are, at the same time, public and private, with *li* structuring *ren* and encouraging and shaping the full participation of individuals in the life of their community.[59]

In turns, *ren*'s basis (*ren zhi benyu* 仁之本与) comprises two other concepts: filial piety (*xiao* 孝) and fraternal submission (*di* 弟).[60] According to Confucius, genuine concern for another human being originates within the life of the family. Just as it cannot exist in a void, *ren* cannot exist outside everyday family-based lives of the people who realise it in their role relationships.[61] Only through the deepening of the role relationships – i.e.: taking on the responsibilities and obligations of family and then, by extension, of communal living – can one become a *junzi*.[62] Not surprisingly, x*iao* is the root of *de*, the concept of potency/virtue/excellence mentioned above:

> When *xiao* is functioning effectively within the home, all is well within the community, the polity, and indeed, the cosmos;[63] they are few who, being filial and fraternal, are fond of offending against their superiors. There have been none who, not liking to offend against their superiors, have been fond of stirring up confusion.[64]

The aspects described so far show how Confucianism perceives moral development as practice-oriented.[65] It is only by behaving with filial piety that one

57 Ames (n 374); Zhu (n 374) 2.

58 Confucius and Lau (61*n*44) 12.22 Yan Yuan-颜渊

59 David Wong, 'Cultivating the Self in Concert with Others' (2013) 10.

60 Confucius and Lau (61*n*44) 1.2 Xue Er-学而.

61 Ames and Rosemont (62*n*54) 21.

62 Ibid.

63 Henry Rosemont and Roger T Ames, 'Introduction' in Henry Jr Rosemont and Roger T Ames (eds), *The Chinese Classic of Family Reverence: A Philosophical Translation of the Xiaojing* (University of Hawai'i Press 2008) <https://doi.org/10.21313/hawaii/9780824832841.003.0019> accessed 17 May 2023.

64 Confucius and Lau (61*n*44) 1.2 Xue Er-学而.

65 Zhu (62*n*56) 3.

can become distinguished as a person who behaves with filial piety: 'one *xiaos* in order to be *xiao*, or perhaps better, one *xiaos* and is *xiao*.'[66]

This is a peculiar approach to virtues, at least from a Western point of view. Confucian virtues are not metaphysical principles or predetermined, static ideals, as is instead the case in Kantianism, utilitarianism or virtue ethics. Instead, Confucian virtues are in a constant state of formation through an ongoing relationship between a person's inner self and the world outside him or her, following an approach that we have already seen to be typical of the Chinese language. They are 'an open-ended and always provisional virtuosity in our continuing patterns of relations,' the 'activity of relating itself,' 'a matter of continuing, collateral, or multilateral negotiation within the complexity of particular circumstances.'[67] Considering the concept of health in the positive sense, as a state of complete well-being, Confucian virtues also become the means to achieve personal health.[68] In the previous section, we took the two-syllable compound *shenxin* as an example of a way of understanding human reality that differs from Cartesian mind-body dualism.[69] In his essay 'Confucian virtues and personal health,' Ni accurately analyses the use of the characters *shen* and *xin* in the Confucian classical texts.[70] He notes that *shen*, commonly translated as person or body, refers to the embodiment of a person and, thus, does not exclude but rather includes the spiritual aspects of an individual.[71] *Xin*, on the other hand, is often translated as 'mind' but, etymologically, it means heart.[72] Far from being disembodied, it refers to an organ of thinking and feeling.[73] Consequently, Ni affirms that personal cultivation (*xiu shen* 修身), one of the fundamental stages of moral development according to Confucius, refers not only to the cultivation of the mind, i.e.: a person's intellectual and moral faculty, or merely to a cultivation of the body as an aggregate of physical organs and limbs[74] but encompasses all these aspects. In the Analects, it is Confucius himself who relates a person's moral improvement and their physical health, stating that 'those who are *ren*

66 Ames and Rosemont (62*n*54) 33.

67 Ibid 34.

68 Ni Peimin, 'Confucian Virtues and Personal Health' in Ruiping Fan (ed), *Confucian Bioethics* (Springer Netherlands 2002) 27 <https://doi.org/10.1007/0-306-46867-0_2> accessed 19 May 2023.

69 See *supra*, Morality, Ethics, and Bioethics in the Chinese Context

70 Ni (64*n*68) 28.

71 Ibid.

72 Ibid.

73 Ibid.

74 Ibid 29.

have longevity' (*renzhe shou* 仁者壽).[75] Therefore, living in accordance with a set of fixed moral rules would not only contribute to social harmony but also to personal well-being, which includes a long, healthy life.[76]

Another trait that differentiates Confucian and Western ethics is its hierarchical, meritocratic approach to moral development.[77] To achieve its aim of creating a harmonious society (*hexie shehui* 和谐社会), Confucianism requires that each individual behave according to his or her social role, and fulfil the duties deriving from such role,[78] following the model of the five basic relationships (*wulun* 五伦), i.e.: father and son, ruler and minister, husband and wife, elder and younger siblings, and between friends. Confucius also references the different virtues that underlying each of these relationships. It is for this reason that, according to Confucius, the first duty of a ruler is to rectify names (*zhengming* 正名):[79] Only when people know their correct names, i.e., know their rightful place in the family or society, can they behave properly. It has been noted how every basic relationship – including between friends, akin to the relationship between siblings – more or less explicitly implies a hierarchy.[80] According to Confucius, harmony depends on social differentiation: 'The noble man is in harmony but does not follow the crowd (*budong* 不同, litt.: is not alike). The inferior man follows the crowd (*dong* 同, litt.: is alike) but is not in harmony.'[81] In a context of hierarchy and differentiation by social roles, it seems natural that the moral concern towards the others decreases with distance. It is what Qin Zhu calls 'love with distinction,'[82] a kind of ethical partiality very different from the ethical impartiality advocated by deontology, consequentialism and even care ethics. In connection to this, note how the notion of differentiation is embedded in the very characters used to express the concept of ethics in the Chinese term 'bioethics:' *lunli* 伦理. In fact, combining the character *lun* 伦, meaning 'human relations' (as conceived in trad-

75 Confucius and Lau (61*n*44) ch 6.23 Yong Ye-雍也.

76 Unschuld (n 93) 27; Lisa Raphals, 'Embodied Virtue, Self-Cultivation, and Ethics' in Chris Fraser, Dan Robins and Timothy O'Leary (eds), *Ethics in Early China: An Anthology* (Hong Kong University Press 2011) <https://doi.org/10.5790/hongkong/9789888028931.003.0008> accessed 22 May 2023.

77 Zhu (62*n*56) 3.

78 Ibid 4.

79 Confucius and Lau (61*n*44) ch 13.3 Zi Lu-子路.

80 Daniel A Bell and Wang Pei, *Just Hierarchy* (2020) <https://press.princeton.edu/books/hardcover/9780691200897/just-hierarchy> accessed 18 May 2023.

81 Confucius, 'Analects of Confucius 论语' (A Charles Muller tr) ch 13.23 Zi Lu-子 路 <http://www.acmuller.net/con-dao/analects.html#div-14> accessed 18 May 2023.

82 Zhu (62*n*56) 2.

itional China), as well as 'logic' and 'order,' with the character *li* 理, meaning 'texture, grain' (in wood, skin etc.), or 'inner essence,' 'moral rule,' indicates that people in different hierarchies should obey different rules.[83] In recent years, several authors have pointed out the need to draw on Confucian ethical partiality to address some of the problems affecting postmodern societies, such as care for the elderly.[84] According to Ann Pang-White, traditional Confucian ethics, based on mutual care across three generations (grandparents, parents, and grandchildren) living together could succeed where the universalist approach based on individual self-determination, typical of Western ethics, has failed.[85] In the second part, we will see whether and how the Chinese regulatory approach is following this path. Let us now turn to another fundamental doctrine in the development of Chinese culture: Daoism.

2.2 *Daoism*

Compared to Confucianism and its different approaches to ethics, the case of Daoism is even more complex. Unlike Confucianism, Daoism did not develop from a Master's thought, and only retrospectively can it be defined a 'school.' The Han court historiographer Sima Tan (司马谈, 165 BCE–110 BCE) first listed a 'Daoist school' (*Daojia* 道家, litt.: school of the Way) among the Six Schools reported in the *Shiji* (史記, litt: Historical Records).[86] Until then, the names of the philosophers who would later be regarded as the initiators of Daoism, Laozi (老子 approx. sixth century BCE) and Zhuangzi (庄子, approx. fourth century BCE), had not been connected,[87] since their works had little in common, apart perhaps from their intended audience. The *Zhuangzi*, named after its author, is a collection of short stories written for and about people who prefer private life to official duty.[88] The *Daodejing* (道德经, litt.: the Classic of the Way and the virtue, or – as suggested by Graham – the Classic of the Way and its potency), also known as Laozi, reads like a long philosophical poem.[89] Like the *Zhuangzi*, it is written for outsiders, however, unlike the *Zhuangzi*, it presents itself as a guide to the art of governing.[90] The reference to mystical statecraft was not the only aspect that made the *Daodejing* more

83 Cong Yali (2018) 243.
84 Ann A Pang-White, 'Reconstructing Modern Ethics: Confucian Care Ethics' (2009) 36 Journal of Chinese Philosophy 210, 221.
85 Ibid 221–222.
86 Graham (60n41) 170.
87 Ibid.
88 Ibid.
89 Ibid 218.
90 Ibid 170.

attractive to the Han court. The two books show also a very different attitude towards death. In fact, some varieties of syncretism had developed around the *Daodejing*, which drew from the thought of several other so-called schools, in particular the 'legist school' (*fajia* 法家). Among them, flowed a current of thought called *Huang-Lao*, merging Laozi's name with that of the Yellow Emperor, *Huangdi*.[91] Huang-Lao would become a reference for literature on alchemy, medicine, and magic, the goal of which was to find the secret of immortality.[92] Since one of the Han Emperors' dreams was to find the elixir of long life, it is not surprising that the *Zhuangzi*, which invoked reconciliation with death, did not enjoy great popularity at the time.[93] Only after A.D 200, following the breakdown of the Han dynasty, did the *Zhuangzi* begin to be considered as one of the classics of philosophical Daoism.

The retrospective acknowledgement of Daoism as a school, combined with its varying vision, *inter alia*, of death, makes it difficult to frame its approach to ethics. Further complicating matters, philosophical Daoism coexisted with religious Daoism (*Daojiao* 道教, litt.: Doctrine of the Way). Religious Daoism was founded by Zhang Daoling (张道陵, traditionally 34–156 AD) in 142 AD, combining *Huang-Lao* and the *yin-yang* philosophy (*yinyang jia* 阴阳家) complemented by folk belief.[94] It is considered the 'indigenous religion of China'[95] and, as such, it has influenced Chinese ethics, medical practice, and the conception of the human body, especially among the lower strata of the population, for centuries. Conversely, the interpretation of philosophical Daoism's values as fundamentally egocentric has led some authors to question whether it ever developed a concept of ethics.[96] The latter opinion, however, it is not generally accepted. On the contrary, it is commonly acknowledged that philosophical Daoism great affected the Chinese ethical approach, with some authors remarking that it was altruistic ideals (and not selfish ones) that constituted the essence of philosophical Daoism from the very beginning. In his article 'The Roots of Altruism in the Taoist Tradition,' Kirkland demonstrates this from a textual analysis of the *Daodejing*, where selflessness is described as the essential quality of the *Dao*:[97] since the sage is a person who successfully

---

91 Ibid 170–171.

92 Ibid 171.

93 Ibid.

94 Ibid.

95 Ibid.

96 J Russell Kirkland, 'The Roots of Altruism in the Taoist Tradition' (1986) LIV Journal of the American Academy of Religion 59, 60.

97 Ibid 69.

imitates the Dao, selflessness should be also the essential quality of the sage.[98] The altruistic ideal of Daoism is reiterated in many passages of the *Daodejing* where, for example, it is said that:

> The sage has no invariable mind of his own; he makes the mind of the people his mind. To those who are good (to me), I am good; and to those who are not good (to me), I am also good; – and thus (all) get to be good. To those who are sincere (with me), I am sincere; and to those who are not sincere (with me), I am also sincere; – and thus (all) get to be sincere.[99]

In fact, 'The more that he [the sage] expends for others, the more does he possess of his own; the more that he gives to others, the more does he have himself.'[100] It is worth mentioning that the idea of placing the needs and interests of others before one's own was put in practice by Daoist monasteries in the Six Dynasties period (between early third century AD and late sixth century AD) by introducing social services, hospitals, orphan care and community quarantine procedures. Even though the idea of permanent hospitals was introduced into China by the Buddhists, who established in the state of Southern Qi the first of such primary medical facilities in the fifth century AD,[101] *wuwei*'s selfless kindness and concern for human health certainly had a part in the development of public institutions. In fact, despite the predominance of Confucian medical ethics, all Three Teachings (San jiao 三教: Confucianism, Daoism, and Buddhism) provided physicians with various set of values and ethical frameworks to be applied to healthcare moral issues.[102] In this sense, we can say that the coexistence of competing forms of medicine and the combination of values and beliefs is a long-standing feature of the Chinese experience.[103] Nowadays, alongside a combination of Chinese and Western medicine, the official Chinese medical system includes traditional Chinese medicine, and modern Western biomedicine,[104] and it operates in a context that is a sort of 'melting pot of concepts,'[105] the origins of which can be traced

98 Ibid 70.

99 Sturgeon Donald, 'Dao De Jing – Chinese Text Project' s 49 <https://ctext.org/dao-de-jing> accessed 31 May 2023.

100 Ibid 81; Kirkland (67*n*96) 70.

101 Unschuld (13*n*75) 19.

102 Nie Jing-Bao (11*n*61) 92.

103 Ibid 91.

104 Ibid 94.

105 Ibid.

back to socialism, collectivism, filial piety, but also individual happiness, self-realisation, and self-perfection. In Imperial times, Chinese doctors – a very assorted category ranging from the already mentioned Confucian medical scholars (*ruyi* 儒医) to itinerant physicians (*lingyi* 领医) – [106] had to interact with various sets of values and concepts, both domestic and foreign. Over the centuries, they drew from this 'pool of ideologies'[107] whenever they needed to answer moral questions about health and the body.[108] Among these, Daoism stands out, at least since 100 A.D., for its (perceived) opposition to Confucianism, which had by then become the state ideology. It is no coincidence that Daoism is considered 'the other side of Chinese culture.'[109] In fact, as pointed out by Graham, Confucianism was public, respectable, conventional, and practical, whereas Daoism was perceived as private, disreputable, magical, spontaneous, and poetic.[110] Similarly, in his book on *Medical Ethics in China: A Transcultural Interpretation*, Nie Jingbao compares the communitarian, familyist, authoritarian, and moralist Confucianism with the highly individualistic, anti-paternalist, anti-statist Daoism.[111]

It is not easy to find a thread linking the many definitions of Daoism found in various periods of Chinese history. However, the thought of Laozi and Zhuangzi have at least one aspect in common that somehow justifies their posthumous inclusion in the same 'school': the insight that while other things move spontaneously in harmony with the Dao, following their own course, men – being capable of speculating, posing alternatives and formulating principles of action [112] – have separated themselves from it. According to both the *Daodejing* and the *Zhuangzi*, the only way to discover the Dao is to follow natural processes and return to the natural flow of life, thus joining either one of the opposites (yin and yang 阴阳). This implies abandoning behaviours that Confucians and other thinkers tried to formulate in words. As in Confucianism, even in Daoism, language is at the centre of the scene[113] but, instead of calling for the 'rectification of names,' the *Daodejing* suggests that its practitioners unlearn the rigid divisions fixed by names, and learn instead 'the spontaneous harmonizing of the qi 气,'[114] the foundation of body and life,

106 Unschuld (13*n*75) 15.
107 Ibid 7.
108 Ibid 92.
109 Graham (60*n*41) 172.
110 Ibid 171–172.
111 Nie Jing-Bao (11*n*61) 35.
112 Graham (60*n*41) 172.
113 Ibid 199–202.
114 Ibid 220.

'moving on the same course as heaven and earth through their natural cycle.'[115] This has consequences on Daoist ethics and bioethics, even with the *caveat* (valid for Confucianism as well) that many issues considered central to contemporary bioethical debate are completely alien to the traditional Daoist vision. In fact, walking the Way – which is 'constantly nameless,' since 'the name that can be named is not the enduring and unchanging name' – [116] means following what is 'natural,' without interfering with the harmony of *yin* and *yang*, or with the interaction among the five elements (wood, fire, earth, metal and water).[117] To this end, non-action (*wu wei* 无为) is crucial.[118]

We have already mentioned this principle when referring to Confucianism, underlining that in Daoist thought it would acquire a different nuance. In fact, in the *Daodejing*, the character *wei* 为 indicates ordinary human action juxtaposed with the spontaneous processes of nature, which are 'so on themselves' (ziran 自然).[119] In this sense, the sage must 'do nothing:' 'The Dao in its regular course does nothing (for the sake of doing it), and so there is nothing which it does not do. If princes and kings were able to maintain it, all things would of themselves be transformed by them.'[120]

In this context, artificiality and arbitrariness contrast with naturalness and spontaneity: whatever follows the flow of the Dao is natural and spontaneous, and whatever is natural and spontaneous is ethical, while diverging from the Dao, going against the movement of nature would be arbitrary and unethical,[121] resulting in frustration and unhappiness.[122] It is worth remarking that some modern bioethicists have interpreted these statements as a call to refrain from the excessive use of medical remedies, in particular when birth, sickness, and death are involved.[123] With particular reference to Chinese bioethicists, we can mention the position of Michael Cheng-Tek Tai of the College of Medical Humanities and Social Sciences of Chung Shan Medical University (Taichung, Taiwan). In his article 'Natural or Unnatural – An Application of the Taoist Thought to Bioethics,' Prof Tai affirms that, according to the Daoist view, all endeavours and any attempt to prolong or shorten

115 Ibid 223.
116 Sturgeon, 'Dao De Jing – Chinese Text Project' (68*n*99) s 1.
117 Michael Cheng-Tek Tai, 'Natural or Unnatural An Application of the Taoist Thought to Bioethics' (2009) 21 Tzu Chi Medical Journal 270, 273.
118 Graham (69*n*41) 232.
119 Ibid.
120 Sturgeon, 'Dao De Jing – Chinese Text Project' (68*n*99) s 37.
121 Tai, 'Natural or Unnatural An Application of the Taoist Thought to Bioethics' 70*n*117, 273.
122 Ibid 270.
123 Ibid 273.

life are artificial, arbitrary, unnatural, and should be avoided.[124] The same conclusions apply to reproductive technology, which in his view not only has changed the nature of parenthood but also the relationship and even the attitude towards children. As evidence, he mentions the expression used by a mother to refer to her biological child: *qinsheng* 亲生 (litt.: I gave birth to this baby myself and this baby bears my genes).[125] This 'natural' way of expressing the link between mother and child loses its significance in the context of modern reproductive techniques, where a child can be conceived by embryo donation and in vitro fertilisation, or even be carried and delivered by a surrogate mother.[126] The fact that reproductive technologies are not natural is almost a tautology, since they are also referred to as 'artificial' reproductive technologies. In Tai's interpretation of the Daoist perspective, this also makes them unethical. Nevertheless, Tai is aware that the definition of 'natural' in the twenty-first century is extremely vague: taken to its extreme, such a position would lead to the rejection of any intervention outside the body and, thus, in essence, of any treatment, rendering scientific progress in the field of medicine meaningless. Therefore, he seeks to establish a criterion that would allow man to intervene in the 'natural' flow of life, seemingly finding it in the aptitude of the treatment to 'restore the body's ability to function according to the goodness of Tian' 天 (litt. Sky, Heaven),[127] understood in the Daoist texts as a naturalistic order[128] that, let's not forget, is neither intentional nor moral.[129] In practice, 'unnatural' measures are acceptable insofar as they become ways to help patients return to the way of the Dao. For example, it would allow for the provisional use of a machine temporarily performing the cardiac function so that a surgeon can repair an ailing heart, or to treat a woman's body so that she can bear a child. On the contrary, cloning or using a surrogate mother would go against the flow of Dao because using donated eggs and sperm to allow pregnancy, or keeping a person on life-support machines indefinitely would be considered unnatural. Regarding the end of life, Daoist ethics would lean towards palliative care and the hospice movement rather than euthanasia or keeping patients alive at all costs.[130]

124 Ibid 270.
125 Ibid 272.
126 Ibid.
127 Ibid 273.
128 Csikszentmihalyi (14*n*77) 43.
129 Ibid 44; Graham (60*n*41) 195–199.
130 Tai, 'Natural or Unnatural An Application of the Taoist Thought to Bioethics' (70*n*117) 273.

In the second part of this book, we will assess whether Tai's interpretation of Laozi and Zhuangzi's view about what is natural and unnatural reflects, as he argues, 'the understanding of most people in far Eastern Asia until recent times.'[131] For the time being, let us return to Daoist ethics, and look at how compares in general to Western Stoic philosophy, with which it shares the idea that death should be accepted as a natural part of life, as well as an emphasis on acting in harmony with nature.[132]

The need to restore lost harmony between man and the universe is not unique to Daoism. However, the Daoist concept, especially when compared to Confucianism, is characterised by a greater emphasis on harmony within the individual and harmony within society and the cosmos.[133] Daoist scholars have sometimes interpreted the idea of harmony inside the individual as referring to physiological practices designed to enhance individual health and prolong physical life. Nevertheless – and even if certain Daoists indeed meant to solve the problem of restoring individual harmony by treating physical diseases – it was a general assumption that physical symptoms remit only once the bio-spiritual integrity of the individual has been restored and rebalanced. This is not surprising, given the non-dualistic concept of mind and body. Many accounts of Chinese medicine explain disease as the result of an imbalance of *qi* 气, the natural vital force, which makes no distinctions between body and mind. This is where the principles of yin and yang come into play. Yin represents the female aspect, and means shade, dark, hidden, secret, and cool, while yang represents the male aspect, meaning sunshine, bright, light, open, and warm. They are different but equal; they originate in each other, depend on each other, nourish each other, and struggle with each other.[134] Prof Nie remarks that, since the Han Dynasty, Confucians had used the yin-yang concept to justify men's power over women and the latter's inferior status in socio-cultural life. However, in early Daoism, the passive member, yin, plays the more critical role in the everlasting metamorphoses of nature.[135] In fact, the yin-passive is the foundation on which the yang-active rises. In the *Daodejing*, yin is described as vital, fluid, fecund: indeed, 'when alive man is soft and weak, when dead he is hard and strong.'[136] Thus, according to Nie,

131 Ibid 272.

132 Nie Jing-Bao (11*n*61) 35.

133 'Daoism, Bioethics in | Encyclopedia.Com' <https://www.encyclopedia.com/science/encyclopedias-almanacs-transcripts-and-maps/daoism-bioethics> accessed 31 May 2023.

134 Nie Jing-Bao (11*n*61) 175.

135 Ibid.

136 Graham (60*n*41) 224; Sturgeon, 'Dao De Jing – Chinese Text Project' (68*n*99) s 61,76.

ancient Daoism could help Chinese feminist bioethicists articulate how the two sexes, though different, are nonetheless equal.[137]

According to Chinese medicine, a healthy life balances the forces of yin and yang; when one becomes dominant, it creates an imbalance and disharmony. Diseases result from the loss of this balance and disharmony among all the internal organs of a human body, which, in turn, correspond to one of the Five Elements: water (kidneys and lower orifices); wood (liver and eyes); earth (spleen and mouth); fire (heart and ears); and metal (lungs and nose).[138] Furthermore, each organ and its corresponding element is related to an hour of the day, a season of the year and to certain foods and medications. A good physician should know these relationships and the ways in which all these elements interact.[139] Only by treating the disease holistically can the original balance can be restored so that the *Dao* in the form of *qi* can smoothly flow within the microcosm of the body;[140] according to Daoism, this will contribute to universal healing. In this sense, the process of self-refinement to which a Daoist life should be devoted, which involves the imperative of 'fostering life' (*yang sheng* 养生) has a value that goes beyond enhancing individual health and prolonging physical life, and even beyond a person's moral and spiritual cultivation: It is how one contributes to the health and wholeness of society, nature and the cosmos.[141]

2.3 *Mohism*

Although Chinese culture is generally described as Confucian, Confucianism was just one of the main philosophies originating or developed in China.[142] Among the indigenous ones, Mohism deserves at least a brief mention, in spite of the relatively short period in which this school flourished, only to disappear at the beginning of the Han era (third to second centuries BC).[143] The posi-

137 Nie Jing-Bao (11*n*61) 175.

138 Tai, 'Natural or Unnatural An Application of the Taoist Thought to Bioethics' (70*n*117) 271.

139 Ibid.

140 Cheng-tek Tai, 'Natural and Unnatural – A Taoist Perspective' (2004) 2 Etica & Politica/ Ethics & Politic 271 <https://www2.units.it/etica/2004_2/CHENG-TEK_TAI.htm> accessed 22 May 2023.

141 Russell Kirkland, 'A World in Balance: Holistic Synthesis in the "T'ai-p'ing Kuang-Chi"' [1993] Journal of Song-Yuan Studies 43, 9; 'Daoism, Bioethics in | Encyclopedia.Com' (72*n*133).

142 Nie Jing-Bao (11*n*61) 92.

143 Graham (60*n*41) 34; Sturgeon Donald, 'Mozi : Book 9 : Anti-Fatalism I – Chinese Text Project' para 2 <https://ctext.org/mozi/anti-fatalism-i> accessed 26 June 2023.

tioning of Mohism as an intermediate solution between the conservative and elitist vision of Confucianism and the liberal and aloof vision offered by Daoism meant that this philosophy, traces of which had been lost after the seventh century AD, came back into vogue in the nineteenth century as a typically Chinese response to the challenges posed by values from the West.[144] It is precisely in this capacity that it could be useful again today, according to some authors, by providing criteria based on collective advantage, measured in terms of concrete benefits for the greatest number of people, to inspire the regulation of life-relevant technologies.[145] In fact, its founder, Modi, also known as Mozi (墨子, litt: Master Mo, c. 470–391 BCE) was Confucius's first rival.[146] Mohist thought is also considered Consequentialist and it is therefore included among the basic approaches of Western ethics and bioethics.[147] Moreover, the *Shiji* describes Mozi as a high officer in the State of Song 'who excelled at defensive warfare' and 'who practiced the frugal use of resources,'[148] which has led some authors to describe Mohist social theory as based on the conservation and the equitable distribution of scarce assets.[149] As we have seen,[150] many bioethical issues find their *raison d'être* precisely in the need for an ethically acceptable allocation of limited resources.

Mohism values the moral rightness of conduct by the goodness of its consequences.[151] According to Mozi, to decide whether a doctrine or a behaviour is ethically correct, it is necessary to subject it to the 'Three Tests:' identifying the basis of the doctrine, its verifiability, and its applicability.[152] In Mozi's words:

> How is it [a doctrine] to be based? It should be based on the deeds of the ancient sage-kings. How is it to be verified? It is to be verified by the senses of hearing and sight of the common people. How is it to be

---

144 Qianfan Zhang, 'Equality and Universal Love: Human Dignity in Mohism', *Human Dignity in Classical Chinese Philosophy: Confucianism, Mohism, and Daoism* (Springer 2016) 251.

145 Hong'en 宏恩 Xiao 萧, ' You Moxue duanshi dangdai yiliao kejixia renzhi shenming zunyan 由墨学端视当代医疗科技下人之生命尊严 La dignità della vita umana nell'ambito della tecnologia medica contemporanea nella prospettiva del Mohismo' (2018) 20 Wuhan keji daxue xuebao 武汉科技大学学报 635, 637.

146 Chris Fraser, *The Philosophy of the Mòzǐ: The First Consequentialists* (Columbia University Press 2016) 33; Fraser.

147 Csikszentmihalyi (14*n*77) 35.

148 Ibid.

149 Ibid; Fraser (74*n*146) 211–216.

150 See *supra*, Introduction.

151 Csikszentmihalyi (14*n*77) 35.

152 Graham (60*n*41) 37.

applied? It is to be applied by adopting it in government and observing its benefits to the country and the people.[153]

Graham points out an interaction between the first and third of these criteria, with the third outweighing any ancient authority: In practice, all conduct and traditions are evaluated in light of the utilitarian principle.[154] Applying the 'Three Tests' to the Confucian tradition is a case in point.[155] A classic example is the length of the mourning period one observes after the death of one's father, which, according to the Confucian principle of filial piety, should last three years.[156] Since both the supporters and critics of long mourning periods claimed to be honouring the Way of the Sage Kings as passed down from their ancestors, Mozi suggested assessing the effects of long mourning on governing 'the myriad of people of the state,'[157] to check whether long mourning periods would 'enrich the poor, increase population, secure the endangered and order the disordered' so as to be judged as 'benevolence, the right, the service of a filial son.'[158] Mozi's test showed that long mourning periods interrupted work and affected health, thus impoverishing the population and weakening the state.[159] Given this lack of advantageous outcomes, akin to the meaning of the English word 'profit,'[160] Mozi held that long mourning periods should be avoided. This example raises another consideration: who benefits and how to maximise that benefit? According to Mozi, since material welfare, an abundant population, and sociopolitical order comprise the benefits, the greatest beneficiary is the state.[161] Not surprising, Mohism has been considered as a form of 'state consequentialism.'[162]

The idea that behaviour should be judged by its consequences rather than its underlying psychological motivation differentiates the Mohist from the Confucian ethical approach.[163] Incidentally, according to Csikzszentmihalyi,

153 Sturgeon, 'Mozi' (73*n*143) para 2.
154 Graham (60*n*41) 33.
155 Ibid.
156 Ibid 39–40.
157 Sturgeon Donald, 'Mozi : Book 6 – Chinese Text Project' 3 <https://ctext.org/mozi/book-6> accessed 26 June 2023.
158 Graham (60*n*41) 40.
159 Ibid.
160 Ibid 41.
161 Philip J. Ivanhoe and Bryan W Van Norden (eds), *Readings in Classical Chinese Philosophy* (Seven Bridges Press 2001) 56; Csikszentmihalyi (14*n*77) 36; Fraser (74*n*146) 16.
162 Ivanhoe and Van Norden (75*n*161) 56.
163 Csikszentmihalyi (14*n*77) 35–36.

such a materialist view of benefits – intended as material rewards for the whole state rather than an aggregate of individual psychological benefits – might explain why Bertold Brecht and other twentieth-century writers influenced by Marxism admired Mohism.[164] The notion behind the maximisation of benefits and distribution of scarce resources radically sets Mohism apart from Confucianism. I am referring to the doctrine of *jian'ai* (兼爱) generally translated into English as 'universal love' or 'concern for everyone.'[165] Following authors such as Ivanohe, Van Norden and Csikzszentmihalyi, I prefer the translation 'impartial caring.' Graham describes *jian'ai* as 'a concern for each person irrespective of relations of kinship with oneself.'[166] Accordingly: 'one must treat one's friend body as if it were one's own, and one must treat one's friend's parents as if he or she were one's own,'[167] so that 'those with sharp ears and keen eyes will listen and look out for others. Those with stout legs and strong arms will work for others, and those who understand the Way will educate and instruct others. And so men who reach old age without finding a wife and having children will get the support they need to live out their years.'[168] Charity should be directed to those who need it most, even if they are not one's relatives.[169] This is the only way to maximise the good. In Mozi's words:

> Of course I should first love others' parents in order that they would love my parents in return. Hence those who desire to be filial to one another's parents, if they have to choose (between whether they should love or hate others' parents), had best first love and benefit others' parents.[170]

Mozi's view is clearly in contrast, not just with Confucianism but also with Chinese civilization as a whole, starting from the early centuries of the Imperial Era. It is worth mentioning that, in later Mohism, the ethical system was refined and, while reaffirming that concern for the others should not take into account kinship, for the general good, people should include the care of their own kin among their duties.[171] I would also add that, according to the Mohists,

164 Ibid 36.
165 Graham (60*n*41) 41.
166 Ibid 424–43; Fraser (74*n*146) 158–184.
167 Csikszentmihalyi (14*n*77) 35; Sturgeon Donald, 'Mozi : Book 4 – Chinese Text Project' para 4 <https://ctext.org/mozi/book-4> accessed 27 June 2023.
168 Ivanhoe and Van Norden (75*n*161) 65.
169 Fraser (74*n*146).
170 Sturgeon, 'Mozi' (73*n*143) 10.
171 Graham (60*n*41) 43.

the principle of impartial care should inspire both the governance of the state and its external relationships. In fact, alongside the principle of utility in relations with other states, the principle of impartial care implies the 'Rejection of aggression,' which was considered the first of the 'six evils' to be eliminated by the practice of *jian'ai*.[172] Moreover, the ruler capable of applying this principle in domestic affairs would lead to the ideal society by transforming the behaviour of his subjects, 'just as clothes are coloured by a strong dye.'[173]

2.4 *Buddhism*

The separation and coexistence of the Three Teachings as equally important in Chinese culture has been acknowledged since antiquity. As early as the sixth century, the scholar Li Shijian stated that 'Buddhism is the sun, Daoism the moon, and Confucianism the five planets.'[174] A popular proverb begins by describing the differences among these Three Teachings only to conclude that they are essentially the same: 'The three teachings – the gold and cinnabar of Daoism, the relics of Buddhist figures, as well as the Confucian virtues of humanity and righteousness – are basically one tradition.'[175] However, among the 'schools' forming such 'one tradition,' only Buddhism originates outside of China, a religion introduced by non-Chinese merchants in the later years of the Han dynasty. Its acceptance and transformation over the centuries not only disproves the idea that Chinese culture rejects external influences, but also shows the extent to which it can absorb and incorporate teachings from other traditions.[176] As pointed out by Wang Youru:

> Chinese culture has never been the same ever since Buddhism was assimilated into this culture and in the meantime, Chinese Buddhism is still not the same as Indian Buddhism. The Chinese assimilation and appropriation of Indian Buddhist soteriological messages and para-

172 Ibid 43–44.

173 Csikszentmihalyi (14*n*77) 36.

174 Stephen F Teiser, 'Introduction: The Spirits of Chinese Religion', *Introduction: The Spirits of Chinese Religion* (Princeton University Press 2018) 296 <https://www.degruyter.com/document/doi/10.1515/9780691188140-022/html> accessed 7 June 2023.

175 Ibid.

176 Nie Jing-Bao (11*n*61) xv; Youru Wang, 'Introduction: Chinese Buddhist Philosophy and Its "Other"' in Youru Wang and Sandra A Wawrytko (eds), *Dao Companion to Chinese Buddhist Philosophy* (Springer Netherlands 2018) 2 <https://doi.org/10.1007/978-90-481-2939-3_1> accessed 4 June 2023.

> digms is a process, and not a stage, of interaction, interchange and interpenetration.'[177]

According to some scholars, the Chinese name for Buddhism clearly indicates its peculiarity and alien origin.[178] Each character used to indicate the Three Teachings in Chinese has a different semantic value. In Confucianism (*Rujiao* 儒教, litt.: school of scholars), the character *ru* refers to a group of people, while in Daoism (*Daojia* 道教, litt.: school of *Dao*), the character *dao* refers to a concept. In contrast, the character *Fo* 佛 in *Fojiao* 佛教, Buddhism, has no real meaning and may have been chosen for purely phonetic reasons, since its ancient pronunciation 'bud' resembles the first syllable of the Sanskrit word 'Buddha,' meaning 'one who has achieved enlightenment.' The choice of the first Chinese Buddhists to use a translation of sound (i.e.: a character with a sound similar to the foreign word) instead of a translation of meaning[179] has been interpreted as a way to underline the foreign origins of Buddhism.[180]

Buddhism's use of a Chinese character with no semantic value demonstrates the challenges its teachers faced when entering China. Unlike in India, Buddhism did not threaten China's prevailing social order; it could coexist with the principles underpinning the Confucian state.[181] Yet, its arrival marks the first clash with non-native values and notions. How do you take a philosophy expressed in another language, based on alien concepts and make it intelligible to a Chinese society? To facilitate its introduction, Buddhist teachers began by explaining the Buddhist interpretation of human existence, i.e., the problem to which Buddhism provided a solution. This is why Mahāyāna (or Great Vehicle) Buddhism, instead of Theravāda (Pāli, literally 'School of the Elders') Buddhism, established itself in China, then spreading to Korea, Japan, and Vietnam.[182] A thorough comparison between these two schools of Buddhism exceeds the scope of this section. However, from an ethical perspective, they differ in three main aspects. First of all, Mahāyāna Buddhism does not distinguish between clergy and laity, maintaining instead that anyone can achieve enlightenment regardless of gender, age or social status.[183]

177 Wang, 'Introduction' (77*n*176) 2–3.

178 Teiser (77*n*174) 307.

179 Deborah Cao, *Chinese Law: A Language Perspective* (1° edizione, Routledge 2004).

180 Teiser (77*n*174) 306.

181 Thomas P Kasulis, 'Cultural Differentiation in Buddhist Ethics', *Encyclopedia of Religious Ethics* (John Wiley & Sons, Ltd 2022) 617 <https://onlinelibrary.wiley.com/doi/abs/10.1002/9781118499528.ch72> accessed 3 June 2023.

182 Ibid.

183 Ibid 616.

Moreover, Mahāyānists emphasised that the only difference between the real world and the illusory is how we observe it. Our ignorance stems not from false appearances but from our tendency to indulge in distorted projections. From this perspective, the ordinary world (*samsāra*, comprising birth, death, and rebirth in a better or worse form according to one's prior actions, or *karma*) and the world of enlightenment (*nirvāṇa*) are fundamentally the same.[184] So Mahāyāna Buddhism presented an ideal of enlightenment that, in accordance with Confucian and Daoist ideas, could be enjoyed in everyday social and natural life. Finally, Mahāyāna Buddhism features a more collective, rather than individual, interpretation of the process of illumination.[185] In general, Mahāyāna's vows and precepts are very similar to those used by Theravāda monks and laity. However, the Mahāyānists introduced a new vow, to which they gave special importance: the bodhisattva vow.[186] Bodhisattvas are present in various forms of Buddhism, but their role is particularly emphasised in Mahāyāna Buddhism. According to Theravāda Buddhism, there is only one Buddha (*the* Buddha), an exceptional man called Gautama Siddhartha, born as a prince around the sixth or fifth century BC, who renounced his privilege, followed certain religious teachers and eventually achieved enlightenment and the final 'extinction' from the afflictions of existence.[187] According to Mahāyāna Buddhism, every human being can achieve illumination and become *a* buddha.[188] The bodhisattvas – those who have not achieved enlightenment yet, but are in an advanced stage along the path towards it – often assist as mediating figures between believers and the buddhas, whom they also serve by being role models for, and protectors of, their followers. In this context, the bodhisattva vow is understood as the promise to defer full enlightenment until everyone else is also ready.[189]

Chinese Buddhists even reformulated the notion of the Three Jewels (in Chinese: *sanbao* 三宝).[190] The First jewel, the Buddha, is not only interpreted in accordance with Mahāyāna Buddhism but also concerns material aspects of the sect: objects, statues, buildings to house the statues, and even the funds needed to finance such paraphernalia, and rituals.[191] The Second jewel, the

184 Ibid 617–618.
185 Ibid 618.
186 Ibid.
187 Teiser (77*n*174) 308.
188 Ibid.
189 Kasulis (78*n*181) 618.
190 Teiser (77*n*174) 308.
191 Ibid 309.

dharma (in Chinese: *fa* 法) means 'truth' or 'law' and it encompasses the teachings of the Buddha, which are comparable to universal law and have been passed on in oral or written form.[192] The Chinese version of *dharma* is very concrete and includes all the ways to spread the *dharma,* such as the stages at which sermons were delivered, the rituals, and the books containing Buddha's law.[193] The *dharma* has been passed on through various literary genres, the most important of which is called *sutra*, a Sanskrit word indicating the warp in a fabric and, by analogy, the basis of the doctrine. It is interesting to note that *sutra* was translated into Chinese using the character *jin* 劲, which has the same meaning and is also the general term traditionally used for Confucian and Taoist classics,[194] thereby affirming in a linguistic way that the Three Teachings belong to a single tradition. The third jewel is *sangha* (in Chinese: *sengqie* 僧伽), which indicates the monastic community.[195] As pointed out by Teiser, some sources interpret the term in a broader sense that includes all the orders of monks, nuns, lay men, and women, while other sources use it to refer only to monks and nuns.[196] In China, the relationship between lay people and monks was characterised by a close interdependence and by tension between the spiritual power traditionally attributed to the monks, and hostility towards their lifestyle. In fact, leaving home, forgoing family life and taking the vow of celibacy all ran counter to the fundamental values underpinning Chinese society. In an apparent attempt to soften the contrast, monks and nuns referred to one other as 'brothers' and 'sisters,' as did Christian and many other monastic orders. They also participated in rituals dedicated to the ancestors. As we have seen with the first and second treasures, the Chinese used the term *sangha* to refer to any aspect of everyday monastic life, from the land on which the monastery stood to the animals on its farms.[197]

Although Chinese Buddhism sets *sangha* as the Third Jewel, let's not forget that, according to Mahāyānists, no spiritual difference separates monks and lay people:[198] Anyone can become a buddha, can attain the wisdom to see the impermanence and emptiness of the ordinary word, or *samsara*,[199] where all things change and eventually vanish, causing pain and suffering. The third aspect, i.e.: the lack of permanent self, in China was reinterpreted in the

192 Ibid.
193 Ibid.
194 Ibid.
195 Ibid.
196 Ibid.
197 Ibid 310.
198 Kasulis (78*n*181) 619.
199 Teiser (77*n*174) 307.

light of rebirth. For Buddhists, existence does not end with death and funeral rites; one reincarnates into other bodily forms that, according to prior conduct, can be one of the following: god, demigod, human being, animal, hungry ghost, or infernal being.[200] According to the notion of impermanence, though, what passes from one form to the other is not the impermanent ego, but 'some aspects of psychophysical life that might endure for a few lifetimes – or a few thousand – but would eventually cease to exist.'[201] Human suffering stems from the vain attachment to impermanent things, and any attempt to hold on to them in spite of their transience perpetuates desire through subsequent reincarnations. To avoid this, one must free oneself from the idea of a permanent self to achieve the state of no-self, or *anātman*. In the Chinese context, this goal tends to be understood as a harmonisation with the impermanent world, rather than as detachment from it.[202]

In practice, 'to have wisdom is to engage, and not to escape, from the suffering of existence,'[203] which also explains why the wisdom of enlightenment is linked to the wisdom of compassion.[204] Here we can see how the Confucian and Daoist ideal of harmony merged with Chinese Buddhism: One should not depart from the flux of *samsāra*, but use 'compassion and wisdom to harmonize ordinary and enlightened activity.'[205] The shift from detachment to openness (towards the others) – which mirrors the Mahāyāna concept of emptiness, influenced (once again) by the Daoist idea of non-being as the source of being – inevitably reverberates in ethics.[206]

In the Buddhist tradition, salvation requires abiding by certain moral precepts, which include the prohibition of killing, stealing, lying, drinking intoxicating beverages, or fornicating.[207] However, many variants of Mahāyāna Bud-

200 Ibid 306–307.

201 Ibid 307.

202 Kasulis (78*n*181) 619.

203 Ibid 618.

204 Vincent Shen, 'The Ethics of Generosity in Chinese Mahayana Buddhism: Theory and Practice' in Youru Wang and Sandra A Wawrytko (eds), *Dao Companion to Chinese Buddhist Philosophy* (Springer Netherlands 2018) <https://doi.org/10.1007/978-90-481-2939-3_3> accessed 4 June 2023.

205 Yoshito Hakeda and Ryūichi Abé, *The Awakening of Faith: Attributed to Asvaghosha* (Columbia University Press 2005) 21; Sandra A Wawrytko, 'The Sinification of Buddhist Philosophy: The Cases of Zhi Dun and The Awakening of Faith in the Mahāyāna (Dasheng Qixin Lun)' in Youru Wang and Sandra A Wawrytko (eds), *Dao Companion to Chinese Buddhist Philosophy* (Springer Netherlands 2018) 37 <https://doi.org/10.1007/978-90-481-2939-3_2> accessed 7 June 2023.

206 Kasulis (78*n*181) 618.

207 Teiser (77*n*174) 306–307.

dhism (such as Chan Buddhism, better known in its Japanese version: i.e. Zen Buddhism) adopted a situational approach to ethics. Assuming at some level that the ordinary world and *nirvāṇa* are indistinguishable, the morality of an act is assessed not so much by what has or has not been done, but by the way in which such act has been carried out.[208] Consequently, an act has *per se* no value, but it can be 'skillful' or 'unskillful' depending on the person performing it and on the situation in which has been performed. Hence, any activity – from martial arts to practicing calligraphy or preparing and serving tea – can express one's harmony with the world as it is, and his or her capacity to look at it with a 'buddha mind-heart' (*Foxin* 佛心).[209] Even more important for our purpose is the way in which Chinese Buddhism's approach to ethics interacts with the principle of compassion. During the sixth and seventh centuries, in the so-called Third Period School of Buddhism, the Buddhist principle of compassion gave rise to permanent hospitals in China,[210] and a treasury was set to help the needy.[211] In fact, according to some forms of Mahāyāna Buddhism, compassion is so important that it can override other imperatives, such as the prohibition on lying, stealing or even harming others. What makes it possible is the principle of *upaya* (skillful means), which allowed the historical Buddha to use suitable means to explain the Dharma. The same notion is applied to bodhisattvas, who use effective tools to help people in need. Sometimes the 'skillful means' employed can go against the precepts. In principle, when the 'wrong' conduct results from compassion, it can still be considered 'skillful.' An example in the field of bioethics is abortion. In general, Buddhism condemns abortion,[212] but in some cases, for example, when a family cannot support and nurture any more children,[213] it might be justified. Not by chance, in China and Japan abortion is described as 'a necessary sorrow,'[214] and Buddhists monks are often involved in special rituals and prayers to reduce its karmic consequences.[215] In the second part of this book, we will analyse this aspect in detail to understand whether it could have favoured the acceptance

208 Kasulis (78*n*181) 619.

209 Ibid.

210 Unschuld (20*n*10) 19.

211 Kasulis (78*n*181) 619.

212 Nie Jing-Bao (11*n*61) 43.

213 William E Deal, 'Buddhism (Bioethics In)', *Encyclopedia of Bioethics* (Macmillan Reference USA 2004) 334 339.

214 William R LaFleur, *Liquid Life: Abortion and Buddhism in Japan* (Princeton University Press 1994) <https://press.princeton.edu/books/paperback/9780691029658/liquid-life> accessed 7 June 2023.

215 Deal (82*n*213) 339.

of abortion as a means of implementing the PRC's one-child policy. For the moment, we note that the attitude towards abortion mirrors the Buddhist approach towards other bioethical issues, such as euthanasia and cloning. Even in these cases, the issue revolves around the tension between the duty not to harm and the duty of compassion.[216]

Buddhism, however, was not the only foreign philosophy to profoundly impact China's culture and society. More recently, another philosophy from afar would bring new values and approaches that, re-elaborated in the light of the Chinese context, would become an integral part of the Chinese cultural and ethical fabric. This section, therefore, cannot but end by briefly describing the relationship between Sino-Marxism and ethics.

2.5 *Sino-Marxism*

In 1969, Eugene Kamenka pointed out that, if an anthology entitled 'Marx on Ethics' were to be published, 'it would contain no passages that continue to be strictly relevant for more than three or four sentences.'[217] Despite my more modest aim, reconstructing Marx's ethical thought still presents a certain degree of complexity. None of Marx's prolific body of work specifically addresses ethics,[218] and he used very little 'moral language' in his writings, often openly disdaining ethical discourse, and even declaring that 'communists do not preach morality at all' and 'capitalism had either destroyed morality or turned it into a palpable lie.'[219] Nevertheless, his writings are steeped in ethical reflections,[220] even if in a 'scattered and unsystematic' way.[221] In his book on 'Marxism and Ethics. Freedom, Desire, and Revolution,' Paul Blackledge argues that Marx's random references to ethics explain why his ethical approach is frequently considered inconsistent. Academic discussions on Marxist or Marxian ethics generally focus on single sentences taken out of context, which can very easily be misunderstood.[222] Thus, Marx's critique of

216 Ibid.

217 Eugene Kamenka, *Marxism and Ethics* (Palgrave Macmillan UK 1969) 6 <http://link.springer.com/10.1007/978-1-349-00592-5> accessed 17 June 2023.

218 Paul Blackledge, *Marxism and Ethics: Freedom, Desire, and Revolution* (SUNY Press 2012) 47.

219 Lawrence Wilde, 'Introduction: Marx, Ethics and Ethical Marxism' in Lawrence Wilde (ed), *Ethical Marxism and its Radical Critics* (Palgrave Macmillan UK 1998) 1 <https://doi.org/10.1007/978-1-349-26865-8_1> accessed 17 June 2023.

220 George G Brenkert, *Marx's Ethics of Freedom* (1° edizione, Routledge 2013) 15; Blackledge (83*n*218) 47.

221 Blackledge (83*n*218) 47.

222 Ibid.

moral theories is commonly juxtaposed with his moral condemnation of capitalism, which can making his thought seem contradictory or even illogical. In 2016, during his *Speech at the Symposium on Philosophical and Social Science Work*, Chinese President Xi Jinping criticised this interpretation of Marxist thought by 'some Western scholars,' recalling how, since the very beginning, Marxism has always 'occupied the high ground of truth and morality.'[223] Paul Blackledge, among others, agrees, and – following Brenkert's advice – suggests reading Marx's apparently contradictory statements on ethics in light of his broader social theory.[224] Blackledge's interpretation of Marxism and its ethics of freedom is very popular among Chinese authors.[225] According to him, Marx's critique of moral theory should be better understood as a rejection of the assumption that moral behaviour involves the suppression of our naturally egoistic desires.[226] The best expression of this is found in Kant who, in forerunning the Marxian perspective, put human freedom at the centre of social theory, though he failed to identify the historical roots of the lack of freedom affecting what he imagined as universally isolated individuals.[227] In Marx's view, the narrowness and historical contingency of Kant's moral vision would emerge from the virtue of solidarity deployed by the working masses in the struggle against capitalist exploitation and alienation. In this sense, Marx's ethics can be considered as a modern version of Aristotle's 'account of the acts supporting the virtues through which individuals are able to flourish within communities.'[228] According to Marx, perceiving oneself as an individual in opposition to society is the outcome of modern social relations. In the eighteenth century, with the conversion to capitalism, production acquired a social dimension, while appropriation remained an individual matter.[229] In that context, private interest became an ethics cornerstone, and individuals started interacting merely as competitors. This is why – in spite of different

223 Xi Jinping 习近平, *Zai zhexue shehui kexue gongzuo zuotanhui shang de jianghua* 在哲学社会科学工作座谈会上的讲话 (*Speech at the Symposium on Philosophical and Social Science Work*) (Renmin chubanshe 人民出版社 2016).

224 Blackledge (83*n*218) 47.

225 Xie Tingyu 谢廷玉, 'Makesi zhuyi lishi lilun yu lunli sixiang de rong tong – Yinguo xuezhe Bauluo Bulaike liqi jiaoshuo fangtan 马克思主义历史理论与伦理思想的融通——英国学者保罗·布莱克里奇教授访谈 (The Connection between Marxist Theory of History and Ethical Thought: An Interview with Professor Paul Blackledge)' [2022] Makesi zhuyi ye xianshi 马克思主义与现实 95, 95.

226 Blackledge (83*n*218) 3.

227 Ibid 24.

228 Ibid 3.

229 Friedrich Engels, *Anti-Dühring* (Wellred Books 2020) 329–330.

approaches (utilitarian, Kantian, or modern virtue ethics) – Western modern moral theory has never questioned the assumption that the community is made up of a collection of egoistic individuals. In fact, Locke, Hobbes, Bentham, Smith, Kant, and other modern philosophers found themselves living in a society characterised by the contradictions between production and appropriation. Not surprisingly, they had to address the problem of defining the common good in a world dominated by the selfish interest of individuals.[230] Indeed, China's first sociologist and anthropologist, Fei Xiaotong (1910–2005), called this conception of society as the sum of its individual members one of the distinguishing features of Western societies. In his work entitled 'From the Soil. The Foundation of Chinese Society,' Fei states that Western societies are organised in the same way 'we [Chinese] collect rice straw to use to cook our food.'[231] Just as each stalk of rice is tied into a small bundle that becomes part of a larger bundle piled up eventually to form a haystack, in the West, individuals gather into larger and larger groups that eventually form a society.[232] According to Fei, this model differs radically from the Chinese one, where individuals relate to one another as 'the circles that appear on the surface of a lake when a rock is thrown into it.'[233] There, 'everyone stands at the centre of the circles produced by his or her own social influence,' which are interrelated, so that 'one touches different circles at different times and places.' The network thus woven 'can be extended to embrace countless numbers of people – in the past, present, and future,' so much that 'everyone has a cousin three thousand miles away.'[234] This can make it difficult to predict how many guests will come to dinner when someone Chinese says he will 'bring the whole family.'[235]

In Marx's perspective, however, Fei's model of society is neither 'Western' nor defined by latitude. Instead, it belongs to a certain historical period, the modern age, and it is the direct consequence of capitalist production. Different ages have different modes of production, which reverberate in different ideas of what is good or right, causing a different perception of the relationship between duty and desire. For example, unlike in modern moral theory in which being good presupposes acting against our desires, with individuals

230 Blackledge (83*n*218) 24–33.

231 Fei Xiaotong, Gary G Hamilton and Wang Zheng, *From the Soil: The Foundations of Chinese Society* (1° edizione, University of California Press 1992) 60.

232 Ibid 60–62.

233 Ibid 62.

234 Ibid 63.

235 Ibid 62.

opposed to the community, Ancient Greek ethics, in particular Aristotelian, interprets the concept of good as the principle 'at which all things aim.'[236] For Aristotle, being good as a man implies the already mentioned[237] concept of *eudaimonia*, rendered in English as 'flourishing,' which individuals can only achieve within communities.[238] For this reason, he famously defined man as a 'political animal,' and claimed that ethics and politics are closely related.[239] As we will see, Aristotle's view of the relationship between ethics and politics, to which Marx subscribed, will get flipped in the Chinese Maoist context. Indeed, a feature of Chinese Marxism is to let politics define the parameters of ethical behaviour, i.e., political correctness equals ethics.

According to Blacksledge, Marx goes beyond Aristotle's idea of man as a 'political animal,' arguing that it is in our 'gregarious nature' to identify ourselves only 'in the midst of society,'[240] but this cannot happen at just any time: a particular historical conjuncture is required. MacIntyre pointed out that both Kantian morality and Aristotelian ethics tend to consider the social context as 'natural,' or 'ahistorical.'[241] Hegel was the first to synthesise the two thinkers, starting to overcome their limitation, a process that Marx would later complete.[242] Like Aristotle, Hegel assumed that the goal of life is self-realisation, but while Aristotle considered happiness as the purpose of life, the German philosopher believed that self-realisation could only be achieved through freedom.[243] By linking freedom and happiness, Hegel reconcile Kantian dichotomies in which individuals, prompted by a sense of duty, must repress their desires; if they succeed, they will be rewarded with happiness. For Hegel, 'to act freely involved acting in accordance with necessity, that is, in line with our human needs and desires.'[244] So, the good 'truly becomes good when it is reconciled with our desires.'[245] In this sense, Hegel dealt with subjective and objective aspects of ethics, which can be understood only in the context of a particular community. Hegel thus historicised the concept of self-realisation but he conceived history as the history of consciousness, and not as

236 Blackledge (83*n*218) 21.
237 See *supra*, Chapter 2, 2.1 C).
238 Blackledge (83*n*218) 21.
239 Alasdair MacIntyre, *A Short History of Ethics: A History of Moral Philosophy from the Homeric Age to the 20th Century* (1° edizione, Routledge 2002) ch 7.
240 Blackledge (83*n*218) 23.
241 MacIntyre (86*n*239) 159.
242 Blackledge (83*n*218) 33.
243 Ibid 34.
244 Ibid.
245 Ibid 35.

the process of evolving modes of production. This is why Marx considered Hegel's vision limited by 'the horizon of capitalism,' and unable to recognise the capitalist nature of alienation and the anti-capitalist nature of the struggle for freedom.[246]

All of Marx's theories grow from the working-class standpoint he used to analyse society,[247] which allowed him to recognise the historical nature of individualism and the lack of freedom and alienation under the formal freedom offered by capitalism.[248]

By further developing Smith's argument, Marx demonstrated how the modern division of labour has actually downgraded workers, both intellectually and physically, to the level of a machine: They are mere commodities; they cannot buy anything but must sell themselves and their humanity.[249] Capital is 'the power to command labour and its products,' which acts as 'an ever-expanding power' against which not even capitalists can consider themselves free.[250] It is here that the concept of alienation comes up: What salaried workers produce becomes alien not just to them, but even to the capitalists behind them. Alienation, according to Marx, operates on four levels that are all consequences of the wage-labour system. By selling their work, not only do workers lose control over what they produce, but they also transform the act of producing to meet their needs i.e.: their life essence, their purpose, into the means through which they can preserve their existence.[251] Thus, the first aspect of workers' alienation is from the output of their labour; the second is from the labour process itself; the third is from their human essence; and the last is the alienation from their fellow human beings.[252] Although alienation is not just interclass, but even between genres, Marx and Engels consider the former more important. It is their brutal condition that will force proletarians to rebel against their situation and unite to achieve what in Kant's thought was just an abstract imperative: to treat others not as means, but as an end in themselves.[253] By observing the discussions within English and French workers' associations of his time, Marx understood that they did not only concern proletarians' immediate needs as workers, but also as human beings. From there he deduced the potential of the class struggle to lead to complete

246 Ibid 37.
247 Ibid 45.
248 Ibid 47.
249 Ibid 72.
250 Ibid 73.
251 Ibid 74.
252 Ibid 73.
253 Ibid 76.

human emancipation, unobtainable through a bourgeois revolution. By focusing on middle class rights, bourgeois revolutions had produced constitutions that, while defending freedom from feudal power, created value systems based on individual egoism, which hindered the full realisation of 'social' individuality.[254]

Individuals can only obtain their freedom 'in and through their association,' as socialism can only come from proletarians' class struggle, and 'it is only through the struggles of this class that solidarity become a real human desire.'[255] On this basis, Marx criticised also what he considered as 'reactionary socialism,' which – by minimizing the 'realization of the sharpness' of class struggle and abstracting human essence from its real manifestation in history' – constitutes a barrier to the 'real diffusion of socialist consciousness.'[256] However, what distinguishes communism from reactionary socialism above all is the principle of resource distribution. According to Marx, reactionary socialism allocates 'to each according to his abilities,' while communism follows the adage 'to each according to his needs.'[257] This concept is of particular interest for our purposes, especially when compared to 6 of the Constitution of the People's Republic of China of 1982, transposed from the Constitutions of 1975 and 1978,[258] which states that 'The system of socialist public ownership supersedes the system of exploitation of man by man; it applies the principle of 'from each according to his ability, to each according to his work.'

This phrasing opens up ethical and bioethical scenarios entirely different from the ones posited by the Marxist original, with which it shares only formal aspects. I mention it here because I believe it clarifies how we might understand the expression 'Marxism-Leninism with Chinese characteristics.' As Eugene Harris points out, following the example of Stalinist Russia, the 'Marxims' that the Communist Party of China (hereafter: CPC) embraced had very little to do with Marx's theoretical foundations, but were instead based on contingency and practice.[259] This was not just because of Mao's modest philosophical background,[260] but also due to China's specific situation in the early twentieth century, which differed from the conditions that had led to the

254 Ibid 76–77.

255 Andrew Collier, *Socialist Reasoning: An Inquiry in the Political Philosophy of Scientific Socialism* (Pluto Pr 1990) 54.

256 Blackledge (83*n*218) 81–82.

257 Ibid 82.

258 See Article 9 of the Constitution of 1975 and Article 10 of the Constitution of 1978.

259 Nigel Harris, *The Mandate of Heaven: Marx and Mao in Modern China* (Haymarket Books 2015) 313.

260 Lowe (58*n*27) 108.

Russian revolution; unlike Lenin, Mao did not have to understand his country and the global context.[261] Understanding the military potential of the area in which the National Liberation Army was operating was sufficient for Mao; practice, or better, military tactics, took the place of political theory.[262] According to Harris, this also gave rise to CPC-specific elitism as the 'vanguard of the proletariat' and the only entity that (like the emperor in Traditional China) had the 'great public in mind' and therefore was capable of seeing the people's 'long-term interests.' In the Chinese context, class struggle should be read as 'whatever the party does,' and 'orthodoxy' as 'whatever the party has done.' This notwithstanding CCP's policies are always supported by appropriate doctrine citations:[263] in fact, and as Article 6 of the PRC's Constitution demonstrates, Marxist terminology, although always present, in some cases hides rules and policies that are very different from those contained in Marx's works, with any deviation always justified in the light of 'Chinese characteristics.'

With this in mind, one can better understand the (rather vague) theoretical references contained in the various calls to 'promote the Chinese-ization, modernization and popularization of Marxism' and to 'Adhere to Xi Jinping Thought on Socialism with Chinese Characteristics in the New Era,' which can be found in the 'Opinions on Accelerating the Construction of Chinese Characteristics in Philosophy and Social Sciences' (*Guanyu jiakuai goujian Zhongguo tese zhexue shehuikexue de yiijian* 关于加快构建中国特色哲学社会科学的意见), issued in 2017 by the Central Committee of the Communist Party of China,[264] or in the more recent 'Opinions on Strengthening Legal Education and Legal Theory Research in the New Era' (*Guanyu jiaqiang xin shidai faxue jiaoyu he faxue lilun yanjiu de yijian'* 关于加强新时代法学教育和法学理论研究的意见), jointly published by the General Office of the CPC Central Committee and by the General Office of the State Council on 26 February 2023.[265]

261 Harris (88*n*259) 313.

262 Ibid.

263 Ibid.

264 Xinhua she 新华社, 'Zhonggong Zhongjian Yinfa "Guanyu Jiakuai Goujian Zhongguo Tese Zhexue Shehuikexue de Yiijian" 中共中央印发《关于加快构建中国特色哲学社会科学的意见》_最新政策_中国政府网 (Opinions on Accelerating the Construction of Philosophical and Social Sciences with Chinese Characteristics Issued by the Central Committee of the Communist Party of China)' <https://www.gov.cn/zhengce/2017-05/16/content_5194467.htm> accessed 17 June 2023.

265 Zhonghua renmin gongheguo jiaoyubu zhengfu menhu wangzhan 华人民共和国教育部政府门户网站, 'Zhonggong Zhonjian Bangongting Guowuyuan Bangongting Yinfa "Guanyu Jiaqiang Xin de Daifa Jiaoyu He Faxue Lilun Yanjiu de Yijian" 中共中央办公厅国务院办公厅印发《关于加强新时代法学教育和法学理论研究的意见》

Underlying these documents is the need to put implement a 'new type of ethics developed under the guidance of Chinese Marxist ethics, with Marxism as its guiding ideology and the construction of socialism and socialist ethical culture with Chinese characteristics as its main theme.'[266] This 'new ethics' inherited and carried forward 'the spirit, order and values of five thousand years of ethical civilization', transformed them creatively and developed them innovatively, while adding 'many new contents, concepts, ideas and wisdoms to them, as well as some unprecedented new disciplines, propositions and theories,' such as, among others, 'the ethics of biotechnology.'[267]

Let us now see whether Chinese regulation on biotechnology reflects this new ethics and its values regarding the beginning of human life. This analysis is necessary since, as Chinese authors fondly remind us, such regulations represent 'the spirit and backbone of a great Eastern country that is rapidly emerging and moving towards the centre of the world stage, as well as leading the trend of ethics in the world.'[268]

[General Office of the Central Committee of the Communist Party of China General Office of the State Council Issued the Opinions on Strengthening Legal Education and Legal Theory Research in the New Era]' <http://www.moe.gov.cn/jyb_xxgk/moe_1777/moe_1778/202302/t20230227_1047943.html> accessed 17 June 2023.

266 Wang Zeying 王泽应, 'Xin Zhongguo lunlixue de lilun tezhi, lishi diwei he weilai zhanwan 新中国伦理学的理论特质、历史地位和未来展望 (Theoretical Qualities, Historical Status and Future Prospects of New Chinese Ethics)' (2023) 52: Shanghai Shifan Daxue Xuebao 上海师范大学学报(哲学社会科学版) 35.

267 Ibid.

268 Ibid.

PART 2

Law, Bioethics, and Birth-Related Biotechnologies in China

CHAPTER 4

Introduction: When Does Human Life Begin?

1 The Beginning of Human Life: A Cultural-Related Concept

For centuries, the question of when human life truly begins has captivated the thoughts of philosophers, jurists, and theologians around the world, giving rise to different answers depending on the cultural backgrounds, religious beliefs, and the historical contexts of the respondents, and leading to different moral and legal attitudes towards voluntary miscarriage. An illuminating example of this complexity can be found in Europe within the realm of Christian theology. Since at least the thirteenth century, the Catholic Church had embraced a creationist perspective largely influenced by thinkers like Thomas Aquinas, who integrated Aristotle's metaphysics into Christian doctrine.[1] According to this viewpoint, the embryo receives its soul from God at the point when it assumed a human-like form. The crucial juncture, often associated with a pregnant woman's sensation of foetal movement, was referred to as 'hominisation,' and marked the moment when the termination of a foetus was considered a serious offence.[2] This perspective held sway until 1869, when Catholic moral doctrine definitively declared that a human being should be 'respected and treated as a person from the moment of conception.'[3] In contrast, Protestantism, which emerged in various forms after its separation from the Latin Church in the sixteenth century, initially rejected what was at that time the Catholic standpoint on the moral status of the foetus, adopting a stringent stance against voluntary miscarriage.[4] However, as the theological dialogue evolved, scientific advancements unfolded, and Protestantism displayed a proclivity for adapting to contemporary cultural shifts, with a gradual lessening of condemnation for abortion. This transformation occurred exactly as the Catholic Church fully embraced the concept of immediate hominisation, meaning that Catholics and Protestants essentially flipped their positions, although the original ideological polarisation was unchanged.[5]

---

1 Ronald Cole-Turner, 'Embryo and Fetus. IV. Religious Perspectives', *Encyclopedia of Bioethics* (3rd edn, Macmillan Reference USA 2004) 604 735.

2 Ibid.

3 Congregation for the Doctrine of the Faith, 'Donum Vitae (Respect for Human Life)' pt I.1.

4 Cole-Turner (93*n*1) 735.

5 Ibid 735–736.

 | DOI:10.1163/9789004754300_006

The moral status of the foetus has been a subject of debate also within Judaism and Islam. In Judaism, Chapter 21 of Exodus contains a pivotal passage addressing human life in the womb. This passage discusses the legal consequences for those who unintentionally cause a miscarriage, prescribing different penalties, depending on whether the act results in an abortion, harms the pregnant woman, or causes her death. These penalties range from a fine, to be determined by the husband, in cases of abortion, to the death penalty ('life for life') if the pregnant woman dies.[6] In early Judaism, this passage was generally interpreted as not conferring legal and moral status upon a foetus as a person.[7] Nevertheless, abortion was discouraged because it was seen as conflicting with God's creative work, a transgression of the commandment to procreate, and a means to depriving a family of the prospect of another child.[8] Over time, Jewish perspectives underwent some transformation, leading to a viewpoint that does not categorise abortion as murder but considers it morally acceptable only in exceptional circumstances. Moreover, for the first 40 days of pregnancy, the Talmud considers the foetus as 'if it were simply water,' with legal status granted to the embryo only on the 41st day of gestation; before then, embryos in or outside the womb lack legal status.[9] In contrast to Judaism and akin to Christianity for many centuries, Islam perceives the commencement of human life as a developing process. The text of reference is verse 23: 12–13 of the Quran, which elucidates human creation by God as commencing from a minute droplet, gaining the breath of life once it attains the appropriate size and shape.[10] Consequently, Islam traditionally equates the foetus to a person only from a certain stage of its development, often corresponding to the point when it begins to manifest human-like features and voluntary movement. This leads certain Islamic theologians to make a distinction between 'ensouled' and 'un-ensouled' foetuses, as Catholics did for centuries. Notwithstanding these variations, Islam explicitly prohibits abo-

6 'Bible Gateway Passage: Exodus 21:22–23 - New International Version' (*Bible Gateway*) <https://www.biblegateway.com/passage/?search=Exodus%2021%3A22-23&version=NIV> accessed 11 August 2023.

7 For a discussion on the Judean Canon in comparison with the Code of Hammurabi and Assyrian and Hittites' laws see Qiu Renzong 邱仁宗, *Shengming lunli xue* 生命伦理学 [*Bioethics*] (n 70) 59.

8 Cole-Turner (93*n*1) 732.

9 Ibid 737.

10 'Surat Al-Mu'minun [23:12–14] – The Noble Qur'an – القرآن الكريم' <https://legacy.quran.com/23/12-14> accessed 11 August 2023.

rtion at least from the end of the fourth month of pregnancy, and this prohibition is upheld without exception.[11]

Elsewhere in the world, determining the exact moment when a group of cells in a woman's womb becomes a human being has not been a crucial issue. For example, the subject elicits relatively little interest in East Asian philosophies and religions. Nevertheless, advances in medical and pharmacological knowledge in recent decades, coupled with the development of biotechnology for human reproduction and the treatment of life-threatening diseases through genetic engineering, have widened the range of ethical dilemmas surrounding the beginning of human life. Today, the issue goes beyond determining whether an intentional or negligent abortion constitutes murder, and becomes more complex, profound and capable of affecting the lives and futures of the entire global population. Consequently, no country or legal system can now avoid addressing this issue.

Unfortunately, despite considerable advances in our understanding of genetics and biology, we find ourselves on ground that would be familiar to our ancestors. Just as the legal principle *res ipsa loquitur* is a construct – no legal or social phenomenon exists that does not require interpretation –, biological data also lack self-evident interpretation.[12] This process of acquiring knowledge is universal to all scientific disciplines. As Pierre Durhem once remarked, theoretical scientists cannot leave outside the laboratory the theory they wish to confirm through their laboratory experiments.[13] Marjorie Grene echoed a similar sentiment, affirming that even the most objective judgments depend on prior evaluative actions.[14] As we delve into the intersection of bioethics and law in China, we must consider the prior evaluative actions that have guided Chinese legislators and legal interpreters in regulating the use of biotechnology related to the beginning of human life.

What are the key issues in this area from a Chinese perspective? An examination of the first embryo case decided by a Chinese court may provide valuable insights.

---

11 Cole-Turner (93*n*1) 737.

12 Daniel J Callahan, *Abortion: Law, Choice, and Morality* (First Edition, Macmillan Pub Co 1970) 351.

13 Pierre Duhem, 'Physical Theory and Experiment' in Sandra G Harding (ed), *Can Theories be Refuted? Essays on the Duhem-Quine Thesis* (Springer Netherlands 1976) 237 <https://doi.org/10.1007/978-94-010-1863-0_1> accessed 11 August 2023.

14 Marjorie Glicksman Grene, *The Knower and the Known* (First Paperback edition, University of California Press 1974) 160.

2 Key Ethical Issues in the Regulation of Birth-Related Biotechnology in the PRC: The 'First Embryo Case before a Chinese Court'

Grief over a loss does not always unite those left behind; it often spawns disputes over inheritance, which are frequently settled in courts. Such was the case of *Shen Xinnan and Shao Yumei v. Liu Jinfa and Hu Xinxian* (hereinafter: the Yixin case) decided by the Wuxi Intermediate People's Court in 2014, notable for its unusual subject matter: four frozen embryos fertilised following an assisted reproductive treatment undertaken by a young couple who tragically perished in a car accident.[15] The spouses, Liu Xi and Shen Jie, died on the 20th and 25th, respectively, of March 2013, a few months after undergoing in vitro fertilisation (hereafter: IVF) at Nanjing City Gulou Hospital in August 2012. Unable to reach an agreement with their deceased son's in-laws on the right to inherit and control the embryos, Shen Xinnan and Shao Yumei initiated a lawsuit in the Basic People's Court of Yixing (Wuxi, Jiangsu), contending that, in accordance with the law and tradition, they should exercise the right to oversee and dispose of any surviving embryos.[16] During the trial, the court added Gulou Hospital as a third party to the litigation, since it was the facility where the embryos were stored.[17] The Basic People's Court acknowledged the deep sorrow experienced by both sets of parents due to the loss of their only children, but ruled that embryos resulting from IVF were unique entities with the potential for future life development; consequently, they could not be treated like ordinary property and were ineligible for inheritance.[18] Moreover, even the right of a couple over their embryos was limited, mandated to 'comply with laws and regulations on population and family planning in China, not violate social ethics and morality, and merely use the embryos for the purpose of procreation.' Since Shen Jie and Liu Xi were deceased, the purpose of procreation through IVF could no longer be fulfilled, and their limited rights over the frozen embryos could not be inherited. Thus, the trial court dismissed Shen Xinnan and Shao Yumei's claims.[19]

Unsatisfied with the trial judgment, the plaintiffs appealed to the Wuxi Intermediate People's Court, arguing that the first instance ruling lacked a

15 *Jiangsu Wuxi Yixing Lengdong Peitai Jiufen An* 江苏无锡宜兴冷冻胚胎纠纷案 *Shen Xinnan and Shao Yumei v Liu Jinfa and Hu Xinxiang* 沈新南,邵玉妹 v劉金法, 胡杏仙 [2014] Intermediate People's Court of Wuxi, Jiangsu Province 江苏省无锡市中级人民法院 Xi Min Zhong Zi No. 01235 锡民终字第01235号.

16 Ibid.

17 Ibid.

18 Ibid.

19 Ibid.

legal basis. They contended that the embryos were the lawful property of Shen Jie and Liu Xi and, as such, should be categorised as 'other lawful property of the citizens' under Article 3(7) of the Law of Successions. They further argued that, since the embryos were left behind by Shen Jie and Liu Xi, they should be inherited by the Appellants. Additionally, they asserted that Gulou Hospital could have disposed of the remaining embryos only after the IVF operation was successful. Since Shen Jie and Liu Xi were dead and the procedure could not been carried out, Gulou Hospital lacked the right to dispose of the embryos, per the relevant agreement between the hospital and the deceased couple.[20] In response, Gulou Hospital contended that embryos were special entities posing ethical issues, thereby precluding their inheritance, citing regulations governing human-assisted reproductive technology and other Ministry of Health directives, which prohibited the donation, transfer, or surrogacy of embryos, and urged the Appellate Court to uphold the initial judgment.[21]

The Appellate Court confirmed the facts established in the original trial but concentrated on determining the party entitled to custody and disposal rights over the embryos. Citing the protection of citizens' lawful rights and interests under the law, the court ruled that both appellants Shen Xinnan and Shao Yumei, and appellees, Liu Jinfa and Hu Xingxian, should jointly enjoy the right to custody and disposal of the embryos. Several factors influenced this decision. In particular:

1. Shen Jie and Liu Xi had signed an informed consent form with Nanjing Gulou Hospital, specifying that the embryos would remain cryopreserved for one year and that they agreed to their disposal following this period. However, the unforeseeable demise of Shen Jie and Liu Xi prevented the fulfilment of this contract, rendering it inoperative. Consequently, Nanjing Gulou Hospital could not unilaterally dispose of the embryos as outlined in the informed consent form.[22]
2. Given the lack of specific provisions concerning the legal status of embryos in Chinese law, the court considered three factors in determining rights pertaining to the embryos: ethics, emotion, and the protection of special interests. Ethically, IVF embryos have the potential for future life, containing genetic material from both parents and their respective families. Emotionally, the court recognised the profound grief experienced by both sets of parents at the loss of their only children, suggesting that the embryos served as the sole link to their family lineage and

20 Ibid.
21 Ibid.
22 Ibid.

offered solace and consolation. The third and final factor to consider pertains to safeguarding special interests. An embryo represents a transitional existence, residing between the realm of human beings and inanimate objects, possessing the potential to develop into a human life. As such, it holds a higher moral status than non-living entities and should be given special respect and protection. Following the tragic demise of Shen Jie and Liu Xi, their parents not only exhibited the deepest concern for the fate of the embryos in question but also shared the closest alignment of interests with these embryos. Therefore, the court could reasonably assert that Shen Jie and Liu Xi's parents possess the right to oversee and dispose of them. Naturally, in the exercise of this right, the parties involved must adhere to legal principles and refrain from contravening public order and moral standards or harming the interests of others.[23]

3. Regarding Gulou Hospital's contention that the relevant regulations of the Ministry of Health prohibit surrogacy and the trade or transfer of embryos, the court has determined that these regulations do not negate an individual's rights over embryos. These administrative regulations chiefly manage and regulate the activities of medical institutions and personnel engaged in Assisted Reproductive Technology (ART) activities and cannot serve as the basis for Gulou Hospital to impede the legitimate rights of private individuals.[24]

Prior to issuing its ruling, the court redefined the nature of the legal dispute as a matter of custody and disposition, considering the Appellants' claim during the trial and the legal relationship between the parties involved.[25] Using a formula that interestingly draws upon the traditional Chinese legal principle that emphasises making reasonable decisions that are contextually appropriate and legally sound (*heqing heli hefa* 合情合理合法),[26] the Court asserted:

'Shen Xinnan, Shao Yumei, Liu Jinfa and Hu Xingxian's request for the right to oversee and dispose of the embryos involved in the case is reasonable (*heli* 合理), aligned with the circumstances (*heqing* 合情), and does not violate any legal prohibitions (*bu weifan fa* 不违反法), thus, the Court shall support it.'[27]

23 Ibid.

24 Ibid.

25 Ibid.

26 Richard Fellows, AMM Liu and Shuibo Zhang, 'What Is Fair? Perceptions of Justice' (2011) 2 J. Quant. Surv. Constr. Bus. 20, 25.

27 *Jiangsu Wuxi Yixing Lengdong Peitai Jiufen An* 江苏无锡宜兴冷冻胚胎纠纷案 *Shen Xinnan and Shao Yumei v. Liu Jinfa and Hu Xinxiang* 沈新南,邵玉妹 *v.*劉金法, 胡杏仙 (n 601).

Consequently, in accordance with Articles 5, 6 and 7 of the General Principles of Civil Law of the People's Republic of China, and Article 170(1)(b) of the Civil Procedure Law of the People's Republic of China, the Court overturned the trial court's decision, ruling that the Appellants, Shen Xinnan and Shao Yumei, and the Appellees, Liu Jinfa and Hu Xingxian, would jointly oversee and dispose of Shen Jie and Liu Xi's four frozen embryos stored at Nanjing Gulou Hospital.[28]

It is evident from the judgment that both the Trial Court and the Court of Appeal concurred in their assessment of the embryos as 'special objects,' recognising their potential to develop into human beings. This perspective is reminiscent of the 'property deserving special respect' theory first introduced in 1992 by the Tennessee Supreme Court in *Davis v. Davis*, which has since gained widespread acceptance in the United States as a means to address embryo disputes, albeit with variations based on specific case circumstances.[29] This approach allowed the court to circumvent treating embryos solely as property or as human beings, resulting in a resolution that avoids the legal presumptions typical of family law, including the 'best interests of the child' criterion.[30]

Moreover, in this case, the adoption of the same theory by both Chinese courts did not preclude them from reaching divergent conclusions. Specifically, regarding the final judgment, the Court of Appeal's consideration of embryos as 'special objects' facilitated the shift from an inheritance-based claim (deemed inappropriate given the subject matter) to one of custody and disposition, leading to a resolution that recognised the rights of both families of the deceased couple over the embryos. Even if the court did not explicitly mention the 'best interests of the child' by acknowledging the embryos' status between inanimate objects and human beings, it seems to me that it recognised a sort of 'best interests of the embryos,' entrusting them to those most invested in their welfare.

Nonetheless, for our purposes, the most intriguing aspect of the decision lies in the court's reasoning. In elucidating the criteria that informed the ruling, the judges shed light on crucial intersections of clinical practices, population policy, biotechnology, ethics, and the law concerning the beginning of life. These intersections encompass family planning, notably the impact of

---

28 Ibid.

29 *Davis v Davis* [1992] Tennessee Supreme Court 842 S.W.2d 588.

30 Fei Lanfang and Zhou Peng, 'The Law Itself Is Not Above Human Beings: Comments on China's First Case on Frozen Embryos' (2015) 29 International Journal of Law, Policy and the Family 260, 265.

China's one-child policy on citizens' rights and obligations regarding reproduction in general and abortion in particular, and the growing adoption of human artificial reproductive techniques by Chinese couples and corresponding legal trends in post-mortem fecundation and gestational surrogacy.

Let's start with one of the oldest technologies related to reproduction: abortion.

CHAPTER 5

Abortion

1 Abortion in China: An Ethical Non-issue?

In the 2004 film *Dumplings*, the novelist and scriptwriter Lillian Lee, in collaboration with director Fruit Chan, narrates the tale of Mrs Li, a former Hong Kong actress whose beauty and youth are slowly slipping away.[1] In a desperate bid to win her husband back from his mistress, Mrs Li seeks assistance from Aunt Mei, famed for her dumplings rumoured to possess rejuvenating properties. Mrs Li later discovers something shocking: Mei's prized and incredibly expensive dumplings are made from aborted foetuses sourced from Mainland China. Mei was once a gynaecologist there, where she also served as a Red Guard during the Cultural Revolution and performed abortions under the one-child policy.[2] The film depicts Mei's journey from the revolutionary 'serve the people' ethos of the Mao era to the 'feast on the people' attitude of post-Mao capitalist Hong Kong, with a detour through 'killing the people' population control for the nation.[3] Through this narrative, the movie offers a critique of Chinese society and its relentless pursuit of rejuvenation, even at the expense of its own offspring.[4]

The cannibalism metaphor, which has roots in social criticism dating back to Lu Xun's 'A Madman's Diary,' resonates deeply.[5] However, what particularly struck Western viewers was the casual manner in which the characters discuss foetuses and abortions, even when conducted at an advanced stage of pregnancy.[6] Does this the attitude, as depicted in a horror movie, truly reflect Chinese regard for intrauterine life? At first glance, it might seem so. As early

1 Jessica Tsui-yan Li, 'Fate, Reincarnation and Medicinal Cannibalism in Lillian Lee's Dumplings,' *Fate and Prognostication in the Chinese Literary Imagination* (Brill 2019) 87 <https://brill.com/display/book/edcoll/9789004427570/BP000005.xml> accessed 29 September 2023.

2 Ibid.

3 Yun-Chu Tsai, 'You Are Whom You Eat: Cannibalism in Contemporary Chinese Fiction and Film' (University of California 2016) 127 <https://escholarship.org/uc/item/7nk4v18m>.

4 Ibid 116.

5 Ibid 138; Tonglin Lu, 'Fruit Chan's "Dumplings" New "Diary of a Madman" in Post-Mao Global Capitalism' (2010) 10 China Review 177, 183.

6 See: <https://www.imdb.com/title/tt0472458/reviews> accessed 29 September 2023; <https://www.rottentomatoes.com/m/dumplings> accessed 29 September 2023.

 | DOI:10.1163/9789004754300_007

as 1899, the French military doctor Jean Jacques Matignon, attaché to the French legation in Beijing, had shocked the European public by recounting how the Chinese considered 'Children's eyes, nose, tongue, and brain,' and especially those of the foetus, to be the ultimate therapeutic remedy, so much so that many caesarean sections were performed precisely to remove these organs and use them for curative purposes.[7] Intriguingly, Lilian Lee claims to have written one of the film's pivotal scenes after unknowingly consuming a delicious soup made from foetuses at a Chinese clinic.[8]

Beyond the grislier aspects, in both fiction and reality, China's family planning policies have often been linked to abortion practices, sometimes through non-consensual enforcement by local authorities keen on meeting demographic targets. Numerous scandals related to these practices have emerged in recent decades. Take, for example, the case of the blind, self-made lawyer and human rights activist Cheng Guangcheng. Around the time *Dumplings* hit theatres in August 2005, Chen was arrested and subsequently sentenced to four years in jail for property damage and 'organizing a mob to disturb traffic' after exposing abuses related to the one-child policy in Linyi village, Shandong Province, where local officials had coerced thousands of women into undergoing abortions or forced sterilisations.[9] A few years later, in June 2012, there was the case of Fei Jianmei, a young woman forced to undergo an abortion in the seventh month of her pregnancy because she could not afford a 40,000 yuan fine for breaking birth control rules.[10] The story triggered a surge of outrage, as a picture of Feng beside the miscarried baby circulated widely on Chinese websites and microblogs, which led to the provincial family planning commission to launch an investigation into potential misconduct by local officials where the incident occurred.[11] Despite frequent declarations by Chinese authorities underscoring the significance of safeguarding the rights of pregnant women and even following the discontinuation of the one-child pol-

7 Jean Jacques Matignon, *Superstition, crime et misere en Chine* (*Souvenirs de biologie sociale*) (Lyon : A Storck et cie; Paris, Masson et cie 1899) 228 <http://archive.org/details/superstitioncrimoomati> accessed 19 July 2024.

8 Tsai (101*n*3) 132.

9 For a chronology of the case see <https://www.hrw.org/news/2010/11/13/chronology-chen-guangchengs-case> accessed 29 September 2023,

10 Tania Branigan, 'Photograph of Woman with Aborted Foetus Sparks Fury in China' *The Guardian* (15 June 2012) <https://www.theguardian.com/world/2012/jun/14/china-forced-abortion-photograph> accessed 12 October 2023.

11 Ibid.

icy in 2015, reports of forced abortions and coerced sterilisations continue to surface, particularly affecting the Uyghur community.[12]

The picture described above has become more complex in recent years, especially after the State Council of the People's Republic of China published its fourth 'Programme' for the Development of Chinese Women (2021–2030)' (*Guowuyuan yinfa Zhongguo funü fazhan gangyao*国务院印发中国妇女发展纲要, hereafter: 2021–2030 Programme).[13] The document sets out the actions that national and local authorities must take over in the next decade to 'promote gender equality and women's comprehensive development at a higher level.' Among them, the call to 'reduce the number of medically unnecessary abortions' caused particular concern, since many observers inside and outside the PRC considered it yet another intrusion of Chinese public power into the private lives of their citizens, albeit in the opposite direction. In its general formulation, however, the goal of reducing the number of induced abortions is not new, since it was already listed in the second and third Programmes as a goal for both decades 2001–2010 and 2011–2020.[14] Moreover, PRC is certainly not the only country recently attempting to limit women's freedom to decide whether they carry gestation to term. Japan, for instance, starting from 2023, mandated the partner's consent not only for surgical termination of pregnancy but also for the administration of the abortion pill.[15] Similarly, in the RoC (Tai-

---

12 'Uighurs Tell of Forced Abortions and Torture in China' (*The Independent*, 3 June 2021) <https://www.independent.co.uk/asia/east-asia/china-uighur-muslim-abortion-torture-b1859027.html> accessed 12 October 2023.

13 'Guowuyuan Yinfa Zhongguo Funǚ Fazhan Gangyao He Zhongguo Ertong Fazhan Gangyao 国务院印发中国妇女发展纲要和中国儿童发展纲要' (*Zhong xin wang* 中新网) <https://www.chinanews.com.cn/gn/2021/09-27/9574812.shtml> accessed 30 May 2022.

14 Zhang Zhengjun 张正军, 'Guowuyuan Guanyu Yinfa Zhongguo Funǚ Fazhan Gangyao He Zhongguo Ertong Fazhan Ganya de Tongzhi 国务院关于印发中国妇女发展纲要和中国儿童发展纲要的通知 (Notice on the State Council Programme for the Development of Chinese Women and Children)' (2001) 21 Guowuyuan Gongbao 国务院公报 (State Council Gazette) pt 3.4.2 <https://www.gov.cn/gongbao/content/2001/content_60887.htm> accessed 6 October 2024; Ma Juan 马娟, 'Guowuyuan Guanyu Yinfa Zhongguo Funǚ Fazhan Gangyao He Zhongguo Ertong Fazhan Ganya de Tongzhi (2011–2020) 国务院关于印发中国妇女发展纲要和中国儿童发展纲要的通知 中国妇女发展纲要 (2011–2020 年) (Notice on the State Council Programme for the Development of Chinese Women and Children 2011–2020)' (2011) 23 Guowuyuan Gongbao 国务院公报 (State Council Gazette) pt 3.1.7; 3.1.8 <https://www.gov.cn/gongbao/content/2011/content_1927200.htm> accessed 6 October 2024.

15 Kathleen Benoza, 'Consent Issue Casts Shadow on Safe Abortion in Japan' (*The Japan Times*, 28 September 2023) <https://www.japantimes.co.jp/news/2023/09/28/japan/science-health/international-safe-abortion-day/> accessed 13 October 2023.

wan), in accordance with articles 9 of the Genetic Health Act (*Yousheng baojian fa* 优生保健法, enacted by the Legislative Yuan on 9 July 1984, and revised in 1999 and 2009), a woman can voluntarily terminate a pregnancy in cases of rape or incest, medical considerations, risk to a woman's mental health, or impact on family life.[16] However, in accordance with article 10 of the same law, such termination is conditional upon obtaining spousal, parental, or guardian authorisation.[17] Despite criticism from feminist groups and the government's stated intention to amend the law in 2020 to remove the need for the husband's consent, the provision remains unchanged; moreover, abortion is still a punishable offence under Taiwan's Penal Code.[18] Nor is the issue unique to Asian countries: the United States and even Europe recently seem to be leaning toward less liberal positions on abortion. For example, in October 2020, the Polish Constitutional Tribunal declared unconstitutional 4, sec. 1, pt. 2 of the 'Family Planning, Protection of the Foetus and Conditions for the Admissibility of Abortion Act' (better known as the Anti-Abortion Act) of 1993,[19] considering the exception to the prohibition of abortion in case of 'high probability of a severe and irreversible foetal defect or incurable illness that threatens the foetus' life' as inconsistent with the right to life of every human being provided for by 38 of the Constitution of the Republic of Poland. As a result, doctors can now only terminate a pregnancy if the woman's life or health is at risk (including mental health risks with a psychiatric diagnosis) or if there is reasonable suspicion that the pregnancy resulted from rape or incest.[20] In the United States, on 24 June 2022, with the ruling in the case of *Dobbs v.*

16 Kathleen Benoza, 'Consent Issue Casts Shadow on Safe Abortion in Japan' (*The Japan Times*, 28 September 2023) <https://www.japantimes.co.jp/news/2023/09/28/japan/science-health/international-safe-abortion-day/> accessed 13 October 2023.

17 Chao-ju Chen, 'Compulsory Motherhood Challenged and Remade in the Name of Choice: Framing the Right to Choose Under Old and New Maternalism' in Chang-fa Lo, Nigel NT Li and Tsai-yu Lin (eds), *Legal Thoughts between the East and the West in the Multilevel Legal Order: A Liber Amicorum in Honour of Professor Herbert Han-Pao Ma* (Springer 2016) <https://doi.org/10.1007/978-981-10-1995-1_12> accessed 16 January 2024.

18 Chia-Ling Yang, 'Competition and Change in the Discourse on Abortion in Taiwan' in Rebecca Selberg, Marta Kolankiewicz and Diana Mulinari (eds), *Struggles for Reproductive Justice in the Era of Anti-Genderism and Religious Fundamentalism* (Springer International Publishing 2023) 134 <https://doi.org/10.1007/978-3-031-31260-1_6> accessed 27 May 2024.

19 The Family Planning, Human Embryo Protection and Conditions of Permissibility of Abortion Act 1993.

20 Magdalena Furgalska and Fiona de Londras, 'Rights, Lawfare and Reproduction: Reflections on the Polish Constitutional Tribunal's Abortion Decision' (2022) 55 Israel Law Review 285, 285.

Jackson Women's Health Organization,[21] the Supreme Court rejected the notion that the right to abortion is constitutionally protected. This decision effectively overturned the precedents set by *Roe v. Wade* (1973) and *Planned Parenthood of Southeastern Pa. v. Casey* (1992),[22] returning the power to regulate abortion to 'the people and their elected representatives,'[23] that is, in practice, to the legislatures of the individual American states. As of today, numerous states have implemented regulations that either prohibit or significantly limit the option for voluntary pregnancy termination.[24]

Within the framework of the Western Legal Tradition (hereinafter: WLT), restrictions on voluntary termination of pregnancy are typically rooted in ethical and religious principles, with a particular emphasis on Christian-Catholic beliefs. In this context, equating abortion with murder has hindered the acknowledgment of this right until very recently, paving the way to the U.S. Supreme Court to affirm, as it did in *Dobbs v. Jackson*, that abortion 'lacks a historical and traditional basis' and is not an integral element of the concept of 'ordered liberty' in Western countries,[25] whether they adhere to common law or civil law systems. Notwithstanding, abortion was and continues to be one of the most contentious and hotly debated issues in the Western world, provoking ethical, religious, and political disputes.[26] On the contrary, at least at a first sight, in China, it has never been considered as a moral problem,[27] but rather as a means of demographic control akin to other methods,[28] or at most, as a 'lesser evil' that can be utilised or restricted according to political and social needs.[29]

The scarcity of discussion on this matter and what is commonly perceived as a lack of interest in the subject by Chinese people is highlighted in the

---

21 *Dobbs v Jackson Women's Health Organization, 597 US* ___ (2022) [2022].

22 *Planned Parenthood of Southeastern Pa v Casey, 505 US 833 (1992)* [1992] US Supreme Court 505 U. S. 833.

23 *Dobbs v. Jackson Women's Health Organization, 597 U.S.* ___ (2022) (n 638) 1, 8–79.

24 For an up-to-date overview of the situation regarding abortion rights in individual American states, see Center for Reproductive Righs, 'After Roe Fell: Abortion Laws by States,' https://reproductiverights.org/maps/abortion-laws-by-state/ > accessed 4 January 2024.

25 *Dobbs v. Jackson Women's Health Organization, 597 U.S.* ___ (2022) (n 638) pt II, B.

26 Nie Jing-Bao (14*n*79) 20.

27 Ibid 67.

28 Stephen TS Lam, 'Abortion, Sterilization and Genetic Control – the Hong Kong Perspectives,' *Chinese Scientists and Responsibility. Ethical Issues of Human Genetics in Chinese and International Context* (Mitteilungen Des Instituts Für Asienkunde Hamburg 1999) 85.

29 Nie Jing-Bao (14*n*79) 74, 77, 190, 191, 207.

majority of Western studies addressing the issue.[30] Significantly, in his 2003 (English) depiction of bioethics in China, Cong Yali mentions abortion only to highlight that much of the Chinese population does not perceive it as an ethical issue.[31] Moreover, in one of his infrequent articles intended for an international audience, Qiu Renzong does not even allude to abortion when discussing the ethical challenges confronting Chinese doctors.[32] It is intriguing to remark, however, that in his Chinese publications, Qiu delves into the topic, typically within the context of fertility control.[33] In his renowned book on bioethics from 1987, for instance, he enumerates various justifications for abortion, encompassing risks to the mother's life or physical health, pregnancies resulting from criminal acts, potential birth of a seriously ill baby, and the inconvenience that a new birth might pose to the mother or the couple due to their work commitments or economic challenges.[34] Additionally, Qiu acknowledges a state's prerogative to restrict births as a measure to curb population growth.[35] Linking attitudes towards abortion to the ontological and moral status of the foetus in the different cultures and philosophical or religious orientations,[36] Qiu quotes ancient Chinese philosophers Xun Zi and Hanfei Zi, who stated that 'Birth is the beginning of man; death is the end of man.'[37] Derived from this conventional belief, he constructs an argument that culminates in asserting that the foetus is, ontologically, a special entity with a human biological life;[38] yet, it remains distinct from being considered a person, which he defines instead as 'a self-conscious entity that fulfills a distinct role in social relations.'[39] Regarding the moral status of the foetus, and specifically its right to life, Qiu – after having defined a right as 'the permission that society gives to an individual'[40] – specifies that a person's right to life is not absolute, but may have limitations, and even be denied. This happens, for example, when an

30 Ibid 6.
31 Cong Yali (20*n*8) 252.
32 Qiu (23*n*23) 25–29.
33 Qiu Renzong 邱仁宗, *Shengming lunli xue* 生命伦理学 [*Bioethics*] (13*n*70) ch 3.
34 Ibid 53.
35 Ibid.
36 Ibid 53; 55–56.
37 Ibid 65.
38 Ibid 63.
39 Ibid 62.
40 Ibid 63. On the concept of 'right' in the Chinese context see also Mark Savage, 'The Law of Abortion in the Union of Soviet Socialist Republics and the People's Republic of China: Women's Rights in Two Socialist Countries' (1988) 40 Stanford Law Review 1027, 1070–1072.

individual does not follow social rules, as in the case of crimes punishable by death,[41] but it can also occur to innocent people in special conditions, such as self-defence.[42] The foetus does not align with these examples, as it is not yet a person: in fact, it constitutes one of the initial stages in the development of a person, much like the corpse represents the latter. As such, and similar to the corpse, it certainly has intrinsic value and deserves respect, but cannot have the same rights as an adult individual, or even a child.[43] Therefore, if the interests of the foetus ever conflict with those of its parents or society, the latter must always prevail.[44] This is why Qiu considers the foetus' value as 'primarily external,'[45] meaning that it can be compressed or increased for social reasons, resulting in the extension or limitation of the use of abortion. When population growth threatens production and social welfare, abortion can be used as a means of birth control, but it can also be strictly regulated if population growth stalls or shrinks, and policymakers decide they need to manage the risk of long-term labour shortages and an ageing population by encouraging births and curtailing abortions.[46]

Qiu's opinions seem to have influenced (or to reflect) the position of PRC leaders about demographic control. Certainly, in the past few decades, many Chinese authors have expressed the same view, sometimes articulating it in slightly different words. Take for example the case of Zhang Hongzhu and Zhang Jingzhong, who in their 1995 book on medical bioethics highlighted the foetus's right to be born and the need for abortion to have 'sufficient moral reasons,' taking into consideration factors as such the purpose of family planning and the need to improve the quality of the population, among others.[47] They argued that the interests of society and the family take precedence over the woman's right to control her own body. Only after these interests have been adequately considered can a woman freely choose whether to have an abortion: In fact, (only) 'in these conditions does the woman's right to happiness exceed the rights of the foetus.'[48]

These arguments fail to account for the silence that surrounds abortion in China,[49] but they provide us with interesting insights into the hierarchy of

41 Qiu Renzong 邱仁宗, *Shengming lunli xue* 生命伦理学 [*Bioethics*] (13*n*70) 65.
42 Ibid 64.
43 Ibid 65.
44 Ibid.
45 Ibid 66.
46 Ibid.
47 Nie Jing-Bao (23*n*23) 61.
48 Ibid.
49 Nie Jingbao has devoted an entire book to this topic. See Nie Jing-Bao (23*n*23).

rights and interests considered in the current Chinese bioethical discourse on abortion. Nevertheless, the authors are not arguing for the foetus's right to be born so much as the extent of other subjects' interest *in* the (possible) birth of that (potential) child. The notion of children as a 'good' or 'assets' in relation to the state, the 'whole of society' (*juguo* 举国) or the family is a hallmark of Chinese law, and it has been meticulously documented with reference to rules on the protection of children's rights.[50] This raises the question of whether this attitude affects the 'value' of the foetus. Is this a recent phenomenon? What are the long-term implications of this attitude? What insights can be gained from an analysis of past and current Chinese legislation and case law regarding the value placed on the foetus and, consequently, the moment when human life begins and requires protection? Before embarking on this analysis, however, it is first necessary to examine how the concept of abortion is expressed in Chinese.

2 Abortion in Chinese Language

The limited attention traditionally given by both the Chinese public and scholars to abortion stands in stark contrast to the abundance of Chinese terms that articulate the notion. Among them, *duotai* (堕胎 literally: dropping foetus-placenta) or *zhuitai* (坠胎 lit. falling or dropping a foetus-placenta)[51] stand out for the frequency of use and the breadth of meaning. The two words, particularly *duotai,* historically conveyed premature delivery, usually resulting in the death of the child, without distinguishing between spontaneous and procured abortion.[52] Other expressions for terminating pregnancy

50 Yin Li 尹力, 'Liangfa shi yu xia Zhongguo ertong baohu falü zhidu de fa zhan 良法视域下中国儿童保护法律制度的发展 (Advances of legal framework for protecting Chinese children from fine law perspective)' (2015) 249 Beijing Shifan Daxue xuebao (shehui kexue ban) 北京师范大学学报(社会科学版) 40, 40–50; Orna Naftali, 'Rights of Children and Youth in China: Protection, Provision, and Participation,' *Handbook on Human Rights in China* (Edward Elgar Publishing 2019) 274, 288; '(95) The Chinese View of the Rights of the Child | Juha Hämäläinen – Academia.Edu' 174–175 <https://www.academia.edu/105742664/The_Chinese_View_of_the_Rights_of_the_Child?auto=download&email_work_card=download-paper> accessed 12 September 2024.

51 Sarah Mellors Rodriguez, *Reproductive Realities in Modern China: Birth Control and Abortion, 1911–2021* (New edition, Cambridge University Press 2023) 77.

52 Bernard Hung-kay Luk, 'Abortion in Chinese Law' (1977) 25 The American Journal of Comparative Law 372, 373.

have been more specific regarding the voluntariness of the occurrence: as is the case with the expression *datai* (打胎 litt. hitting a foetus-placenta) or *xiatai* (下胎 sending down foetus-placenta), while *xiaochan* (小产 small delivery) or *liuchan* (流产 slippery delivery) were generally used to indicate spontaneous abortion or miscarriage.[53] During the Republican Era (1912–1949), the meaning of *duotai* was restricted to procured abortion,[54] and it was exactly with this connotation that the word was eventually replaced by the expression *rengong liuchan* (人工流产 artificially slipping delivery) shortly after the foundation of the People's Republic of China.[55] The linguistic shift was less due to technical reasons than to political ones, as noted by Sarah Mellors Rodriguez. While the medical procedures stayed essentially the same, Communist reformers wanted a lexical shift that could mark the difference between the outdated, unlawful, and hazardous abortions conducted in capitalist Old China and their modern, scientifically advanced approach adopted by the New China under the leadership of the CPC.[56] *Rengong liuchan*, frequently abbreviated as *renliu* 人流, is now the common Chinese expression for abortion, alongside *rengong yinchan* 人工引产 (induced birth or induced labour), or *yinchan* 引产:[57] *renliu* typically denotes a terminated pregnancy at any stage, whereas *yinchan* specifically refers to termination in the later stages of pregnancy, ranging from fourteen to twenty-seven weeks and, notably, beyond the 28th week.[58] It is noteworthy that, since the 1990s, when national and local legislation incorporated the right to abortion, the term legislators most frequently employed is *rengong zhongzhi renshen* (人工终止妊娠, induced interruption of pregnancy), which covers a broad scope.

The growing semantic diversity of terms referring to abortion marks important changes in its social perception. To measure this evolution, we must also look closely at how Chinese law reflects those changes in its treatment of abortion.

---

53 Ibid; Nie Jing-Bao, 'The Problem of Coerced Abortion in China and Related Ethical Issues' (1999) 8 Cambridge Quarterly of Healthcare Ethics 463, 7.

54 Luk (108*n*52) 373.

55 Ibid; Rodriguez (108*n*51) 77; Weiwei Cao, '"Glorious Mothers" and "Rational Women": A Comparative Analysis of the Chinese and English Regulatory Models of Abortion' (2019) 67 The American Journal of Comparative Law 745, 749; Nie Jing-Bao (n 79) 6.

56 Luk (108*n*52) 373; Rodriguez (108*n*51) 77; Cao, '"Glorious Mothers" and "Rational Women"' (109*n*55) 749; Nie Jing-Bao (14*n*79) 6.

57 Cao, '"Glorious Mothers" and "Rational Women"' (109*n*55) 749; Nie Jing-Bao (14*n*79) 7.

58 Nie Jing-Bao (24*n*79) 7.

3 Abortion in Chinese History, among Philosophical Approaches, Medical Assumptions, and the Law

3.1 *Abortion in Pre-modern China*

While surgical abortion became available only in recent times, the knowledge and use of various methods of terminating unwanted pregnancies, e.g., through the use of abortifacient drugs, can be found in medical texts dating back to the second millennium BC.[59] In the world's first systematically written book of forensic science, the 'Collected Cases of Justice Rectified' (*Xi Yuan Lu* 洗冤录) – first published in 1127 and still in use in revised form into the twentieth century – one-third of the space devoted to special problems related to the examination of female corpses dealt with death from abortion.[60] The attention dedicated to the topic suggests that deaths from abortion attempts were not rare during imperial times, while the instructions on how to conduct the autopsy clarify that the intention was to ascertain the cause of the woman's death and not the legal culpability of the person who had performed the abortion. In fact, from the Tang dynasty (618–906) to the Late Qing era (1644–1912), abortion was generally considered a private household matter, completely outside the interest of the emperor and, therefore, of Chinese statute law.[61] Only under specific circumstances was the unintentional act of causing a pregnant woman to abort deemed a crime:[62] the primary case was abortion-in-assault (*dou ou* 斗殴), first outlined in the section of the Tang Code detailing an assault's potential consequences, including knife wounds, breaking of one or more ribs, and partial loss of sight in both eyes. Abortion was listed among them and carried the same punishment for the offender: two years of penal servitude. The penalty could be decreased or increased depending on the status of the woman who had been assaulted, not that the foetus, because – as explained by Zhangsun Wuji, the draftsman of the Tang Code, in his Commentary on assault – the assailant intended to harm her, not the child.[63]

Subsequent legal codes made minor adjustments to the penalties while maintaining the overall approach. Over time, the rule grew more refined.[64]

59 Cao, '"Glorious Mothers" and "Rational Women"' (109*n*55) 749; Susan M Rigdon, 'Abortion Law and Practice in China: An Overview with Comparisons to the United States' (1996) 42 Social Science & Medicine 543, 547–548; Nie Jing-Bao (14*n*79) 68–69.

60 Luk (108*n*52) 376; Rigdon (110*n*59) 545.

61 Luk (108*n*52) 373.

62 Ibid 374.

63 Ibid.

64 Ibid 375.

In the Ming and Qing codes, for example, the severity of the offense was proportional to the age of the foetus at the time of abortion, and the codes even specified how long after the assault could a premature birth be considered a consequence.[65] In particular, for the abortion-in-assault statutes to be applicable, the foetus must have assumed human form (*chengxing* 成形, which was believed to occur 90 or more days after conception), and the abortion must have taken place within fifty days (Ming Code, before 1525) or 70 days (Ming Code thereafter and Qing Code) after the assault that allegedly caused it.[66] It is for this reason that the 'Xin Yuan Lu' mentioned above furnished the medical examiner with comprehensive instructions extracted from medical literature on determining the age of the foetus. It also gave guidance on identifying the cause of its death[67] to differentiate between cases where foetal demise resulted from the assault versus attempted abortion that also proved fatal for the mother. The introduction of a cut-off point in the law was intended to protect the mother, who was considered more vulnerable from a certain stage of pregnancy onwards, as her condition made her less able to defend herself from attacks.[68] Nevertheless, imperial law undoubtedly regarded the foetus as a life. At least since the Han dynasty, a pregnant prisoner could not be executed until 100 days after the birth of her child.[69] But if the foetus was considered a (human?) life, why didn't Chinese Imperial Codes punish abortion as murder? What was the status and value of a prenatal human life under traditional Chinese law? To answer this question without branding traditional Chinese law as contradictory, we need to adopt the perspective of Traditional Chinese Medicine (hereafter: TCM), considering its systematic approach and its Daoist roots.[70]

3.1.1 Abortion in Traditional Chinese Medicine (TCM) and Medical Ethics

3.1.1.1 *Abortion in TCM*

First off, TCM does not distinguish between the placenta and the embryo (or foetus). Linguistically, classical Chinese used a single term, *tai* 胎 or *taiyuan* 胎元, to refer to both. Rarely was it necessary to use terms like *taiyi* 胎衣or *taipan* 胎盘 (placenta), and *taier* 胎儿 (foetus), because TCM does not consider the

65 Rigdon (110*n*59) 544.
66 Luk (108*n*52) 374–375.
67 Ibid 377.
68 Cao, '"Glorious Mothers" and "Rational Women"' (109*n*55) 749.
69 Luk (108*n*52) 382; Rigdon (110*n*59) 546.
70 Luk (108*n*52) 382.

foetus a part of the mother's body, the way Western organ-based medicine does, but rather as 'integrated with' it.[71] Furthermore, following the principles of Daoist thought, the embryo's transition from an insensible blood clot to a living person was not deemed to occur in a single, specific moment, as in the (Western) case of ensoulment. Upon conception, the foetus – 'formed by the harmony of the *yin* and *yang* of both parents, and sustained by different circuits [of acupuncture points] during each lunar month of its development' –[72] was viewed as a human being, which developed in a 'horizontal and multicausal' way,[73] receiving all the cosmic forces necessary to complete its organic unity, conceived as neither spiritualistic nor materialistic.[74] This integration with the mother's body implied that the mother could no more dispose of the foetus than she could her own body. In fact, from cradle to grave, a woman had no decision-making power, but should obey first her father, then her husband and mother-in-law, and (if she was a concubine) her husband's official wife.[75] Her first duty was to procreate to give offspring to her husband's ancestors; it was therefore her husband and his family who possessed and disposed of her body and of the contents of her womb. For this reason, and as we have already remarked, if abortion did not cause the woman's death and was not due to a third party's fault or malice – as in the case of assault, or of termination of pregnancy due to an extramarital affair – abortion was considered a private family matter, which the state neither had to nor wanted to deal with.

3.1.1.2 *Abortion in Traditional Medical Ethics*

Medical deontology mirrored the law's attitude towards abortion. Just as the Imperial Codes do not regulate abortion in any capacity, premodern texts dedicated to medical ethics – in particular Sun Simiao's (581–682) Tang Dynasty treatise 'Absolute Sincerity of a Great Physician' (*Dayin jin Cheng* 大医精诚), considered the basis of TCM ethics – in no way prohibit physicians from giving women abortion remedies, as does the Hippocratic Oath.[76] This led many authors to conclude that, in traditional China, abortion did not raise any moral issue, based on the Confucian belief that 'life begins at birth.' In the past few decades, numerous scholars have disputed this overarching char-

71 Ibid 383.
72 Ibid.
73 Ibid.
74 Ibid.
75 Ibid 384.
76 Nie (109*n*53) 469.

acterisation from different perspectives[77] demonstrating that the premodern Chinese attitude towards abortion was not as permissive as has been generally assumed. While it is challenging to uncover explicit Confucian and Daoist texts that assign the foetus the same value as an adult person, an examination of medical case reports reveals that, in medical practice, efforts were made to minimise abortion, reserving it for cases where it was 'the lesser of two evils.' This reluctance was certainly justified by technical-medical reasons inspired by Daoism and its theory that the interruption of a natural process could be harmful: since terminating pregnancy runs counter to the natural order, voluntary abortion could potentially be a threat to the mother's health and life, and therefore should be avoided, unless necessary.[78] However, in imperial times, warnings against the use of abortion were based not only on physiological assumptions, but also on the medical profession's moral and social rules. While the former derived from Daoist philosophy, the latter were inspired by Confucianism and Buddhism.[79] Therefore, we must look to these teachings to understand the (possible) ethical issues abortion raised in premodern China.

3.1.1.2.1 Abortion and (Chinese) Buddhism

As detailed in the first chapter, Buddhism's initial precept prohibits 'depriving a human being of life,' and Buddhist scriptural tradition is clear in its opposition to abortion, which becomes more accentuated with the advancement of pregnancy or when a pregnancy is terminated for trivial reasons.[80] Even though Buddhists adopt a permissive view in practice, and generally do not oppose the legalisation of abortion,[81] we can find the moral censure inherent in this doctrine in some of the most relevant texts on Chinese medicine. In Sun Simiao's 'Absolute Sincerity,' for example, Confucian, Daoist, and Bud-

77 For an analysis of the topic from a feminist perspective, see Francesca Bray, *Technology and Gender: Fabrics of Power in Late Imperial China* (0 edition, University of California Press 1997). Cao Weiwei, 'The Regulation of Reproduction in New China: Seven Decades On' (2022) 30 Feminist Legal Studies 97; Cao, '"Glorious Mothers" and "Rational Women"' (109*n*55); Cao Weiwei, 'The Regulatory Model of Abortion in China through a Feminist Lens' [2013] Asian Women <http://www.e-asianwomen.org/_common/do.php?a=full&b=22&bidx=73&aidx=826> accessed 17 January 2024. For an exam of the reasons behind Chinese silence on the topic, see Nie Jing-Bao (14*n*79).

78 Bray (113*n*77) 325; Nie Jing-Bao (14*n*79) 77.

79 Nie Jing-Bao (14*n*79) 72.

80 Peter Harvey, *An Introduction to Buddhist Ethics: Foundations, Values and Issues* (1st edn, Cambridge University Press 2000) 350 <https://www.cambridge.org/core/product/identifier/9780511800801/type/book> accessed 4 February 2024.

81 Ibid.

dhist elements intertwine; while the text does not explicitly proscribe abortion, it states that humans and animals are equal 'when love of life is concerned,' and discourages using living creatures as medicament, and allowing the use of animal eggs before hatching only in extreme cases.[82] Some authors have interpreted this as Sun's clear, albeit implicit, condemnation of abortion.[83] Another work, Zhang Gao's 'Medical Compendium' (*Yi Shuo* 医说 litt.: medical narrations), incontrovertibly expresses the Buddhist view on the subject. The 'Yi Shuo,' written during the Southern Song dynasty (1127–1279),[84] contains a section on 'Retribution for medical services' (*Yigong baoying* 医功报应), considered one of the most authoritative ethical texts in Chinese medical literature.[85] In this text, the author links the practice of medicine to the Buddhist concept of rewards and punishments for earthly conduct by the powers of the afterlife through twelve episodes exemplifying virtuous or bad medical practice and the respective consequences.[86] Among them, the episode entitled 'retribution for abortion' (*Xiatai guobao*下胎果报) tells the story of a woman who earned her fortune selling abortion drugs.[87] The woman is haunted by the vision of hundreds of babies sucking her brain out, which makes her cry out in pain. As a result, she loses her beauty and health and eventually dies in excruciating torment, aware that her suffering is the punishment for destroying 'the fruit of the womb.'[88] In his book on 'Medical Ethics in Imperial China,' Unschuld describes the author, Zhang Gao (1149–1227), as 'a Confucian who practiced medicine as a Confucian physician' (*Ruyi* 儒医),[89] and the above-mentioned episode is frequently cited in recent studies as evidence that Confucians shared with Buddhists the idea that abortion entails the destruction of human life. This is not to say that in pre-modern China abortion was universally and absolutely considered morally reprehensible, but it certainly renders a more nuanced picture of Ancient Chinese attitudes towards abortion.

3.1.1.2.2 Abortion and Confucianism

Detailed knowledge of human physiology led even Confucian thinkers to consider the foetus a living human being, at least from a certain stage of preg-

82 Unschuld (10*n*10) 31.
83 Nie Jing-Bao (14*n*79) 78–79.
84 Unschuld (n 93) 42–53.
85 Nie Jing-Bao (14*n*79) 72.
86 Unschuld (10*n*10) 43–44.
87 Ibid 43.
88 Ibid 49.
89 Ibid 42.

nancy. Interesting in this regard is the Confucian doctrine concerning the 'education of the foetus' (*taijiao* 胎教). Notably inspired by the Confucian assumption that human nature, initially identical in every human being, differs in response to upbringing and external environment, it held that the mother's behaviour during gestation influenced the physical, intellectual, moral and, in some cases, even the sex of the unborn child. From this, it derived a series of prescriptions regarding readings, behaviours, and foods that the pregnant woman should take, depending on the characteristics she wished her child to have.

The fact that human existence was conceived not only in its physical and social dimensions but also in its psychological and spiritual ones provides additional elements for assessing the status of the foetus in traditional China. The spiritual dimensions were defined by a series of terms that are generally, and not too accurately, translated in English as 'soul': *hun* 魂, *po* 魄, *shen* 神, *ling* 灵, *linghun* 灵魂, *hunpo* 魂魄.[90] Without going into details, we can say that the fundamental difference was between the *hun*-soul, a spirit within a human being that can exist independent of the body, and the *po*-soul, a spiritual component that coexists with the body.[91] Both develop in the foetus at a certain stage of gestation and are necessary for the material body to live, but separate upon death. The infusion of the souls into the embryo and foetus should not be confused with the process of ensoulment in Western monotheistic religions,[92] not even in the case of the 'foetus soul,' also known as the 'Placenta god,' a popular belief mentioned by Emily Aher in her paper on the power and pollution of Chinese Women.[93] While the 'Placenta God' comes into existence at conception, it is not physically confined within the foetus or the womb, but 'it moves around outside the mother's body.' Only four months after delivery, does it attach firmly to the baby's body; nevertheless, not even at that point is the child deemed fully human, since its personhood is still evolving.[94] As pointed out by Luk: 'unlike the Western dichotomy where the only choice is between one human life (animated, viable) and zero, the Chinese duality allows much variation in between.'[95] This variation makes

90 Gao Xinmin, Zhang Yu and He Guanqi, 'The Truth-Seeking Objective of Chinese Philosophy of Mind' (2023) 13 Open Journal of Philosophy 195.

91 Nie Jing-Bao (14*n*79) 82–83.

92 Luk (108*n*52) 380–381; Rigdon (110*n*59) 546.

93 Emily M Ahern, 'The Power and Pollution of Chinese Women' <https://ehrafworldcultures.yale.edu/cultures/ad05/documents/029> accessed 7 February 2024.

94 Rigdon (110*n*59) 546.

95 Luk (108*n*52) 383.

conception 'a continuum of events,'[96] in which the value of the foetus will never be cosmologically equal to its mother. The idea of the foetus as a (kind of) human life is further confirmed by popular belief in foetus ghosts (*yingling* 婴灵) and foetus demons (*xiaogu*i 小鬼, litt.: little demons[97] that would 'come back' (*hui* 回)[98] to haunt the women who aborted them, and even to the practitioners who willingly caused their deaths. The phenomenon has been recently studied with reference to Japan and Taiwan,[99] but records of remedies against these uncanny entities were found in mainland China dating back to the late Warring States Period.[100] Besides, the 'haunting foetus' has always been a *topos* in Chinese ancient Buddhist-inspired texts, such as the 'Yi Shuo,' and it still surfaces in post-Maoist literature and films dealing with family planning policies, such as Mo Yan's novel 'Frog' (Wa 蛙, 2009) or Wang Nanfu's documentary 'One Child Nation' (2019).

In the light of what we have examined so far, we can conclude that even in pre-modern China, the foetus had at least some limited intrinsic value, as mentioned by Qiu Renzong. At least from a certain stage of gestation, the foetus was considered a human life, and some doctors and thinkers of the Imperial Era considered practices aimed at its destruction morally questionable. At the same time, the practise of abortion was fairly common and tolerated.

Legal provisions confirmed that the value of human life was not the same from conception to death. The imperial codes never prosecuted people for abortion, and the punishment for parents who committed infanticide or killed their impious and disobedient offspring also gradually grew less harsh over time: In the Han code, it was punished as ordinary homicide, but by the Yuan, Ming, and Qing eras, it was no longer a crime.[101] The Confucian principle of *xiao*, or filial piety, likely accounted for the decriminalisation of these behaviours; however, the idea of family autonomy in internal decisions also played a part in the process. At the time, the 'primarily external value' of the foetus, as mentioned by Qiu, was almost exclusively ascribed to the family

96 Rigdon (110*n*59) 546.

97 Moskowitz (14*n*80) 6.

98 David Der-Wei Wang, *The Monster That Is History: History, Violence, and Fictional Writing in Twentieth-Century China* (2004) 266.

99 Helen Hardacre, *Marketing the Menacing Fetus in Japan: 7* (University of California Press 1999); Moskowitz (14*n*80).

100 Donald Harper, '23. Spellbinding,' *23. Spellbinding* (Princeton University Press 2018) < https://www.degruyter.com/document/doi/10.1515/9780691188140-028/html> accessed 7 February 2024.

101 Luk (108*n*52) 381.

unit. Consequently, the family was responsible for determining the fate of the foetus, as it did for all of its members (particularly women and children) into adulthood. The emperor, regarded as the 'father' of the entire country, possessed similar authority over his subjects. As Rigdon observed, in imperial times 'the worthiness of a life was tied not only to age and ability but to gender and class.'[102] Whatever the philosophical justification, valuing human life based on age, gender and status is hardly an exclusive feature of pre-modern China. The classical example is the Roman *pater familias' ius vitae necisque* (right to life and death) over the members of his family; recent studies have also shown that early modern Europe exhibited a similar approach, especially over women, to abortion and infanticide.[103]

In any case, limiting the discourse to termination of pregnancy, in Europe between the seventeenth and early nineteenth centuries, Canon Law completely banned abortion from conception on, countries passed laws criminalising abortion.[104] At this time, Western powers began to impose on China their cultural and legal models, which coincides with the first Chinese legislation to ban abortion.

3.2 *Abortion in Early Republican and Nationalist China (1912–1949)*

Unlike Japan, which reacted to its military defeat at the hand of the West by embarking on radical reforms at the beginning of the Meiji era (1868–1912), China did not move to modernise its legal system until the early years of the twentieth century, and even then, only with great reluctance, as reflected in its pursuit of two parallel approaches to legal reform: one to revise the Qing code, the other to draft modern codes inspired to those in force in European countries.[105] The Qing government never got the chance to implement the draft codes of criminal and civil procedure, commercial law, civil law, and criminal law completed between 1910 and 1912.[106] However, in the late Qing to early

102 Rigdon (110*n*59) 547.

103 Josephine Billingham, '2. European and Medieval Contexts of Infanticide,' 2. *European and Medieval Contexts of Infanticide* (Amsterdam University Press 2019); Anne-Marie Kilday, *A History of Infanticide in Britain, c. 1600 to the Present* (Palgrave Macmillan 2013); Rodriguez (n 669); 'Death Control in the West 1500–1800: Sex Ratios at Baptism in Italy, France and England' (Routledge & CRC Press, 2023); Francisco J Beltrán Tapia and Francisco J Marco-Gracia, 'Death, Sex, and Fertility: Female Infanticide in Rural Spain, 1750–1950' (2022) 26 European Review of Economic History 234.

104 Luk (108*n*52) 381.

105 Philip CC Huang, *Code, Custom, and Legal Practice in China: The Qing and the Republic Compared* (Stanford University Press 2001) 15.

106 Ibid.

Republican Period, the Supreme Court's predecessor, the Central Judicial Office (*Dali yuan* 大理院), did reference these draft provisions for legal interpretation.[107] Only the first version of the criminal code would later become state law in 1912 under the Provisional Government of the Republic of China. Renamed the New Criminal Code Temporarily in Force (*Zanxing xin xinglü* 暂行新刑律), it formed the basis of criminal law in the Republic of China and had a lasting impact on certain sectors of Chinese society.[108] Most pertinent to our discussion, it abolished the distinction between different kinds of homicide based on rank, and for the first time in Chinese law, gave the state a monopoly over life and death. In fact, as reported in the 'New Decrees of the Qing Emperor Guanxu' (*Da Qing Guangzu xin faling* 大清光绪新法令), published in 1909 to summarise the legislative activity conducted in the first years of the reforms,[109] 'subjects and people are the first substance of the State';[110] therefore, only the State could decide on their fate, even before birth. By comparison with the norms at that time common in Western countries – especially in accordance with Japanese law, borrowed from Germany and a reference model at that stage of legal modernisation[111] – the New Criminal Code defines abortion (*duotai*) as 'cruel to humanity, damaging to [social] order and contrary to the public interest.'[112] Chapter 27 (arts. 317–323) of the new codes focuses entirely on abortion-related offenses and prohibits abortion in any form, under any circumstances, with no exceptions, even for therapeutic abortion, and establishes punishments for both the mother and the abortionist, with more severe punishments if the abortion takes place due to violence or malice perpetrated against the woman, if the woman suffers permanent damage, or dies, or if the abortion is performed by persons engaged in medical activities.[113]

The definition of these new crimes affected the Chinese language, which from this time on began to distinguish between induced abortion (*duotai*) and spontaneous miscarriage (*xiaochan*). While the linguistic change seems stra-

107 Chun-Fu Lee, 'A Study on The Extraordinary Appeal Decisions of Dali Yuan in the beginning of Republic of China' (2017) 29 Dong Wu fa lü xue bao. Soochow law review 47.

108 Huang (116*n*105) 18; Luk (108*n*52) 385.

109 Shangwu yin shuguan bianyi suo bian 商务印书馆编译所编 (ed), *Da Qing Guangxu Xin faling* 大清光绪新法令 (*New Decrees of the Qing Emperor Guangxu*) (Shanghai Shangwu yin shuguan 上海商務印書館 1909).

110 Ibid 20.

111 Luk (108*n*52) 386.

112 Shangwu yin shuguan bianyi suo bian 商务印书馆编译所编 (n 727) vol 20.

113 Ibid; Luk (108*n*52) 385–386.

ightforward, it was rather complicated for legal practitioners to adapt to the new scenario, not only due to the uncertainty about the laws in force typical of the early years of the Republic.[114] Accustomed to working in a context where abortion was only relevant to the law if it harmed the mother, they struggled to understand new rules based on an ethical vision so different from their own. The idea that the foetus deserved legal protection was so foreign that they ended up asking absurd questions (in the eyes of Westerners anyway), such as whether someone responsible for the murder of a pregnant woman should be liable for two deaths or just one under the New Criminal Code Temporarily in Force.[115]

The Penal Codes enacted under the Nationalist government from 1928 onwards did not significantly modify the new criminal codes for abortion, apart from an exemption for therapeutic abortion (i.e.: abortion performed for medical reasons) in case of illness or 'for averting danger to the [mother's] life' introduced by the 1935 revision of Article 288(3). However, the ban on abortion remained in place for women who had become pregnant as a result of rape.[116] This is not surprising: despite the Republican lawmakers intention to reshape gender and family relations – embodied, for example, in the articles on freedom of marriage, divorce and the possibility of inheritance also granted to women in the Civil Code of 1929–1931 –[117] family values underwent little change under the Guomindang (国民党, hereafter: GMD) government, either in mainland China or, after 1949, in Taiwan, at least as long as martial law remained in force (1987).[118] Nor did the purpose of abortion regulations changed from what the Qing reformers had proclaimed, i.e.: 'to maintain good social customs and protect the public interest.'[119] Indeed, irrespective of women's inability to control the fate of their own bodies, a near universal and timeless condition, China's abortion ban was less about protecting the foetus than about strengthening the state, at a time when a country's power was also measured by its demographic strength.

---

114 Huang (116*n*105) 18–20.

115 Luk (108*n*52) 387.

116 Ibid 388.

117 Kathryn Bernhardt and Philip CC Huang, *Civil Law in Qing and Republican China* (Stanford University Press 1994) 188.

118 Norma Diamond, 'Women under Kuomintang Rule Variations on the Feminine Mystique' (1975) 1 Modern China 3; Adrian Chiu, 'Transformation of Women's Status in Taiwan, 1920–2020' (*Taiwan Insight*, 17 March 2023) <https://taiwaninsight.org/2023/03/17/transformation-of-womens-status-in-taiwan-1920-2020/> accessed 20 May 2024.

119 Luk (108*n*52) 388.

In any case, the Criminal code of the Republic did not last long. On mainland China, Article 17 of the Common Programme (*Zhongguo Renmin Zhengzhi xieshang huiyi gongtong ganglin* 中国人民政治协商会议共同纲领, issued by the Chinese People's Political Consultative Conference on 29 September 1949) abrogated 'All laws, decrees and judicial systems of the GMD reactionary government which oppress the people.' (The Republican era codes lived on in Taiwan's criminal law, however.) Yet, the principle that the lives of citizens, even the unborn, belong to the state had by then taken root in the minds of Chinese leaders, regardless of ideological differences. In the following decades, under both the GMD on Taiwan and the CPC on the mainland, the Chinese version of what Foucault described as 'anatomo and biopolitics'[120] would have 'normalized the surveillance of birth, sexuality, illness, and health,'[121] resulting in the state's extreme control over its citizens' bodies, especially women; a close link between birth control and eugenics[122] (on Taiwan, one reproduction law even as the termed baked into its name: the already mentioned Eugenic Health Law, *Yousheng baojian fa* 优生保健法); and, last but not least, a commitment to preserving the patriarchal family unit.[123] Now, let's look at how the PRC has implemented this new kind of state power and the impact on its legal system.

3.3 *Abortion in the People's Republic of China (1949–2024)*

3.3.1 Abortion in the Maoist Era (1949–1978)

The founding of the People's Republic of China was expected to put an end to feudal inequalities and discriminations within Chinese society, including those related to gender. Although the CPC's mobilisation of women during the War of Resistance against Japan was probably intended to increase women's role in production to support the military effort rather than to achieve gender equality,[124] it cannot be denied that by the 1930s and 1940s Communist women in the liberated areas had achieved a level of emancipation and parity with men that was unthinkable not only during the imperial era but also under the Nationalist government. It is no coincidence that for decades the GMD based part of its propaganda against Maoist China precisely

120 Michel Foucault, *The History of Sexuality: 1: The Will to Knowledge* (1° edizione, Penguin Classics 2020) 140–141.

121 Rodriguez (108*n*51) 4.

122 Ibid 23; Yang (104*n*18) 134.

123 Rodriguez (108*n*51) 5.

124 David SG Goodman, 'Revolutionary Women and Women in the Revolution: The Chinese Communist Party and Women in the War of Resistance to Japan, 1937–1945' [2000] The China Quarterly 915, 918.

on women's participation in combat, their dressing 'like boys' and their sharing of daily work with men, taken as tangible proofs of the sexual immorality and unnatural behaviour resulting from gender equality.[125]

From a statutory point of view, equality between the sexes in the PRC was established by 1954 constitution, Article 96 of which states: 'Women in the People's Republic of China shall enjoy equal rights with men in all aspects of political, economic, cultural, social and domestic life.' When it comes to family planning, this promise has certainly been kept, but instead of giving women the same right to reproductive choice as men, women and men alike have increasingly been prevented from deciding whether to reproduce, when to reproduce and how many children to have. The transfer of power over citizens' lives and bodies from the family to the state that began in the late Qing era was taken to extremes in the PRC, so much so that decisions about a couple's private lives have become state policy, with abortion becoming a tool of birth control; it can be banned, encouraged, or even forced, depending on party leaders' perception of demographic needs, or for eugenic reasons. The intertwining of state-centric abortion regulation with population-control policies and eugenics remains a defining feature of Chinese family planning.[126] In light of these considerations, the subsequent discussion will address these topics in a comprehensive manner.

Authors usually divide the PRC's reproductive policy into three main periods: Maoist pronatalist policy (1949–1979), post-Maoist birth control policy (1980–2015), and the recent removal of birth limits (2016-present).[127] This timeline generally remains valid, but recent critics have highlighted its excessive rigidity in portraying a linear and clearly top-down process that belies repeated rethinking and changes of direction, and by uneven implementation across the territory.[128] In recent decades, even authors close to the Party have recognised these fluctuations, which (not surprisingly) correspond to the alternation of revolution and reconstruction in the political, legal, and economic spheres. In an article published in the People's Daily in 2013,[129] for example, Ni Liangduan describes the history of birth control in the PRC through the slogans launched by communist leaders, from the mottos 'a

125 Diamond (119*n*118) 13–14.

126 Cao, '"Glorious Mothers" and "Rational Women"' (109*n*55) 770.

127 Cao, 'The Regulation of Reproduction in New China' (113*n*77) 97.

128 Rodriguez (108*n*51) 6.

129 Ni Liangduan 倪良端, 'Jihua shengyun yu Shao Lizi 计划生育与邵力子(Family Planning and Shao Lizi)' (*Zhongguo gongchangdang xinwen wan* 中国共产党新闻网, 25 February 2013) <http://dangshi.people.com.cn/n/2013/0225/c85037-20590077.html> accessed 19 June 2024.

great population is a great good thing' and 'every miracle on earth can be made' to 'only one child per couple.' It is worth remarking that the first two slogans were created by Mao Zedong on the eve of the founding of the PRC in response to the then U.S. Secretary of State's concern about China's ability to feed its rapidly increasing population.[130] Mao's approach was not only ideologically faithful to Marx's critique of Malthusian thought; at the time of the outbreak of the Korean War, a large population also seemed to be a practical means of ensuring the defence of the territory.[131] Thus, following the example of its Soviet ally,[132] the People's Republic of China implemented a pronatalist policy, awarding prizes and honours to the most fertile women, now called 'glorious mothers' (*guangrong muqin* 光荣母亲) or 'heroic mothers' (*yingyong muqin* 英勇母亲).[133] Due to the poverty of resources, however, state support could not go much beyond declamations. In the absence of aid and subsidies, large families were often driven to infanticide or to abandoning infants, while many women lost their lives or suffered permanent harm either from too many gestations or from abortion practices.[134] At a time when abortion was criticised and prohibited as an old-society and bourgeois feature, many women were forced to resort to dangerous methods to end their pregnancies, such as throwing themselves off cliffs, or ingesting poisonous herbs.[135] Yet, the pronatalist policy was successful. Between 1949 and 1953, China experienced its first population peak, and with it, the difficulty of sustaining such rapid population growth. In 1953, Deng Xiaoping, then Vice-Premier of the State Council, ordered the Ministry of Health to formulate and issue the 'Measures on Contraception and Abortion' (*Biyu ji rengong liuchan banfa* 避孕及人工流产办法). A year later, Premier Liu Shaoqi said, 'the Party is in favour of birth control… [. .].'[136] The trend continued during the 'Hundred Flowers campaign' (1956–1957) when, among other topics, many intellectuals were invited to

130 Ibid.

131 Ibid.

132 Savage (106*n*40) 1052.

133 Ni Liangduan 倪良端 (121*n*129).

134 Cao, '"Glorious Mothers" and "Rational Women"' (109*n*55) 756.

135 Ibid 752.

136 Shanxi sheng difangzhi bangongshi陕西省地方志办公室 (Local records office of the Shaanxi Province, 'Renkou He Jihua Shengyu Shi – Disi Pian Renkou He Jihua Shengyu Gongzuo Diyicheng Gonzuo Lishi Di Yijie Yunniang Chuzhi Shijian 人口和计划生育志 – 第四篇 人口和计划生育工作 第一章 工作历程 第一节 酝酿初始时期(1950–1970) Population and Family Planning, Title IV Population and Family Planning Work Chapter I. History of Work Section I. The Initial Period of Conception (1950–1970)' (22 September 2017) <http://dfz.shaanxi.gov.cn/sqzlk/xbsxsz/szdel/rkhjhsyz/201709/t20170922_934742.html> accessed 29 July 2024.

express their view on 'How Malthusian Population Theory should be evaluated' and 'Whether the propaganda for birth control is in conflict with the superiority of socialist system.'[137] In 1956, Mao Zedong himself, speaking to a Yugoslavian women delegation, advocated state planning of 'human beings' production' similar to that already implemented in other fields of the economy and society; in 1957, the national government established the Central Committee for Birth Control (*Zhongjian shengyu xianzhi weiyuanhui* 中央生育限制委员会), and in the same year, the Department of Geography at East China Normal University established China's First Population Research Unit (*renkou yanjiu shi* 人口研究室).[138] While this was happening, the situation suddenly changed. In the spring 1957, the 'Anti-Rightist Movement' began targeting intellectual, scientific, and technological circles, and within a few months, the general situation in China became decidedly hostile to the 'dissenting voices' in favour of family planning, which was (again!) seen as an 'anti-Marxist-Leninist view.'[139] Mao Zedong's words sanctioned the new policy. In his article 'Introducing cooperative society,' Mao clearly stated that with more people, 'the heat is high, and the energy is great,' endorsing the abandonment of the recently drawn up 'new population theory' (*xin renkou lun* 新人口论)[140] and the embrace of a new 'manpower theory' (*renshou lun* 人手伦).[141] The problem of sustaining a huge population resurfaced in 1963, when China, trying to recover from the disaster of the Great Leap Forward (*Da yuejin* 大跃进, 1953–1960), experienced a second fertility peak, with a population growth rate of 33.33 per thousand. To solve the issue, Zhou Enlai and other communist leaders proposed the campaign 'two children per couple is enough' and the implementation throughout the country of late marriage (*wan hun* 晚婚: after the age of 28 for men and 25 for women)[142] which culminated in 1964 with the establishment of the State Council's Family Planning Commission (*Jihua shengyu weiyuanhui* 计划生育委员会). In this context, Mao's attitude changed again, to the extent that in September 1965, he

137 Ni Liangduan 倪良端 (121*n*129).

138 Ibid.

139 Ibid.

140 Ma Yinchu 马寅初, 'Zai di yi ju quanguo renmin daibiao dahui di si ci huiyishang de fayan "Xin koulun" Ma Yinchu de shumian fayan 在第一届全国人民代表大会第四次会议上的发言 新人口论 马寅初的书面发言 (Speech at the Fourth Session of the First National People's Congress: 'New Population Theory Written statement by Ma Yinchu' *Renmin Ribao* 人民日报 (Beijing 北京市, 5 July 1957Cn) <http://politics.people.com.cn/ywkx/n/2015/0728/c363762-27371444.html> accessed 25 July 2024.

141 Ni Liangduan 倪良端 (121*n*129).

142 Ibid.

expressed to the American journalist Edgar Snow his dissatisfaction with the implementation of birth planning, which he felt was not being effectively promoted in the countryside.[143] The Great Cultural Revolution (*Da wenhua geming* 大文化革命, 1966–1976) intervened before Maoist family planning could be properly implemented: in that period, today remembered as 'the ten years of catastrophe' (*shinian haojie* 十年浩劫),[144] everything was out of control, including population growth. To slow it down, on the 8th of July 1971, the State Council issued the 'Report on Doing a Good Job in Family Planning' (*Guanyu zuohao jihua shengyu gongzuo de baogao* 关于做好计划生育工作的报告),[145] while in the same year birth control was included for the first time among the targets of the national economic development plan.[146] Then, in December 1973, China's first national conference on family planning proposed the policy of 'late, sparse and few' (*wan xi shao* 晚稀少), which Ni Liangduan recalled as:

> 'late' means that a man marries after the age of 25 and a woman after the age of 23, and that a woman gives birth after the age of 24; 'sparse' means that the interval between births is three years or more; and 'few' means that a couple has no more than two children.[147]

By the late 1970s, this slogan had been superseded by the infamous 'only one child is good' (*zhi sheng yige hao* 只生一个好).

---

143 Ibid.

144 Xi Jinping 习近平, 'Xi Jinping Zia Shenbuji Zhuyao Lingdao Ganbu Xuexi Guanche Dang de Shiba Jie Wu Zhong Quanhui Jingshen Zhuanti Yantao Ban Shang de Jianghua 习近平在省部级主要领导干部学习贯彻党的十八届五中全会精神专题研讨班上的讲话_共产党员网 (Xi Jinping's Speech at the Seminar for Provincial Level Leading Cadres to Study and Implement the Spirit of the Fifth Plenary Session of the 18th CPC Central Committee)' (*Gongchandang yuanwan* 共产党员网) <https://news.12371.cn/2016/05/10/ARTI1462820587609178.shtml> accessed 25 June 2024.

145 'Guowuyuan Zhuanfa Weisheng Bù Junguan Kuai, Shangye Bu, Ranliao Huaxue Gongye Bu "Guanyu Zuo Hao Jihua Shengyu Gongzuo de Baogao" 国务院转发卫生部军管会、商业部、燃料化学工业部 "关于做好计划生育工作的报告" (The State Council Forwarded to the Ministry of Health's Military Commission, the Ministry of Commerce and the Ministry of Fuel and Chemical Industry the "Report on Improving Family Planning")' <https://www.gov.cn/zhengce/content/2015-11/19/content_10304.htm> accessed 25 June 2024.

146 Ni Liangduan 倪良端 (121*n*129).

147 Xinhua wang 新华网, 'Guanyu "sheng haizi" de naxie zhengce zhongguo renkou zhengce yanbian "bian nianshi" 关于 "生孩子" 的那些政策——中国人口政策演变"编年史" (*Xinhua wang* 新华网, 9 February 2015) <http://www.xinhuanet.com/politics/2015-02/09/c_1114311252.htm> accessed 25 June 2024.

The central government's endorsement of contradictory and frequently changing policies could not help but confuse local officials, not to mention ordinary people, especially given the lack of formal regulations on the subject. It is worth mentioning that, although planned population policies have been formulated since the early years of the PRC,[148] the term 'family planning' does not appear in Chinese legislation until 1978, with the enactment of 53 of the Third Constitution of the PRC.[149] A statutory provision on abortion doesn't exist until the adoption of 19 of the Maternal and Infant Health Care Law (*Muying baojian fa* 母婴保健法, hereafter: MIHCL) by Tenth Meeting of the Standing Committee of the Eighth National People's Congress on October 27, 1994.

Before then, the rules on birth control and termination of pregnancy only existed in what Mark Savage has described as 'an amalgam of constitutional duties, regulation of the Ministry of Health, state policies, Party policies, Party enactments, provincial policies, provincial administrative regulations, and even local supplementary regulation.'[150]

Among the first of these documents, the 'Methods on controlling abortion among female cadres' (*Kongzhi nüganbu duotai fangfa* 控制女干部堕胎方法) issued in 1950 by the Ministry of Health allowed abortion in specific situations: if a woman suffered from severe physical or genetic mental diseases, or her life was at risk, and in the case of women who had at least one child, but were physically unable to have another one.[151] However, except in an emergency, a woman needed her husband's written consent, the permission of both spouses' work units and a physician's certificate of authorisation to apply for an abortion.[152] A reading of this provision makes it clear that, despite declarations of gender equality and changes in ideology, the approach to abortion had not changed since 1935. Exceptions were made to protect pregnant cadres, who were nevertheless denied full control over their bodies, even when their lives were at stake. Similar rules directed at all Chinese women, regardless of party affiliation, surfaced in the 'Interim Measures to restrict birth control and abortion' (*Xianzhi jieyu ji rengong liuchan zanxing banfa* 限制节育及人工流产暂行办法) issued by the Ministry of Health on 31st December 1952; in

148 Savage (106*n*40) 1072.

149 Ibid 1081.

150 Ibid 1067.

151 Peng Peiyun 彭珮云, *Zhongguo jihua shengyu quanshu* 中国计划生育全书 (*China Family Planning Compendium*) (Zhongguo renkou chubanshe 中国人口出版社 1997) 889.

152 Cao, 'The Regulation of Reproduction in New China' (113*n*77) 99; Cao, '"Glorious Mothers" and "Rational Women"' (109*n*55) 752; Rigdon (110*n*59) 544.

response, the central government specified the criminal liability of those who illegally undertook induced abortion.[153] A few months later, on 20 August 1953, the evolution of China's political and demographic situation led the same State Council to issue the 'Measures on Contraception and Abortion' (*Biyu ji rengong liuchan banfa* 避孕及人工流产办, hereafter: Measures 1953), which established a few medical exceptions for the use of abortion, in response to the country's first demographic peak, diminishing at the same time women's mortality due to clandestine abortions and improving maternal and child health care. However, an analysis of the discourse between officials and political leaders for and against abortion reveals that within a few years, the primary focus of family planning shifted from the protection of women and children to the realisation of the economic plan.[154] It was probably also to achieve this goal, which needed more working women than mothers, that in the middle 1950s the government started relaxing rules against contraception and interruption of pregnancy.[155]

It is not easy to access the original text of most of the provisions issued in the first decades of the PRC. One reason could be that they were often internal departmental rules (*neibu* 内部) and therefore, as was common practice until the 1990s, generally not published, even if they applied to everyone. Therefore, their content must be derived from secondary sources, as the reports published on institutional websites or the statements of the people at the time involved in population control. These documents show that, in the perpetual motion of the PRC's demographic policies, the one unchanging feature has been the law-in-action's almost total disregard for a woman's autonomous will to continue or terminate her pregnancy. This is unsurprising, given Chinese culture's specific approach to the relationship between the individual and the community, and more generally the global reluctance to allow women the capacity to decide the fate of their own bodies. On mainland China, the concept of a foetus's right to life has never been the primary ideological opponent to a woman's reproductive rights, at least not the same way that it takes precedence in most Western countries struggling with the issue of abortion, and to some extent also in the island of Taiwan.[156] This feature further confirms what Qiu Renzhong says about the limited intrinsic value that Chinese tradition ascribes to the foetus, and the tendency to give it 'primarily' an external value, which varies according to the importance given to the (possible) new-

153 Ni Liangduan 倪良端 (121*n*129).

154 Savage (106*n*40) 1074.

155 Rodriguez (108*n*51) 77.

156 Yang (104*n*18) 135, 142.

born by the net of relationships in which it will be included. It is precisely the external value of the foetus, as understood in this way, that serves to balance the interests involved in the issue of abortion. This is the key to understanding Chinese demographic policies and norms. From the Maoist era to the Xi Jinping era, the policies governing population control have fluctuated in line with the varying degrees of value attributed to the child as an asset by the entities that comprise this net. These entities include the state and society, with the patrilineal family playing a role only to a limited extent and not consistently.

This also explains the minimal, if any, consideration given to a woman's will. Since the external value of the foetus reverberates only marginally on her, logically, she is but one among many subjects whose consent to abortion is required, even in cases where her own life or health is put at risk by gestation. Take as an example the 'Interim Measures on Revision of Contraception and Abortion' *Guanyu xiugai biyun ji gongren liuchan zanxin banfa* 关于修改避孕及人工流产暂行办法, hereafter: Interim Measures 1954), issued by the Ministry of Health on 20 July 1954, and usually considered to have 'appropriately relaxed the scope of abortion' in the Maoist era.[157] It stipulated that 'there is no restriction on contraception and birth control for married men and women,'[158] allowing abortion 'when the continuation of the pregnancy is considered medically undesirable, or the spacing of childbirth is too close, or the mother had a baby only four months old and had trouble in breastfeeding.'[159] However, meeting these requirements was not sufficient to initiate the abortion procedure. To this end, the norm also required a joint application from the couple, a medical certificate, and the approval of the responsible organisation to which the couple belonged.[160] Furthermore, if abortion was requested because of the woman' special or too heavy workload, or for study reasons, the application should first be certified and supported by the key personnel of the responsible organisation and approved by a medical organisation.[161]

According to Fu Lianzhang, then vice-minister of health, Interim Measures 1954 excluded any possibility that a woman could obtain abortion at will because its objective was to protect women's health.[162] Chinese doctors, no strangers to the idea that women were unfit to choose what was in their best

---

157 Shanxi sheng difangzhi bangongshi 陕西省地方志办公室 (Local records office of the Shaanxi Province (122*n*136).

158 Ibid.

159 Savage (106*n*40) 1074.

160 Ibid.

161 Ibid.

162 Ibid.

interest, had discretion over not only the choice to terminate a pregnancy, but even the decision to inform the couple of the possibility to do so. The fact that Interim Measures 1954 was *neibu*, coupled with the invitation not to advertise the new provisions on contraception and birth control contained in the 'Circular on Improving Contraception and Abortion' (*Guanyu gaijing biyun ji rengong liuchan wenti de tongbao* 关于改进避孕及人工流产问题的通报) issued by the Ministry of Health on 10 November 1954, put completely in doctors' hands the duty 'to provide correct guidance on birth control to anyone who requests it.'[163] In a few months, the Party would change its approach due to shifting political and social developments. As early as 1 March 1955, the CPC Central Committee called on local Party committees to 'properly publicise this Party policy among cadres and the masses (except in ethnic minority areas) so that the people have a correct understanding of the issue of birth control.'[164] Nevertheless, the attitude of doctors to women's freedom of choice in the matter remained critical: when, on 11 April 1957, the Ministry of Health issued a new Notice on abortion and sterilisation (hereafter: Notice 1957), which for the first time prohibited any special approval procedure for abortion, the Chinese Medical Association rejected it as a violation of the principle of health.[165]

Notice 1957 represented a drastic change from the past. It only applied to healthy and married women, to whom it granted the right of abortion irrespective of their age or the number of children. The interruption of pregnancy should be performed within ten weeks after conception, and at least one year after any previous abortion. Furthermore, in case of induced abortion, all third-party approvals were prohibited, including the spouse's consent, which still required in case of sterilisation.[166]

The repeal of the husband's approval marked a break between the written law of the PRC and the tradition not only of China, but of Far East Asia as a whole. As noted above, even nowadays in countries influenced by Chinese culture, such as Taiwan and Japan, laws still require the husband's consent for an abortion. Mainland China, on the contrary, in the mid-1950s rejected this part of its own legal tradition, depriving the patrilineal family of control over the existence of its new members, and (in theory) giving the woman

---

163 Shanxi sheng difangzhi bangongshi 陕西省地方志办公室 (Local records office of the Shaanxi Province (122*n*136).

164 Ibid.

165 Savage (106*n*40) 1074.

166 Ibid; Nie Jing-Bao (14*n*79) 43.

exclusive rights over the decision to carry a pregnancy. In practice, however, things did not turn out this way. Firstly, most doctors refused to consider abortion as a means of contraception, a position shared by the government, which felt the need to educate the masses about the potential harm to women's health from induced abortions;[167] however, given the difficulty and costs of obtaining contraceptives, particularly condoms, and the cultural taboos linked to sex, especially extramarital sex, abortions became a common option to end unplanned pregnancy. In this situation, doctors often effectively restricted abortion by exercising their discretion and by imposing additional requirements in local practice, such as setting a lower limit of gestational weeks within which the pregnancy of could be terminated, or by requiring the consent of parties other than the woman, particularly her husband.[168] The tendency not to follow the letter of the (unpublished) rule was then reinforced by how it was transposed into local regulations. According to Savage, 'regional governments either disapproved or generally adopted the notice; but each enacted regional variations.'[169]

Additional political events would eventually nullify the (already limited) impact of Notice 1957 on Chinese society. From the latter half of 1957 until 1961, the expansion of the Anti-Rightist Movement and the Great Leap Forward initially created an illusory labour shortage – later followed by actual decline in population growth precipitated by natural disasters and misguided economic policies. Then problem of overpopulation resurfaced, and with the implementation of the policy of 'readjusting, consolidating, strengthening, and enhancement' (expressed as an eight-character slogan: *tiaozheng, gonggu, chongshi, tigao* 调整、巩固、充实、提高)[170] the objective of birth control resumed, this time in a planned form. On 18 December 1962, the CPC Central Committee and the State Council issued the 'Instructions Concerning the Serious Promotion of Family Planning' (*Guanyu renzheng ti gao jihua shengyu de zhishi* 关于认真提倡计划生育的指示), calling for the promotion of family planning in cities and densely populated rural areas, and for the appropriate control of the natural population growth rate.[171] Family planning committees were set up at the central and local levels, and many provinces created family

---

167 Savage (106*n*40) 1075.

168 Ibid 1076.1077.

169 Ibid 1075.

170 Jianfu Chen, *Chinese Law: Context and Transformation* (Expanded, Revised edizione, Martinus Nijhoff 2015) 53.

171 Shanxi sheng difangzhi bangongshi 陕西省地方志办公室 (Local records office of the Shaanxi Province (128*n*163).

planning surgical teams, 'to publicise and popularize knowledge of contraception and birth control, and to guide and carry out technical services for birth control.'[172] Then in 1963, the Ministry of Health issued the Notice on Revising the Required Conditions for induced abortion and Male and Female ligation Surgery' (*Guanyu xiugai rengong liuchan ji nannü jieza shoushu tiaojian guiding de tongzhi* 关于修改人工流产及男女结扎手术条件规定的通知, hereafter: Notice 1963), removing the restriction on induced abortion and sterilisation. In particular, the notice stipulated that married men's vasectomy or women's tubal ligation surgery could be carried out at the request of either man or woman if they had been examined by a physician and there were no contra-indications to the surgery.[173] It also re-affirmed that abortion did not require spousal approval and specified that, without contraindication to the operation, a woman should be granted abortion at will and the medical unit should also perform it as early as possible, preferably within the third month of pregnancy.[174] Furthermore, in case of abortions requested in the third or fifth month or later, the health administrative departments at all levels should designate hospitals where experienced physicians can induce abortion.

As the content of Notice 1963 shows, the time limits on induced abortion were based on concerns about the health risks for a woman at an advanced stage of pregnancy: no weight was given to foetal development and its greater or lesser value depending on gestational age. The concern for women's health also inspired the MoH's advice to promote vasectomy over tubal ligation, which was considered a much more complex and dangerous procedure. While the latter appeal was to go unheeded – at least according to the published data, which in some provinces show a 1:6 ratio between male and female sterilisations in the first half of 1960s[175] – as far as abortion was concerned, the 'new' indication was followed, with a significant drop in pregnancies carried to term between 1962 and 1965. The advent of the Cultural Revolution, with its objective of breaking down the 'Four olds' (*Sijiu* 四旧: old ideas, culture, customs and habits) and denouncing the traditional family structure, initially appeared to provide an opportunity for the promotion of birth control. However, the establishment of revolutionary committees at all levels from 1968 onwards resulted, among other things, in the *de facto* elimination of all family planning agencies and the disbandment of the entire workforce

172 Ibid.
173 Ibid.
174 Ibid.
175 Ibid.

specialised in this field;[176] in some provinces, such as Shaanxi, occasionally the birth rate reached 40 per thousand per year.[177]

It was not until the early 1970s that family planning was reintroduced to the political agenda, albeit in relation to urban areas and based on vague and unclear criteria. In this context, it is unsurprising that cultural resistance to birth control prevailed over the official promotion of it, with both women and healthcare providers continuing to adhere to the traditional norm of having large families. According to Savage, such resistance is confirmed by state statistics, which show that the use of abortion remained relatively constant during the 1970s, notwithstanding governmental promotion of birth control.[178] Radical change came from the CPC decision to formulate birth control rules more as positive law than as Party and state policy, and to set definitive quantitative limits on population growth. These were the prodromes of the reform and opening-up period that Deng Xiaoping inaugurated in December 1978.

3.3.2 Abortion in the Reform and Opening-Up Period (1978–2021)

In March 1978, nine months before the meeting of the CPC Central Committee that would have change the PRC's destiny, the Fifth NPC adopted a new constitution which stated for the first time that '[t]he state advocates and encourages family planning.' At the same session of the NPC, Hua Guofeng, at the time the Chairman of the CPC, set the goal to lower China's annual population growth rate to less than 1% within three years.[179] From that point on, and for the next forty years, the focus of birth control shifted from education to results. This does not mean that the previously implemented instruments of propaganda, training, and persuasion lost their importance. However, making local family planning commissions responsible for reaching precise demographic targets led them to use abortion as a means to meet their targets, sometimes against a woman's will and at a late stage of pregnancy. We began this section by recounting precisely the impressions aroused outside and inside China by the stories (or silence) of the women and men who had such experiences. These stories seem to confirm, once again, the Western prejudice regarding the low value that Chinese culture attributes to life in general, and to life of the foetus in particular. The narrative now shifts perspective, no longer focusing on the foetus itself, but on how a relevant social group, most notably the state assigns value to potential new members of their

176 Ibid.
177 Ibid.
178 Savage (106*n*40) 1080.
179 Ibid 1081.

society. This is clearly expressed in the speeches of political leaders in the 1980s: births should be planned in the same way as one plans the economy, to foster national construction and improve the standard of living of the entire Chinese population, particularly women, who in this way will gain more freedom from traditional family duties and can finally take an active part in socialist construction.

For a long time, however, these precepts did not take the form of actual legislation. In fact, until the enactment of the Population and Family Planning Law (*Renkou yu jihua shengyu fa* 人口与计划生育法, hereafter: PFPL) approved by the SC of the Ninth NPC on 29 December 2001, formal laws in the field of birth control did not go much further than the family planning reference in Article 53 of the 1978 Constitution. The expression 'practice of family planning' was included in Article 2 of the Marriage Law (*Jiehun fa* 婚姻法, hereafter: ML) passed by the NPC on 10 September 1980, which also introduced in Article 12 the duty of both husband and wife to practice it, lately (and more importantly) reiterated in Article 49.2 of the 1982 Constitution. For many years, however, no law explained what this duty meant. Just like during the Maoist era, the contents of population policy in the early reform period had to be uncovered in party decisions and declarations, or at best in the local regulations they inspired.

Even the one-child policy itself originates from one such document: the 'Open letter to All Members of the Party and the Communist Youth on controlling population growth' (*Guanyu kongzhi renkou zengzhang wenti zhi quanti gongchandang yuan, gong qingtuan yuan de gongkai xin* 关于控制人口增长问题致全体共产党员、共青团员的公开信, hereafter: the 9.25 Open Letter), written on 25 September 1980 by Central Committee of the CPC.[180] The 9.25 Open Letter states:

> To control the total population of China to less than 1.2 billion by the end of this century, the State Council has issued a call to the whole country to promote the idea of having only one child per couple. This is a major measure that has a bearing on the speed and future of the four modernisations, on the health and well-being of future generations, and

180 Fang Yuanzheng 方圆震, 'Guanyu "Sheng Haizi" de Naxie Zhengce Yanbian' Nianbian Shi – Zhongguo Renkouy Zhengci 关于"生孩子"的那些政策——中国人口政策演变"编年史" (Policies on "Having Children": A Chronicle of the Evolution of China's Population Policy)' (*Xhonguan zhengfu menhuwangzhang* 中央政府门户网站 (*Central govermment Portal*, 9 February 2015) <https://www.gov.cn/zhengce/2015-02/09/content_2816919.htm> accessed 25 June 2024.

is in the long-term interests of the people of the country as well as their immediate interests.[181]

Susan Greenhalgh recently noted that the notion of limiting couples to one child did not originate demographic research, but rather a group of missile-strategy scientists led by an aerospace engineer named Song Jian.[182] Given its political origins, it is not surprising that its effects on Chinese demographic growth have since been downplayed. A substantial body of evidence from numerous studies shows that three quarters of the decline in fertility, generally ascribed to the one-child policy's success, actually occurred during the 1970s, well before its inauguration, as a result of China's improving socio-economic conditions.[183]

In contrast, the impact of the 'one-child policy' on the practice of abortion is indisputable: induced abortions grew steadily from the late 1970s and early 1980s and remained at more than 41.5% of live births through 1995.[184] In fact, even though the 9.25 Open Letter made clear that 'Birth control measures should focus on contraception, with methods chosen voluntarily by the masses,' many provincial authorities infringed upon this right to choose, forcing women to abort in case of 'unplanned births,' or when a pregnant woman did not meet the quantitative requirements set by local regulations.[185] This did not happen everywhere. Given the lack of national provisions, some local authorities applied the policy flexibly, adapting it to their local circumstances – and in some cases mitigating its impact.[186] In other cases, local authorities took advantage of the new rules to force families to comply with the population plan to meet economic goals. For example, the so-called household responsibility contracts (*Jiating lianchan chengbao hetong* 家庭联产承包合同) at the heart of the Chinese system designed to modernise agri-

181 The content of the '9.25 Open Letter' can be found at: '9.25 Gongkaixin 9.25 公开信 (Open Letter of the 25 September)' (*Baidu baike* 百度百科) <https://baike.baidu.hk/item/9.25%E5%85%AC%E5%BC%80%E4%BF%A1/8632026> accessed 8 August 2024.

182 Susan Greenhalgh, *Just One Child: Science and Policy in Deng's China* (2008) 48–58; Thomas Scharping, *Birth Control in China 1949–2000: Population Policy and Demographic Development* (Routledge 2013).

183 Martin King Whyte, Wang Feng and Yong Cai, 'Challenging Myths About China's One-Child Policy' (2015) 74 The China Journal 144, 145. Contra see: Zhenwu Zhai and Guangzhao Jin, 'China's Family Planning Policy and Fertility Transition' (2023) 9 Chinese Journal of Sociology 479.

184 Rodriguez (108*n*51) 178.

185 Savage (106*n*40) 1085–1086; Cao, '"Glorious Mothers" and "Rational Women"' (n 673) 754–755.

186 Rodriguez (108*n*51) 185.

culture and solve the problem of underproduction in rural areas often incorporated the 'duty to abort.'[187] This created a contractual bond between the production team and the individual family added a commitment to have a certain number of children (usually none) while reaching their production quota. If a woman exceeded the number of pregnancies her family had agreed to in the contract, she not only had to pay a fine but also had to have an abortion as a specific remedy for the breach of contract,[188] a liability defined in Article 12 of the new Economic Contract Law (*Jingji hetong fa* 经济合同法), approved by the Fifth NPC on 13 December 1981.

However, in the age of the 'legislation of democracy' (*minzhu falü hua* 民主法律化),[189] the extensive use of (voluntary?) abortion to meet population growth targets probably wouldn't have been possible without another statutory development: the enactment of the PRC's first Criminal Law (*Xingfa* 刑法, hereafter Criminal Law 1979) adopted by the Fifth NPC on 1 July 1979. Not by chance, the Criminal Law 1979 did not include any provision regarding induced abortion. Thus, following its approval, the PRC became the first and only country in the world not to punish under any circumstances either the woman or the person performing the abortion on her.[190]

Similarly, as far as civil law is concerned, the General Principles of Civil Law (*Minfa tongze* 民法通则, hereafter GPCL) adopted by the Sixth NPC on 12 April 1986, made no mention of the rights of the foetus. We will have to wait until the Civil Code (*Minfa dian* 民法典, hereafter: CC) adopted by the Thirteenth NPC on 28 May 2020, and in force since 1 January 2021, for the law to recognise the capacity of the foetus to enjoy civil rights in cases involving the protection of its interests, such as inheritance or the acceptance of a gift, subject to the event of birth (CC, Article 16).

This did not mean that abortion was always allowed, or that it was allowed to any woman, regardless of her marital status. After the promulgation of Criminal Law 1979, for example, some municipal regulations preserved eco-

---

187 Justin Yifu Lin, 'The Household Responsibility System in China's Agricultural Reform: A Theoretical and Empirical Study' (1988) 36 Economic Development and Cultural Change S199.

188 Savage (106*n*40) 1088–1089.

189 Deng Xiaoping 邓小平, 'Jiefan sixiang, shishi qiushi, tuanji yishi xian qiankan (1978 nian 12 yue 13 ri)) 解放思想,实事求是,团结一致向前看(1978年12月13日)(Emancipate the mind, seek truth from facts, and unite as one to look forward) (13 December 1978),' *Deng Xiaoping wenxuan – Dier Juan* 邓小平文选 – 第二卷 (*Selected Works of Deng Xiaoping*), vol 2 (1983rd edn, Renmin chubanshe 人民出版社) 146 <https://www.marxistphilosophy.org/Deng/Dengxiaowen2.pdf>.

190 Savage (106*n*40) 1083.

nomic penalties for unmarried couples having an abortion.[191] It is challenging not to view these provisions as a vestige of the long-standing skepticism surrounding extramarital sex, which originated in the imperial era and still endures. Remarkably, in the Qing dynasty, concern over extramarital sex's potential threat to the social order and stable gender roles gave rise to a new crime, 'fornication' (*jian* 奸).[192] The Maoist era took a similar approach in labelling premarital and extramarital sex as 'the most bourgeois of acts,'[193] with transgressors becoming a 'primary target' during the Cultural Revolution.'[194] The punishments and torture reserved for those caught indulging in extramarital affairs did not spare even the Red Guards, particular in the case of the female revolutionary youths who became pregnant while travelling the country 'to create networks' (*chuanlian* 串联). Many Chinese novels, memoirs, and movies have since recounted the drama of these women and their companions who were convicted of sexual crimes even for consensual sex and often killed themselves out of shame.[195] The implementation of regulations to control citizens' sexual activity and protect the traditional family unit has persisted to varying degrees throughout the reform era. In the early 1990s, premarital sex was often labelled 'hooliganism' (*liuman huodong* 流氓活动) and punished under Article 160 of the Criminal Law 1979.[196] An amendment in 1997 revoked this provision, yet the legal system persists in its disapproval of out-of-wedlock relationships, which it tries to discourage in many ways, including measures that make abortion more onerous for unwed women. As evidenced by Irene Zhang in 2023, for example, the reimbursement of abortion procedures by national insurance, though subject to local variations, seldom includes voluntary abortions, particularly when sought by unmarried women.[197]

I have elaborated on these aspects because censorship related to certain behaviours, especially taboos regarding sex, is a long-standing feature of Chinese cultural and legal tradition. Some scholars believe that censorship has exacerbated the lack of sex education among young Chinese and contributed

---

191 Ibid 1069.

192 Rodriguez (108*n*51) 206.

193 Ibid 147.

194 Ibid 144.

195 Ibid 1456–148.

196 Teemu Ruskola, 'Law, Sexual Morality, and Gender Equality in Qing and Communist China' (1994) 103 The Yale Law Journal 2531, 1554.

197 Irene Zhang, 'In China, a Fight for Reproductive Rights' (*Asia Pacific Foundation of Canada*) <https://www.asiapacific.ca/publication/china-fight-reproductive-rights> accessed 13 November 2023.

to the recent exponential growth of sexually transmitted diseases and unwanted pregnancies among teenagers in the PRC.[198]

This also sheds light on our discussion of abortion. Despite government initiatives to disseminate information on birth control and sexual hygiene practices,[199] abortion appears to have become the dominant method of contraception, particularly among younger women.[200] Both Chinese and international statistical data corroborate this. According to data published in the 2020 Health Statistical Yearbook, compiled and released by the PRC's National Health Commission,[201] and available on the Guttmacher Institute's website,[202] the number of induced abortions has increased year on year since 2017, reaching 9.762 million in 2019.[203] Furthermore, the proportion of high-risk abortions among multiple repeat abortions and abortions among those under the age of 20 is rising.[204] Recent surveys indicate that abortions among unmarried adolescents under the age of 24 now account for more than 40% of total abortions per year in China. Additionally, nearly 20% of unmarried adolescents' abortions are repeat abortions.[205]

These figures are cause for concern for the Chinese government, particularly considering the possible impact on the future health of young Chinese women. According to an article published in 2021 in the Chinese Journal of Practical Gynecology and Obstetrics (*Zhonguo shiyong nüke yu chanke zazhi* 中国实用妇科与产科杂志) and frequently referenced in Chinese articles pertaining to the subject, voluntary abortions, especially when repeated and experienced at a young age, are among the causes of rising female infertility

198 James Wang, Nanlin Griffiths, and Serenitie Fang, 'China's Lack of Sex-Ed Putting Young People at Risk' (*CNN*, 30 November 2016) <https://www.cnn.com/2016/11/30/health/china-sex-education-world-aids-day/index.html> accessed 13 August 2024.

199 Qin Qian and Zhang Jiali, 'Sex Education in China: Actors and Dynamics of China's Policies and Practices' (2023) 10 Cogent Education 2270289.

200 Guo Chao and others, 'Risky Sexual Behaviors and Repeat Induced Abortion Among Unmarried Young Women in China: Results from a Large, Nationwide, Population-Based Sample' (2019) 28 Journal of Women's Health (2002) 1442.

201 http://www.nhc.gov.cn/mohwsbwstjxxzx/tjtjnj/202112/dcd39654d66c4e6abf4d7b1389becd01.shtml

202 https://www.guttmacher.org/regions/asia/china.

203 'Qingshaonian shengzhi jiankang bu "liu" shi' '青少年生殖健康不"流"失' (Adolescent reproductive health is not 'lost') <https://wsjkw.zjtz.gov.cn/art/2022/2/21/art_1229568733_58941170.html> accessed 28 August 2024.

204 Liu Jinlin and others, 'Is Repeat Abortion a Public Health Problem among Chinese Adolescents? A Cross-Sectional Survey in 30 Provinces' (2019) 16 International Journal of Environmental Research and Public Health 794.

205 Qingshaonian shengzhi jiankang bu 'liu' shi '青少年生殖健康不"流"失' (136*n*203).

in China.[206] Moreover, research has demonstrated that they have a detrimental impact on the efficacy of assisted fertilisation treatments,[207] which have become commonplace in the PRC, now experiencing a significant population decline, similar to other economically developed countries.

China's current demographic crisis seems to be a kind of 'retaliation law,' following decades of the one-child policy, in which sterilisations and abortion have been often imposed on individuals 'for the benefit of the nation.' The projected number of births by 2024 is the lowest since 1949: 10,478 per 1,000 inhabitants,[208] placing mainland China among the least fertile countries in the world, on a par with Finland and Switzerland.[209] Even the amendments to the PFPL have failed to increase the birth rate. Although Article 18 of the PFPL has allowed Chinese (married) couples to have up to two children since 2015, and up to three after 2021, the PRC's fertility decline has yet to bottom out, and according to some experts, may be approaching irreversibility.[210]

In this situation, we can't ignore the infertility associated with repeated voluntary abortions at a young age, a phenomenon that scholars consider peculiar to the PRC.[211] The same can be said about another 'Chinese characteristic' of abortion, which is also linked to demographic decline: gender-related interruption of pregnancies, leading to a lower-than-expected number of women of childbearing age in the PRC currently.[212] In fact, in the PRC the ratio at birth is 120 boys to 100 girls, compared with a typical ratio of 106 boys to 100 girls.[213] The implementation of the one-child policy in a patriarchal and

---

206 Global Times, 'China's Family Planning Roadmap Aimed at Protecting National Fertility, Not Banning Abortion: Experts – Global Times' <https://www.globaltimes.cn/page/202202/1252012.shtml> accessed 31 August 2024; Qingshaonian shengzhi jiankang bu "liu" shi '青少年生殖健康不"流"失-健康报网——健康门户' (Adolescent reproductive health is not 'lost') <https://www.jkb.com.cn/news/industryNews/2022/0216/483796.html> accessed 28 August 2024.

207 Zou Linbing and others, 'The Association between Previous Induced Abortion and in Vitro Fertilization Outcomes: A Retrospective Cohort Study in Hefei, China' (2021) 262 European Journal of Obstetrics & Gynecology and Reproductive Biology 124.

208 https://www.macrotrends.net/global-metrics/countries/CHN/china/birth-rate

209 https://www.cia.gov/the-world-factbook/field/birth-rate/country-comparison/

210 Jacob Funk Kirkegaard, 'China's Population Decline Is Getting Close to Irreversible | PIIE' (18 January 2024) <https://www.piie.com/research/piie-charts/2024/chinas-population-decline-getting-close-irreversible> accessed 2 September 2024.

211 Wang Tian and Jiang Quanbao, 'Recent Trend and Correlates of Induced Abortion in China: Evidence from the 2017 China Fertility Survey' (2022) 22 BMC Women's Health 469.

212 Ibid.

213 Hao Luo and others, 'Repeat Induced Abortion in 30 Chinese Provinces: A Cross-Sectional Study' (2021) 154 International Journal of Gynaecology and Obstetrics: The

patrilineal society has resulted in the disappearance of up to 40 million women, including those aborted, killed at birth, or abandoned.[214] In an attempt to prevent what is now considered a veritable gendercide, as early as 1986, the National Commission for Family Planning and the Ministry of Health prohibited prenatal diagnosis at the request of mothers, except when conducted by licensed hospitals for the diagnosis of hereditary diseases.[215] The prohibition has been reiterated in different forms in various regulations enacted over the decades at the central and local levels, and now backed by the second paragraph of Article 32 of the MiHCL and Article 39 of the PFPL. Interestingly, it was precisely to prevent gender-selective abortions that the first and only time limit on a woman's autonomy to terminate a pregnancy was introduced in the Chinese national legislation at the beginning of the new millennium. According to Article 7 of the Regulation on the prohibition of foetal sex identification and sex-selective artificial termination of pregnancy for non-medical needs (*Guanyu jinzhi fei yixue xuyao de tai'er xingbie jianding he xuanze xingbie de rengong zhongzhi renshen de guiding* 关于禁止非医学需要的胎儿性别鉴定和选择性别的人工终止妊娠的规定, promulgated by the National Family Planning Commission, the Ministry of Health and the State Drug Administration on 29 November 2002: hereafter Regulation 2002), those who 'intend to undergo non-medically necessary pregnancy termination surgery at the mid-term stage or later (more than 14 weeks gestation), must obtain the approval of the family planning administrative department of the county people's government or the people's government of the township (town) where they live, or the family planning work agency of the sub-district office, and obtain the corresponding certificate.' This provision was eventually repealed by Article 15 of a regulation having the same title, approved by the State Administration for Industry and Commerce and the State Food and Drug Administration, effective since 1 May 2016 (hereafter: Regulation 2016). The recently introduced legislation does not impose any restrictions on the termination of pregnancies at the woman's discretion, which is currently possible until the end of gestation, unless otherwise stipu-

Official Organ of the International Federation of Gynaecology and Obstetrics 532; Nie Jing-Bao, 'Non-Medical Sex-Selective Abortion in China: Ethical and Public Policy Issues in the Context of 40 Million Missing Females' (2011) 98 British Medical Bulletin 7, 9; Yongai Jin and Wenbo Hu, 'Diverging Destinies: Changing Trends of Induced Abortion in China' (2023) 7 China Population and Development Studies 63.

214 Nie (138*n*214).

215 Ibid 13.

lated by local regulations. We will return to this point in a moment. For now, we note that none of the listed rules has been able to effectively counter the traditional preference for male offspring still prevalent in Chinese society, with rippling effects on Chinese demographic growth in the short and medium run.

We must evaluate the recent developments concerning abortion with this background in mind. They can be divided along three principal lines: demographic policy, eugenics, and patrilineal tradition. These, in turn, reflect the three key centres of interest that, as we have seen, have shaped the external value of the foetus since at least the late Qing era: the state, society, and the family. The following section will examine how this trend is impacting China's contemporary legal system.

4 Abortion in Post-Covid-19 PRC

The Report on Human Rights Violations in the United States in 2022 (*2022 nian Meiguo qinfan renquan baogao* 2022 年美国侵犯人权报告) released by the State Council Information Office of the PRC in March 2023, defines the overturning of *Roe v. Wade* by the U.S. Supreme Court as a 'major setback in the protection of the rights of women,'[216] which 'lands a huge blow to gender equality'[217] and confirms, once again, the inability of the country 'to respond to the basic demands of ordinary people'[218] and to solve its own 'structural problems of human rights.'[219] In particular, Section V of the report, dedicated to 'Historic retrogression in Women's and Children's Rights,' echoes the statements made by the then-spokesperson of the Chinese Ministry of Foreign Affairs a few days after the ruling was issued. In response to a journalist asking his opinion on the matter, Zhao Lijian not only criticised U.S. reproductive policy, which he regarded as detrimental to women's rights and therefore inconsistent with the country's claim to be the international champion of human rights, he also highlighted the negative impact on lives of American

216 The State Council Information Office of the People's Republic of China, 'Full Text: The Report on Human Rights Violations in the United States in 2022' (2023) para V. Historic Retrogression in Women's and Children's Rights <http://ge.china-embassy.gov.cn/eng/xwdt/202303/t20230328_11050361.htm> accessed 16 September 2024.

217 Ibid Foreword.

218 Ibid.

219 Ibid.

women, and presented China as a country that prioritises and defends gender equality.[220]

It is challenging to accept that legal protection of abortion should be regarded as the sole criterion for assessing a country's respect for women's rights. Assuming this to be the case, however, Zhao Lijian's assessment, regarding China's greater recognition of gender equality compared to the United States, may be less paradoxical than it initially appears. Not only has the U.S. Congress failed to pass any laws explicitly protecting a woman's reproductive freedom but even *Roe v. Wade* itself, as Justice Ruth Bader Ginsburg pointed out as early as 1985,[221] regarded abortion as a matter of privacy, implicitly covered by the Due Process Clause of the Fourteenth Amendment, rather than as equal protection for women.

On the other hand, Chinese national legislation has explicitly guaranteed the right to abortion since the 1990s, with the relevant provisions in Article 32 (formerly Article 51) of the Law on the Protection of Women's Rights and Interests (*funü quanyi baozhang fa* 妇女权益保障法, adopted by the 5th Session of the Seventh NPC on April 3, 1992, and emended in 2005, 2018, and 2022; hereafter: PWRIL) and Article 19 of the MIHCL, amended in 2009 and 2017. Article 32 of PWRIL states that: 'Women have the right to bear a child and also the freedom not to bear a child in accordance with the law,' while under Article 19 of the MIHCL: 'Termination of gestation or performance of ligation operations carried out in accordance with the provisions of this Law shall be subject to the consent and signature of the person per se.' According to this provision, only when 'the person per se has no capacity for civil conduct' is abortion subject to the consent and signature of the person's guardian. Moreover: 'Whoever is to terminate gestation under this Law shall receive such services free of charge.'

As comparative law teaches, the legislative formant represents just one element among several components that contribute to the formation of a legal rule within a specific legal system. Furthermore, as is the case with all other formants, the legislative formant comprises operational rules and declamations. The right of a woman to have a child as enshrined in Article 32 of

220 Ma Juan 马娟, 'Guowuyuan Guanyu Yinfa Zhongguo Funǚ Fazhan Gangyao He Zhongguo Ertong Fazhan Ganya de Tongzhi (2021–2030) 国务院关于印发中国妇女发展纲要和中国儿童发展纲要的通知 中国妇女发展纲要(2021–2030年) (Notice on the State Council Programme for the Development of Chinese Women and Children 2011–2020)' (2021) 16 Guowuyuan Gongbao 国务院公报 (State Council Gazette) <https://www.gov.cn/zhengce/content/2021-09/27/content_5639412.htm> accessed 6 October 2024.

221 Ruth Ginsburg, 'Some Thoughts on Autonomy and Equality in Relation to Roe v. Wade' (1985) 63 North Carolina Law Review 375, 376.

the PWRIL falls into the latter category, to put it mildly. It is evident that the exercise of this right has been subject to significant restrictions since its introduction at the close of the twentieth century, despite the statutory reservation provided for by Article 32 itself and the absence of any legal provision on the content of family planning at that time. Even after the implementation of the PFPL (2001), which stipulates at Article 18 the 'one-child policy' in order to rectify this anomaly, the right to reproduce has been subject to such stringent limitations that its practical implementation is questionable.

Surprisingly, the criticism directed at Zhao's assertions in 2022 did not pertain to the initial section of Article 32. Instead, the discrepancy highlighted between the tangible circumstances and the leader's pronouncements pertained to the latter part of the same article, namely the freedom not to have a child, which Chinese netizens recently see as somewhat vulnerable within the PRC.

While many authors agree that the PRC won't adopt the kind of restrictive abortion policies that numerous U.S. states have enacted after the *Dobbs* ruling, they have observed a shift in perspective regarding this right in post-Covid -19 Mainland China.[222] As was the case previously, the evidence of this transformation is not as readily discernible in state legislation as it is in national development plans, local regulations that implement them, and judicial decisions.

4.1 *Abortion and the State in Post-Covid-19 PRC: Demographic Policy*

As mentioned at the beginning of this chapter, the 2021–2030 Programme, published by the State Council on 27 September 2021, proved to be a source of significant concern with reference to the protection of abortion rights in China. The document calls on 'the people's governments of all provinces, autonomous regions and municipalities directly under the central government, all ministries and commissions of the State Council, and all agencies under the State Council' to support 'women in giving full play to their role as half of the sky and accelerating action to promote women's comprehensive development.' The goal is to achieve equality between men and women, which it regards as a 'basic national policy' (*jiben guoce* 基本国策), as defined by the Party Central Committee at the 18th Party Congress.[223] From this perspective, the PRC's domestic women's rights policy, as expressed in its

222 Mary Brophy Marcus, 'Abortion in China | Think Global Health' (Council on Foreign Relations, 7 October 2021) #x003C;https://www.thinkglobalhealth.org/article/abortion-china> accessed 30 September 2024.

223 Zhang Zhengjun 张正军 (14*n*103) pt Qian yan 前言 (Preface).

2021–2030 Programme, doesn't conflict with its international women's rights policy, as expressed in Zhao Lijian's critique of the *Dobbs v. Jackson* decision. However, the two discourses contradict each other when it comes to the role of abortion in the pursuit of such a fundamental goal, according to those who, in the wake of Zhao's remarks, have pointed out the paradox of a country that claims to be a champion of gender equality, and *thus* of the right to abortion, when it comes to criticising the U.S., while at the same time calling on Chinese public organs at all levels to restrict that very right to achieve equality between woman and men *inside* China.[224] In fact, the 2021–2030 programme not only lists 'disseminating knowledge on reproductive health and eugenics, promoting healthy motherhood and reducing unwanted pregnancy' among the objectives to be pursued to promote the development of women's health. It also includes the 'reduction of medically unnecessary induced abortions' (*fei yixue xuyao de rengong liuchan* 非医学需要的人工流产) under point six of the strategic measures to be used for this purpose.

The idea of reducing abortion to improve women's health is not entirely new: a general call to 'prevent unwanted pregnancies and decrease the rate of induced abortions' was included in the last two national plans for the development of women (2001–2010 and 2011–2020). At that time, however, the one-child policy was still in force; therefore, reducing the rate of abortions, especially coerced abortion, could reasonably be seen as protecting women's health and promoting gender equality, not to mention women's rights. The PRC now finds itself in a very different situation, where the call to avoid abortion, except for health reasons, coupled with the national media's dissemination of information on the risks associated with these practices, points local governments in a new direction: towards restricting abortion rights and women's freedom of choice, with the aim of having healthier women who can become healthier mothers, thus improving the quality and quantity of children for the good of the nation.

In the previous section, we noted that the central government initially restricted full abortion freedom at the beginning of the twenty-first century

224 Analysis by Jessie Yeung and Nectar Gan CNN, 'Analysis: China Says It's Restricting Abortions to Promote Gender Equality. Experts Are Skeptical' (*CNN*) <https://www.cnn.com/2021/10/01/china/non-medical-abortions-mic-intl-hnk/index.html> accessed 20 May 2022; Yi Fuxian, 'China's Abortion Problem Can't Be Regulated Away | by Yi Fuxian' (*Project Syndicate*, 14 April 2022) <https://www.project-syndicate.org/commentary/china-abortion-restrictions-demographic-crisis-by-yi-fuxian-2022-04> accessed 20 May 2022; Kaamil Ahmed, 'China to Clamp down on Abortions for "Non-Medical Purposes"' *The Guardian* (27 September 2021) <https://www.theguardian.com/world/2021/sep/27/china-to-limit-abortions-for-non-medical-purposes> accessed 20 May 2022.

to prevent sex-selective abortions and to try to rebalance the ratio of male to female births. In the following years, many local governments amended their family planning rules to comply with Article 7 of the 2002 Regulation, sometimes (perhaps to take account of local conditions, perhaps in recognition of the changing political winds) setting much stricter limits on abortion at a woman's request than those approved by the State Council. For example, that was the case in the 2005 amendment to the Administrative Measures for Population and Family Planning of Guangzhou Municipality (*Guangzhou shi renkoy yu jihua shengyu guangli banfa* 广州市人口与计划生育管理办法 hereafter: Guangzhou Measures), which required any induced abortion, except in an emergency, to be approved in advance by the family planning department at the county level or above,[225] in accordance with Article 20, number 3 of the 2008 amendment of 'Guangdong Provincial Regulations on Population and family planning' (*Guangdong sheng renkou yu jihua shengyu tiaoli* 广东省人口与计划生育条例).[226] The Guangzhou Measures were amended again in 2015, specifying in Article 53 that only married women and women more than 14 weeks pregnant should seek government approval.[227] It is hard to imagine that in the period between the two amendments such permission was ever refused by family planning officials, who at the time often forced women in the eighth month of pregnancy to abort to meet demographic targets. The content of the provision shows how little weight was given to women's reproductive freedom and, at the same time, how much discretionary power local authorities enjoyed in a context where no effective system exists to enforce conformity with higher-ranking sources of law.

This confirms the historical trend of provincial or lower-level legislators being more sensitive to the nuances of political discourse than to the content of legal rules, and it could probably also explain why many provinces continue to restrict abortion at will even after 2016 when they were eliminated at the national level due to their limited impact on sex ratios among newborns.[228] A study published in 2018 found that at least ten local regulations – in Guangxi, Liaoning, Nanchang (Jiangxi), Shandong, Hubei, Guizhou, Fujian, Henan, Gansu and Hunan –[229] still required compulsory approval for abortion after

---

225 https://www.gz.gov.cn/zwgk/fggw/zfgz/content/post_2837894.html

226 https://baike.baidu.com/item/广东省人口与计划生育条例（第四次修订）/18560549

227 https://www.gz.gov.cn/zwgk/fggw/zfgz/content/post_4756941.html

228 Zhang (136*n*199).

229 Liang Hongxia 梁洪霞, 'Wo guo duo shengshi "xianzhi funü duotai" guiding de he xianxing tanjiu – jianyi shengyu quan de xianfa baohu 我国多省市"限制妇女堕胎"规定的合宪性探究* — — —兼议生育权的宪法保护 (Constitutionality Research

a certain week of pregnancy. Some Chinese feminist activists and bloggers consider the persistence of these provisions evidence that 'Chinese women's loss of abortion rights began a long time ago.'[230] Whether this is the case, or whether it is instead, as its critics claim, an interpretation tainted by anti-nationalist and pro-Western sentiments, is difficult to say, not least because government censors quickly remove posts of this tenor. In any case, the trend does not appear to be abating. Just to give a few examples, Article. 11 of the Hunan Provincial Regulation on the Prohibition of Nonmedical Foetal Sex Identification and Sex Selective Abortion (*Hunansheng jinzhi fei yixue xuyao jianding tai'er xingbie he xuanze xingbie zhongzhi renshen de guiding* 湖南省禁止非医学需要鉴定胎儿性别和选择性别终止妊娠的规定)[231] revised for the second time on 8 October 2022, prohibits abortion on request after the fourteenth week of pregnancy, except in one of the following circumstances (1) if the foetus has a serious genetic disease or severe defect; (2) if the pregnant woman suffers from a serious disease and continuation of the pregnancy may endanger her life or seriously endanger her health; (3) if a medical institution approved by the provincial health administration department diagnoses that the pregnancy must be terminated; (4) if the abortion is requested due to divorce, widowhood, etc. In the cases referred to in points (1)–(3), the woman must present a medical certificate issued by a health institution at or above district level, which provides prenatal diagnosis.

Similar provisions are contained in the Nanchang Municipal Regulations Prohibiting the Identification of the Sex of the Foetus for Non-medical Purposes and Sex-Selective Termination of Pregnancy (*Nanchang shi jinzhi fei yixue xuyao jianding tai'er xingbie he xuanze xingbie zhongzhi renshen de guiding* 南昌市禁止非医学需要鉴定胎儿性别和选择性别终止妊娠的规定 last amended on 14 November 2019, hereafter: Nanchang Regulations),[232] which in Article 1 states the purpose 'to maintain the normal sex composition of the birth population in accordance with the Population and Family Planning Law of the People's Republic of China, the Maternal and Infant Health Care Law of the People's Republic of China, the Population and Family Planning Regula-

---

on Restricting Abortion in the Local Legislations of China With Discussion on the Constitutional Protection of Reproductive Right)' (2018) 12 Beifang faxue 北方法学 37, 37.

230 Zhang (136*n*199).

231 See (in Chinese): <https://www.hunan.gov.cn/hnszf/xxgk/zfgz/202110/20738529/files/cb97c8134d084191a5a66613f3b7da01.pdf > accessed 20 October 2024.

232 See (in Chinese): <https://www.nc.gov.cn/ncszf/yfzgz/202112/eba7f2b2f542434db8dda692cc01fb63.shtml> accessed 20 October 2024.

tions of Jiangxi Province and other laws and regulations, and in the light of the actual situation in the city.' To this end, Articles 9 and 10 stipulate that 'pregnant women who meet the legal requirements for childbirth and are more than 14 weeks pregnant may not terminate their pregnancies,' except in cases of serious genetic diseases or severe foetal defects (Article 10, comma 1, nos. 1) and when the continuation of the pregnancy may endanger the life, safety or seriously harm the health of the woman (Article 10, comma 1, no. 3); other circumstances in which termination of pregnancy is not necessary for sex selection (Article 10, comma 2, no. 4). In order to obtain an abortion under circumstances in points 1) to 3), a woman must present proof of identity and a certificate issued by an institution that carries out foetal sex identification or a health institution at or above the county level that is qualified to carry out prenatal diagnosis (Article 10, comma 2); pregnant women over the age of 20 must also present relevant marriage and childbearing certificates issued by the rural (township) people's government or the health and health work agency of the sub-district office (Article 9).

In the case of Nanchang in particular, Article 1's reference to compliance with the Jiangxi provincial regulations could explain, if not justify, a deviation from the regulations in force at the national level; as of 2018, it requires women who are more than 14 weeks pregnant and seek an abortion to obtain the signed consent of three medical professionals to confirm that the abortion is medically necessary.[233] Interestingly, the Jiangxi government's explanation for enacting such a burdensome regulation was based precisely on the official media's widely disseminated rhetoric that repeated abortions can damage fertility.[234] Apparently, the media is considered a more authoritative source than formal state law.

Although abortion remains fully legal in Mainland China, the interplay among local regulation, health care institutions, and social pressure can severely limit access in practice. Not only rules that require the consent of parents to perform abortion on minor women, or that exclude unmarried women, as Article 9 of Nanchang Regulation, forced them to visit private clinics, at best. As noted by Irene Zhang in 2023, government directives describing

233 'CHINA – Jiangxi Province Has Restricted Abortion after the 14th Week of Pregnancy Because of the Sex Ratio Imbalance' (*International Campaign for Women's Right to Safe Abortion*, 27 June 2018) <https://www.safeabortionwomensright.org/news/china-jiangxi-province-has-restricted-abortion-after-the-14th-week-of-pregnancy-because-of-the-sex-ratio-imbalance/> accessed 20 October 2024.

234 'Jiangxi Abortion Rule Seeks Sex Ratio Balance' <https://www.ecns.cn/news/society/2018-06-25/detail-ifyvmiee7354538.shtml> accessed 20 October 2024.

abortion as a self-inflicted tragedy rather than a regularly performed medical procedure have also persuaded vulnerable patients that they are wrong to seek health care.[235]

Once again, these campaigns aren't aimed at protecting the foetus, but at defending what is now perceived as the 'best interest' of the nation: its fertility rate. In fact, 'to protect the fertility of the nation' is the ultimate goal set by the Highlights on the work of the Chinese Family Planning Association for year 2022 (*Zhongguo jihua shengyu xiehui 2022 nian gongzuo yaodian* 中国计划生育协会2022年工作要点), whose call to 'promote reproductive health of adolescents, [..] intervene in abortion among unmarried people, reduce abortions among teenagers'[236] is now mirrored in many local family association highlights, such as the ones in Shanxi province, or Taicang municipality (Jiangsu). Equally meant to 'promote the achievement of moderate fertility levels and the long-term balanced development of the population' is the Guidance on further improving and implementing active reproductive support measures (*Guanyu jingyibu wanshan he luoshi jiji shengyu zhichi cuoshi de zhidao yijian* 关于进一步完善和落实积极生育支持措施的指导意见) issued on 16 August 2022 by the Department of Population Monitoring and Family Development, which again include the reduction of medically unnecessary abortions among the measures to be adopted to strengthen reproductive health services, asking at the same time to improve the level of eugenic and fertility services.[237] The above-mentioned calls have been reiterated at the local level in 2023[238] and 2024.[239]

But what is the link between eugenics and abortion in post-Covid PRC?

4.2 *Abortion and Society in Post-Covid-19 PRC: Eugenics*

Since the end of the Qing dynasty, a section of China's intellectual elite has supported eugenic policies to strengthen China by enhancing the quality of its

235 Zhang (136*n*199).

236 See (in Chinese): <http://qianjin1.one/good/08a793182.html >accessed 20 October 2024.

237 See (in Chinese): <https://www.gov.cn/zhengce/zhengceku/2022-08/16/content_5705882.htm>accessed 20 October 2024.

238 See (in Chinese) Henan Province Family Planning Association Highlights for 2024 (*Henan sheng jihua shengyu xiehui 2023 nian gongzuo yaodian* 河南省计划生育协会2023 年工作要点)<http://222.143.34.138:86/xiehui/contents/907/51585.shtml>accessed 20 October 2024.

239 See (in Chinese) Guiyang City Family Planning Association Highlights for 2024 (*Guiyang shi jihua shengyu xiehui 2023 nian gongzuo yaodian* 贵阳市计划生育协会 2024 年工作要点):<https://wsjkj.guiyang.gov.cn/sjsx/wjhb/202404/t20240428_84365278.html>accessed 20 October 2024.

population.[240] In the Republican era, this resulted in a proposal for premarital screenings and marriage bans for those deemed 'unifit.'[241] This approach continued after 1949, with the 1950 ML – one of the few formal laws enacted during the Maoist era – prohibiting marriage when 'the man or the woman is suffering from leprosy, a cure not having been effected, or from any other diseases that are considered by medicine to be reasons not to marry' in Article 5 (3). An identical provision was included in 1981's revision of the same law, at Article 6 (2), while the rhetoric of 'quality birth control' (*yousheng youyu* 优生优育, first used in the context of the nationalist Counciling Department for Birth Control (*Shengyu jieyu zixunbu* 生育节育咨询部)[242] became one of the slogans of the one-child campaign from the 1980s onwards.

However, it was not until 1994, when the MIHCL came into force, that the international community began to raise concerns about the ethical implications of pursuing a eugenic policy in a country with controlled births.[243] It is worth mentioning that law was initially proposed, in December 1993, under the name of the Eugenic and Health Protection Law.[244] The latter title would have resembled those of similar laws in force in other East Asian countries, such as Taiwan and Japan. These countries appear to be less inclined than other parts of the world to associate certain vocabulary with Nazism.[245] The change in the title of the Chinese law did not affect its main goal: to improve the quality of the newborn population (MIHCL, Article 1) and reduce the perceived burden of disability on Chinese society.[246] To have not only fewer, but also healthier babies, the law made premarital medical examination compulsory to check whether either prospective partner suffered from 'genetic dis-

240 Leon Antorio Rocha, 'Translation and Two "Chinese Sexologies" Double Plum and Sex Histories' in Heike Bauer (ed), *Sexology and Translation: Cultural and Scientific Encounters across the Modern World* (Temple University Press 2015) 154–155; Rodriguez (n 669) 23–30.

241 Rodriguez (108*n*51) 209.

242 Ibid 208.

243 Daniel S Gewirtz, 'Toward A Quality Population: China's Eugenic Sterilization of the Mentally Retarded' (*134994*, 1994) <https://repository.library.georgetown.edu/handle/10822/526049?show=full> accessed 29 October 2024; Mao Xin, 'Chinese Eugenic Legislation' (1997) 349 The Lancet 139; Graciela Gómez, 'China's Eugenics Law as Grounds for Granting Asylum' (1996) 5 Washington International Law Journal 563; 'Western Eyes on China's Eugenics Law' (1995) 346 The Lancet 131; D Dickson, 'Concern Grows over China's Plans to Reduce Number of "Inferior Births"' (1994) 367 Nature 3.

244 Mao (147*n*244).

245 Yuehtsen Juliette Chung, 'Better Science and Better Race?: Social Darwinism and Chinese Eugenics' (2014) 105 Isis 793.

246 Gómez (147*n*243) 569.

eases of serious nature,' 'target infectious diseases' and 'relevant mental diseases' (MIHCL, Article 8). In case of infectious or mental diseases, the couple had to postpone their marriage until the end of the treatment (Article 9); if the exam found the man or woman to have a serious genetic disease considered inappropriate for childbearing, the couple could not marry unless they took long-term contraceptive measures or underwent a ligation operation that rendered them infertile; this, however, subject to compliance with the rules prohibiting marriage under the ML (MIHCL, Article 10). Article 16 of the MIHCL then stipulated that even after marriage, and as long as they were able to procreate, the couple would be subject to medical checks; if a doctor discovered or even suspected that they had serious genetic diseases, they would have to follow his instructions and undergo the recommended treatments (presumably, although the rule does not specify, those listed in Article 10). During pregnancy, prenatal testing would be compulsory; if the foetus had a serious genetic or somatic defect (Article 18 (1) and (2)), the doctor should explain the situation to the couple, and advise on termination, which was subject to the consent and signing of the person per se (Article 19). It should be noted that, although the last rule suggests that the decision to abort ultimately rested the woman, a couple accepting the risk of having a handicapped child was certainly a remote possibility in the early 1990s. Since Chinese citizens could only have one child, they wanted it to be as healthy as possible[247] and (hopefully) male. While the second aspiration (or rather the selection of foetuses to fulfil it) was contrary to the spirit of the MIHCL, the first was perfectly in keeping with the legislation's intent.

Foreign critics voiced concerns that the application of these rules would disproportionaly harm vulnerable groups, especially ethnic minorities and impoverished rural populations. Their suspicion rested on the vagueness of the MIHCL's provisions, which, for example, did not define what characteristics a genetic disease had to have to be considered 'serious,' leaving, at least in appearance, a great deal of discretion to the interpreters, whether they were local officials or the doctors in charge. Statements by Chinese central leaders and academics reinforced these fears. In December 1993, Public Health Minister Chen Minzhang pointed to high 'inferior birth' rates among minority and economically disadvantaged areas, while Scholar Deng Bihai[248] characterised minorities as a 'population of low quality,' broadening 'genetic disease' to include traits like 'mental retardation, illiteracy and physical deformities

247 Rodriguez (147*n*243) 209.

248 Gómez (108*n*51).

such as short stature,'[249] suggesting an expansive interpretation of eugenic policy.

Although forced abortions seemed to be more common in certain areas than in others,[250] since the mid-2010s it is not really easy to distinguish between abortions aimed at limiting the number of births and those aimed, instead, at increasing the quality of births.[251] The shift away from the one-child policy, and the demographic, political and legal developments of the past decade have changed the situation in a way that confirms the concerns described above, strengthening the link between abortion and eugenics.

The new emphasis on reproduction has not led to any substantial changes in the provisions discussed so far, with the sole exception of the rules on marriage. The ban on marriage for people with serious viral, genetic or mental illnesses, provided for by the ML in 1950 and 1981, was softened in its 2001 revision, which made them grounds for invalidating a marriage if they were not cured after the marriage itself (ML 2001, Article 10 (3)). The rule was completely abolished in 2020, when the ML was incorporated into the CC; only a hint of it remains in the provision of Article 10153 of the CC, which allows one of the spouses to request the annulment of the marriage within one year discovering serious illness in the other spouse, but only if he or she was aware at the time of the registration of the marriage and had concealed it. On the other hand, the articles of the MIHCL regarding premarital and prenatal examinations have not undergone significative modifications, despite two amendations (the last in 2017). Furthermore, the latest revision of the PWRIL (2022) has confirmed in Article 62 the invitation to future spouses to jointly undergo medical examinations before registering the marriage. The possibility to do so is now guaranteed by Article 35 of the PFPL (2021 revision, formerly Article 30), according to which 'The State shall establish the pre-marriage health care system and the pregnancy and childbearing period health care system to prevent or reduce the birth defects, and to improve the condition of health of the babies born.'

In addition, the 2021 amendment to the PFPL includes for the first time objectives to improve the quality of the population, along with regulating

249 Ibid 572.

250 'Thousands at Risk of Forced Sterilization in China' (*Amnesty International*, 22 April 2010) <https://www.amnesty.org/en/latest/news/2010/04/thousands-risk-forced-sterilization-china/> accessed 1 November 2024.

251 Steven W Mosher, 'China's One-Child Policy Itself Leads to Forced Abortions' (2012) 380 The Lancet 1558; Jonathan Watts, 'Chinese Officials Accused of Forcing Abortions in Shandong' (2005) 366 The Lancet 1253.

and controlling population targets, raising the fertility rate to an appropriate level, optimising population structure and promoting balanced, long-term population development (PFPL 2021, Article 2).

This represents the legislative implementation of the objectives set out in the 2021–2025 Five-Year Plan, which had drawn considerable criticism from the foreign press, especially Catholic media organisations,[252] due to its references to 'optimising birth policy' and 'improving the quality of the population.'

The effort to achieve these goals even led the PRC's legislature to review Article 18 of the PFPL, which now allows married couples to have three children, while also urging couples 'to marry and give birth at an appropriate age' (*heling jieyu yousheng youyu* 适龄婚育、优生优育, litt: Marriage and childbirth at the right age, giving birth to healthy children). It is interesting to compare this 'suggestion' with the original version of the same article (2001), which had called on Chinese citizens to 'marry and have children at an advanced age' (*wanjiewanyu* 晚婚晚育). Indeed, the article currently in force does not define the appropriate age for marriage, nor does it make explicit who should marry at that age to produce children of superior quality. Although it cannot be ruled out that the invitation is directed at both women and men, the propaganda aimed at young Chinese women in recent years suggests that the message is primarily directed at them.

State Council First Vice Premier Ding Xuexiang's speech on 23 October 2023 during the 13th National Women's Congress in Beijing offers an example of what I am saying. After emphasising Chinese women's enormous contributions to scientific, technological and social development, First Vice Premier Ding clarified that 'doing a good job in women's work' is not only related to women's own development,' but also to 'family harmony, social harmony, national development and national progress.'[253] To this end, it is necessary to 'actively cultivate a new culture of marriage and childbearing and strengthen guidance on young people's view on marriage, childbirth and family.'[254]

252 'China's Five-Year Plan Proposal Stresses Eugenics in Birth Policy, Says Expert' (13 November 2020) <https://angelusnews.com/news/world/chinas-five-year-plan-proposal-stresses-eugenics-in-birth-policy-says-expert/> accessed 29 October 2024.

253 '13th National Women's Congress Opens in Beijing | English.Scio.Gov.Cn' <http://english.scio.gov.cn/topnews/2023-10/24/content_116769544.htm> accessed 2 November 2024.

254 Ibid; 'Changes in Rhetoric to China's Women's Congress Push Patriarchal Values' (*IR Insider*) <https://www.irinsider.org/home/9kf4dzaqcoy6454vq316i07i7viro6> accessed 2 November 2024; 'Beijing's Message to the National Women's Congress: Gender Equality Is Out, Family and Childbirth Are In | Council on Foreign Relations' <https://www.cfr

His words go hand in hand with the campaigns launched by the All-China 'women' Association on Chinese media targeting so-called 'left-over women,' a euphemism for unmarried, highly educated, urban professional women aged twenty-five or older.[255] The campaigns aim to persuade these women to redirect their effort from achieving professional goals to marrying and having healthy babies.[256] In her book on left-over women, Leta Hong Fincher identifies two aspects of this propaganda. Firstly, it is designed to protect social stability by encouraging women to marry, thereby reducing the number of unmarried men, who are statistically more prone to violence and crime than their married counterparts.[257] Second, and more relevant to our discussion, it aims to make their high-quality genes available to the state and at an earlier age. In fact, the state media describes the decision to have children at an increasingly advanced age as the main cause of the growing number of children born with genetic defects.[258] According to Rodriguez, Chinese regulations on egg-freezing should be seen as further evidence of the state's intention to force women to consider the implications of postponing marriage and procreation, especially given significant social and cultural resistance to pregnancy outside marriage. In fact, only married women are allowed to freeze their eggs, a widespread practice among young women pursuing professional careers.[259]

Not all young (and not so young) Chinese women are in the same situation, however, and it is here that I believe the use of abortion for eugenic purposes in post-Covid-19 China becomes apparent. Highly educated young Han women no longer seem to face the risk of forced abortion – their duty now is to produce quality children[260] – but rather pressure to carry an unwanted pregnancy to term. Women from ethnic minorities face a very different situation. As early as 2018, the government of China's Xinjiang Uyghur Autonomous Region admitted that the birth rate had fallen by almost a third, with much of the decline

.org/blog/beijings-message-national-womens-congress-gender-equality-out-family-and-childbirth-are> accessed 2 November 2024.

255 Leta Hong Fincher, *Leftover Women: The Resurgence of Gender Inequality in China, 10th Anniversary Edition* (Bloomsbury Academic 2023) 13.

256 Ibid 44.

257 Ibid 53.

258 Ibid 57.

259 Rodriguez (n 669) 207–208.

260 Vivian Wang, 'So, Are You Pregnant Yet? China's In-Your-Face Push for More Babies.' *The New York Times* (8 October 2024) <https://www.nytimes.com/2024/10/08/world/asia/china-women-children-abortions.html> accessed 2 November 2024; Cao, 'The Regulation of Reproduction in New China' (113*n*77) 104.

attributed to 'better implementation of family planning policies.'[261] Since then, the number of reports on pregnancy tests and forced abortions, sterilisations and IUD implantations among Uyghurs and other minorities living in the same region has steadily increased.[262]

In sum, for Chinese women as a whole, the obligation or impossibility of having an abortion depends on the value (in this case also measured in terms of genetic heritage) that society places on what they carry in their wombs, even though, as we have seen, Article 32 of the PPCC is supposed to guarantee 'the right to bear a child and the freedom not to bear a child' to all Chinese women, without distinction.

In recent years, however, this right and freedom have not only been restricted in the light of the greater interest of the state or society, the family (in patrilinear sense) has also (re)gained an important role, which has increasingly been recognised by case law. The following sections will provide a number of illustrations to demonstrate this tendency.

4.3 *Abortion and (Patrilinear) Family in Post-Covid-19 PRC: The Right to Reproduce*

By the mid-1950s, PRC regulations had begun to guarantee pregnant women the freedom to decide for themselves whether to undergo a voluntary abortion.[263] This set the country's legal system apart from others in the region, such as Taiwan and Japan, where spousal consent is still required for a legal abortion. It is noteworthy that a woman's right to self-determination in this matter, which could be implicitly derived after the enactment of the PWRIL (1992) granted the 'right to bear a child and the freedom not to bear a child,' was made explicit in the 2022 revision of the same law. Paragraph 3 of Article 21 now states:

> When medical institutions perform a reproductive surgery, special examination, or special treatment, women's own consent shall be obtained,

261 'China's Five-Year Plan Proposal Stresses Eugenics in Birth Policy, Says Expert' (n 870).

262 Ruining Jin, 'Eugenics in China through the Lens of Cultural Additivity'; 'Uighurs Tell of Forced Abortions and Torture in China' (n 628); 'Torture, Forced Abortions: Key Allegations in UN Report on Xinjiang' (*France 24*, 1 September 2022) <https://www.france24.com/en/asia-pacific/20220901-torture-forced-abortions-key-allegations-in-un-report-on-xinjiang> accessed 2 November 2024; Mary Brophy Marcus, 'Abortion in China | Think Global Health' (*Council on Foreign Relations*, 7 October 2021) <https://www.thinkglobalhealth.org/article/abortion-china> accessed 30 September 2024.

263 See Notice 1957, *supra* 128.

> and respect women's own will if they disagree with their family members or related persons.

This represents a significant acknowledgement, especially in a culture where medical practice involves family members in deciding whether to proceed with a particular course of treatment, regardless of the patient's gender. We will examine this more closely in sections on suffering and end-of-life decisions.

In cases of abortion, however, the clarity of the rule does not seem to have curbed the tendency of local family planning institutions, hospitals, and medical units to require spousal permission before performing the operation.[264] This trend emerged at the beginning of the twenty-first century, when, following the enactment of Article 17 of the PFPL, which states that 'citizens have the right to bear children,' medical institutions that performed abortions began to fear being sued by the husbands of their patients for violating their right to reproduce. In fact, Article 17 of the PFPL, still regarded as a relatively unique feature of the Chinese legal system, was at the time celebrated in the Chinese media as the world's first recognition of men's right to procreate.[265] The same Article 17 states that spouses must engage in family planning; it seems reasonable to assume that legislators intended to make clear that both spouses are responsible for contraception, and not just the wife, along with their procreative rights. In the years immediately following the enactment of the PFPL, many husbands brought court cases citing infringement of their reproductive rights. One example is the case of Mr Zhang, who in 2003 sued his wife, Ms You, seeking compensation from the Xicheng district court in Beijing for the alleged violation of his right to fatherhood.[266] Mr Zhang and Ms You had been married for approximately six years, but the couple had been living separately the previous year due to conflicting desires regarding parenthood.[267] While Ms You did not wish to have children because of her precarious economic and psychological situation, Mr Zhang, an only child, was keen to become a father, motivated by his parents' desire for a grandchild. While the judge expressed regret over the breakdown of the marriage, the divorce was granted on gro-

264 Zhang (136*n*199).

265 Ibid.

266 'Liuchan Shoushu Zhangfu Qianzi Zhineng Guibi Shengyu Quan Jiufen Ma 流产手术丈夫签字真能规避生育权纠纷吗 (Can a Husband's Signature on a Miscarriage Procedure Really Avoid Disputes over Reproductive Rights?)' (Xinhua wang 新华网, 15 September 2003) <https://news.sina.cn/sa/2003-09-15/detail-ikknscsi1244828.d.html> accessed 5 November 2024.

267 Ibid.

unds of irreconcilable differences, and Mr Zhang was awarded no compensation.[268] Another example involves an octogenarian man who sued his wife in Nanjing for having undergone three abortions during their marriage. The wife had terminated her pregnancies out of concern that, once he had a biological child of his own, he would neglect her children from a previous marriage. In his old age, the husband felt deprived of the chance to have his own offspring and sought compensation for emotional damage.[269] This trend was common across the provinces. For instance, in two cases filed under Article 17 in Sichuan, one man had raised the child his wife had with another man under the assumption it was his own, and another case involved a worker in Chengdu who sued his wife for aborting without his consent.[270] In a 2003 interview reported by the Xinhua Agency, President Xu Lin, then a judge of the Fengtai district court in Beijing, stated that the emphasis on PFPL implementation had led to a significant rise in divorce petitions citing the infringement of reproductive rights as a primary reason for marriage dissolution.[271] According to the judge, even if, in the absence of specific rules or interpretations by the Supreme Court, the courts were not in a position to recognise damage solely on the grounds of infringement of reproductive rights under Article 17, the existence of such cases should have been taken into account.[272]

The Supreme People's Court responded to this situation a few years later with its third interpretation 'Concerning questions on the application of the Marriage Law (No. 18)' (*Guanyu shiyong zhonghuorenmin gongheguo jiehun fa ruogan wenti de jieshi (san) fashi 18 hao*) 关于使用中华人民共和国结婚发若干问题的解释 (三) 法释18号 hereafter: 2011 SPC's Interpretation). Article 9 of the 2011 SPC's Interpretation states: 'If a husband requests compensatory damages because his wife terminated a pregnancy without authorization, the court will not support such an award of compensatory damages.'

This rule has not deterred frustrated husbands from seeking redress through the courts, as demonstrated by research conducted by Bodhurta, Liebman, Li and Wu on divorce cases published in the *China Judgments Online* database from 2014 to 2018.[273] The authors identified 949 out of 15,152 divorce cases in which men complained of unilateral or unauthorised abortions by

268 Ibid.

269 Ibid.

270 Ibid.

271 Ibid.

272 Ibid.

273 Molly Bodurtha and others, 'Contesting and Controlling Abortion in China's Courts' (Social Science Research Network, 17 February 2024) <https://papers.ssrn.com/abstract=4730082> accessed 3 November 2024.

their wives.[274] Claims on this basis included requests for the recognition of emotional damages due to the violation of the husband's and his family's interest in having a child;[275] return of the 'bride price';[276] request for the husband to have custody of the child;[277] and demand to grant or refuse the divorce.[278] In some cases, abortion without the husband's consent was used to counter the wife's accusations of violent or abusive behaviour by the husband,[279] or to discredit her by casting doubt on her morality.[280]

The authors observe that in only a few instances have courts awarded damages for emotional distress,[281] thereby explicitly disregarding the 2011 SPC's interpretation. However, even in cases where the plaintiff's claims were dismissed, the latter claims were rarely deemed unlawful; cases were often rejected due to inadequate evidence of damage or suffering allegedly caused by the abortion.[282] On the other hand, in around 50% of cases involving claims for the return of the bride price, courts accepted the husband's request, at times reducing the reimbursement amount in favour of the woman.[283] Finally, it appears that the wife's unilateral decision to have an abortion does not significantly impact courts' decisions on who gets child custody in a divorce.[284] Courts generally deny women custody at a disproportionately high rate;[285] in the cases examined, men granted custody at twice the rate of the women.[286]

When a husband is reluctant to grant the divorce, the wife's unilateral decision to undergo an abortion is frequently presented by the judge as proof of sexual relations between the spouses. This often leads to the denial of the wife's divorce request, even in cases where there is clear evidence of sexual abuse and violence by the husband.[287] As mentioned, a woman's decision to have an abortion against her husband's wishes is commonly used to justify the male perpetrator's violent behaviour or to conceal his abuse, a strategy that

274 Ibid 18.
275 Ibid 21–24.
276 Ibid 24–29.
277 Ibid 29–30.
278 Ibid 31–32.
279 Ibid 32–39.
280 Ibid 39–43.
281 Ibid 23.
282 Ibid 24.
283 Ibid 26.
284 Ibid 29.
285 Ibid 30.
286 Ibid 29.
287 Ibid 31.

often succeeds in court.[288] In other instances, the same act is cited as evidence during the proceedings to portray the woman as an unfaithful spouse, engaging in sexual activities outside reproductive purposes and contrary to traditional gender roles.[289] It is noteworthy that, while husbands appear more inclined than their wives to characterise the foetus as a 'child' (*xiao hai* 小孩, *haizi* 孩子), 'little life' (*xiao shengming* 小生命, *yi tiao shengming* 一条生命), or 'flesh and blood' (*xin gurou* 新骨肉), the foetus' right to life is never acknowledged.[290] The judges' adoption of the plaintiffs' terminology, emphasising the gestational stage at which the abortion occurred or using the term 'child' for the foetus, does not imply recognition of the foetus's interest but rather serves to reinforce criticism or moral condemnation of the woman's reproductive autonomy. This illustrates how husbands' arguments align with values upheld by the courts.[291] As the authors aptly note, the 'courts assigned ethical and moral obligations to women that do not exist in the law, and privileged patriarchal norms over legal ones.'[292]

Chinese courts do not seem to have changed their stance in the post-Covid -19 era. Indeed, evidence suggests it has become more entrenched, as shown by the following case, decided by the Gaoxin District Court (Chengdu, Sichuan) in February 2023.[293] The case involved Mr Liu and Ms Zhao, a couple of old friends who initiated a romantic relationship in September 2021. In December, Ms Zhao became pregnant and was diagnosed with uterine fibroids. In the same month, the couple registered their marriage, but they soon separated. On 27 February 2022, Ms Zhao filed for divorce and decided to have an abortion. Despite Mr Liu's objections, Ms Zhao proceeded with the procedure and subsequently sought a divorce, which was granted through judicial mediation. On 4 August 2022, Mr Liu sued Ms Zhao in the Gaoxin District Court, seeking compensation for the emotional damage caused by her infringement of his reproductive rights. The court dismissed his claims, stating that the couple's strained relationship made Ms Zhao's decision to

288 Ibid 35.

289 Liang Linjun 梁林军、 and Liu Tiantian 刘甜甜, 'Qisi Zhongzhi Rengsheng How Zhangfu Qisu Qinfan Shengyu Quan 妻子中止妊娠后丈夫起诉侵犯生育权法院这么判 (After His Wife Terminated Her Pregnancy, the Husband Sued for Infringement of Reproductive Rights. The Court Ruled as Follows)' *Hongxing xinwen* 红星新闻 (13 February 2023) <https://static.cdsb.com/micropub/Articles/202302/208b8ceb48836607f10f50cf91b2f46e.html> accessed 5 November 2024.

290 Bodurtha and others (154*n*273) 41.

291 Ibid.

292 Ibid 43.

293 Liang Linjun 梁林军、 and Liu Tiantian 刘甜甜 (156*n*289).

abort entirely legitimate. Furthermore, Ms Zhao's uterine fibroids would have entitled her to terminate the pregnancy on health grounds.[294] The judge explained that a woman's freedom to undergo an abortion, enshrined in Article 32 of the PWRIL, is balanced by a man's right to procreate, enshrined in Article 17 PFPL. After marriage, decisions regarding procreation are at the spouse's discretion. However, if a woman becomes pregnant and wishes to terminate the pregnancy, her husband's consent is a prerequisite. Terminating a pregnancy without the husband's consent or without valid reasons constitutes a violation of the husband's reproductive rights. In such circumstances, while the husband may request a divorce, he cannot seek compensation for emotional damage. In its decision, the court delineates the grounds upon which a woman may exercise the right to decide autonomously to have an abortion, in line with legal practice. These grounds include (1) instances where the woman has a medical condition that makes continuation of the pregnancy inadvisable; (2) situations where the husband and wife are in a strained relationship and have been living apart; and (3) cases where the woman has initiated divorce proceedings against her husband.[295]

It is important to note that these principles are not outlined in any specific legislation or Supreme Court interpretations. However, the case above received extensive coverage in the Chinese press, emphasising the ongoing limitation of reproductive freedom for Chinese women, which has historically been subject to state and societal control since the early twentieth century, to the desires of their spouse and family. This reversion to traditional norms aligns closely with the recent emphasis of Chinese leaders on traditional values and fits neatly with the demographic needs of China's New Era. Furthermore, along with other aspects of post-Covid China's abortion policy discussed previously, this shift unexpectedly brings the PRC's stance closer to those of countries that claim to base their attitudes toward abortion entirely on different ideological, religious, and moral beliefs concerning the beginning of a human life and the value of the foetus.

However, it is imperative to acknowledge that this observed similarity should not obscure the significant differences that have emerged from the analysis conducted thus far. Firstly, the notion that pregnancy constitutes a continuum that is only completed with the birth of a new child, which can be traced back to philosophical and medical concepts deeply rooted in Chinese tradition. Secondly, the tendency to de-emphasise the 'absolute' value of the foetus, instead placing its importance 'in relation' to other subjects, particu-

294 Ibid.
295 Ibid.

larly the family, society and the state. As has emerged in the discourse, the interests of the family are prioritised over those of the individual, even before birth. However, the family's interests, even the most important one related to its continuity, are superseded by the interests of broader social groups. This could explain both the fluctuations experienced by Chinese demographic policies, from the founding of the PRC to the period of reforms, and the more recent trends observed above.

The issue becomes more complicated, and the differences, even within WLT, widen, when the focus shifts from abortion to other, more recent biotechnologies related to the birth of human beings and the early stages of their development. I am referring, in particular, to the regulation of Human Assisted Reproduction Technologies (hereafter: HART), particularly in its more ethically controversial expressions, such as post-mortem fertilisation and surrogacy. Are there any Chinese characteristics in the PRC's approach to these issues? What principles, from the Chinese perspective, inform the regulation of these practices? In the following chapters, I will address these questions, starting from the events surrounding the four frozen embryos of the Yixin case described in Chapter 4.

CHAPTER 6

Law, Bioethics, and Human Assisted Reproduction Technology (HART)

1 The 'First Embryo Case before a Chinese Court': The Epilogue

Our analysis of the relationship between law, bioethics, and the beginning of life in the twenty-first century PRC commenced with the 'Yixing case,' i.e.: the ruling in which the Wuxi Intermediate People's Court granted the parents of a married couple the right of custody and disposition of the four frozen embryos resulting from the assisted reproduction treatment their children had undergone shortly before dying in a car accident. We shall now briefly return to this case to ascertain the fate of the four embryos following the transfer of their custody to the four elderly parents. Both Chinese and Western media have widely reported the story:[1] After numerous Chinese medical institutions refused to become involved, the family sought assistance from a surrogacy agency based in Laos, where gestational surrogacy, at that time, was not regulated by law. Upon payment of 200,000 RMB plus 100,000 RMB of expenses, the agency facilitated the transfer of the embryos to a local hospital by car, since no airline was willing to accept a thermos-sized bottle of liquid nitrogen, and the selection of a surrogate mother of Laotian nationality. Two of the four embryos were then implanted in the womb of the woman whom the families chose based on her physical health and appearance. On 9 December 2017, the grieving parents of Shen Jie and Liu Xi became the happy grandparents of a baby boy, Tiantian. The infant was born in China, where it was initially gra-

1 'Chinese Baby Born Four Years after Parents' Death' (12 April 2018) <https://www.bbc.com/news/world-asia-china-43724395> accessed 14 December 2024; Wangyi 网易 (NetEase), 'Fumu lishi sinian hou haizi cai chusheng? Shuangfang fumu ai ru zhenbao: qin sunzi 父母离世四年后孩子才出生?双方父母爱如珍宝: 亲孙子 (The child was born four years after the parents died? Both sets of parents loved him like a treasure: their own grandchildren)' (*Wangyi* 网易 (*NetEase*), 18 April 2024) <https://www.163.com/dy/article/J025P180054179DD.html> accessed 18 January 2025; Liu Yajing 刘雅静, 'Zhongguo zhe ming ying'er shi chuanqi! Ta zai fumu qushi si nian hou shusheng 中国这名婴儿是传奇!他在父母去世四年后出生 (This baby in China is legendary! He was born four years after his parents died)' (*Jinri huawen* 今日华闻, 12 April 2018) <https://ihuawen.com/article/index/id/50864> accessed 18 January 2025.

 | DOI:10.1163/9789004754300_008

nted Laotian nationality in accordance with the citizenship of the gestational mother. However, following the results of the DNA analysis, which confirmed the child's lineage to the Shen and Xu families, and since the biological grandparents were willing to assume responsibility for the child's care while the gestational mother was not at all interested, Tiantian was finally granted Chinese nationality.[2]

In contrast to Western reports that generally express dismay over the story, Chinese blogs presented it as a fairy tale with a happy ending. The latter narrative portrayed the successful posthumous artificial reproduction (hereafter: PAR) through a surrogate mother as a just reward, a sort of prize achieved by four elderly parents devastated by the death of their only children at the end of long vicissitudes. The underlying causes of these events are generally not explored; it is worth remarking, though, that most of the obstacles so 'heroically' overcome were not due to chance, as is often the case in fairy tales, but rather (and much more prosaically) to more or less explicit prohibitions imposed by the Chinese legal system through administrative regulation. Reading the enthusiastic comments published online, however, one cannot help but question the incongruity between what the majority of Chinese (seem to) consider as 'just' or at least 'acceptable' in extreme situations and the provisions in force in the PRC.[3]

Regarding PAR, this inconsistency is confirmed by a 2022 quantitative study, which investigated the attitudes of three distinct groups – the general public, in vitro fertilisation (IVF) couples, and HART practitioners – towards the management of frozen embryos in instances of familial-structure changes, such as the accidental death of one of the intended parents.[4] According to the findings, a considerable proportion of individuals from the three categories exhibited approval for PAR in specific circumstances, reaching 79.20% among the general public.[5] With reference to surrogacy, the tension between the prevailing sentiment of Chinese citizens and the government's regulatory will was brought to the fore by the 2015 amendment to the PFPL. As mentioned in the previous chapter, its promulgation on 27 December 2015 has been globally welcomed for ending the infamous Chinese one-child policy. However, the event aroused the interest of Chinese citizens and legal scholars for another

2 'Chinese Baby Born Four Years after Parents' Death' (n 914); Wangyi 网易 (NetEase) (n 914); Liu Yajing 刘雅静 (159*n*1).

3 Jiliang Huang and others, 'Attitudes toward Posthumous Assisted Reproduction in China: A Multi-Dimensional Survey' (2022) 19 Reproductive Health 122.

4 Ibid 124.

5 Ibid 126.

reason: the removal, from its final version, of the prohibition of 'any form of surrogacy' contained in the draft initially proposed by the State Council and announced both in the *People's Daily* and the NPC's website less than one week before the final approval.[6] Although it is rare for a law to be changed so radically after its contents have been published,[7] the decision of the Chinese legislature did not come as a complete surprise. In fact, the article anticipating the contents of the draft had devoted only a brief space to the possibility of having two children per couple, focusing mainly on the doubts expressed by parliamentarians over whether surrogacy should be banned completely.[8] These concerns primarily related to the potential risks associated with incorporating such a provision into a law meant to be passed 'in one shot,' and thus without the possibility of broad popular consultation. According to the deputies, the proposed ban could potentially infringe upon the reproductive rights of couples, particularly in cases where the female partner is biologically unable to conceive, infertile, or where there is a risk of giving birth to an unhealthy child. This could also have implications for the stability of marriage; consequently, robust popular support and profound reflection were deemed necessary, in addition to comparison with legal systems that had recently embraced gestational surrogacy and the ongoing discourse in Taiwan.[9] It is unclear whether these or other considerations prompted the NPC to remove the ban on surrogacy from the final version of the law.[10] In any event, and notwithstanding the government's frequent campaigns against surrogacy, the level of public approval for this type of HART has continued to grow, as confirmed by

6 'Cong "Jingzhi" daiyun dao "guifang" fatiaoboyi beihou de shi yu 从"禁止"代孕到"规范"法条博弈背后的是与非|青岛|半岛网 (From "prohibiting" surrogacy to "regulating" it: the pros and cons behind the legal battle)' (*Bandao wang – Bandao doushi bao* 半岛网- 半岛都市报, 1 January 2016) <https://news.bandao.cn/news_html/201601/20160101/news_20160101_2598426.shtml> accessed 19 January 2025; Sui Suli 睢素利, Li Jingru 李京儒 and Liu Hang 刘欢, 'Guanyu daiyun wenti de falü he linlun bianxi 关于代孕问题的法律和伦理辨析 (Legal and theoretical analysis on the problem of surrogacy)' (2017) 25 Zhongguo ji hua shengyu xue zazhi 中国计划生育学杂志 804.

7 Saibal Dasgupta, 'China Reverses Planned Surrogacy Ban to Encourage More Births' (*Voice of America*, 1 January 2016) <https://www.voanews.com/a/china-reverses-planned-surrogacy-ban-to-encourage-more-births/3127177.html> accessed 18 January 2025.

8 Yang Cheng 杨成, 'Renkou Ji Sheng Fa Xiugai: Weiyuan Jianyi Na Diao "jingzhi Daiyun" Tiaokuan 人口计生法修改: 委员建议拿掉"禁止代孕"条款 (Amendment to the Population and Family Planning Law: Committee Members Propose Removing the Clause Prohibiting Surrogacy)' (*Renda xinwen wang* 人大新闻网, 23 December 2015) <http://npc.people.com.cn/n1/2015/1223/c14576-27967873.html> accessed 19 January 2025.

9 Ibid.

10 Dasgupta (161*n*7).

the results of regular opinion polls launched by both official newspapers and institutional websites.[11]

The discrepancy between the regulatory intentions of Chinese leaders and popular sentiment on the matter was arguably a contributing factor to the delay in Chinese lawmakers taking a position on the two HART(s) successfully used by Yixing case's plaintiffs, leaving the issues unanswered even in the 2021 PFPL revision. The contrast among law-in-the-books, people's attitude and legal practice in this field can be easily dismissed as yet more proof of how little weight formal rules carry in the Chinese context, and the lack of moral qualms or taboos typical of a notoriously materialistic country. However, legal comparison teaches us to be wary of simplistic answers, and to ask whether these inconsistencies might not be the expression of cryptotypes or path dependency phenomena that influences how the Chinese legal system approaches PAR and gestational surrogacy.

In the following pages, an analysis of this approach will be conducted to ascertain how it fits within the global legal landscape, as well as its relationship with the Chinese ideological-cultural substratum and the PRC's prevailing political context. The goal is to determine the presence of any distinguishing Chinese characteristics in the governance of what are probably the two most controversial biotechnologies associated with the commencement of human life at a global level. I will also offer some predictions on the trajectory of future development in this domain.

To this end, it is essential to undertake a preliminary investigation on the evolution of HART within the PRC, as well as the general regulatory framework for assisted reproduction in China.

2 The Development of HART in the PRC

The first test tube-baby in the PRC was born at the Third Hospital of Beijing University in 1988, precisely a decade after the birth of Louise Brown, the first human being conceived following In Vitro Fertilisation (hereinafter: IVF), on 25 July 1978 in Oldham, northwest England.[12] The main contributing factors to China's delayed implementation of these technologies appear to be the legal

11 Zhan Zhongle 湛中乐, 'Lun Daiyun Ji Qi Xingwei de Gongfa Guizhi 论代孕及其行为的公法规制 (On Surrogacy and Its Public Regulation)' (2024) 16 Yixue yu faxue 医学与法学 27, 33.

12 Huang Qi 黄祺, 'Shijie Shang Di Yi "Shiguan Ying'er" – Lu Yi Si 世界上第一个"试管婴儿"露易丝 (The World's First "Test-Tube Baby," Louise)' *Xin min zhoukang* 新民周刊

and social complexities inherent in the implementation of the one-child policy rather than any absence of adequate medical facilities, personnel, and resources. It was not until the early 1980s that advocates of HART research managed to persuade the Chinese authorities that allowing infertile couples to become parents was not at odds with the strict demographic controls in place at the time.[13] On the contrary, the technology could be useful in mitigating some of its side-effects while also increasing the number of high-quality births. Consequently, from 1984 onward, the National Natural Science Foundation began to support HART research initiatives at the Third Hospital of Beijing University. In 1986, a programme run by the same hospital and entitled 'High Quality Birth: Research on the Protection, Preservation and Development of Early Embryos' was designated as a pivotal national 'Seventh Five-Year Plan' key research project.[14]

The stories of babies conceived via IVF in the initial years serve to substantiate the interpretation of these technologies as a solution to the unintentional consequences of family planning. Although the first test-tube baby born in China was to a 38-year-old woman who had been infertile for 10 years,[15] the second was born to a 29-year-old woman who had previously given birth to a child. Unfortunately, the infant died and the woman, who had undergone a sterilisation procedure right after delivery as part of a family planning programme, could no longer naturally generate another child.[16] Only the newly available HART made this possible through the donation of an embryo from another patient.

Adopting a cultural tradition standpoint, several Chinese authors regard it as 'obviously regrettable' that the infant was not genetically related to the family into which it was born; nevertheless, they admit that such an event had the potential to reinvigorate the 'hope for life' of the parents.[17] As a matter of fact, in the late 1980s, the implementation of HART enabled many sterilised

(19 October 2023) <https://m.xinminweekly.com.cn/content/19238.html> accessed 1 May 2025.

13 Liu Yinliang, 'The Development of the Human-Assisted Reproductive Technology and Its Regulation in China: A Historical Narrative' (2024) 12 Peking University Law Journal 1, 6.

14 '31 Nian Qian Chusheng de Zhongguo Dalu Shou Li Shiguan Yin'er Jintian Dang Mama Le! 31 年前出生的中国大陆首例试管婴儿今天当妈妈了！(The First Test-Tube Baby Born in Mainland China 31 Years Ago Became a Mother Today!)' *Beijing wanbao* 北京晚报 (15 April 2019) <https://news.cctv.com/2019/04/15/ARTINznFdJxdc1ydzOMlm0Ec190415.shtml> accessed 1 May 2025.

15 Ibid.

16 Liu (163*n*13) 6.

17 Ibid.

couples who had previously experienced the loss of their only child to once again procreate. This clearly had a positive impact on social stability, strengthening public confidence in the leadership of the CPC, as the authorities sought to demonstrate their commitment to supporting the population's reproductive aspirations, provided that such actions did not contradict the prevailing family planning policies.

It is therefore unsurprising that, following a gradual introduction, HART underwent rapid development. In 1992, just four years after the first IVF birth, the first baby was born from donated eggs, followed in 1995 by the first birth from frozen-thawed embryos, in 1996 by the first intracytoplasmic sperm injection, and in 2006 by the first 'three frozen' baby (i.e.: a childbirth from frozen sperm, frozen eggs and frozen embryos).[18] This marked only the second time when the latter technology had been successfully employed on a global scale. By the onset of the 2020s, the PRC not only equalled the achievements of so-called developed states in this field, but had ascended to the pre-eminent position in the global HART market, distinguished by its exceptional success rate and technical proficiency.[19]

It is worth remarking that since the mid-1990s, significant advancements in HART, particularly gestational surrogacy, have finally rendered it feasible to ensure the birth of genetically related offspring even for women who, due to health issues or (again!) sterilisation, would have been unable to carry a pregnancy to term. The first birth through surrogacy was documented in 1996.[20] In this case, the intended mother had been authorised to undergo the procedure after being sterilised following a series of unfortunate pregnancies that had resulted in miscarriages, induced abortions and even a ruptured uterus. At the turn of the twentieth and twenty-first centuries, a significant number of children were born through this method,[21] concurrent with the development of services aimed at preserving the reproductive cells of intended parents.[22] This was facilitated by sperm banks (hereafter: SB), the first of which was established in 1981 at the Xiangya School of Medicine of Central South Univer-

18 Ibid.

19 Ren Zeping 任泽平, 'Zhongguo Fuzhu Shengzhi Yanjiu Baogao 中国辅助生殖研究报告 2023 (China Assisted Reproductive Technology Research Report 2023)' (28 February 2023) <https://finance.sina.com.cn/cj/2023-02-28/doc-imyieiem8146136.shtml> accessed 2 May 2025.

20 Liu (163*n*13) 6.

21 Ayo Wahlberg, 'The Birth and Routinization of IVF in China' (2016) 2 Reproductive Biomedicine & Society Online 97, 104.

22 Liu (163*n*13) 6.

sity,[23] and egg banks.[24] However, while sperm self-storage services were initiated in 2003, egg preservation remains inaccessible to single women in the PRC, as well as married women without a diagnosed medical condition who want to postpone motherhood for academic or career reasons.[25] The preceding chapter dealt with the subject in relation to systems currently established to persuade couples to procreate at 'an appropriate age,' as outlined in Article 18 of the PFPL 2021 from the perspectives of pronatalism and eugenics. The persistent disparity in treatment, irrespective of prevailing policies and net of concerns regarding the impact of egg retrieval on the reproductive health of young women,[26] underscores the constrained autonomy that PRC women have historically been accorded, particularly when their traditional roles as wives and mothers are at stake.

To confront the challenges posed by the emergence of gamete banks, as well as to prevent abuse and restore order to the increasingly chaotic reproductive services market, the Minister of Health (hereafter: MoH) initiated the process of issuing the first regulatory documents on the subject at the beginning of the twenty-first century.[27] Until that time, the accelerated development of HART in China had been further enabled by the absence of specific norms at the national level,[28] which allowed research institutes, hospitals and clinics to undertake experiments and implement new technologies with minimal restrictions, apart from those related to family planning. The sole exception was probably 1989's 'Urgent Notice on Strictly Prohibiting the Use of Medical Techniques to Determine Foetal Sex and the Abuse of Artificial Insemination Techniques' (*Guanyu yanjin yong yiliao jishu jianbie tai'er xingbie he lanyong rengong shoujing jishu de jinji tongzhi* 关于严禁用医疗技术鉴别胎儿性别和滥用人工授精技术的紧急通知, MoH, doc. N. 13/1989). It is pretty evident from the title that the intention of the notice was not to regulate HART; instead, the objective was to prevent the utilisation of recently available technologies for the purpose of determining the sex of unborn chil-

23 Wahlberg (164*n*21).

24 Zhang Yan 张园, Diao Feiyang 刁飞扬 and Liu Jiayin 刘嘉茵, 'Renlei "luanzi ku" jianshe shuping 人类"卵子库"建设述评 (Commentary on the construction of human "egg bank" in China)' (2022) 42 Zhonghua shengzhi yu biyun zazhi 中华生殖与避孕杂志 219.

25 Sun Jingzhou, 'The Social and Legal Implications of Elective Egg Freezing in China' (2024) 12 Peking University Law Journal 61.

26 Zhang Jiakai and others, 'Current Status and Reflections on Fertility Preservation in China' (2022) 39 Journal of Assisted Reproduction and Genetics 2835, 2841.

27 Ren Zeping 任泽平 (164*n*19).

28 Wahlberg (164*n*21) 103.

dren. This was part of the broader fight against gender-selective abortion, which was examined in the preceding chapter. A considerable time elapsed before the government felt obliged to tackle the issue by means of a series of departmental regulations and administrative documents. The implementation of these measures would have resulted in the illegality of certain practices previously implemented, most notably gestational surrogacy.

2.1 HART's *Regulatory Framework*

By the close of the 1990s and the dawn of the 2000s, it became clear that the challenges and possibilities presented by HART extended far beyond, though were inextricable from, the foundational realm of demographic policy. The qualitative and quantitative development of these techniques and their concomitant increase in sophistication has transformed practices that until recently were the province of science fiction into routine protocols. These advances have forced a re-evaluation of the long-standing concept of parenthood as between two individuals of different genders, thereby giving rise to ethical and social issues that could threaten the maintenance of public order. To guarantee the safety of those involved and protect them from possible abuse, it therefore became a priority not only to bring order to the technical and structural chaos surrounding assisted reproduction services, but also to establish the ethical principles that should inspire the use of HART. Chinese leaders chose an approach that would allow them to control the application of these technologies at the source, through instruments aimed at regulating the activities of medical institutions and professionals involved in their use. Thus, on 20 February 2001, the MoH issued the Measure on the Administration of Human Assisted Reproductive Technology (*Renlei fuzhu shengzhi jishu guanli banfa* 人类辅助生殖技术管理办法, Min. ord. n. 14, hereafter: MAHART 2001) and the Measure on the Administration of Human Sperm Bank (*Renlei jingzi ku guanli banfa* 人类精子库管理办法, Min. ord. n. 15) both of which came into force on the 1st August 2001. These documents officially stated that HART services could only be provided by medical institutions approved and registered with national and provincial health authorities (MAHART 2001, arts. 3 and 12), subjecting anyone practising them without such approval to the penalties provided for in the Regulations on the Administration of Medical Institutions and its implementation rules (MAHART 2001, arts. 12 and 21). Not only that: Article 24 of MAHART 2001 also provides the first legal definition of HART, understood as "the use of medical techniques and methods to artificially manipulate gametes, zygotes, or embryos to achieve the purpose of conception.' According to the same article, HART can be divided into artificial insemination and in vitro fertilisation-embryo transfer technology. Artificial insemination refers both to intrauterine insemination using the husband's semen and intrauterine insemination using donor semen. On the other hand, in vitro-insemination-embryo transfer technology and its derivative technologies refer to 'the process of retrieving ova from a woman's body, culturing them in a container, adding technically processed sperm, allowing fertilisation to occur, continuing cultivation until early-stage embryos form, and then transferring them to the uterus for implantation, development into a foetus, and delivery.' It is evident that, according to MAHART 2001, PAR and surrogacy fall under the latter category. In order to continue this concise historical excursion into the realm of HART regulations, it is important to note that, on 14 May 2001, the MoH issued the Ethical Principles for the Implementation of Human Assisted Reproductive Technology (*Shishi renlei fuzhu shengzhi jishu de lunli yuanze* 实施人类辅助生殖技术的伦理原则, hereafter: EPIHART 2001), the Technical Specifications on Human Assisted Reproductive Technology (*Renlei fushu shengzhi jishu guifan* 人类辅助生殖技术规范, hereafter: TSHART 2001) the Basic Standards for Human Sperm Bank (*Renlei jingzi ku jiben biaozhun* 人类精子库基本标准, hereafter: BSHSB 2001) and the Technical Specifications for Human Sperm Bank (*Renlei jingzi ku jishu guifan* 人类精子库技术规范, hereafter: TSHSB 2001).[29] Nonetheless, within several months of their implementation, the provisions became obsolete due to the rapid development of scientific and bioethical knowledge in this field, both nationally and internationally. Therefore, in March 2002, the Ministry of Health initiated 'the establishment of expert groups with the objective of leveraging and adapting the technical specifications, fundamental standards and ethical principles of advanced nations, whilst considering the prevailing conditions in China.'[30] The purpose of this project was to comprehensively revise the original EPIHART, TSHART, BSHSP, and TSHSB, with a view to establishing higher standards for institutions utilising relevant technologies and the qualifications of their personnel. Moreover, the initiative sought to provide further clarification on the ethical principles that should govern the implementation of HART. It also sought to establish, for the first time, ethical principles for SB, incorporating both sets of principles in one norm: the Ethical Principles for the Imple-

29 Weisheng bu 卫生部, 'Weisheng bu guanyu xiuding renlei fuzhu shengzhi jishu yu renlei jingzi ku xiangguan jishu guifan, jiben biaozhun he luli yuanze de tongzhi 卫生部关于修订人类辅助生殖技术与人类精子库相关技术规范、基本标准和伦理原则的通知 (Notice of the Ministry of Health on the Revision of Technical Specifications, Basic Standards, and Ethical Principles Related to Human Assisted Reproductive Technology and Human Sperm Banks).'

30 Ibid.

mentation of Human Assisted Reproductive Technologies and Sperm Bank (*Shishi renlei fuzhu shengzhi jishu he renlei jingzi ku lunli yuanze* 实施人类辅助生殖技术和人类精子库伦理原则). The new regulations were published on 27 June 2003 as annexes to the same 'Notice on the Revision of Technical Specifications, Basic Standards, and Ethical Principles Related to Human Assisted Reproductive Technology and Human Sperm Bank ' (*Guanyu xiuding renlei fuzhu shengzhi jishu yu renlei jingzi ku xianguan jishu guifan, jiben biaozhun he luli yuanze de tongzhi* 关于修订人类辅助生殖技术与人类精子库相关技术规范、基本标准和伦理原则的通知, hereafter: Notice 2003) through which the MoH informed the local health authorities of the amendments to the 2001 provisions. They came into force on 1 October 2003 and have remained unamended since that date (hereafter: EPIHARTSB 2003, TSHART 2003, BSHSP 2003, and TSHSB 2003).[31] Simultaneously, the MoH proceeded to delineate the more pragmatic elements of the supervision of HART through the 'Administrative Procedures for the Review, Audit and Approval of Human Reproductive Assisted Technology (*Renlei fushu shengzhi jishu yu yu renlei jingziku pingshen, shenhe he shenbi guanli chengxu de tongzhi* 发人类辅助生殖技术与人类精子库评审、审核和审批管理程序的通知) also issued on 27 June 2003,[32] and the 'Implementation Rules for the Inspection and Verification of Human Reproductive Assisted Technology and Human Sperm Banks' (*Renlei fuzhu shengzhi jishu yu renlei jingzi ku jiaoyan shishi xize* 人类辅助生殖技术与人类精子库校验实施细则) issued on 7 February 2006.[33]

Notwithstanding the passage of more than two decades and their comparatively subordinate position within the legal hierarchy, the aforementioned norms persist in their role as the fundamental regulatory framework for HART within the PRC. The definition of HART has remained the same since 2001, and the objectives pursued by the system are still those indicated by

31 Ibid.

32 Weisheng bu 卫生部, 'Weisheng Bu Guanyu Yinfa Renlei Fushu Shengzhi Jishu Yu Renlei Jingziku Pingshen, Shenhe He Shenbi Guanli Chengxu de Tongzhi 卫生部关于印发人类辅助生殖技术与人类精子库评审、审核和审批管理程序的通知 (Notice of the Ministry of Health on the Issuance of the Review, Examination, and Approval Management Procedures for Human Assisted Reproductive Technology and Human Sperm Banks)' <http://www.nhc.gov.cn/bgt/pw10303/200708/6998a89f66c247469a179482dd9f930c.shtml> accessed 26 April 2025.

33 Weisheng bu 卫生部, 'Weisheng Bu Guanyu Yinfa Renlei Fuzhu Shengzhi Jishu Yu Renlei Jingzi Ku Jiaoyan Shishi Xize de Tongzhi 卫生部关于印发人类辅助生殖技术与人类精子库校验实施细则的通知 (Notice of the Ministry of Health on the Issuance of the Implementation Rules for the Inspection and Verification of Human Assisted Reproductive Technology and Human Sperm Banks)' <http://www.nhc.gov.cn/bgt/pw10604/200606/9ce14a2958214ef5936153115707d827.shtml> accessed 26 April 2025.

the 2003 Notice. Consistent with the general provisions of Article 1 of the MAHART 2001, the Notice 2003 states that the revision aims 'to ensure the safe and effective implementation of human assisted reproductive technology and human sperm banks in China, and to effectively protect the health rights and interests of the people.' More specifically, it intends 'to prevent the misuse of human assisted reproductive technology and human sperm bank technology due to the pursuit of economic benefits, to earnestly implement the national population and family planning policy, uphold the ethical dignity of human life, and minimise the negative impacts and harms that this technology may bring to society, ethics, morality, law, and future generations.' The MoH also identifies areas that require special attention, both from a technical and ethical point of view, due to their central importance in achieving these goals. These include the control of multiple pregnancies, the improvement of embryo reduction techniques, the strict regulation of indications, the strict prohibition of the commercialisation of sperm and egg donation, and oocyte cytoplasmic transfer technology.[34]

Indeed, the MAHART 2001 already covered many prohibitions. Article 3, after stating that the application of HART shall be 'in accordance with the national family planning policy, ethical principles and relevant laws and regulations,' stipulates that: 'The sale of gametes, zygotes and embryos in any form is prohibited. Medical institutions and medical personnel shall not carry out any form of surrogacy technology.' Furthermore, its Article 15 prohibits the 'private collection of sperm,' while Article 17 restates the ban on selecting embryos based on gender without specific authorisation.

The 2003 regulations reiterated these prohibitions, while introducing new and more specific bans. In particular, Part III of the TSHART 2003 sets out which actions are prohibited for medical institutions and their staff in the practise of HART, including: oocyte cytoplasm transfer and nuclear transfer when performed for the purpose of treating infertility; hybridisation of gametes between humans and other species; transplantation of gametes, zygotes and embryos of other species; transplantation of gametes, zygotes and embryos of other species into humans; transplantation of human gametes, zygotes and embryos into other species; genetic manipulation of human gam-

34 Weisheng bu 卫生部, 'Weisheng bu guanyu xiuding renlei fuzhu shengzhi jishu yu renlei jingzi ku xianguan jishu guifan, jiben biaozhun he luli yuanze de tongzhi 卫生部关于修订人类辅助生殖技术与人类精子库相关技术规范、基本标准和伦理原则的通知 (Notice of the Ministry of Health on the Revision of Technical Specifications, Basic Standards, and Ethical Principles Related to Human Assisted Reproductive Technology and Human Sperm Banks)' (167*n*29).

etes, zygotes and embryos for reproductive purposes; combining of sperm and egg between close relatives; the use, in the same cycle, of gametes and zygotes coming from different men and women; transferring gametes, zygotes and embryos to others, or conducting scientific research without the patient's knowledge and consent; implementing HART for couples or single women who do not meet the requirements of the national population and family planning laws; conducting human chimera embryo experiments and research; and human cloning. It is important to note that while the ban on surrogacy is mentioned in all the administrative rules pertaining to HART, no provision, either within the MAHART 2001 or within the TSHART 2003, or in any other current regulation in force in the PRC, makes any reference to PAR.

In relation to ethical principles referred to HART, the most significant change is the introduction in the EPIHARTSB 2003 of the 'principle of beneficence for patients' (*youli yu gongshouti de yuanze* 有利于供受体的原则). In fact, the EPIHART 2001 stipulated at point 2 the duty 'to protect the interests of patients and future generations' exclusively in terms of nonmaleficence. The 2003 EPIHARTPB, besides confirming the protection of future generations in the sense of minimising the harm which the performance of HARTS can caused them,[35] has expanded the responsibility of the professionals operating in the field to include the obligation to maximise the benefit of HART towards the interest of donors and recipients and their family.'[36] Apart from this addition, the list of the principles is the same as the EPIHART 2001. They are as follows: the principle of informed consent (*zhixing tongyi* 知性同意),[37] the principle of protecting the offspring (*baohu houdai liyi* 保护后代利益),[38] the principle of social public interest (*shehui gongyi* 社会公益),[39] the principle of confidentiality (*baomi* 保密),[40] the principle of strictly forbidding commercialisation (*yanfang shangye hua* 严防商业化),[41] and the principle of ethical supervision (*lunli jiandu* 伦理监督).[42]

The newly introduced principle of 'beneficence towards patients' clearly recalls the principle of beneficence developed by Beachamp and Childress in 1979 discussed in Chapter 2 a principle that constitutes the basis of bioethical regulation at a global level. Among other provisions, it is incorporated into the

---

35 Ibid 3, Part I (3), Part II (3).
36 Ibid 3, Introduction.
37 Ibid 3, Part I (2), Part II (2).
38 Ibid 3, Part I (3), Part II (3).
39 Ibid 3, Part I (4), Part II (4).
40 Ibid 3, Part I (5), Part II (5).
41 Ibid 3, Part I (6), Part II (6).
42 Ibid 3, Part I (7), Part II (7).

preamble of the Council of Europe's 'Convention for the Protection of Human Rights and Dignity of the Human Being with regard to the Application of Biology and Medicine: Convention on Human Rights and Biomedicine,' signed in Oviedo (Spain) on 4 April 1997 (hereafter, Oviedo Convention),[43] and into Article 4 of the United Nations Educational, Scientific and Cultural Organization (hereafter: UNESCO), and the 'Universal Declaration on Bioethics and Human Rights,' signed in Paris on 19 October 2005 (hereafter: UNESCO Declaration 2005). The Oviedo Convention was the first, and still the only, binding international text designed to preserve human dignity, rights and freedoms through a series of principles and prohibitions against the misuse of biological and medical advances,[44] albeit limited to a regional context. On the other hand, the UNESCO Declaration 2005 is the first international norm to explicitly establish the conformity of bioethics with international human rights law.[45] An in-depth analysis of these norms goes beyond the scope of this work; I mention them here to note that, at least at first glance, the ethical principles underlying Chinese legislation on HART are entirely consistent in spirit, if not identical in wording, with those formulated by leading international organisations mainly as a result of Western philosophical reflection, and replicated in national legislation at various levels. To limit the examples to the international instruments mentioned above: the duty of informed consent is enshrined in Article 5 of the Oviedo Convention and Article 6 of the UNESCO Declaration 2005; the protection of future generations is enshrined in Article 16 of the UNESCO Declaration 2005 ; social responsibility is enshrined in Article 16 of the UNESCO Declaration 2005 ; respect for privacy is enshrined in Article 10 of the Oviedo Declaration and Article 9 of the UNESCO Declaration 2005 ; the prohibition of financial gain is enshrined in Article 21 of the Oviedo Declaration; and the duty of ethical supervision is enshrined in Article 19 of the UNESCO Declaration 2005.

However, a (almost) literal equivalence does not always correspond to a similar equivalence in meaning. A thorough investigation of the 2003 norms reveals the validity of this statement. Indeed, in a manner analogous to its 2001 predecessor, the EPIHARTSB 2003 follows each principle with a concise des-

---

43 Council of Europe, 'Oviedo Convention and Its Protocols – Human Rights and Biomedicine – Www.Coe.Int' (*Human Rights and Biomedicine*) <https://www.coe.int/en/web/human-rights-and-biomedicine/oviedo-convention> accessed 30 April 2025.

44 Treaty Office, 'Details of Treaty No.164' (*Treaty Office*, 4 April 1997) <https://www.coe.int/en/web/conventions/full-list> accessed 30 April 2025.

45 UNESCO, 'Universal Declaration on Bioethics and Human Rights |' <https://www.unesco.org/en/ethics-science-technology/bioethics-and-human-rights> accessed 30 April 2025.

cription, the purpose of which is to provide healthcare operators with a framework for its implementation. Reading those descriptions, one cannot help but see a reflection of Chinese cultural, ideological, and political needs and values, albeit situated within a conceptual framework of external origin. This phenomenon can be attributed to the theoretical integration of Western bioethical principles in the PRC since the 1988 work of Qiu Renzong, a process that has been filtered and made congruent with prevailing local ethical values. In Chapter 2 we noted that, particularly with reference to Beauchamp and Childress' renowned 'four principles of bioethics,' this has resulted in two key outcomes. Firstly, it has led to the pre-eminence of the concept of beneficence over that of autonomy. Secondly, it has led to a sort of relativisation of the latter, according to the principle that the common good must always prevail over the individual good in cases of conflict.[46] This approach is evident in the EPIHARTSB 2003 introduction, which specifies that, in addition to the interests of individuals and future generations, the application of HART must also protect and enhance the interests of the family.

As has been repeatedly emphasised throughout this book, the concept of family plays a fundamental role in Chinese culture and tradition. Indeed, the family represents the foundation of the Chinese political and social system, and the focal point of philosophical reflection, including medical ethics. Its inclusion in the 2003 norms is therefore unsurprising; nevertheless, it constitutes a peculiar (Chinese) characteristic and gives rise to scenarios with potential ramifications for the two biotechnologies to be discussed in the following pages.

This is not the only feature that can influence the way in which PAR and surrogacy are perceived and practiced in today's PRC. Still, with reference to the principle of 'beneficence to the patients,' the EPIHARTSB 2003 also specifies that ovulation induction for the purpose of multiple pregnancies or commercial egg donation is prohibited,[47] and that infertile couples have the right to choose how to handle gametes and embryos obtained through HART.[48] Service providers must maintain detailed records of such decisions and obtain written informed consent from the husband, the wife or both parties;[49] gam-

46 See *supra*, Chapter 2, 2.1 B) a).

47 Weisheng bu 卫生部, 'Weisheng bu guanyu xiuding renlei fuzhu shengzhi jishu yu renlei jingzi ku xiangguan jishu guifan, jiben biaozhun he luli yuanze de tongzhi 卫生部关于修订人类辅助生殖技术与人类精子库相关技术规范、基本标准和伦理原则的通知 (Notice of the Ministry of Health on the Revision of Technical Specifications, Basic Standards, and Ethical Principles Related to Human Assisted Reproductive Technology and Human Sperm Banks)' (n 942) apps 3, Par I (1) 2.

48 Ibid 3, Par I (1) 3.

49 Ibid 3, Part I (1) 3.

etes and embryos of patients may not be processed in any manner without their informed consent, nor may they be bought or sold.[50] The principle of informed consent, on the other hand, elucidates that HART can only be implemented with the voluntary agreement and signature of both spouses on a written informed consent form.[51] Medical personnel must inform the couple of the necessity of implementing the technology, the procedures for doing so, the potential risks, and the measures taken to avoid these risks.[52] Furthermore, they have to inform the recipients of their right to propose the termination of the implementation of the technology at any time, and that this will not affect their future treatment.[53] With reference to the protection of future generations, the recipients must acknowledge that children born through HART are endowed with the same rights and obligations as offspring conceived and born naturally.[54] Simultaneously, the recipients possess ethical, moral and legal obligations towards children born through HART, including children with birth defects.[55] Moreover, medical professionals must discontinue the implementation of HART when there is clear evidence that its introduction will result in significant physical, psychological, and social harm to offspring.[56] It is then essential that HART not be employed in relation to sperm or eggs of close relatives, nor on any sperm or eggs that do not adhere to ethical and moral principles.[57] In accordance with the aforementioned objective, the number of women who can receive the same sperm or egg from the same donor is limited to five.[58] Moreover, the performance of surrogacy and embryo-donation-assisted reproduction technology is prohibited.[59] The same applies to human oocyte cytoplasmic transfer and nuclear transfer, and to chimera embryo technology for the purpose of treating infertility.[60]

The principles of social public interest, as well as the principle of 'strictly preventing commercialisation,' give rise to a number of prohibitions that can deeply influence the performance of PAR and surrogacy. The first principle proscribes the implementation of HART on single women or couples who do

50 Ibid 3, Part I (1) 4.
51 Ibid 3, Part 1 (2) 1.
52 Ibid 3, Part I (2) 2.
53 Ibid 3, Part 1 (2) 3.
54 Ibid 3, Part I (3) 1.
55 Ibid 3, Part I (3) 2.
56 Ibid 3, Part I (3) 3.
57 Ibid 3, Part I (3) 4.
58 Ibid 3, Part I (3) 8.
59 Ibid 3, Part I (3) 5,6.
60 Ibid 3, Part I (3) 7, 9.

not comply with national population and family planning laws and regulations.[61] It further prohibits gender selection for non-medical reasons[62] and reproductive cloning,[63] as well as the use of gametes and embryos from other species in HART.[64] Conversely, the principle of strictly preventing commercialisation implies that institutions and medical personnel must adhere to the indication for the use of HART and must not be driven by economic interest to abuse these technologies.[65] As a corollary to this rule – which recalls Kant's imperative to use humanity 'always at the same time as an end, never merely as a means' – the sale and purchase of sperm and eggs is prohibited.[66] Nevertheless, donors can be remunerated for any loss of income, as well as for any medical and transportation expenses incurred.[67]

In a recent article on the development of HART in China, Liu Yinlian noted that the decision to regulate the tasks of institutions and personnel engaged in HART activities comprehensively through administrative norms referring to 'relevant laws and regulations' for broader issues, has enabled the legal framework designed at the beginning of the twenty-first century to maintain, to a certain extent, the security and efficiency of the system up to the present day.[68] As demonstrated in the preceding chapter; however, the technological, economic, social, cultural and, most significantly, demographic shifts experienced by the country over the past two decades have profoundly transformed the official approach to procreation. This has resulted in the repeated amendment of the most relevant legislation in the field, namely the PFLP and the MIHCL. Furthermore, this situation has resulted in the dissolution of the ministry which issued the HART regulatory framework outline. In 2013, the MoH underwent a merger with the National Planning Commission, resulting in the formation of the National Health and Family Planning Commission (NHFPC). Subsequently, in 2018, the NHFPC was formally renamed the National Health Commission (hereafter NHC).

In a context so divergent from that in which, and for which, this operational system was designed, inevitable contradictions and aporias have increasingly emerged. In fact, contemporary legal issues pertaining to HART cannot help but prove challenging for the Chinese people's courts, which find themselves

61 Ibid 3, Part I (4) 1.
62 Ibid 3, Part I (4) 2.
63 Ibid 3, Part I (4) 3.
64 Ibid 3, Part I (4) 4.
65 Ibid 3, Part I (6).
66 Ibid.
67 Ibid.
68 Liu (163*n*13) 21.

tasked with harmonising specific yet outdated rules, with legal sources at a higher level that are more recent but too generic and ambiguous to be of any practical use in this scientifically, legally and ethically intricate domain. To illustrate this point, it is sufficient to remark that Article 1009 of the recently promulgated CC merely provides that: 'Medical and scientific research activities concerning human genes and human embryos, among others, shall be carried out according to the laws and administrative regulations, and relevant provisions issued by the state, without endangering human health, violating moral principles, or damaging public interests.' The game of references thus created continues to leave unanswered the thorniest questions with which the courts have been grappling in recent years, and which have been encapsulated in the case that initiated the present study. These include, among others, the nature of frozen embryos and doubts about their endowment with personality; the definition of parent and/or the possibility that a child may have more than one mother or father; issues relating to the nationality of children born through surrogacy. In a similar manner, within the criminal sphere and despite the frequent amendments to the Criminal Law, the only relevant provision remains its Article 136 (1), which was added in 2020 as a reaction to the emergency caused by the already mentioned DNA-modified twins' scandal. This article punishes 'Whoever implants any genetically edited or cloned human embryo into the body of a human being or animal or implants any genetically edited or cloned animal embryo into the body of a human being, shall be punished.'

Considering all this, the 'contradictions' among public opinion, legal practice and the rules in force highlighted in the previous pages seem to find an initial justification. Not surprising, in recent years, numerous authors have begun to call on the NPC to legislate on the issue, putting an end to the uncertainty surrounding a matter as personal and intimate as reproduction and the rights associated with it.[69]

But what is the reason for the legislature's hesitation in tackling this issue? In the absence of clear legislative rules, what principles (legal, ethical, cultural, or traditional) inspire the solutions found by legal practitioners? Is it possible, on the basis of these principles, to imagine what the future of legislation in this area might be in the PRC?

The analysis will commence with a reproductive technology that was not considered within the regulatory framework established at the beginning of the twenty-first century: PAR.

---

69 Ibid.

CHAPTER 7

Posthumous-Assisted Reproduction (PAR)

1 Introduction

In 1997, the bioethicist Leon Kass coined the expression 'wisdom of repugnance' to describe the instinctive sense of disgust that human beings feel in the face of certain products of scientific development, such as cloning, genetic manipulation or (as far as we are concerned here) posthumous reproduction.[1] The author posits that, in controversial issues such as the aforementioned, 'repugnance' constitutes an emotional expression of profound wisdom that transcends the limits of reason's capacity to articulate,'[2] serving as 'prima facie evidence of foulness and violation.'[3] According to Kass, it is essential to recognise the emotional dimension of this issue and to prohibit the use of technologies that cause deep distress or moral repulsion, such as those that cross the boundary between life and death. This concern is symbolised by the literary figure of Dr Frankenstein,[4] the scientist from Mary Shelley's nineteenth-century novel[5] who creates a sentient being from human corpses, embodying man playing God,[6] and has since become the epitome of the 'yuck factor.'[7]

Kass's hypothesis has faced ongoing criticism,[8] mainly for the risk of giving emotions a central role in ethics. Critics argue this could lead legal and political systems to set limits on personal freedom based on public sentiment and

1 Leon R Kass, 'The Wisdom of Repugnance. Why We Should Ban the Cloning of Human' [1997] The New Republic 17, 18–19.
2 Ibid 20.
3 Ibid 21.
4 Ibid 20.
5 Mary Shelley and Charlotte Gordon, *Frankenstein: The 1818 Text* (1st edition, Penguin Classics 2018).
6 Kass (1776*n*1) 20.
7 Charles W Schmidt, 'The Yuck Factor When Disgust Meets Discovery' (2008) 116 Environmental Health Perspectives A524.
8 John A Terrizzi, Natalie J Shook and W Larry Ventis, 'Disgust: A Predictor of Social Conservatism and Prejudicial Attitudes toward Homosexuals' (2010) 49 Personality and Individual Differences 587.

 | DOI:10.1163/9789004754300_009

prejudice, rather than on rational, objective standards like preventing harm to others.[9]

Despite recognising that instinctive reactions don't determine objective morality or justify broad prohibitions, the unease felt when life and death boundaries blur,[10] such as in cases of babies 'brought into being by a parent from the grave,'[11] is hard to dismiss. This phenomenon endures, notwithstanding the awareness that PAR unequivocally excludes practices such as nocturnal grave-robbing and incursions into slaughterhouses, as dramatised in Mary Shelley's famous novel. As previously stated, current practices in reproductive medicine encompass the implementation of advanced technologies that enable the utilisation of cryopreserved reproductive tissues in a laboratory setting, even long after their extraction from the individuals from whom they originated. These technologies also permit the maintenance of human subjects previously categorised as deceased for a designated duration of time through artificial means, with the objective of retrieving reproductive cells or sustaining a foetus in a gestating female body until the point of delivery. For these reasons, PAR is divided in as planned and unplanned classifications.[12] Planned PAR involves the cryopreservation of gametes, embryos, or tissues prior to death, as exemplified by fertility preservation (FP) prior to gonadotoxic chemotherapy or active-duty military service. In legal systems that recognise PAR, this process generally requires explicit consent from the donor authorising the utilisation of their tissues post-mortem.[13] In contrast, 'unplanned PAR' denotes the retrieval of tissue or gametes from deceased individuals in cases of unexpected death or illness.[14] In particular, male gametes can be retrieved post-mortem within the first hours after death, or (more commonly) taken from the biobank in which they have been previously

9 Martha C Nussbaum, 'Danger to Human Dignity: The Revival of Disgust and Shame in the Law' (*The Chronicle of Higher Education*, 6 August 2004) <https://www.chronicle.com/article/danger-to-human-dignity-the-revival-of-disgust-and-shame-in-the-law/> accessed 10 May 2025.

10 Yael Hashiloni-Dolev and Silke Schicktanz, 'A Cross-Cultural Analysis of Posthumous Reproduction: The Significance of the Gender and Margins-of-Life Perspectives' (2017) 4 Reproductive Biomedicine & Society Online 21, 23.

11 Jason D Hans, 'Attitudes Toward Posthumous Harvesting and Reproduction' (2008) 32 Death Studies 837.

12 Emma Trawick and others, 'Posthumous Assisted Reproduction Policies among a Cohort of United States' in Vitro Fertilization Clinics' (2020) 1 F&S Reports 66.

13 Ibid; Zhang and others (165*n*26) 2841.

14 Trawick and others (177*n*12).

stored. In the case of eggs, retrieval can be performed post-mortem from the woman; alternatively, her eggs may have been frozen.[15] Moreover, as in the initial Chinese case concerning frozen embryos, supernumerary pre-embryos may have been stored by fertility clinics prior to the demise of one or both parents.[16]

It is evident that posthumous births, although not occurring with great frequency, present several challenges from the legal, ethical, social and even anthropological perspective. This is because they pertain to, and interweave, the most significant events in the life of a human being, i.e.: its end and its beginning, questioning their definition and highlighting the different cultural approaches to them. In fact, extending life beyond its physical limits through procreation disrupts the alternation between death and reproduction, which Schopenhauer regarded as the eternal pulse-beats of the human species.[17] Depending on the cultural and social contexts, it can be considered as a source of emotional solace or a fringe scientific anomaly,[18] a way to offer grieving individuals and families a renewed sense of hope in the future that ensures the continuity of the lineage, or a practice associated with necrophilia and incest.[19] We have already found examples of these different attitudes comparing the reactions of Western and Chinese commentators to the birth of Tiantian four years after the death of his parents. However, PAR not only triggers a culturally specific 'yuck factor,' it also raises issues regarding the interests and welfare of the future child, respect for the autonomy of the deceased, and the interest of the living, to which different societies and different legal systems give different answers.[20] This is why no international consensus has emerged, even though PAR has been a controversial issue in Western countries since 1980, when technological progress made it possible.[21] In the last four decades, many states have issued legal provisions to regulate or prohibit it. Among oth-

15 Hashiloni-Dolev and Schicktanz (177*n*10) 24.

16 Usha Ahluwalia and Mala Arora, 'Posthumous Reproduction and Its Legal Perspective' (2011) 2 International Journal of Infertility & Fetal Medicine 9, 10–11.

17 Arthur Schopenhauer, *The World As Will And Idea: 3 vols in 1* (CreateSpace Independent Publishing Platform 2016) 677.

18 Hashiloni-Dolev and Schicktanz (177*n*10) 24.

19 Charlotte Halmø Kroløkke and Stine Willum and Adrian, 'Sperm on Ice: Fatherhood and Life after Death' (2013) 28 Australian Feminist Studies 263.

20 Ahluwalia and Arora (178*n*16) 9–10.

21 CM Rothman, 'A Method for Obtaining Viable Sperm in the Postmortem State' (1980) 34 Fertility and Sterility 512.

ers, Germany,[22] Sweden,[23] the state of Victoria (Australia),[24] France[25] and Italy[26] have passed legislation that forbids PAR, while the UK, the US, and Israel all permit it, under certain conditions.[27] Lin Yun-Hsien Diana has described these policies and regulations' different level of openness toward PAR as a spectrum.[28] One end of this continuum is restrictive, framing the ban on posthumous reproduction generally in terms of human dignity and respect for the body of the deceased, as well as protecting the interests of the child born already orphaned of one of its parents.[29] Moving along the spectrum, some countries have adopted a pro-restrictive approach, i.e., where the written consent of the deceased is required to proceed with posthumous fertilisation (e.g. the province of British Columbia, Canada, or the state of California, USA).[30] In such legal systems, the deceased is required to provide a document stipulating their wishes regarding the utilisation of their gametes for procreative purposes in the event of their demise, while the decision regarding the initiation of posthumous procreation rests with the deceased's spouse.[31] A step removed would be the pro-permissive framework, in which only a reasonably inferred consent by the decedent is required, as is the case for the guidelines set forth by the New York Hospital or Israel.[32] However, only men undergoing fertility

---

22 Sect. 4, paragraph 1, number 1–3, Act for the Protection of the Embryos of the 13th Dec 1990 (BGBI.I p. 2746), last amended by Article 1 of the Law of the 21st Nov. 2011 (BGBI.I p. 2228). See also Matthias Krüger, 'The prohibition of post-mortem-fertilization, legal situation in Germany and European Convention on human rights' (2011) 82 Revue internationale de droit pénal 41.

23 Ch. 6, Article 4 (Choice of Sperm Donor) of the Genetic Integrity Act, Swedish Code of Statutes no 2006:351 of the 18th of May 2006.

24 Ahluwalia and Arora (178*n*16) 11.

25 L. 2141–2, number 1 of the Public Health Code of the 8th November 2023.

26 Article 5 of the Rules on Medical Assisted Procreation, Law 19th February 2004, n. 40. See also 'Dalle tecniche di preservazione della fertilitá all'utilizzo con finalitá riproduttiva post mortemdi embrioni e gamete crioconservati l'esperienza giuridica italiana, francese e spagnola a confronto' (*Revista Actualidad Jurídica Iberoamericana*) <https://revista-aji.com/dalle-tecniche-di-preservazione-della-fertilita-allutilizzo-con-finalita-riproduttiva-post-mortemdi-embrioni-e-gamete-crioconservati-lesperienza-giuridica-italiana-francese-e-spagnola-a-c-2/> accessed 22 May 2025.

27 Ahluwalia and Arora (178*n*16) 11.

28 Lin Yun-Hsien Diana, 'Posthumous Assisted Reproduction in the East Asian Context: Towards a Comprehensive Framework of Regulation' (2013) 5 Asian Bioethics Review 93, 95.

29 Ibid.

30 Ibid.

31 Ibid 95–96.

32 Ibid 95.

treatment, who are trying to conceive, or who have specifically expressed a wish to become parents in the near future, are considered eligible for post-mortem procreation.[33] At the other far end of the spectrum is the permissive approach, predicated on the assumption that the decedent's desire to become a parent is an inherent aspect of the individual's character, unless there is explicit evidence to suggest otherwise.[34] Here, respect for the deceased is understood to imply the fulfilment of their natural procreative interest.[35] This category is somewhat borderline, as virtually no legal system in the world falls into it.

An additional category of states, although not incorporated in the classification under discussion, nevertheless possesses numerical significance: countries that have not (yet?) regulated PAR. As we have noted, this is the case with the PRC; however, many other so-called 'Sinic societies,' i.e.: those influenced by Chinese cultural norms,[36] such as Vietnam, Japan, Korea and Taiwan, also lack explicit rules for PAR.[37] To be precise, over the years, Vietnam and Taiwan in particular have promulgated regulations that could effectively prevent the performance of PAR. With regard to Vietnam, the provision is contained in Article 8 of Decree 12/2003/ND-CP, which states that 'in the event of the death of the sperm donor, the sperm storage facility must destroy that person's sperm count.'[38] Until recently, Vietnamese practitioners interpreted this rule as a general duty to dispose of gametes after death, thus making it impossible (at least in theory) to proceed with PAR.[39] As has been noted by several scholars, it is not clear whether the Vietnamese legislature at the beginning of the twenty-first century genuinely intended to proscribe PAR, or whether this was a mere oversight.[40] Conversely, the introduction of a similar rule in Taiwan followed the first request for posthumous reproduction. The incident occurred in 2005, when Sun Chi-hsiang, a Taiwanese military officer, succumbed to injuries sustained from being struck by a tank.[41] In the aftermath,

33 Ibid 96.
34 Ibid 95.
35 Ibid 96.
36 Hai Thanh Doan, Diep Thi Phuong Doan and Nguyen Kim The Duong, 'Post-Mortem Reproduction from a Vietnamese Perspective an Analysis and Commentary' (2020) 12 Asian Bioethics Review 257, 258.
37 Lee Kyung-hee 이경희, 'A Study on the Decision-Making framework for Posthumous Reproduction' (2007) 21 Korean Journal of Family Law 207.
38 Doan, Doan and Duong (180*n*36) 259.
39 Ibid.
40 Ibid.
41 Diana (179*n*28) 93.

his fiancée, Li Hsin-yu, requested the retrieval of Sun Chi-hsiang's sperm for the purpose of artificial insemination, with the intention of conceiving a child. The Taiwanese Department of Health (DoH) initially expressed opposition to the request for the extraction of sperm from a corpse. However, following significant public pressure, the DoH ultimately granted approval for the procedure and its subsequent cryopreservation. The latter operation enabled the DoH to convene a panel of scholars and experts to determine whether PAR should be permitted in the country. The panel expressed opposition to Li's request, and Sun's sperm was destroyed.[42] The rule was subsequently incorporated into the Artificial Reproduction Act (*Rengong shengzhi fa* 人工生殖法) of the Republic of China, which was enacted on 21 March 2007 and last revised on 3 January 2018. In accordance with Article 11 of the Act, the performance of HART in Taiwan is restricted to married couples who 'have been diagnosed as suffering from infertility or as being diagnosed as suffering from a major hereditary disease designated by the competent authority, and it is suspected that natural conception and birth will cause abnormal children' (Article 11, point 2). Furthermore, at least one of the spouses must be capable of producing healthy gametes (Article 11, point 3). In any event, as stated in Article 21, paragraph 2, number 2, cryopreserved gametes must be destroyed upon the death of one of the gamete providers.[43]

It is interesting to note that in both Vietnam and Taiwan, the enactment of these regulations has not brought the debate on the issue to a conclusion,[44] nor has it ended the use of this reproductive technology. On the contrary, the Vietnamese and Taiwanese public and relevant public bodies and courts often recognise PAR as legitimate,[45] as is also the case in Japan, Korea or the PRC. In Japan, for example, between 2001 and 2004, at least four children were born through PAR,[46] and the courts have decided cases on the subject since then.[47]

It is imperative to emphasise this point because in numerous authoritative publications dedicated to the comparative analysis of PAR, Sino-Confucian

42 Ibid.

43 Ibid 94.

44 Ethan Dean-Richards Lih Kris, 'The Unusual Shape of the Debate Around Fertility Treatment in Taiwan' (*Domino Theory*, 3 May 2024) <https://dominotheory.com/the-unusual-shape-of-the-debate-around-fertility-treatment-in-taiwan/> accessed 13 May 2025.

45 Doan, Doan and Duong (180*n*36) 259–261.

46 Noriyuki Ueda and others, 'Study of Views on Posthumous Reproduction, Focusing on Its Relation with Views on Family and Religion in Modern Japan' (2008) 62 Acta Medica Okayama 285, 285.

47 Ibid.

countries, including the PRC, are frequently listed among those with an explicit legal ban on PAR.[48] As we can see from more detailed cases in the PRC, this is a mistake, or at least an oversimplification, that completely overlooks the role of case law and ignores statute law, or the lack thereof, in these countries, failing to take into account the cultural and ethical issues related to PAR in this part of the world.

Fortunately, not all authors succumb to this misconception. Indeed, recent studies devoted specifically to Japan,[49] Vietnam,[50] Korea,[51] and Taiwan[52] recognise the complexity of the issue, which they often explain by resorting to the Sino-Confucian legacy and its influence on cultural and legal attitudes towards the practice. Authors in the PRC adopt a similar approach when discussing the cultural and moral rational that underpin the support for PAR from Chinese citizens and, to a certain extent, the people's courts.

In the ensuing pages, I will pursue this model, with a view to identifying which elements of traditional Chinese culture may influence the Chinese 'yuck factor' (or the lack of it) in relation to this biotechnology, and which principles, as determined by contemporary Chinese bioethicists, should be given due consideration when assessing its morality. This will serve as background for understanding the *de iure condendo* solutions proposed by Chinese doctrine, and the solutions adopted by the people's courts in deciding posthumous procreation cases.

2 PAR in the PRC, between Chinese Traditional Ethics and Contemporary Bioethics

Posthumous reproduction, defined as the process of conception subsequent to the demise of one or both of the gamete suppliers, is the consequence of a scientific advancement that would have been inconceivable until a few decades ago. Before this, the only posthumous births that took place were the

---

48 'Posthumous Reproduction Practice Is Regulated' (*WHO Data*) <https://platform.who.int/data/sexual-and-reproductive-health-and-rights/national-policies/srh/practices-that-are-regulated-posthumous-reproduction> accessed 5 June 2025; 'Chapter 7: Posthumous Insemination' (2007) 87 Fertility and Sterility S26.

49 Ueda and others (181*n*46).

50 Doan, Doan and Duong (180*n*36).

51 Lee Kyung-hee 이경희 (189*n*37).

52 Diana (179*n*28).

result of conceptions from sexual intercourse during the deceased's lifetime.[53] From an ethical perspective, such births were no more problematic than other births. In this sense, PAR differs from abortion, a custom observed in China and elsewhere since antiquity, and from surrogacy, which in its 'traditional' form has been a part of Chinese culture and legislation since imperial times. The first reported instance of PAR in the PRC occurred in 2001 in Zhejiang Province, where the wife of an executed prisoner, Zheng Xueli, demanded the retrieval of sperm following her husband's death. The court rejected the plaintiff's request.[54] The first planned PAR happened four years later, in 2004, in Guangdong Province, when a married man undergoing fertility treatment died in a traffic accident. The wife demanded to continue the HART procedure, using the 13 embryos stored at the Reproductive Centre of Guangdong Maternal and Child Health Hospital so that she could give birth to a posthumous child. The hospital refused, in accordance with the stipulations of EPIHARTSB 2003, which prohibits the implementation of HART for single women as a way to protect the principle of public interest.[55] The wife appealed and, after three months, the MoH sent a letter to the Guangdong Provincial Department of Health allowing the wife to continue her treatment. After another three months and a succession of complaints, the MoH issued a second letter to the Guangdong Provincial Department of Health, which eventually authorised the wife to complete the artificial reproduction process. This constitutes the inaugural clinical case in China in which a wife was treated with HART using existing frozen embryos subsequent to the death of her husband.[56]

---

53 Li Yan 李琰, Li Jun 李军 and Lan Liji 兰礼吉, 'Sihou Shenzhi Wenti de Shengming Sikao 死后生殖问题的生命伦理学思考 (Thinking on Bioethics in the Reproduction after Death)' (2007) 28 Yixue yu zhexue 医学与哲学 32, 32.

54 Wang Liqing 汪丽青, 'Lun Meiguo Fa Shang Sihou Shengzhi Haizi de Liyi Baohu Ji Qi Dui Woguo de Qishi 论美国法上死后生殖孩子的利益保护及其对我国的启示 (Study on the Protection of the Interests of the Children Born by Posthumously Reproduction in the U.S. and Its Enlightenment to China)' (2020) 33 Yixue yu shehui 医学与社会 130, 133; Zhang and others (136*n*199) 2841; Yu Jiajia 于佳佳, 'Renlei fuzhu shengzhi jishu yinyong fanwei de falü tiaozheng lun 类辅助生殖技术应用范围的法律调整论 (A Discussion on the Legal Adjustments to the Scope of Application of Assisted Reproductive Technologies)' [2024] Jiao Da faxue 交大法学 94, 103.

55 Weisheng bu 卫生部, 'Weisheng bu guanyu xiuding renlei fuzhu shengzhi jishu yu renlei jingzi ku xiangguan jishu guifan, jiben biaozhun he luli yuanze de tongzhi 卫生部关于修订人类辅助生殖技术与人类精子库相关技术规范、基本标准和伦理原则的通知 (Notice of the Ministry of Health on the Revision of Technical Specifications, Basic Standards, and Ethical Principles Related to Human Assisted Reproductive Technology and Human Sperm Banks)' (n 942) apps 3, Part I (4) 1.

56 Li Lei 李磊 and Shen Yanru 沈燕如, 'Sihou Renlei Shengzhi de Lunli Sikao 死后人工生殖的伦理思考 (Ethical Thinking of Post-Mortem Artificial Reproduction)' (2021) 42

Despite the recent cases related to PAR and the novelty of the biotechnologies it involves, when commenting on the phenomenon from a legal or ethical point of view, Chinese authors invariably refer to values and principles that are deeply rooted in Chinese cultural tradition. In the following discussion, I will briefly examine these principles and how they may influence the moral evaluation of this controversial HART.

2.1 *PAR and Chinese Traditional Ethics*

In earlier sections, it was noted how Confucian thought assigns a central role to the family unit, conceptualised as the foundational 'cell of society.' It is imperative to return to this subject to accentuate an additional characteristic of the family: namely, its capacity to overcome temporal and spatial limitations.[57] In fact, unlike its constituent individual members, family is not subject to birth and death; rather, it can endure in perpetuity.[58] In order for the family, as a sacred entity, to bestow immortality upon its past members, its current members must uphold the integrity, continuity, and prosperity of the family unit.[59] Procreation functions as a foundational mechanism for the perpetuation of the lineage in a patrilineal context, thereby ensuring the veneration and respect of its ancestors. From this perspective, the commitment to nurturing offspring and honouring ancestors becomes a fundamental obligation and an integral component of the self-realisation and self-fulfilment of the noble man, the *junzi*.[60] Conversely, the failure to fulfil these responsibilities is deemed '*bu yi*' (不义), i.e.: a violation of the fundamental principle of righteousness.[61] In practice, a man's most significant obligation is to ensure the continuation of his lineage by producing at least one (ideally male) heir who will inherit his ancestors' qi 气 (vital energy), oversee the ritual offerings to their spirits, and contribute sons to perpetuate the lineage.[62] The traditional Chinese concep-

Yixue yu zhexue 医学与哲学 34, 34–35; Wang Liqing 汪丽青 (n 1036) 133; Zhang and others (136*n*199) 2841.

57 Sun Jitao, 'Between Emotion and Reason: The Judicial Practice of Disputes Involving Frozen Embryos in China' (2024) 12 Peking University Law Journal 83, 97.

58 Ibid.

59 Fan Ruiping 范瑞平, *Dangdai Rujia shengming lunli xue* 当代儒家生命伦理学 (*Contemporary Confucian Bioethics* (Beijing daxue chubanshe 北京大学出版社 2011) 9.

60 Wang Qingjie, 'The Confucian Filial Obligation and Care for Aged Parents', *Confucian Bioethics* (Springer, Dordrecht 1999) 248–249 <https://link.springer.com/chapter/10.1007/0-306-46867-0_10> accessed 8 June 2025.

61 Ibid 249.

62 Francesca Bray, 'Becoming a Mother in Late Imperial China: Maternal Doubles and the Ambiguities of Fertility', *Chinese Kinship* (Routledge 2008) 185.

tion of the ideal family unit is encapsulated by notions of 'blood continuation' (*xueyuan yuanxu* 血缘延续) and 'son and grandson fill the hall' (*zisun mantang* 子孙满堂).[63] In addition, Confucian orthodoxy regarded the notion of 'continuing the lifeline of the family' (*yangxu jiazu mingmai* 延续家族命脉) as paramount within the context of childbirth,[64] and the absence of a male heir as the gravest of the three cardinal sins against filial piety (*buxiao you san wu hou weida* 不孝有三无后为大).[65] In this context, as dictated by social public morality, marriage is considered a prerequisite for reproduction.[66] This results in a model defined as 'marriage-reproduction-heir' (*jiehun-shengyu-jisi* 婚姻 – 生育 – 继嗣) in which women not only lack independent family status or even a personality, but are also regarded as a mere instrument for producing offspring and continuing the family line.[67] Women's reproductive rights are thus both absorbed by the marital relationship and subordinate to it as a status relationship. The question of whether a woman is in a marital relationship therefore becomes a crucial factor that affects her fertility.[68]

The traditional gender-based reproductive approach has important implications for the current Chinese legal attitude towards PAR, particularly when the surviving spouse is a woman who wishes to continue assisted reproduction treatment that began while her husband was still alive. In fact, whether widows can independently enjoy reproductive rights remains controversial. In particular, some legal scholars argue that reproductive rights depend on the existence of a marital relationship, based on the specific status of spouses,[69] while others contend that reproductive rights belong to the marital union and

63 Shi Lei 石雷 and Zhan Luxia 占 泸霞, '"Gongneng Jiegou" She Yu Xia Woguo Daiyun Zhidu de Goujian '功能结构' 视 域下我国代孕制度的构建 (The Construction of a Chinese System of Surrogacy from the Perspective of Structural Functionalism)' (2019) 79 Haixia Faxue 海峡法学 74, 79.

64 Ibid.

65 Ibid.

66 Zhu Xiaofeng 朱晓峰, 'Lun Di Shengyu Lü Shidai de Shengyu Quan Xingshi Guize 论低生育率时代的生育权行使规则 (On the Rules for the Exercise of Reproductive Rights in an Era of Low Fertility' (2004) 273 shehui kexue jikan 社会科学辑刊 59, 61.

67 Ibid.

68 Ibid 62.

69 Fan Linlin 樊林林, 'Shengyu Quan Tanxi 生育权探析 (Analysis of Reproductive Rights)' [2009] Faxue 32; Yang Linping 阳林平, 'Shengyu Quan Zhi Gainian Fenxi 生育权之概念分析 (Conceptual Analysis of Reproductive Rights)' Falü shiyong 法律适用 32; Wang Linwei 王林卫, 'Lun Woguo Shengyu Quan Gongfa Tiaojie de Fanwei He Bianjie 论我国生育权公法调节的范围和边界 (On the Scope and Boundary of Public Law Regulation of Reproductive Rights in My Country)' [2020] Renmin luntan – Xuexu qianyan 人民论坛•学术前沿, 108.

should be jointly exercised by both spouses.[70] These two perspectives, combined with the prohibition to perform HART on single women imposed on medical institutions by the EPIHARTSB 2003 make the exercise of reproductive rights contingent upon the 'continuation of the marital relationship.' Therefore, once the husband dies and the marital relationship is dissolved, widows face significant uncertainties in exercising their reproductive rights. It is worth mentioning that in the most recent years, both legal doctrine and judicial courts seem to have overcome this approach, and have started to recognise what define as an 'autonomous' reproduction right for (widowed) women.[71] This important recognition – certainly linked in part to the demographic policy changes underway in China – should not overshadow another trend equally present in Chinese decisions. The widow's ability to exercise her (autonomous?) reproductive right is subject to the court's ascertainment of the husband's wish to continue with the assisted reproduction procedure even after his death. In many cases, the courts also require that the plaintiff's request include the consent of the deceased's parents. Even if the latter role in the decision could be linked to the idea of the parents as 'the best people to determine the intent of their child when it came to procreation,'[72] I consider this tendency as first and foremost a traditional legacy linked to the role of the family in Chinese traditional life, and to what has been framed by certain legal scholarship as the 'deceased's parent interest in grandparenthood.'[73]

From this perspective, the concept of *xiao*, understood in its original meaning, emerges as a fundamental element. As Wang Qinghie has observed,[74] the concept of filial piety in the traditional Chinese context is not perceived as a moral responsibility, as is the case in some Western philosophical interpretations,[75] where it is considered a self-imposed burden, i.e.: a consensual, con-

---

70 Shi Jiayou 石佳友 and Ceng Jia 曾 佳, 'Shou Renlei Fuzhu Shengzhi Shengyu Zinü de Quanyi Baohu 死后人类辅助生殖生育子女的权益保护 (The Protection of the Rights and Interests of Children Born through Human Assisted Reproduction after Death)' [2023] Falü shiyong 法律适用 35.

71 Chen Zhaoyang 陈兆阳 and Zhang Boyuan 张博源, 'Sang'ou nuxing lendong peitai yizhi de hefa xing zhi bian 丧偶女性冷冻胚胎移植的合法性之辩 (Debate on the Legality of Frozen Embryo Transfer for Widowed Women)' (2025) 46 Yixue yu Zhexue 医学与哲学 46.

72 Doan, Doan and Duong (180*n*36) 288.

73 Shelly Simana, 'Creating Life after Death: Should Posthumous Reproduction Be Legally Permissible without the Deceased's Prior Consent?' (2018) 5 Journal of Law and the Biosciences 329, 352–354.

74 Wang, 'The Confucian Filial Obligation and Care for Aged Parents' (184*n*60) 235.

75 Norman Daniels, *Am I My Parents' Keeper?: An Essay on Justice Between the Young and the Old* (Oxford University Press 1988); Jane English, 'What Do Grown Children Owe

tractarian and voluntary obligation.[76] Conversely, Confucian tradition sees it as a moral obligation, characterised by its 'existential, communal and historical' nature;[77] 'filial duty is not limited to the moral obligation towards parents; it extends to all familial predecessors.'[78] Upon entering her husband's family unit, a woman is obligated to honour and care for the family's ancestors as part of her marital duties. This includes fulfilling her husband's reproductive wishes, which focus on ensuring the continuity of their family. In modern times, this traditional moral duty may influence the surviving wife's decision to undergo HART as a sign of respect for the deceased and his ancestors; in particular, if the deceased is a married, childless, only-child male, his friends and relatives may voice the strongest demand for PAR.[79]

According to some Chinese scholars, all the above factors would align medical activities related to PAR with social ethics. The same scholars, however, also remark that, although social ethics and medical ethics are intertwined in the field of medicine, when it comes to evaluating medical activities, medical ethics should take precedence over social ethics. This is because medical ethics has more stringent requirements, making it more compatible with the specificity of medicine, which should not undergo arbitrary changes to its mandate to treat diseases. In their view, the deceased's lack of descendants and the technical feasibility of PAR do not automatically justify its use. On the contrary, before allowing PAR, a preliminary reflection on the phenomenon in light of contemporary bioethical principles is necessary.[80]

On the following pages, I will analyse the bioethical principles that Chinese scholars deem relevant to PAR, to ascertain whether their discourse exhibits Chinese characteristics and, if so, how these align with the primary European and American bioethical theories outlined in the first chapter.

2.2 *PAR and Contemporary Bioethics*

It is noteworthy that the ethical analyses of PAR revolve around a shared principle of respect (*zunzhong* 尊重), which functions as a litmus test to evaluate medical actions in general, and the moral acceptability of this specific biotechnology related to the beginning of life in particular. The concept draws on

---

Their Parents?', *Aging And Ethics* (Humana Press, Totowa, NJ 1992) <https://link.springer.com/chapter/10.1007/978-1-4612-0423-7_6> accessed 10 June 2025.

76 Wang, 'The Confucian Filial Obligation and Care for Aged Parents' (180*n*36) 236.

77 Ibid.

78 Doan, Doan and Duong (180*n*36) 264.

79 Simana (186*n*73) 350; Neil Maddox, 'Children of the Dead: Posthumous Conception, Critical Interests and Consent' (2020) 27 Journal of Law and Medicine 645, 650.

80 Li Lei 李磊 and Shen Yanru 沈燕如 (183*n*56) 36.

Chinese cultural tradition: the existence of the first of the two component characters, *zun* 尊, can be traced to the Shang Dynasty (c. 1600–1046 BC), when it initially denoted the wine vessel used by the ruler for ritual sacrifices. However, over time, it evolved to signify 'noble' or 'respectable,' both in the sense of the elevated status of a class of people or natural beings and the attitude one has to show towards them.[81] It is exactly with that meaning that the principle, expressed as *zunzun* 尊尊, was included in the Rites of the Zhou (*Zhou Li* 周礼, approx. second century BC) and listed among the basic principles the king should implement to 'harmonise Heaven with morality' and earn the continuing right to rule.[82] It later became the model for the elaboration of the Confucian 'Great tradition' supporting the formation and consolidation of the imperial state. In the latter context, the concept of *zun* embodied the principle of distinguishing between classes, the core element of which was the recognition of the king as the head of the political structure, in a manner analogous to the father as the head of the family unit.[83]

Contemporary Chinese bioethicists appear to have re-established *zun* as a central tenet, while revising its content and reinterpreting the predominant modern bioethical theories from Europe and North America to incorporate it. This conclusion is supported by a review of the extant literature on the subject, which, it should be noted, consists of very few examples. In this corpus, the article published in 2007 on *Yixue yu zhexue* (医学与哲学, Litt.: Medical Science and Philosophy) by Li Yan, Li Ji and Lan Liji, which commented on one of the first cases of PAR in the PRC,[84] is of particular interest. The paper argues that the principle of respect is implied in the Kantian Categorical Imperative, expressed here as the duty to 'respect human beings rather than use them as means or tools.'[85] This inclusion of the principle of respect, even if absent from the original formulation, does not significantly alter the meaning of the Kant's Categorical Imperative. However, in other cases, the dissonance between the Western model and its Chinese counterpart is evident. For example, in a paper

81 Jimmy Chia-Shin Hsu, 'Human Dignity in the Jurisprudence of the Taiwan Constitutional Court' in Jimmy Chia-Shin Hsu (ed), *Human Dignity in Asia: Dialogue between Law and Culture* (Cambridge University Press 2022) 88 <https://www.cambridge.org/core/books/human-dignity-in-asia/human-dignity-in-the-jurisprudence-of-the-taiwan-constitutional-court/13B4E1A4A534CDB8BFFD565FFCDE92AD> accessed 17 March 2024.

82 John W Head and Wang Yanping, *Law Codes in Dynastic China. A Synopsis of Chinese Legal History in the Third Centuries from Zhou to Qing* (Carolina Academic Press 2005) 28–30.

83 Ibid 30.

84 Li Yan 李 琰, Li Jun 李 军 and Lan Liji 兰礼吉 (183*n*53).

85 Li Lei 李磊 and Shen Yanru 沈燕如 (183*n*56) 33.

published in 2021 in the same review,[86] Li Lei and Shen Yanru regard the principle of respect (*zuzhong yuanzi* 尊重原则) as one of the fundamental tenets of medical ethics, alongside the principles of non-maleficence (*bu shanghai* 不伤害), beneficence (*youli* 有利), and justice (*gongzheng* 公正).[87] In practice, the authors have adopted the four principles of bioethics developed by Beauchamp and Childress, substituting the principle of autonomy with the principle of respect, which they evidently consider to bear a similar meaning.[88]

From a Western standpoint, perceiving the potential semantic equivalence of these two concepts is challenging, and the situation does not improve when one examines the sense in which the principle of respect is used to assess the ethical acceptability of PAR. Instead, an initial observation suggests that Chinese bioethicists' interpretation of 'respect' (*zunzhong* 尊重,) is closely associated with the concept of dignity (*zunyan* 尊严). The authors reference and even explicitly mention dignity when they discuss, for instance, the morality of post-mortem sperm retrieval. In this case, they emphasise the potential mutilation of the corpse, violating the dignity of the deceased and (therefore) the principle of respect.[89] The same use of 'respect' in the sense of 'dignity' emerges in issues pertaining to the privacy of the deceased. In fact, this right is frequently violated by the Chinese media and newspapers in case involving PAR, due to the public interest aroused by this HART. Chinese scholars posit that, also in such occurrences, PAR constitutes a transgression against the respect owed to a deceased individual, or (more precisely) his or her personal dignity.[90] In my opinion, a more precise analogy can be drawn between the concept of 'respect' as employed by Chinese bioethicists and the Western conception of 'autonomy' in the context of evaluating the ethical acceptability of the decision by relatives and friends to proceed with PAR using the remains of their beloved.[91] In fact, Chinese bioethicists reject the concept of treating the human body or human tissues as legal entities or objects that can be transferred through inheritance. With no legal right to the deceased's gametes, relatives and friends have no control over their disposition.[92] Furthermore, the decision to perform PAR in cases where the deceased has not explicitly given consent when alive would also constitute a violation of their right to

86 Li Lei 李磊 and Shen Yanru 沈燕如 (183*n*56).

87 Ibid 36.

88 Ibid.

89 Ibid.

90 Ibid.

91 Li Yan 李琰, Li Jun 李军 and Lan Liji 兰礼吉 (183*n*53) 33; Li Lei 李磊 and Shen Yanru 沈燕如 (183*n*56) 36.

92 Li Lei 李磊 and Shen Yanru 沈燕如 (183*n*56) 36.

informed consent and contradict the principle of respect, as understood by Chinese authors.[93] This principle still applies even in circumstances where the individual has opted to cryopreserve their gametes before their demise, or when they have given the consent just before dying, i.e.: in situations where they would be extremely susceptible to acquiescing to the wishes of friends or family members.[94] It is only in the presence of a considered and rational declaration, in writing or an audio-visual recording in a reasonable amount of time before the demise of the individual concerned, that PAR can be said to comply with the respect due to the deceased.[95]

Nonetheless, even in circumstances where the deceased has provided informed and explicit consent, PAR may still be deemed to lack moral soundness. Indeed, as posited by Chinese scholars, an additional factor merits consideration when considering these issues: the interests of the child who is yet to be born. The authors consider it in term of 'intergenerational justice' (*daiji zhengyii* 代际正义), quoting Rawls's reference to the notion of 'justice as fairness,' and (again!) respect that the current generation should show to the next generation.[96] In particular, they adopt the standpoint of 'basic family ethics' (*jiben de jiating lunli* 基本的家庭伦理), with marriage regarded as the most significant environment for a child's education and socialisation.[97] The child's right to a 'complete family' is acknowledged, unless the absence of one parent is attributable to unforeseen circumstances. From this standpoint, PAR can be regarded as 'unfair' and therefore unethical, since it condemns the child to exist within the paradigm of an 'incomplete family' even before conception, and to confront the economic, social and psychological challenges typically encountered by children born into single-parent families.[98]

Another aspect Chinese authors always mention involves the damage that PAR can potentially cause to social order. Since a marriage union dissolves when a spouse dies, allowing PAR could transform the right to procreate, originally shared by both spouses, into a unilateral decision exercised by one individual that erodes the principal of equality, a potentially slippery slope. Indeed, the question must be posed: Why should a widow be permitted to use her late husband's gametes, while a widower should not? Furthermore, what

93 Li Yan 李 琰, Li Jun 李 军 and Lan Liji 兰礼吉 (183*n*53) 36; Li Lei 李磊 and Shen Yanru 沈燕如 (183*n*56) 36.

94 Li Lei 李磊 and Shen Yanru 沈燕如 (183*n*56) 36.

95 Ibid.

96 Li Yan 李 琰, Li Jun 李 军 and Lan Liji 兰礼吉 (183*n*53) 33.

97 Ibid.

98 Ibid.

considerations apply in the case of individuals who have never entered into matrimony? In what ways do their requests to procreate differ from the aforementioned case?[99]

In view of these considerations, Chinese bioethicists draw an unambiguous conclusion about the morality of PAR. Since death is not an ailment or a pathology, but integral to the human condition, PAR cannot be considered a medical treatment for a disease. In fact, unlike other HART, PAR does not help an infertile couple establish a sound family; rather, it enables the creation of a life merely to satisfy the emotional needs of the deceased's relatives and friends, or to continue a family's bloodline. Moreover, it could negatively impact the healthy growth of a child, disrupt natural order, and even damage social stability. As with any medical technology divorced from natural, social, humanistic, or ethical factors, it should therefore be prohibited.[100]

This position is well-founded, and motivated both by a sense of prudence and the acknowledgement that 'there are "no-go areas" in medicine, and there are red lines in medical technology.'[101] However, Chinese bioethicists recognise that scientific progress advances at an accelerated rate, rapidly leaving behind legal norms, and even imposing changes to ethical principles and norms.[102] In light of these concerns, as early as 2007, Li Yan, Li Jun, and Li Yiji proposed a series of measures to address the challenges posed by advancements in HART, including the establishment of an interdisciplinary committee for human and embryonic reproduction, which would collaborate with public health bodies to oversee, standardise and update the application of reproductive technologies from an ethical and scientific perspective,[103] as well as the establishment of a robust legal framework to oversee HART.[104] So far, neither measure has been considered. In the meantime, Chinese courts have adjudicated a growing number of PAR cases, lending further credence to the hypothesis that medical ethicists' criticisms little affect its acceptance from a social ethics standpoint.

Consequently, it is imperative to analyse the matter from the perspectives of legal theory and practice.

99 Li Lei 李磊 and Shen Yanru 沈燕如 (183*n*56) 36.
100 Ibid 37.
101 Ibid.
102 Li Yan 李 琰, Li Jun 李 军 and Lan Liji 兰礼吉 (183*n*53) 36.
103 Ibid.
104 Ibid.

3 PAR in Chinese Legal Theory and Practice

3.1 *PAR in Chinese Legal Theory*

The ability to use frozen gametes and embryos for reproductive purposes rendered post-mortem fertilisation a reality. Ever since, Chinese legal scholars have focused on defining the status and nature of these entities. A review of research published as of 2024 found 86 cases concerning frozen embryos, since the first case in 2014; 54 of those cases (representing the first major group and accounting for 63% of all frozen embryos disputes) concerned lawsuits filed by couples against hospitals for the return of their frozen embryos. The second major group comprised twenty-eight cases (33% of all frozen-embryo disputes) involving situations where either one or both parents had died and the surviving partner (or both partners' parents) initiated legal action against the medical institution to either proceed with the implantation, fulfilling the original medical service contract, or return the frozen embryos.[105] In light of the increasing (albeit relative) significance in case law, in particular during the drafting of the CC, certain jurists in the PRC proposed including a provision that would elucidate the topic, thereby providing judges with a definitive foundation for their decisions. It is noteworthy that these recommendations frequently allude to the decision that initiated the present research, suggesting that the legislature should adhere to its interpretation of the status of the embryo as a 'special object with personal interests' (*you renge liyi de teshu wu* 有人格利益的特殊物).[106]

Five years following the ratification of the Civil Code, these appeals have yet to be given due consideration. The absence of a specific provision within the Chinese legal system could thus provide a justification for the continued interest of PRC legal scholars in solutions found in other countries, with particular attention given to foreign case law.

The United States is the primary reference point in this regard. Indeed, as has been demonstrated, the nation has historically dominated the field of biotechnology research, at least until the recent rise of the PRC. Furthermore (or consequently), the major doctrines concerning the status of frozen embryos have been developed in the US. I am referring to the theories set

105 Sun (184*n*57) 87.

106 Wu Guide 吴桂德, 'Deguo Fa Shang Renlei Tiwai Peitai de Falü Baohu Ji Qi Jiejian 德国法上人类体外胚胎的法律保护及其借鉴 Legal Protection of the Human Embryos In-Vitro-Fertilization in German Laws and Its Reference' [2020] Jiaoda Faxue 交大法学 86, 97.

forth in the *York v. Jones* (1989)[107] and *Davis v. Davis* (1992)[108] decisions. In *York v. Jones*, the court was tasked with determining the legal ownership of frozen embryos between the couple who had provided them and the medical institution in which they were stored. The court concluded that the parties had formed a bailment contract by mutually signing a Cryopreservation Agreement, which explicitly considered the embryos the personal property of the embryos' providers.[109] In establishing the rights of the Yorks over their embryos, the court also established the 'object/property theory' for the first time. Conversely, *Davis v. Davis* concerned the right to dispose of frozen embryos in case of divorce. The trial court, adopting the assumption that life begins at birth, considered the frozen embryos to be 'children in vitro' of the couple. Accordingly, within the paradigm of the 'limited natural person theory,' the custody of the embryos was conferred on the wife, who was regarded as being better suited to act in the best interests of the (in vitro) children by ensuring their birth, as opposed to destruction.[110] The initial ruling was reversed on appeal, quoting as reference the precedent set by *Yok v. Jones*;[111] upon a further appeal, the Tennessee Supreme Court eventually provided the final ruling on the matter. Quoting in its decision the Ethical guidelines proposed by the American Fertility Association,[112] the court declared that frozen embryos 'are not, strictly speaking, either persons or property, but occupy an interim category that entitles them to special respect because of their potential for human life.'[113] It is worth remarking that, until very recently, the 'intermediate entity theory' constitutes the majority view in American doctrine and case law, influencing many countries in the world, including the PRC. In fact, as noted in Chapter Four, the Chinese judges drew inspiration from this theory in deciding the first case concerning frozen embryos. Nevertheless, recent events, particularly the infamous overturning of *Roe v. Wade* by the US Supreme Court in 2022, suggest a possible shift in the American approach. The first sign of this change can be found in the February 2024 Alabama Supreme Court decision in *LePage v. Center for Reproductive Medicine*,[114]

107 *York v Jones* (1989) 717 F Supp 421 (Dist Court).

108 *Davis v. Davis* (99*n*29).

109 *York v. Jones* (193*n*107).

110 *Davis v. Davis* (99*n*29) para 42.

111 Ibid 50.

112 'Ethical Considerations of the New Reproductive Technologies. Ethics Committee of The American Fertility Society' (1990) 53 Fertility and Sterility 1S, s 35.

113 *Davis v. Davis* (99*n*29) para 63.

114 *LePage v Center for Reproductive Medicine, PC* [2024] Alabama Supreme Court SC-2022–0515.

where the court ruled on the applicability of Alabama's Wrongful Death of a Minor Act, § 6–5–391, Ala. Code 1975 to the destruction of five embryos stored in a cryogenic nursery. The statute allows parents of a deceased child to recover punitive damages for their child's death; in considering its pertinence to the case, the court recognised that frozen embryos have legal status analogous to that of human children or adults.[115] In a 2025 article on PAR in China, Sun Jitao quotes all of these judgments, focusing on the latter to emphasise the controversy it has sparked, in particular the accusation, by the American Society for Reproductive Medicine, that it is a 'ruling without medical or scientific basis.'[116] The author himself considers it as a product of the current political and religious climate in the United States,[117] which in the last few years has contributed to an even deeper ideological and cultural divide between the PRC and the US. Given the fact that US court decisions concerning the status of embryos principally concern divorce disputes, with little relevance to PAR, Chinese comparative law scholars view the recent US approach with a certain degree of disinterest. Instead, they have directed their attention towards other legal systems, particularly in Europe.[118]

Among those that have been analysed in the greatest detail, the French legal system stands out.[119] In France, PAR has been explicitly prohibited since 1994 by Article 2141–2 of the Code de la Santé Publique (in force since the 7th of October 1953, hereafter: CdlSP).[120] Over the decades, the article has undergone numerous amendments, the latest of which, in 2021, significantly changed the French approach to assisted reproduction. Nowadays, the law no longer regards HART merely as a treatment for infertility but defines it as a means of fulfilling a parental project, to which heterosexual couples, lesbian

115 Ibid.

116 Sun (184*n*57) 84.

117 Ibid 85.

118 Yu Jiajia 于佳佳 (183*n*54) 101.

119 Ye Mingyi 葉名怡, 'Faguo Fa Shang de Rengong Peitai 法国法上的人工胚胎' [2015] Huadong Zhengfa Daxue xuebao 华东政法大学学报 35; Zeng Pingjie 曾品杰, 'Lun Rengong Peitai Zhi Falü Diwei 论人工胚胎之法律地位——从法国法谈起 (The Legality of Artificial Insemination: From the Perspective of French Law)' [2016] Jiao Da faxue 交大法学 97; Wang Liqing 汪丽青, 'Lendong Peitai Si Hou Shengzhi Yunyong de Falü Peitai Si Hou Shengzhi Yunyong de Falü Guizhi 冷冻胚胎死后生殖运用的法律规制 (Legal Regulation of Post-Mortem Reproductive Use of Frozen Embryos)' (2025) 42 中国卫生事业管理 182, 184.

120 For the text of the code, see online: 'Code de La Santé Publique – Légifrance' <https://www.legifrance.gouv.fr/codes/texte_lc/LEGITEXT000006072665/> accessed 22 June 2025.

couples, and single women can access.[121] The new provision makes no reference to male same-sex couples or single men, who still cannot access HART. Their exclusion is based the illegality of surrogacy, as outlined in Article 6.6 of the French Civil Code since its revision by Law No. 94–653 of 19 July 1994. Much more difficult to explain is the rationale to ban widows from using PAR, contained in the new Paragraph 4, point 1 of Article 2141–2 of the CdlSP. Accordingly, for a heterosexual couple, insemination or transfer of embryos cannot be performed or continued in the event of the demise of one of the two partners. As stated by the European Court of Human Rights in 2023 in the *obiter dictum* of a judgment concerning a case prior to the reform, and reiterated by French and international doctrine, the prohibition leads to a rather absurd outcome, raising questions about the consistency of the system.[122] Indeed, the norm prohibits a widow from using her deceased husband's sperm for fertilisation. However, the same Article allows her access to HART using an anonymous donor's sperm for the same purpose, as any other single woman.

The debate surrounding the new French rule has attracted the attention of Chinese jurists for several reasons. Firstly, in France, as in the PRC, most cases regarding frozen embryos focus on the issues of posthumous embryo transfer.[123] Therefore, knowing how the French judges deal with this topic in their cases can be useful in the Chinese context. Another compelling reason is that France has lifted its ban on unmarried women accessing HART. The PRC itself has started to consider this for demographic and eugenic reasons, but it has additional implications for PAR: Recognising that a parental project can involve just one (female) parent implicitly opens the way for a new definition of what a family, especially a 'complete family,' entails, making irrelevant the questions regarding 'intergenerational respect.'[124] As we have seen, the French legislature has not yet properly addressed this issue. However, the discussion over French doctrine and potential new developments there interests Chinese legal given the (not too remote) possibility that it will become an issue also in the PRC. Finally, both the French and Chinese debates on PAR mainly focus on issues connected to the concepts of free will and informed consent. The

121 'Dalle tecniche di preservazione della fertilitá all'utilizzo con finalitá riproduttiva post mortemdi embrioni e gamete crioconservati l'esperienza giuridica italiana, francese e spagnola a confronto' (179*n*26) 92.

122 Ibid 93.

123 Zeng Pingjie 曾品杰 (194*n*119) 101.

124 'Dalle tecniche di preservazione della fertilitá all'utilizzo con finalitá riproduttiva post mortemdi embrioni e gamete crioconservati l'esperienza giuridica italiana, francese e spagnola a confronto' (179*n*26) 93–94.

French ban is frequently justified on the grounds of protecting the widow's right to self-determination and to resisting the influence of her deceased husband's relatives, who wish to maintain a living memory of him. Equally important is the husband's right to decide on the use of his gametes, even after death.[125] Chinese doctrinal discussions also recognise these issues, which identify informed consent, free will and the protection of the unborn child's interests as among the fundamental lenses through which to consider the phenomenon.[126]

Looking through the same lenses, however, does not mean reaching the same conclusions. Chinese legal scholars always remark that a country's approach to PAR is associated with law and medicine and depends on its ethical concepts and cultural and religious traditions. However, they consider a nation's demographic policy and its social conditions to have the greatest influence. This is why, even within analogous cultural contexts, perceptions of the fundamental legal problem pertaining to a given situation can vary considerably. The Japanese case is emblematic in this regard. As noted, Japan belongs to the Sino-Confucian tradition and shares with the PRC certain aspects of its legal approach to PAR, i.e.: the lack of provisions specifically regulating the issue, and the frequency of cases on it. Nevertheless, in contrast to the Chinese judicial system, Japanese courts typically are not tasked with determining the status of embryos in cases pertaining to PAR.[127] Instead, their primary function is to ascertain the paternity of a child conceived subsequent to the death of the child's father.[128]

In this respect, despite the considerable geographical and cultural distance between the two nations, German case-law serves as a more substantial legal reference point. This is not surprising, since the German model has been instrumental in characterising Chinese reforms from the late Qing modernisation to the recent enactment of the Civil Code. Moreover, aside from the

---

125 Ibid 94.

126 Wang Liqing 汪丽青 (179*n*26) 184; Tai Yuru 戴瑀如, 'Sihou Rengong Shengzhi Shi Jingzhi Yu Kaifang – Yi Deguo Ji Taiwan de Caipan Wei Zhongxin 死后人工生殖之禁制与开放- 以德国及台湾的裁判为中心 (The Prohibition and Liberalisation of Post-Death Reproduction: A Study Focusing on Court Rulings in Germany and Taiwan)' [2015] Huadong Zhengfa Daxue xuebao 华东政法大学学报 26, 29.

127 Sun (184*n*57) 86.

128 Zhou Jianghong 周江洪, 'Fazhi Hua Tuzhong de Rengong Peitai Falü Diwei – Riben Fa Zhuangkuang Ji Qi Xueshuo Jian Ping 法制化途中的人工胚胎法律地位- 日本法狀況及其學說簡評 (Legal Status of Human Embryos in Legalization Process – A Brief Review of Japanese Law and Doctrinal Positions)' [2015] Huadong Zhengfa Daxue xuebao 华东政法大学学报 50.

United States, Germany has been among the countries most committed to supporting legal education programmes in the PRC since the start of the reform and opening era in 1978. According to section 4 of the German Embryo Protection Law (ESchG, 1990, last revised in 2011, hereafter: GEPL), unauthorised fertilisation, unauthorised embryo transfer, and artificial insemination after death is prohibited by law.[129] Notwithstanding this, in a few cases, German courts have been called to rule on the restitution to the widow of zygotes that were cryopreserved before the husband's death. Among them, the 'Neubrandenburg case,'[130] decided by the Higher Regional Court in Rostock on 7th May 2010, stands out, and PRC's scholars consider it the most 'typical example of the attitude of German legal theory and practice towards the legal protection of human in vitro embryos.'[131] The most significant aspect of this case, and probably also the reason for the profound interest it has aroused in Chinese legal doctrine, is the similarity between the events that gave rise to it and those that characterised the Yixing case.[132] The German case involves a couple, Ines and Sandro S, who in 2002 turned to a hospital to undergo assisted reproduction treatment.[133] In 2008, following the failure of an initial IVF treatment, nine zygotes were cryopreserved for use in a later procedure. A few months later, however, Sandro was killed in a car accident. Ines asked the hospital to continue the treatment, but the hospital refused, saying that the request fell within the scope of Section 4 (1) point 3 GEPL, which stipulates that anyone who knowingly fertilises an egg cell with the sperm of a man after his death shall be criminally persecuted.[134] Ines brought a lawsuit requiring the hospital to return the cryopreserved zygotes. She argued that the hospital could not invoke GEPL, since her eggs had been fertilised before her husband's death, and the law did not prohibit the implantation of an embryo whose sperm donor had died.[135] The court of first instance ruled against the plain-

129 'Gesetz Zum Scjitz von Embryonen (Embryonenschutzgesetz – ESchG)' <https://www.gesetze-im-internet.de/eschg/BJNR027460990.html>.

130 [2010] OLG Rostock Az.: 7 U 67/09, FamRZ 2010.

131 Wu Guide 吴桂德 (192n106) 91; Yu Jiajia 于佳佳 (183n54) 102; Sun (184n57) 85.

132 Wu Guide 吴桂德 (192n106) 92–93; Si Jingjing 司静静, and Si Yangyu 司衍鲁, 'Si Hou Rengong Shengzhi Hefa Hua de Lifa Qishi 死后人工生殖合法化的立法启示 (Legislative Enlightenment about the Legalisation of Artificial Insemination After Death)' (2018) 26 Chengdu Ligond Daxue xuebao (Shehui kexue ban) 成都理工大学学报 (社会科学版) 54, 54–55.

133 Hashiloni-Dolev and Schicktanz (177n10) 27.

134 Wu Guide 吴桂德 (192n106) 91–92.

135 Ibid 92.

tiff.[136] Ines appealed to the Higher Regional Court in Rostock, which overturned the previous judgment.[137] The Higher Court held that the zygotes were stored in their pronuclear stage (i.e., before the nuclei fuse), so the husband's sperm had already been used before he died and was now inseparably embedded in the oocyte. While acknowledging the illegality of impregnating an oocyte with a dead man's sperm, the court ruled that a pronuclear zygote is the product of a process of impregnation already underway, and that the plaintiff's request neither violated the law's aim to protect the interest of the child, nor the informed consent of the husband, who had agreed with his wife on issues of procreation while he was still alive. Therefore, it ruled that the female partner was the owner of the 'incomplete embryos' and ordered the hospital to release them to her.[138] In Germany, the general public and the legal community reacted differently to the court's interpretation that the legal duty to protect frozen embryos included zygotes, and its consideration for the zygotes' personal interests. Some German legal scholars found the idea problematic that frozen zygotes are special entities with personal interests deserving due consideration of their personal nature, and ethical and emotional factors. In particular, they criticised the case made by the LG Neubrandenburg that 'the terminology of reproductive medicine and biology has to be taken as a basis' for interpreting Section 4 (1) no. 3 GEPL. In their opinion, given the contentiousness and lack of clarity regarding when exactly artificial insemination is completed, both from the scientific and legal point of view, and the inconsistent use of the term 'fertilization' even among scientists, such an approach could only lead to more legal uncertainty.[139] Yet, the German media and public sympathised with the widow's request,[140] especially how she justified her legal battle as the will to have 'a piece of him [the husband] to remain alive.'[141] Interestingly, this deeply human reaction, which we also observed in the case of Yixin, is common when confronted with PAR news like the one in question. This 'heart factor' somehow balances the 'yuk factor' referred to in the introduction to this chapter, and it is unsurprising that it is also taken into consideration by courts deciding PAR cases almost at a global level.

136 [2009] LG Neubrandenburg Az: 2 O 111/09.

137 Wu Guide 吴桂德 (192*n*106) 92–93; Si Jingjing 司静静， and Si Yangyu 司衍鲁, (197*n*132) 54–55.

138 Wu Guide 吴桂德 (192*n*106) 92–93.

139 Krüger (179*n*22) 47.

140 Hashiloni-Dolev and Schicktanz (177*n*10) 27.

141 Ibid.

Chinese legal scholars expressed a similar level of appreciation for the ruling, commending the German court's utilisation of multiple legal interpretation methodologies. According to these commentators, the court did not limit itself to the use of general civil law legal interpretation methods, such as textual, systemic, and purposive interpretation, but also decided the case based on the constitutional interpretation of the protection of the interest of the child and respect for their relevant personal interests.[142] Moreover, the court did not directly incorporate ethics into its reasoning, but used it indirectly as a guide to apply the relevant legal provisions by analogy and fill the legal loopholes, always taking as a basis the coherence of the legal system as whole. In their view, Chinese courts should do the same, using a systematic approach that puts the law at the centre instead of merely resorting to ethical principles, as the court in the 'Yixin case' was forced to do for a lack of relevant provisions dedicated to the protection of frozen embryos.[143] The proposed solution, however, necessitates a preliminary legislative intervention. The need has become particularly urgent in recent years due to increasing use of HART, raising more cases involving this issue. In consideration of this, several Chinese jurists have called for the adoption of the German model,[144] creating a system in which a general provision on the protection of frozen embryos is supplemented by special laws detailing the modalities. This would provide the courts with a solid legal framework, minimising the risk of extra-legal factors influencing their reasoning and undermining predictability and legal certainty.

Nevertheless, although the German model may serve as a useful point of reference with regard to form, it does not necessarily extend to content. Chinese legal experts are aware of this fact. They explain that the focus of the German legal system on embryo protection stems from Christian tradition,[145] as well as from a reaction to the racial discrimination and eugenics policies pursued under the Nazi regime.[146] According to them, the civil and criminal liability for individuals engaging in the abuse, damage, or destruction of embryos is a consequence of two overarching factors. Firstly, it is driven by a profound desire to safeguard the vulnerable nature of human life. Secondly, it is informed by an acute awareness of the imperative to protect human

142 Wu Guide 吴桂德 (192*n*106) 95.

143 Ibid 96.

144 Wu Guide 吴桂德 (192*n*106); Si Jingjing 司静静, and Si Yangyu 司衍鲁 (197*n*132).

145 Wu Guide 吴桂德 (192*n*106) 95.

146 Sun (184*n*57) 86.

embryos in vitro, a practice that is deemed essential for the preservation of the human race and its future well-being.[147] The philosophical and religious conception that underpins this approach is predicated on the premise that the foetus is an entity in itself, distinct from the mother. In a similar fashion, the German legislature establishes the beginning of human life at a very early stage of cellular development.[148] As demonstrated, this notion is inherently incongruent with the Chinese cultural paradigm, which traditionally conceives of birth as the inception of human life. From this standpoint, the significance of the human embryo is predicated on its capacity to carry and transmit the genetic information of its two families to future generations.[149] This phenomenon is not, of course, unique to China; many cultures attribute significant value to new life, including from the perspective of family continuity. In the context of China, however, this aspect assumes a particular significance, as it is intertwined with the Confucian tradition and the perspective that infertility constitutes a grave infringement of the duty of filial piety.

It is probably why some authors consider the German approach, in particular with reference to statute law, too rigid for China. Instead, China should adopt a system capable of balancing the need to control modern medical development and the benefits of this development for society.[150] To do so, legislation must be refined to allow for technological application. Regarding the question of PAR, the law should require written informed consent prior to death, while leaving it to the courts to ascertain the wishes of the deceased on a case-by-case basis where circumstances prevented him from expressing his will explicitly before death.[151] This approach is positioned midway between the pro-restrictive and pro-permissive approaches delineated by Lidia Lin Yun-Hsien. Yu Jiajia's position is that this model corresponds to that employed in the United Kingdom, where the interplay between the provisions of the Human Fertilisation and Embryology Act (2008) and the courts allows for this kind of flexibility.[152]

It is important to note that, due to inherent structural differences, the British legal model may encounter challenges in being implemented in Mainland China, where the relationship between statute law and case law differs significantly from that of the UK. It is perhaps for this reason that Yu Jiajia's proposal

---

147 Wu Guide 吴桂德 (192*n*106) 95–96.
148 Hashiloni-Dolev and Schicktanz (177*n*10) 29.
149 Wu Guide 吴桂德 (192*n*106) 96.
150 Yu Jiajia 于佳佳 (183*n*54) 113.
151 Ibid.
152 Ibid 101, 113.

is decidedly isolated, at least with regard to the legal system taken as reference.

From the analysis of the extant literature, it appears that Chinese legal scholars hold a more favourable attitude towards PAR than bioethicists. However, it remains to be ascertained how the courts are approaching this issue. In the absence of specific legislation, what are the most recent guidelines followed in Chinese legal practice?

3.2 *PAR in Chinese Legal Practice*

As noted, according to the data of a 2024 survey referred to by the most recent articles on the topic,[153] starting from the 2014 Yixing case, Chinese people's courts have decided twenty-eight cases related to PAR. Of these, only the Yixing case involved the deaths of both spouses, while in two cases, the surviving spouse was male. Most suits (twenty-five) were brought by widows who have been denied access to frozen embryo transplantation by assisted reproductive institutions. It is worth noting that judicial authorities have generally shown support for requests related to PAR, notwithstanding the typologies of plaintiffs.[154] This is particularly evident with reference to the cases brought by the surviving wives. In fact, only in four cases has the court has rejected the widow's claim.[155] With reference to the cases in which the plaintiff/female surviving spouse succeeded, in four cases the court has supported the widow's requests to return the embryos, while in seventeen cases the court has supported the request for continued treatment, ordering the hospital to perform the embryo transfer procedure.[156]

In the following pages, I will analyse a number of cases, with a particular focus on those involving surviving wives. First, a methodological clarification is required. In recent years, the task of accessing the original texts of judgments handed down by Chinese people's courts has become increasingly challenging due to a significant step backwards in China's judicial transparency.[157] This has resulted, for example, in the Supreme People's Court (SPC) implementing a substantial reduction in the number of cases available on its China Judgments Online (CJO) website. Established in 2013, the CJO website

153 Chen Zhaoyang 陈兆阳 and Zhang Boyuan 张博源 (186*n*71) 46; Wang Liqing 汪丽青 (194*n*119) 182.

154 Wang Liqing 汪丽青 (194*n*119) 182.

155 Chen Zhaoyang 陈兆阳 and Zhang Boyuan 张博源 (186*n*71) 47.

156 Sun (n 1039) 93; Chen Zhaoyang 陈兆阳 and Zhang Boyuan 张博源 (186*n*71) 46.

157 Benjamin Liebman and others, 'Rolling Back Transparency in China's Courts' (2023) 123 Columbia Law Review 2407.

has since emerged as the primary database for Chinese case law.[158] Excluding a significant number of cases from the CJO, in conjunction with the implementation of additional measures by the SPC with the objective of restricting public access to court verdicts,[159] has resulted in the utilisation of case quotations by Chinese legal scholars, media outlets and institutional reports as the predominant method for accessing PRC's case law, both outside China and, in some instances, even within it.[160] In the ensuing analysis, therefore, I will chiefly draw upon secondary sources.

3.2.1 PAR Cases Where the Surviving Spouse Is Female

3.2.1.1 *Embryo Transfer for Widowed Women: When No Transfer Has Been Performed Yet*

The lawsuit initiated by Yang Yonghui against Zhoushan Women and Children Hospital[161] serves as a paradigmatic illustration of a PAR dispute concerning the continuation of the performance of HART. In this case, the plaintiff and her husband had begun assisted reproduction treatment with the hospital. However, before the embryos were transferred, the husband was involved in a maritime accident while on duty at sea and was declared missing. The wife requested that the hospital continue performing the medical services contract, including embryo implantation surgery. After the hospital's refusal, she filed a lawsuit with the People's Court of Dinghai District (Zhoushan city, Zhejiang Province).[162] During the trail, the hospital raised an issue about informed consent, saying that the 'Embryo freezing Informed consent' signed by the couple contained a clause stating that: 'in the event that either or both of us pass away without leaving a will concerning the disposal of frozen embryos, we allow the hospital to terminate the cryopreservation of the embryo.' In the absence of any will, the hospital held that it had the right to proceed to the in vitro degradation of the embryos. The court rejected this

158 Luo Jiajun and Thomas Kellogg, 'Verdicts from China's Courts Used to Be Accessible Online. Now They're Disappearing.' (*ChinaFile*, 1 February 2022) <https://www.chinafile.com/reporting-opinion/viewpoint/verdicts-chinas-courts-used-be-accessible-online-now-theyre-disappearing> accessed 24 June 2025.

159 Ibid.

160 Chen Zhaoyang 陈兆阳 and Zhang Boyuan 张博源 (186*n*71) 46.

161 *Yang Yonghuui su Zhoushan fuyong baojianyuan* 杨勇会诉舟山市妇幼保建院 (*Yang Yonghui v Zhoushan Women and Children Hospital*) [2016] Zhejinagsheng Dinghai qu Renmin fayuan 浙江省舟山市定海区人民法院 (People's Court of Dinghai District, Zhoushan City, Zhejiang Province) (2016) Zhe 0902 Minchu 598 hao (2016) 浙 0902 民初 3598 号.

162 Yu Jiajia 于佳佳 (183*n*54) 101.

argument, holding that the abovementioned clause was a standard term drafted by the defendant, and according to contract law, when there is more than one interpretation, the interpretation that is unfavourable to the party providing the standard terms should prevail.[163] Instead, the court gave more weight to the fact that the human-assisted reproductive treatment had already commenced, and the plaintiff's husband had not revoked his consent.[164] On the contrary, he had signed multiple informed-consent forms related to embryo transfer during his lifetime, clearly expressing his willingness to have children through human-assisted reproductive technology, including embryo transfer. Additionally, considering the plaintiff's husband's specific actions during his lifetime, the traditional beliefs widely accepted by the local community, and common human nature, there were reasonable grounds to believe that performing embryo transfer for the plaintiff did not violate her deceased husband's wishes, as such consent is typically expressed through words or actions rather than legal documents.[165] In fact, 'when assessing whether consent was given in a specific case, written consent is not the sole evidence; it is generally necessary to consider the relevant circumstances comprehensively and draw inferences from them.'[166] On this basis, the court ruled in favour of the plaintiff.

As we have noted in previous sections, issues concerning informed consent are not the only ones that courts have to address when deciding cases relating to PAR. Other important issues concern the protection of the rights of future generations and the need to protect the public interest. From this point of view, the reasoning of another case,[167] decided in 2019 by the People's Court of Liangxi District (Wuxi City, Jiangsu Province) is particularly interesting. In this case, a couple had undergone HART, but the embryo implantation surgery was postponed for two years due to the wife's physical condition. During this period, the husband passed away. When the wife requested the local Maternal and Child Health Hospital to perform the embryo implantation surgery, the hospital refused to proceed, citing the absence of the husband's signature. The widow filed a lawsuit. In its ruling, the court explicitly considered the parties' right to informed consent, the principle of protecting future generations, and

163 Sun (184*n*57) 95.

164 Yu Jiajia 于佳佳 (n 1036) 101.

165 Chen Zhaoyang 陈兆阳 and Zhang Boyuan 张博源 (186*n*71) 48.

166 Ibid 47.

167 [2020] Jiangsu sheng Wuxi shi Liangxi qu Renmin fayuan 江苏省无锡市梁溪区人民法院 (Liangxi district People's Court, Wuxi city, Jiangsu Province) (2019) Su 0213 Minchu 10672 hao (2019) 苏 0213 民初 10672 号.

the principle of public interest. With reference to the right to informed consent, the court held that the plaintiff's deceased husband had already signed and confirmed in the informed consent form that he agreed to matters such as embryo freezing, thawing, and transplantation. The reason why the embryo implantation was not immediately performed was solely due to the plaintiff's physical condition. Since the existing medical service contract had not yet been fulfilled, the plaintiff, as one of the parties to the contract, separately requested the Maternal and Child Health Hospital to continue fulfilling the medical service contract that her husband had already entered into with it. Her request, therefore, did not constitute a violation of her husband's true intentions or the principle of informed consent. Furthermore, the court held that the plaintiff's request did not violate the principle of protecting future generations. In fact, single-parent families are not necessarily detrimental to the offspring; moreover, according to the law, offspring born through HART enjoy the same legal rights and obligations as those born through natural childbirth, as well as family ethical and moral obligations, while their parents should provide support and assume moral, ethical, and legal obligations towards them. Finally, the plaintiff's request did not violate the principle of public interest. According to the court, a widow's decision to have children does not violate national population and family planning laws and regulations. The court considered the legal status of a widow as distinct from that of an unmarried woman, thus holding that the prohibition on unmarried women using HART did not apply to plaintiff.[168]

In cases where the husband's death occurred prior to the transfer of the embryos, the courts have been largely consistent in supporting the widows' claims. Conversely, when at least an embryo transfer has been conducted during the husband's lifetime, the outcomes of these instances are less predictable, irrespective of the success of the procedure.

3.2.1.2 *Embryo Transfer for Widowed Women: When a Transfer Has Already Been Performed*

An example of this situation can be found in a case[169] decided the People's Court of Xishan District (Kunming city, Yunnan Province) on 20 November 2019. In that case, the court held that when the wife had already under-

---

168 Yu Jiajia 于佳佳 (183*n*54) 102.

169 *Ya Chunli su Yunnan sheng diyi Renmin fayuan* 崖春丽诉云南省第一人民医院 (*Ya Chunli v the first People's Hospital of Yunnan Province*) [2019] Kunminshi Xishanqu Renmin fayuan 昆明市西山区人民法院 (2019) Yun 112 Minchu 370 hao (2019) 云 112 民初 370 号.

gone HART, whether the initial transfer was successful or not, the contract between the parties is considered executed and cannot be continued for the surviving spouse. Therefore, it rejected the widow's requests.[170] A year earlier, the People's court of Qinghai District (Nanning city, Guanxi Zhuang Autonomous Region) had adopted a similar approach in the case brought by Tan Hui Ping against the Guangxi Zhuang Autonomous Region Health and Family Planning Commission Reproductive Centre Medical Services.[171] The court did not recognise the plaintiff's claim for PAR after the death of her husband because the couple had already conceived a daughter through in vitro fertilisation.[172] According to the court, since the couple had already given birth to one child through HART, the purpose of the previously entered contract had been achieved, and the medical service contract relationship between the parties had terminated. Reimplantation effectively constitutes a new contract between the couple and the medical institution. In the absence of the husband's explicit consent to reimplant the frozen embryos for the purpose of having a second child, the reimplantation lacks legal validity. Consequently, the widow's claims were dismissed.[173]

In other similar lawsuits, different courts reached opposite conclusions. This happened, for example, in the litigation between Li Qingyan and the First Affiliated Hospital of Wenzhou Medical University, decided by the People's Court of Outai District (Wenzhou City, Zhejiang Province) on 8 July 2020 (hereafter: Outai case).[174] Even though the plaintiff had already undergone an (unsuccessful) transfer of embryos, the court did not deem the contract fulfilled and ruled for the plaintiff, ordering the hospital to perform the transfer of the embryos cryopreserved before the husband's death.[175]

170 Yu Jiajia 于佳佳 (183*n*54) 101; Sun (184*n*57) 95.

171 *Tan Huiping su Guangzi Zhuangzu zizhiqu weisheng jisheng weizhi zhongxin* 覃惠萍诉广西壮族自治区卫生计生委生殖中心 (*Tan Huiping V the Reproductive Health Centre of the Guangxi Zhuang Autonomous Region Health and Family Planning Commission* [2018] Guanxi zhuangzuzizhiqu Nanning shi Qingxiu qu Renmin fayuan 广西壮族自治区南宁市青秀区人民法院 (People's Court of Qingxiu District, Nanning City, Guangxi Zhuang Autonomous Region) (2018) Zuang 0103 Minchu 5920 hao (2018) 桂 0103 民初 5920 号.

172 Wang Liqing 汪丽青 (183*n*54) 133–134.

173 Chen Zhaoyang 陈兆阳 and Zhang Boyuan 张博源 (186*n*71) 48.

174 *Li Qingyan su Wenzhou yikedaxue fushu di yi yiyuan* 李清艳诉温州医科大学附属第一医院 (*Li Qingyan v The first affiliated Hospital of Wenzhou Medical University*) [2020] Wenzhou shi Outai qu Renmin fayuan 温州市瓯海区人民法院 (Outai district People's court, Wenzhou city) (2020) Zhe 304 Minchu 066 hao(2020) 浙 304 民初 066 号.

175 Yu Jiajia 于佳佳 (183*n*54) 101; Sun (184*n*57) 95.

Another case had the same result,[176] in which the widow not only had already undergone HART, but also had already successfully given birth to a child. In its ruling, the People's Court of Shizhong District (Jinan City, Shandong Province) considered that the spouses possess the right to dispose of the embryos, which is a prerequisite for asserting the right to embryo implantation against the medical institution. Frozen embryos are transitional entities between humans and objects, carrying the personal interests of the widowed woman and her husband; therefore, only the married couple has the right to decide on the use of frozen embryos. This is why, after the husband's death, frozen embryos cannot simply be treated as joint property of the couple and disposed of at the discretion of the surviving spouse; the deceased's wishes must be taken into consideration. However, in this particular instance, the evidence presented indicated that the embryo transfer did not contravene the deceased husband's expressed wishes. Furthermore, all close relatives had provided their consent. Based on this, the court supported the plaintiff's claim and held that the widow possessed full disposal rights over the embryos and could 'independently' request medical institutions to perform the embryo transfer.[177]

Chinese legal scholars mostly attribute the contradictory nature of these decisions and the resulting legal uncertainty to the lack of clear rules on the matter. The legislature's inaction in this regard has already been widely noted and requires no further analysis. What I find interesting, however, is the criticism some authors have levelled at the courts, which they accuse of focusing on the contractual situation between the parties without taking into due account women's reproductive rights.

In an article published in 2025, Chen Zhaoyang and Zhang Boyuan go so far as to consider the right to reproduce, established for all citizens by Article 17 of the PFPL, and reproductive autonomy, guaranteed to all women by Article 32 of the PWRIL, as a human right protected by the Article 33, paragraph 3 of the PRC's Constitution. On this basis, they claim that every woman, regardless of her marital status, has the right to reproduce, even suggesting that the rule contained in the EPIHARTSB 2003 prohibiting single women from undergoing assisted reproduction is invalid. In their view, besides violating the Constitution, the provision no longer aligns with Article 91 of the Law on Laws (*Fali fa*

176 Shandong sheng Jinan shi Shizhong qu Renmin fayuan 山东省济南市市中区人民法院 Shizhong District People's Court (Jinan City, Shandong Province) (2021) Lu 0103Minchu 6739 hao(2021) 鲁 0103 民初 6739 号(.

177 Chen Zhaoyang 陈兆阳 and Zhang Boyuan 张博源 (186*n*71) 48.

法立法, enacted on the 15 March 2000, and revised in 2015 and 20123) as amended in 2015. According to Article 91:

> Without any basis in laws or the administrative regulations, decisions, and orders of the State Council, state Council departmental rules shall not set out any requirements that impair the rights or increase the obligations of citizens, legal persons, and other organizations, nor increase the power or decrease the statutory duties of the department.

Since the EPIHARTSB 2003's prohibition impairs a citizens' right, and the EPIHARTSB is a department rule, the authors suggest that it should be amended to ensure its conformity with the rest of the legislation and with China's new demographic policy.

The permanence of this regulation remains uncertain. What is certain is that, as of 12 January 2023, Chinese courts cannot apply it to widowed women requesting the transfer of embryos. On that date, the SPC released the case 'Zou Moling v. a hospital medical service contract dispute'[178] among the second batch of 'typical cases' (*dianxing anli* 典型案例)[179] that people's courts should follow when implementing the Civil Code.[180] Four months later, a Chinese People's court ruling extended, for the first time, foetal rights to frozen embryos.[181] Let's now see briefly what these important decisions are

178 *Zou Mouling su Mou yiyuan* 邹某玲诉某医院 (*Zou Mouling v A Hospital*) 衡阳市石鼓区人民法院 (People's Court of Shigu district, Hengyang city) (2022) Xiang 0407 Minchu 229 hao (2022) 湘 0407 民初229 号.

179 Supreme People's Court Monitor, 'More on the Supreme People's Court and Typical Cases' (*Supreme People's Court Monitor*, 2 May 2014) <https://supremepeoplescourtmonitor.com/2014/05/02/more-on-the-supreme-peoples-court-and-typical-cases/> accessed 27 June 2025.

180 Linyi shi Lanshan qu Renmin fayuan guanli yuan 临沂市兰山区人民法院管理员 (Administrator of the People's Court of Lanshan District, Linyi City), 'Yi Lingfa Cu Shangshi Quanmian Shenhua Minfa Dian Guanche Shishi – Zuigao Fa Fabu Di Er Pi Renminfayuan Guanche Shishi Mín Fǎ Diǎn Diǎnxíng Ànlì 以良法促善治，全面深化民法典贯彻实施——最高法发布第二批人民法院贯彻实施民法典典型案例（Promoting Good Governance with Good Laws and Comprehensively Deepening the Implementation of the Civil Code – The Supreme People's Court Released the Second Batch of Typical Cases of the People's Courts Implementing the Civil Code)' (31 January 2023) <http://qdzy.sdcourt.gov.cn/lylsqfy/367109/367114/9171392/index.html>.

181 Wan yi 网易, 'Guonei Shou Li! Fuqin Gong Wang Hou, Shiguan Ying'er Suoperi Fuyan Fei, Yishen Xuanpan 国内首例！父亲工亡后，试管婴儿索赔抚养费，一审宣判→(A First in China! After His Father Died in a Work Accident, a Child Conceived through IVF Sued for Child Support, and the First Instance Verdict Was Handed Down)' (19 April 2023) <https://www.163.com/dy/article/I2ML3IJT0514R9KQ.html> accessed 27 June 2025.

about, and how they might impact the development of legal and bioethical reflection on biotechnologies related to the beginning of life.

3.3 *PAR in 2023 PRC's Case Law: From the First SPC's 'Typical Case' regarding PAR to the Decision of the 'First Chinese Case Involving a Claim for Child Support as a Compensation for Its Father's Workplace Death'*

The facts of the first 'typical case' regarding PAR published by the SPC are analogous to those of many cases described above. In October 2020, Ms Zou and her husband, Mr Chen, went to the defendant for the purpose of receiving IVF-assisted reproduction surgery. However, due to Ms Zou's health conditions, the transfer of the embryos was postponed, and four embryos were cryopreserved to be used in the future. In March 2021, Mr Chen passed away. Ms Zou asked the defendant to proceed with the embryo transfer surgery, and upon the defendant's refusal citing the prohibition on performing HART for single women, she filed a lawsuit to the People's Court of Shigong District (Hengyang City, Hunan Province, hereinafter: Zou Mouling case). In its reasoning, the court acknowledged that the plaintiff's husband died after the embryos were created; that the plaintiff's status was substantially different from the one of a 'single woman receiving embryo transfer surgery' mentioned in the EPIHARTSB 2003; that no provision in force in the PRC's legal system prohibits a widowed woman to proceed with the transfer of embryos that have been fertilised with her husband's sperm. The court also considered the plaintiff's motivations. According to the court, the plaintiff wanted to continue the HART procedure not only out of grief for her dead husband, but also as way to assume her responsibility as a mother. This is 'in line with common sense and the general feeling of the public, and did not violate public order and good customs'; therefore, the court ordered the hospital to continue to perform the medical service contract signed with the plaintiff.[182]

In the 'typical case' part dedicated to explaining why Chinese courts should follow the Zou Moling decision in ruling on similar lawsuits, the SPC defined it as: 'a specific practice of protecting women's reproductive rights and interests in accordance with the law, which reflects the effective judicial protection of women's lawful rights and interests, and has positive guiding significance.'[183]

182 'Renmin Fayuan Guanche Shishi Min Fa Dian Dianxing Anli (Di Er Pi) 人民法院贯彻实施民法典典型案例(第二批) (Typical Cases of the People's Courts Implementing the Civil Code (Second Batch))' (1 September 2023) s 5 (2) <http://jningyzfy.sdcourt.gov.cn/jningyzfy/547173/386111/386155/12579963/index.html>.

183 Ibid 5 (3).

With reference to the articles of the CC to be applied in these cases, the SPC interestingly mentions Article 3, regarding the legal protection of personal rights, property rights and other lawful rights and interest of the parties to legal civil relations, and Article 8, which states that civil entities cannot violate the law or public order and morals when engaging in civil activities.[184]

The SPC's endorsement to (at least this kind of) PAR could not help but have a positive impact on the success rate of these cases, and on the number of children born from frozen embryos after their fathers' demise. This has resulted in the emergence of novel legal issues, particularly concerning the question of whether frozen embryos possess the capacity for civil rights (*minshi quanli nengli* 民事权利能力) analogous to those recognised for foetuses under Article 16 of the Civil Code, which states: 'In circumstances where the safeguarding of foetal interests is implicated in the context of a succession or acceptance of a gift, the foetus is to be presumed to possess the capacity for civil rights,' on the condition that it is born alive.

This progression was not wholly unanticipated. In 2020, Wang Liqing had highlighted the urgency of enacting regulations governing the status and rights of embryos, anticipating that people's courts would soon be asked to rule on such matters.[185] While the legislature has yet to take action on this matter, on 18 April 2023, the Intermediate Court of Sanmenxia District decided in first instance what has been immediately called the 'first Chinese case involving a claim for child support as a compensation for its father's workplace death' (*Guonei shouli fusing gongwang hou shiguan ying'er suopei fuyang fei an* 国内首例父亲工亡后试管婴儿索赔抚养费案, hereafter: Sanmenxia case).[186]

The case concerned, once again, two spouses who had undergone assisted reproduction treatment involving in vitro fertilisation and embryo transfer.[187] As an outcome of HART, two embryos had been created, but before they could be implanted in the wife's uterus, the husband was involved in an accident while working at an aluminium company and died. The wife asked the hospital for the continuation of the treatment; the hospital refused, and the wife filed a lawsuit. On second instance, the Luoyang intermediate Court ordered

184 Ibid 5 (4).

185 Wang Liqing 汪丽青 (183*n*54) 134.

186 *Henan sheng Sanmenxia shi Zhongji Renmin fayuan* 河南省三门峡市中级人民法院 (*Intermediate People's Court of Sanmenxia City, Henan Province2022*) 豫 12 民初 *56* 号民事判决 [2022] Henan sheng Sanmenxia shi Zhongji Renmin fayuan 河南省三门峡市中级人民法院 (Intermediate People's Court of Sanmenxia City, Henan Province (2022) Yu 12 Minchu 56 hao (2022) 豫 12 民初 56 号民事判决.

187 Shi Jiayou 石佳友 and Ceng Jia 曾 佳 (186*n*70) 35.

the hospital to fulfil the medical service contract and perform the embryo's implantation surgery. The treatment was successful, and in November 2021, the widow gave birth to a child, who then filed a lawsuit as the plaintiff, demanding that the companies responsible for the father's death pay her maintenance fees until she turns eighteen.[188] In an interview, Judge Chang Hui, the presiding judge of the case, stated that the primary legal problem for the court to resolve was to ascertain whether the child had legal standing to claim compensation for maintenance damage. The court's response was affirmative. In particular, the court held that the embryo transfer was a matter decided by the spouses and had a definite nature. Thus, the interest of a child born as a result of their joint intention should be protected through legal remedies. The husband's unexpected death does not negate the pre-existing certainty of the embryo transfer; although the time at which it became a foetus in the mother's womb differed from that of a naturally conceived foetus, this did not alter its inherent natural attribute as a 'pre-foetus.' On the contrary, 'granting it foetal rights, in the absence of explicit legal provisions, constitutes an appropriate response to technological advancements that can bring about a better life for humanity.' Therefore, on the basis of Article 16 of the Civil Code, and taking into account ethics and reason (*lunli yu qingli* 伦理与情理) the court partially recognised the plaintiff's claim, ordering the defendants to compensate the child's relatives for his living expenses.[189]

This decision is particularly significant for the exceptional issue on which the court was required to rule. The PRC legal system lacks any regulations or judicial precedents that address the status of embryos, and legal scholars have addressed the issue in only a limited number of cases – Wang Liqing may be the exception.[190] In commenting on the ruling, Prof Yang Lixin of the Renmin University School of Law referred many times to the concept of dignity, which Chinese bioethicists consider the fundamental principle with reference to HART in general, and PAR in particular.[191] According to Yang, 'by recognising

188 Ibid.

189 Su Qi 苏琦, Zhang Jing 张静, and Wang Ping 王萍, 'Sihou Rengong Shengzhi Suo Yu Zinü Liyi de Falü Baohu – Yi Guonei Shouli Fuqing Gongwang Hou Shiguan Ying'er Suopei Fuyang Fei an Wei Shijiao 死后人工生殖所育子女利益的法律保护——以国内首例父亲工亡后试管婴儿索赔抚养费案为视角 (Legal Protection of the Interests of Children Conceived through Posthumous Assisted Reproduction after the Death of the Parent— from the Perspective of the First Case of Test Tube Baby's Claim for Alimony after the Father's Death at Work in China)' (2024) 38 Weisheng ruan kexue 卫生软科学 32.

190 Wang Liqing 汪丽青 (183*n*54) 134.

191 Wan yi 网易 (207*n*181).

in vitro embryos as a quasi-foetus and applying Article 16 of Civil Code by analogy, the court has confirmed that in vitro embryos possess the dignity of life and potential personality interests, acknowledged their limited capacity for civil rights, and recognised that their personality interests and dignity must be protected by law.'[192] To summarise, the ruling signifies 'the judiciary's proactive consideration of protecting the dignity of children born through assisted reproductive technology.' By granting foetal rights to embryos under specific conditions, it also fills gaps in legal provisions, judicial rulings, and theoretical research.[193]

The reference to the 'specific conditions' under which the court has recognised an embryo's rights is particularly relevant. In fact, as Xue Dinglan of the Chinese Academy of Social Science's Institute of Law has remarked, the court refrained from directly defining the nature of human embryos or determining the rights that they generally possess; rather, it specified that the extension of foetal rights to the embryonic stage should be limited to specific cases and to embryos that are 'legitimate and certain.'[194] It seems to me that this choice could be justified by the court's awareness of the effect that a general redefinition of frozen embryos outside the body as foetuses can have, for example, on scientific research. That is how I understand Dr Xue's evaluation of the ruling as 'not only protecting the legitimate interests of all parties involved but also leaving room for further legal refinement.'[195]

The case also raises important issues related to the protection of children's interests. Yao Jianlong, Director of the Institute of Law at the Shanghai Academy of Social Sciences, has pointed out that the decision explicitly evokes the 'principle of the best interest of the child,' enshrined in the 1989 UN Convention on the Rights of the Child, and since 2020 incorporated in Article 4 of the PRC's Minors Protection Law (*Wei chengnianren baohu fa* 未成年人保护法, enacted in 1991 and revised in 2006, 2012, 2020, and 2024, hereinafter: MPL). In Prof Yao's view, the decision is simultaneously 'a practical application of the best interest of the child' and a vivid interpretation of the 'socialist judicial philosophy of the New Era' (*Xin shidai shehui zhuyi sifa linian* 新时代社会主义司法理念) of upholding the unity of 'national law, natural justice, and human sentiment' (*Guofa tianli renqing* 国法天理人情).[196]

192 Ibid.
193 Ibid.
194 Ibid.
195 Ibid.
196 Ibid.

The 'socialist judicial philosophy of the New Era' that Prof Yao references can be interpreted as a reinterpretation – or more accurately, an elucidation – of the *hefa, heli, heqing* adage that characterised judicial decisions in imperial times and was invoked in both the Yixing and the Sanmenxia cases. From this standpoint, numerous authors regard both these cases, in conjunction with the Zou Mouling's Case, as exemplifying 'compassionate judgments' (*wenqing panjue* 温情判决)[197] and 'useful explorations by the People's Courts in resolving legal disputes involving human reproductive technology.'[198]

These authors seem unfazed by how these 'compassionate judgments' have exposed gaps in Chinese law involving crucial issues. However, the Yixing case raised the most legally problematic issue, namely, the weight given to natural law and human feelings, which seems to have led the court to overlook both the fragility of the legal standing of the parents of the deceased spouses with regard to the return of frozen embryos and the explicit illegality, under state law, of the actions resulting from its decision. The particulars of the case have previously been delineated in Chapter Two. The question now is whether the right to become a grandparent exists in China, and if so, on which factors it does rely.

3.4 *The 'Elephant in the Room':* PAR *Cases in the Event of the Death of Both Spouses and When the Surviving Spouse Is a Male*

In analysing the cases related to PAR in which the surviving spouse is female, reference was made to the position of women's reproductive autonomy and the need for the courts to give it more consideration, as asserted by some authors. It is important to reiterate that, despite its significance, widows' reproductive autonomy is not absolute. Indeed, the court's recognition of the embryos in question is contingent on the more or less explicit consent previously expressed by the deceased husband of the woman in question, with regard to the utilisation of the embryos that had been formed using his gametes. In the Chinese cultural context, however, the fate of frozen embryos extends beyond the couple who provided the gametes to encompass their families, especially if they were only-children. Virtually all the legal scholars who have written on PAR have emphasised the importance of traditional Chinese ethical values linked to bloodline continuity and how they reflect the public's sense of justice. However, as demonstrated in the preceding jurisprudence, the courts frequently cite the endorsement of the deceased's family members. Prior to the publication of the Zou Mouling case by the SPC, these

197 Ibid.
198 Ibid.

courts used this endorsement to substantiate their decisions regarding a widow's entitlement to pursue artificial reproductive treatment. In certain cases, the courts have been known to remark upon the fact that both parents of the deceased consent to the plaintiff continuing with the embryo transfer and pregnancy. Furthermore, the courts have emphasised that, for the parents of the deceased, the birth of a grandchild would also serve as emotional comfort for the loss of their only child.[199] This statement is analogous to that of the court in the Yixing case, which numerous authors regard as a 'judicial victory of human ethics and reason' (*renlun yu qingli shengsu* 人伦与情理胜诉)[200] and was widely lauded in public opinion.

Public support for PAR is not a secondary issue. As is well known, since at least 2008, with the introduction of three principles that must guide judges in their decisions, the so-called 'Three Supremes' (*san ge zhishang* 三个至上: supremacy of the business of the Party, supremacy of the interests of the people and supremacy of the Constitution and the law),[201] public opinion has been given a prominent role in guiding judicial decisions. Even more prominent, however, at least judging by the order in which the Three Supremes are expressed, is Party leadership. Also in this case, the favour for judicial outcomes that support the use of the embryos for reproductive purposes, even after the demise of one or both parents, is in line with the shift in Chinese demographic

199 *Zhao Moumou su Beijing Daxue diyi yiyan* 赵某某诉北京大学第一医院 (*Zhao v First Hospital of Beijing University*) [2022] Beijing shi Xichengqu Renmin fa yuan 北京市西城区人民法院 (People's court of Xicheng district, Beijing city) (2022) Jing 102 Minchu 822hao (2022) 京 102 民初 822 号; *Yang Yonghuui su Zhoushan fuyong baojianyuan* 杨勇会诉舟山市妇幼保建院 (*Yang Yonghui v. Zhoushan Women and Children Hospital*) (n 1143); *Li lianfeng su Yunnan Jizhou yiyuan* 李连风诉云南九洲医院 *Li Lianfeng v Yunnan Jizhou Hospital* [2020] Kunming shi Panlong qu Renmin fayuan 昆明市盘龙区人民法院 (People's Court of Panlong district, Kunming city) (2020) Yun 103 Minchu 76 hao (2020) 云103 民初76 号; *Sasa su Yunnan Jiuzhouyiyuan* 飒飒诉云南九洲医院 (*Sasa v Yunnan Jizhou Hospital*) [2019] Kunming shi Panlong qu Renmin fayuan 昆明市盘龙区人民法院 (People's Court of Panlong district, Kunming city) (2019) Yun 103 Minchu 897hao (2019) 云 103 民初 897 号.

200 Yang Lixin 杨立新, 'Yi Fen Biaozhi Renlun Yu Qingli Shengsu de Minshi Panjue – Ren de Tiwai Peitai Quan Shu Zhengyi an Ershen Panjue Shi Ping 一份标志人伦与情理胜诉的民事判决——人的体外胚胎权属争议案二审判决释评 (A Civil Judgment That Marks the Victory of Human Ethics and Reason: Commentary on the Second-Instance Judgment in the Case of the Dispute over the Ownership of Human in Vitro Embryos)' (2014) 11 Falü shiyong 法律适用 48.

201 Clarke, 'He Weifang versus China's Legal Establishment on the "Three Supremes"' (*Chinese Law Prof Blog*, 12 August 2009) <https://lawprofessors.typepad.com/china_law_prof_blog/2009/08/he-weifang-versus-chinas-legal-establishment-on-the-three-supremes.html> accessed 27 June 2025.

policy from restrictive to inclusive, as expressed by the slogan 'Optimize fertility policies and enhance their inclusiveness' (*youhua shengyu zhengce, zengqiang shengyu zhengxe baorong xing* 优化生育政策，增强生育政策包容性) launched by the 'Proposal of the CPC Central Committee on the Formulation of the 14th Five-Year Plan for the National Economic and Social Development and the Long Term Goals for 2035 (*Zhonggong Zhongyang guanyu zhiding guomin jingji he shehui fazhan di shisi ge wu nian guihua he er ling sanwu nian yuanjing mubiao de jianyi* 中共中央关于制定国民经济和社会发展第十四个五年规划和二〇三五年远景目标的建议)[202] on the 3rd November 2020.

Sun Jitao acknowledges the negligible effect on promoting population growth of allowing frozen embryos for post-mortem artificial reproduction.[203] Nevertheless, it is possible that the traditional value of reproduction in resolving disputes over frozen embryos has become more prominent as a result of the liberalisation of birth control.[204]

All these factors may have played a role in the Yixing court's decision to grant to the spouses' parents custody of the embryos formed from their gametes – the first and only such decision by a PRC court to date. Nevertheless, China is not the sole nation where a court has legally acknowledged someone's the right to become grandparents. Internationally, the debate surrounding the existence of this right remains unresolved, both from a doctrinal perspective[205] and with respect to case law. In the context of case law, in *Petithory Lanzmann v. France*,[206] the European Court of Human Rights (hereinafter: ECtHR) ruled that Article 8 of the European Convention on Human Rights (hereinafter: ECHR) does not guarantee anyone the right to have a family or to become grandparents.[207] Israel's Attorney General reiterated this point in 2003 when issuing the government's 'National Guideline for Posthumous Reproduction.'

202 Shi Luyan 石璐言, 'Xi Jingpiing; Guanyu "Zhonggong Zhongyang Guanyu Zhiding Guomin Jingji He Shehui Fazhan Di Shisi Ge Wu Nian Guihua He Er Ling Sanwu Nian Yuanjing Mubiao Di Jianyi" de Shouming 习近平: 关于《中共中央关于制定国民经济和社会发展第十四个五年规划和二〇三五年远景目标的建议》的说明 (Xi Jinping: Explanation on the CPC Central Committee's Proposal on Formulating the 14th Five-Year Plan for National Economic and Social Development and the Long-Term Goals for 2035)' *Xin hua shi* 新华社 (3 November 2020) <https://www.gov.cn/xinwen/2020-11/03/content_5556997.htm> accessed 27 June 2025.

203 Sun (184*n*57) 99.

204 Ibid.

205 Cfr. Katheryn Katz, 'Parenthood from the Grave: Protocols for Retrieving and Utilizing Gametes from the Dead or Dying' (2015) 2006 University of Chicago Legal Forum <https://chicagounbound.uchicago.edu/uclf/vol2006/iss1/11>; Simana (186*n*73).

206 *Petithory Lanzmann v France* (*dec*) [2019] European Court of Human Rights 23038/19.

207 *Ibid.*

Nevertheless, Israeli family courts have recently authorised some parents to use the sperm of their deceased sons for reproductive purposes,[208] particularly in cases involving young men who died while serving in the army. The same authorisation has also been granted by some courts in India[209] and in the United States, the latter (it is worth remarking) often in cases brought by families of Chinese origin.[210] The courts' favour towards the deceased's parents' requests for the return of gametes and embryos is easily justified in cultural terms, as it ensures the continuity of the family and the perpetuation of its genes, which would otherwise be destined for extinction. It also helps the parents fulfil their child's desire to procreate and give them 'a piece of their child to love.' These values are certainly important to many cultures, whether Israeli, Indian, Chinese or (to a certain extent) American. However, gestational surrogacy, the only biotechnology that currently can realise these rights and desires, is legal in Israel,[211] India[212] and the US,[213] but not in the PRC. While not a minor

208 Yael Hashiloni-Dolev and Zvi and Triger, 'The Invention of the Extended Family of Choice: The Rise and Fall (to Date) of Posthumous Grandparenthood in Israel' (2020) 39 New Genetics and Society 250.

209 'Why Delhi High Court Approved Parents' Request for Their Dead Son's Sperm' *The Times of India* (11 October 2024) <https://timesofindia.indiatimes.com/etimes/trending/why-delhi-high-court-approved-parents-request-for-their-dead-sons-sperm/articleshow/114153469.cms> accessed 28 June 2025.

210 Olivia Christie, 'Couple Win Legal Fight to Take Their Dead Son's Sperm and Use It to Create a Grandchild' *Daily Mail Online* (9 Oct 2024) <https://www.dailymail.co.uk/health/article-13940647/couple-win-legal-fight-dead-sons-sperm-grandchild.html> accessed 28 June 2025.

211 Vardit Ravitsky and Ya'arit Bokek-Cohen, '"Life after Death": The Israeli Approach to Posthumous Reproduction' in Dani Filc and others (eds), *Bioethics and Biopolitics in Israel: Socio-legal, Political, and Empirical Analysis* (Cambridge University Press 2018) <https://www.cambridge.org/core/books/bioethics-and-biopolitics-in-israel/life-after-death-the-israeli-approach-to-posthumous-reproduction/1D27B44F4BCFBAF95A46E10AC6999CD2> accessed 28 June 2025; Etti Samama, 'Within Me, But Not Mine: Surrogacy in Israel' in Jean-Daniel Rainhorn and Samira El Boudamoussi (eds), *New Cannibal Markets : Globalization and Commodification of the Human Body* (Éditions de la Maison des sciences de l'homme 2015) <https://books.openedition.org/editionsmsh/10755> accessed 28 June 2025; Sigrid Vertommen, 'Surrogacy at the Fertility Frontier: Rethinking Surrogacy in Israel/Palestine as an (Anti)Colonial Episteme' (2024) 14 History of the Present 108.

212 Prithivi Raj, 'Regulating Surrogacy in India: Legal Frameworks, Ethical Considerations and Lessons from Global Practices' (2024) 4 Nyaayshastra Law Review <https://papers.ssrn.com/abstract=5017308> accessed 28 June 2025; Lopamudra Goswami, Stephen Anthony Larmar and Jennifer Boddy, 'The Impacts of the Covid-19 Pandemic on Surrogacy in India: The Role of Social Work' (2021) 20 Qualitative Social Work 472.

213 Carla Spivack, 'The Law of Surrogate Motherhood in the United States' (2010) 58 The American Journal of Comparative Law 97.

detail, this issue has been largely overlooked by the enthusiastic commentators on the Yixing case, as well as the court that decided that dispute and those who have decided PAR cases in which the surviving spouse is male.

The latter category of disputes is seldom referred to the Chinese courts; the 2024 report cites merely two cases[214] (representing approximately 7% of the total), yet these cases consistently achieve success. The judgment in the Gao Wei case against the Nanjing Drum Tower hospital is particularly pertinent in this regard. Mr Wang and Ms Gao underwent successful IVF treatment at the defendant's clinic. A year later, Ms Gao became pregnant but subsequently died of an amniotic fluid embolism. Following her death, her husband and family requested the return of the remaining embryos, which the hospital refused. The husband and his parents sued the hospital to obtain the embryos. The court determined that the husband, as the signatory of the medical services contract, was entitled to the embryos created under that contract. Furthermore, Ms Gao's relatives and husband, as her heirs, had legitimate rights to them. Consequently, their request for the return of the embryos did not constitute a violation of any legal provisions. The legal and moral risks associated with the reasonably foreseeable use of the embryos in question did not constitute a valid reason for the hospital to refuse to return them.[215]

In referencing the 'reasonably foreseeable future use of the embryos,' the court implied the practice of surrogacy, as is typically the case in most instances where it orders the return of embryos to (living) couples or widows who, due to health concerns, are unable to carry the foetus to full term. In such cases, the transfer of embryos to the uterus of a surrogate mother may be the sole viable utilisation and rationale for requesting their return. Nevertheless, the 2024 report indicates that courts adjudicating such cases have upheld the plaintiffs' requests in 93% of instances.[216]

This prompts the question of whether, as asserted by the Research Group of the Jiangsu Provincial Court in 2020, 'the rulings on frozen embryos somehow implicitly reflect an attitude and position on surrogacy.'[217] According in these

---

214 *Gao Wei Deng su Nanjing Gulou yiyuan* 高鬼等诉南京鼓楼医院 (*Gao Wei et al V Nanjing Drum Tower Hospital*) [2018] Nanjing shi Zhongji Renmin fayuan 南京市中级人民法院 (Intermediate People's Court of Nanjing city) Su Minchong 5641 hao 苏民终5641 号; *Xiong Tao deng su Guangdong sheng renmin yiyuan* 熊涛等与广东省人民医院 (*Xiong Tao et al v Guangdong Provincial People's Hospital* (Guangzhou shi Yuexiu qu Renmin fayuan 广州市越秀区人民法院 (People's Court of Yuexiu district, Guangzhou city)).

215 Sun (184*n*57) 93.

216 Ibid.

217 Ibid 88.

rulings, if medical institutions and healthcare professionals who provide HART services cannot cite their fear of potential legal transgressions as a rationale to deny requests for the return of embryos, how does the legal system respond once banned biotechnology, such as surrogacy, has been successfully employed? How does the socialist judicial philosophy of the New Era influence the decisions in these cases? What are the 'laws of the state, natural ethics and human feelings' that the judge must consider and balance, in determining their outcome?

The time has come to examine the last of the issues relating to biotechnology at the beginning of human life raised by the Yixing case: the ethical and legal approach to gestational surrogacy in the PRC.

CHAPTER 8

Surrogacy

1 Surrogacy in the World: A Contentious Issue

The expression surrogacy, or – as it is also called – 'surrogate motherhood' generally refers to a woman bearing a child on behalf of someone else, waiving her parental rights.[1] Surrogacy can be carried out in many ways, the most significant distinction being the one between 'traditional surrogacy' and 'gestational surrogacy.' In the first case, the surrogate mother provides her own genetic material. She becomes pregnant through sexual intercourse with the intended father or (more commonly, in modern times) through IVF; therefore, she is biologically related to the newborn baby. In the case of gestational surrogacy, instead, the embryo is always generated through IVF. The oocyte and the sperm can be provided by the intended parents or by donors. The surrogate mother, thus, has no genetic links with the child.[2] It is worth noting that both traditional and gestational surrogacy can imply an 'altruistic' or 'commercial' arrangement or contract.[3] In altruistic surrogacy the surrogate mother will only be reimbursed medical costs and other pregnancy-related expenses incurred. In commercial surrogacy the intended parents will also remunerate the surrogate mother.[4]

Traditional surrogacy – intended as the use of another woman's body to overcome infertility in a couple – is not a novelty, as its name suggests. On the contrary, and as often recalled in the articles dedicated to the topic, it is a very ancient practice, dating back to thousands of years ago.[5] With reference to the Judeo-Christian tradition, references to this practice can be found in the Old Testament of the Bible. In Genesis 16:2, for example, Sarah offers her hus-

1 Mario Gervasi, 'The European Court of Human Rights and Technological Development: The Issue of the Continuity of the Family Status Established Abroad Through Recourse to Surrogate Motherhood' [2018] Diritti umani e diritto internazionale 213.

2 Ibid.

3 Ibid.

4 Ibid 213–218.

5 Debora L Spar, 'For Love and Money: The Political Economy of Commercial Surrogacy on JSTOR' (2005) 12 Review of International Political Economy, 287, 290–291; Ludovica Poli, 'La Grande Camera e l'ultima parola sul caso Paradiso e Campanelli' (*SIDIBlog*, 21 February 2017) <http://www.sidiblog.org/2017/02/21/la-grande-camera-e-lultima-parola-sul-caso-paradiso-e-campanelli/> accessed 13 July 2025; Gervasi (218*n*1) 216.

 | DOI:10.1163/9789004754300_010

band Abraham her slave Hagar, so that the latter can bear a child on her behalf. In Genesis 30:3 and Genesis 30:6 a similar offer is made to Abraham's grandson, Jacob, by his wives, Rachel first and then Leah, who offer their husband their servants to procreate.[6] Moreover, from the Roman age to recent times, sterile and wealthy women in the West have taken advantage of their social position to avoid the stigma brought by childlessness by adopting illegitimate children of their husbands or by raising as their own the children born out of sexual relationships (that they sometimes even facilitated) between their husbands and their servants.[7]

These ancient practices are of relevance to the discourse surrounding surrogacy in contemporary times, in particular in view of two aspects. Firstly, they corroborate the critique proposed by British anthropologist Marilyn Strathern in 1993 regarding the association between reproduction and kinship. In the introduction to a book dedicated to technologies of procreation, Strathern criticised the emphasis placed on the bodily process, rejecting the axiom that biological aspects should prevail in the social recognition of parenthood. It is her contention that this perspective is confined in both space and time, insofar as it is, in essence, a Euro-American concept that emerged in the twentieth century. In her own words: '[…] While everywhere social arrangements attend to the production and rearing of children, it is not the case that everywhere the fact of procreation are taken to be of prime significance.'[8]

Then, these practices provide insight into a persistent characteristic of surrogate mothers, namely their affiliation with vulnerable groups, which makes it very difficult for them to oppose surrogacy proposals. As Joelle Long has observed, this underscores the imperative to adopt an intersectional framework in the analysis of the issue, emphasising the risk of exploitation and discrimination, particularly against impoverished and migrant women.[9]

It is worth remarking that, due to reproductive technology innovations, in the last decades the link between procreation and parenthood has started to be questioned even in the Euro-(North)American context. Legal systems, in particular but not only belonging to the WLT, have been forced to (re)define

6 Joelle Long and Simona Novaretti, '"You Were an Embryonic Dragon, Nurtured in a Dog's Belly" v. "Children Are a Piece of Heart". Surrogacy in China and Italy among Tradition, Ideology, Gender, and the Law' (2022) 2-Cmoparative Family Law Methodology IUS COMPARATUM 71, 78.

7 Ibid 94.

8 Marilyn Strathern, 'Introduction. A Question of Context,' *Technologies of Procreation: Kinship in the Age of Assisted Conception* (Manchester University Press, 1993) 23.

9 Long and Novaretti (219*n*6) 77–78.

the notions of 'mother' and 'father,' adapting them to situations in which the conception of a child is not always the result of intercourse between two individuals of opposite sex (possibly) in the privacy of their marital bed, but can involve a plurality of subjects in the public space of a hospital.[10] This has resulted in the dissolution of the conventional notions of parentage and 'motherhood,' and (notably in the context of gestational surrogacy) has led to the emergence of a multifaceted division of functions, encompassing genetic, gestational, and social dimensions.[11] These developments, however, have not diminished the risk of exploitation of vulnerable women; on the contrary, this risk has increased, particularly in cases of commercial surrogacy. From this standpoint, it is remarkable that both opposition and support for this particular type of HART are typically articulated in terms of the protection of human rights, adopting, as Mario Gervasi observes, 'an anthropocentric perspective.'[12] In fact, those who oppose surrogacy in general consider it as a threat to women's and children's rights. With regard to the infringement of women's rights, the emphasis is on the freedom of consent given by surrogate mothers to the practice, which is deemed at least questionable in situations of extreme poverty and destitution. This is particularly evident in cases of transnational surrogacy, which fall within the broader context of the exploitation of countries in the Global South by those in the Global North. With reference to children's rights protected by international public law, surrogacy is widely considered as being incompatible with the principle of 'best interests of the child,' as articulated in Article 3 of the UNCRC. Moreover, it is deemed in direct contravention of the ban of 'the abduction or, the sale of or traffic in children for any purpose or in any form,' as set out in Article 35 of the UNCRC, and (in particular in case of transnational surrogacy) it is incompatible with 'the right from birth to a name, the right to acquire a nationality and, as far as possible, the right to know and be cared for by his or her parents,' as established by Article 7 of the UNCRC. On the other hand, supporters of surrogacy argue that this practice is sometime the only means of ensuring the right to reproduce for the intended parents. Furthermore, it signifies an acknowledgement of the surrogate mother's freedom of contract, along with a validation of her full capacity to act. In their view, such full capacity is, on the contrary, implicitly called into question by policies prohibiting a woman from entering a surrogacy contract. The same policies would impede numerous women in

10 Carmel Shalev, *Birth Power: The Case for Surrogacy* (Revised ed edition, Yale University Press, New Haven & London 2009) 16.

11 Ibid.

12 Gervasi (218*n*1) 214.

need from acquiring the means to enhance their living conditions and those of their families.

It is worth noticing that surrogacy is a contentious issue even among schools of thought that are otherwise highly cohesive on other matters. A particularly salient exemplar is provided by feminist thought, which encompasses both of the positions summarised above.[13] In this context, the critique of surrogacy as a manifestation of the subjugation of the female body by the patriarchal system[14] is coupled with an openness towards the practice, which should be freely chosen and managed by women as autonomous individuals capable of making independent decisions about their own bodies.[15]

The aforementioned views are reflected in the legal provisions concerning surrogacy adopted by various legal systems. In general, an initial classification of global jurisdictions divides the various legal systems into two categories. The first category is termed 'receiving jurisdictions,' meaning the countries of origin of couples who resort to international surrogacy, often due to restrictive rules in force in their own countries.[16] The second category is termed 'destination jurisdictions,' i.e. legal systems that are the destination for reproductive tourism.[17] Scherpe and Fenton-Glynn have given these approaches a geographical connotation, referring to Western and Eastern perspectives on surrogacy.[18] This designation is arguably imprecise, and it may be indicative of an Orientalist perspective. Nevertheless, it is a valuable tool for the classification of legal systems, provided one acknowledges the substantial variations in the approach to surrogacy within these macro-categories, and the colonialist origins of the designation of Europe and North America as 'West,' and the rest of the world as 'East.'

---

13 Noemí Terrats, 'Surrogacy and Feminist Movements' (*IDEES*, 29 January 2020) <https://revistaidees.cat/en/gestacio-subrogada-i-feminismes/> accessed 20 July 2025.

14 Joan C Callahan, *Reproduction, Ethics, and the Law: Feminist Perspectives* (Indiana Univ Pr 1995).

15 Katherine B Lieber, 'Selling the Womb: Can the Feminist Critique of Surrogacy Be Answered?' (1992) 68 Indiana Law Journale 205; Sophie Lewis, *Full Surrogacy Now: Feminism Against Family* (Verso 2021); Shalev (n 1209).

16 Jens M Scherpe and Claire Fenton-Glynn, 'Introduction,' *Eastern and Western Perspectives on Surrogacy* (Intersentia 2019) 1 <https://www.cambridge.org/core/books/eastern-and-western-perspectives-on-surrogacy/introduction/4DD3D0AACB5896A81EE50CD3DBBE2780> accessed 20 July 2025.

17 Ibid.

18 Jens M Scherpe, Claire Fenton-Glynn and Terry Kaan (eds), *Eastern and Western Perspectives on Surrogacy* (Intersentia 2019) <https://www.cambridge.org/core/books/eastern-and-western-perspectives-on-surrogacy/2E5076101F2AAD8C4F85DA40EB802E41> accessed 13 July 2025.

Given the above, and for simplicity's sake, I will still use the aforementioned framework in the following pages, which are dedicated to a general overview of surrogacy on a global level.

1.1 *Surrogacy in Legal Systems Belonging to the WLT: The Western Approach*

In the context of legal systems belonging to the WLT, the approaches towards surrogacy can be described along a spectrum analogous to that previously delineated in the case of PAR. The spectrum ranges from 'prohibitive approach' to 'free market approach,' passing through 'tolerant approach' and 'regulatory approach.'[19]

The prohibitive approach is adopted for example by France, Germany, Spain, and Italy. It is interesting to note that, while all these jurisdictions prohibit surrogacy as a matter of principle, when confronted with a child born as a result of an international surrogacy arrangement, some of them recognise the commissioning parents as legal parents of the child on the basis of the best interest of the child concerned.[20] Without delving into the specifics of the matter, it is important to note that in France this outcome was only realised after 2014, as a direct consequence of the ruling delivered by the ECtHR in *Mennesson v. France*.[21] Conversely, on 16 October 2024, the Italian Parliament passed a bill amending Article 12 of Law No. 40/2004.[22] The provision, which punishes any individual who organises or publicises the commercialisation of gametes or embryos, or surrogate motherhood, with a maximum custodial sentence of two years and a pecuniary penalty of up to €1 million, can now also be applied to Italian citizens who commit 'surrogacy crime' abroad, despite the legality of the procedure in the state in which it is performed.[23]

The recognition of intending parents as legal parent of the surrogating child born abroad is also common to the jurisdictions which are considered to have

---

19 Scherpe and Fenton-Glynn (221*n*18) 4.

20 Ibid.

21 *Mennesson v France* [*extracts*] [2014] ECtHR 65192/11.

22 Maia Davies, 'Italy Surrogacy Ban: Couples Banned from Travelling Abroad to Seek Surrogate' (16 October 2024) <https://www.bbc.com/news/articles/c62rmv630690> accessed 20 July 2025; Angela Giuffrida, 'Surrogate Parents Too Afraid to Return to Italy after "Procreative Tourism" Law' *The Guardian* (17 March 2025) <https://www.theguardian.com/world/2025/mar/17/surrogate-parents-too-afraid-to-return-to-italy-after-procreative-tourism-law> accessed 20 July 2025.

23 Susanna Marinelli and others, 'The Newly Enacted Italian Surrogacy Law: Effects on Reproductive Tourism' [2025] Journal of Assisted Reproduction and Genetics 1.

a 'Tolerant Approach' as, for example England and Wales and the jurisdictions of Australia.[24] Whilst these countries prohibit the commercialisation of surrogacy, they do permit altruistic surrogacy to a certain extent, regulating the transfer of parenthood from the surrogate to the commissioning parents through specific mechanisms. In England and Wales, the regulatory framework pertaining to surrogacy is delineated by two key pieces of legislation: the Surrogacy Arrangements Act 1985 (hereinafter: SAA 1985) and the Human Fertilisation and Embryology Act 1990, revised in 2008 (hereinafter: HFEA 1990 and HFEA 2008). The SAA 1985 was enacted in the aftermath of the first UK surrogacy case, which was named 'The Baby Cotton's Case' after the name of the surrogate mother, Kim Cotton.[25] For this reason, the act has been characterised by some commentators as a 'morally panicked' response.[26] This legislation prohibits commercial surrogacy, while also stipulating that surrogacy agreements are not legally enforceable. A regulatory framework for surrogacy arrangements was established only a few years later, with the introduction of a mechanism for the transfer of parenthood. Section 30 of the HFEA 1990 stipulates the conditions that commissioning parents must fulfil in order to be recognised as the legal parents of the surrogate child.[27] This process is known as a Parental Order, and it is now regulated by Section 54 of the HFEA 2008.[28] The fulfilment of certain criteria is a prerequisite for this recognition. This approach has attracted the interest of legal professionals in the PRC, particularly in recent years, due to the guarantees it appears to offer with regard to respect for the surrogate mother's freedom of choice and the protection of the best interest of the surrogate child.[29] Nevertheless, it must be noted that it is not without its drawbacks. These include the fact that it does not eliminate reproductive tourism. Due to the lack of available surrogate mothers in the

24 Scherpe and Fenton-Glynn (183*n*54) 4.

25 'UK Surrogacy Law: History and Reform' (*NGA Law*) <https://www.ngalaw.co.uk/knowledge-centre/uk-surrogacy-law-history-reform/> accessed 27 July 2025.

26 M Freeman, 'Does Surrogacy Have a Future after Brazier?' (1999) 7 Medical Law Review 1, 12.

27 Claire Fenton-Glynn, 'England and Wales' in Claire Fenton-Glynn, Jens M Scherpe and Terry Kaan (eds), *Eastern and Western Perspectives on Surrogacy* (Intersentia 2019) 116 <https://www.cambridge.org/core/books/eastern-and-western-perspectives-on-surrogacy/england-and-wales/F0AC144381E76538FDF44089207A92C0> accessed 27 July 2025.

28 Ibid.

29 He Yue 何悦 and Yu Fenglei 俞风雷, 'Wo Guo Dayun Shengshi Lifa Yanjiu – Yi Yinguo Daiyun Shengzhi Lifa Shijiao 我国代孕生殖立法研究—以英国代孕生殖立法为视角 (Research on China's Surrogate Reproduction Legislation – from the Perspective of UK Surrogate Reproduction Legislation)' (2017) 38 Faxue zazhi 法学杂志 46.

UK, very often UK citizens seek surrogacy abroad, as is the case in 'prohibitive' jurisdictions.[30]

In their book dedicated *Eastern and Western Perspectives on Surrogacy*, Scherpe and Fenton-Glynn list Greece, Israel, South Africa, New Zealand, and Portugal among the Western countries with a 'regulatory approach.'[31] According to the authors, the main characteristic of this approach is the acceptance of surrogacy as a reality, and the attempt to deal with it in a preventive manner. In particular, they regulate surrogacy before the conception of a child, with permission needed to be sought before this can go ahead, rather than find a solution when the child is already in existence, as often happens in countries with a tolerant approach, and (as a matter of fact) also in the ones with a prohibitive approach.[32]

Many US states are among the legal systems that adopt a 'free market approach,' i.e.: a legal framework in which surrogacy contracts are binding and enforceable. This is why some of them, particularly the State of California, are important destinations for international surrogacy.[33] This is particularly true for men, both single and in a homosexual couple, as the practice is often prohibited for these subjects even in countries considered to be surrogacy friendly. Russia used to be an example of it;[34] nevertheless, in 2023 the Duma approved an amendment to s. 11 of the Federal law on the Basic Protection of Citizens' Health, abolishing access to surrogacy for foreign citizens, and thus eliminating the country from reproductive tourism destinations.[35]

1.2 *Surrogacy in East Asia and Greater China: The 'Eastern Approach'*

The frequency of sudden changes of regulatory approaches in the field of surrogacy, like the one just mentioned with reference to Russia, makes it difficult

30 Scherpe and Fenton-Glynn (183*n*54) 4.

31 Ibid.

32 Ibid.

33 Stephanie M Caballero, 'Gestational Surrogacy in California' in E Scott Sills (ed), *Handbook of Gestational Surrogacy: International Clinical Practice and Policy Issues* (Cambridge University Press 2016) <https://www.cambridge.org/core/books/handbook-of-gestational-surrogacy/gestational-surrogacy-in-california/7F41E998A6EF652ACCB9C7546DFB4F10> accessed 20 July 2025.

34 Olga A Khazova, 'Russia' in Claire Fenton-Glynn, Jens M Scherpe and Terry Kaan (eds), *Eastern and Western Perspectives on Surrogacy* (Intersentia 2019) <https://www.cambridge.org/core/books/eastern-and-western-perspectives-on-surrogacy/russia/FC418EC7D4D0C8DE608BBC2D817EFF98> accessed 19 July 2025.

35 Olga A Khazova, 'Chapter 19: Recent Changes in Russian Law on Surrogacy in the Eastern European Context' (2024) <https://www.elgaronline.com/edcollchap/book/9781802207651/book-part-9781802207651-27.xml> accessed 19 July 2025.

to classify legal systems adopting an 'Eastern perspective' on it. The ease in changing approach shown by these countries can be somehow enabled by the low hierarchical level of the regulations governing the topic. This is undoubtedly the case with the 'prohibitive approach' adopted by the PRC, as well as by Taiwan and Singapore.[36] In the legal systems under discussion, the prohibition on surrogacy is contained in administrative regulations governing the activities of medical institutions and their staff. Consequently, it does not apply to subjects other than those specified, namely surrogacy agencies and their clients. In this regard, the Taiwanese scenario merits a concise analysis. Notably, the island stands as a unique case among those territories that fall within the ambit of Greater China, insofar as it mirrors the situation in the PRC with respect to the proportion of the population that opts for surrogacy as a reproductive strategy, when measured against the total population size.[37] It also appears that the Taiwanese legal system is close to adopting a new approach towards this HART, through the introduction of a provision authorising altruistic surrogacy. This was, for example, the content of the amendment presented on 1 May 2020 by legislator Wu Ping-jui of the ruling Democratic Progressive Party to the law on assisted reproductive techniques of the RoC, the Artificial Reproduction Act (*Rengong shengyu fa* 人工生育法, 2007).[38] The proposal was passed at the preliminary discussion stage, but did not receive final approval. In recent years, however, there has been an increasing call to relax restrictions on surrogacy, including by the Ministry of Health and Welfare.[39] These endeavours were evidently influenced by the findings of polls conducted by the ROC government in 2010 and 2013, which revealed that 86% of respondents concurred with the notion that under specific circumstances and following a medical examination, altruistic surrogacy should be legally sanctioned for infertile couples.[40]

36 Scherpe and Fenton-Glynn (183*n*54) 5.

37 Chih-Hsing Ho, 'Taiwan' in Claire Fenton-Glynn, Jens M Scherpe and Terry Kaan (eds), *Eastern and Western Perspectives on Surrogacy* (Intersentia 2019) 378 <https://www.cambridge.org/core/books/eastern-and-western-perspectives-on-surrogacy/taiwan/B21919D856E746A68B19E99159D14C78> accessed 1 February 2025.

38 'Church Concerned as Taiwan Moves to Legalize Surrogacy- UCA News' (*ucanews.com*, 6 May 2020) <https://www.ucanews.com/amp/church-concerned-as-taiwan-moves-to-legalize-surrogacy/87931> accessed 1 February 2025.

39 *Health Ministry Proposes Making Taiwan First in Asia To Legalize Surrogacy | TaiwanPlus News* (Directed by TaiwanPlus News, 2024) <https://www.youtube.com/watch?v=DOyi-NPOVY> accessed 3 August 2025; stephanie, 'Taiwan To Legalize Surrogacy' (17 November 2023) <https://surrogacy-lawyer.com/zh/taiwan-to-legalize-surrogacy/> accessed 3 August 2025.

40 Ho (225*n*37) 381–382.

In contrast, another territory considered as part of Greater China, the Macao Special Administrative Region of the PRC (hereinafter: Macao) has already adopted a legislative (prohibitive) approach to the regulation of surrogacy, enshrining specific provisions within its Civil Code. To elaborate further, until the conclusion of the twentieth century, Macao adhered to a legal perspective on surrogacy analogous to that which had been long followed by the state which had ruled it for 442 years, i.e. Portugal.[41] In essence, the legal framework did not explicitly prohibit surrogacy but rather permitted judicial organs to derive such a prohibition through the interpretation of prevailing legal principles.[42] A notable shift occurred in 1999, when, following its reversion to PRC jurisdiction, Macao promulgated its own Civil Code. Notwithstanding the fact that, in general terms, the latter law is consistent with the Portuguese Civil Code, the two laws differ with respect to surrogacy. In particular, art. 1726 of the Macao's Civil Code includes a provision that makes agreements for procreation or gestation on behalf of a third party invalid.[43] However, surrogacy in Macao is not regarded as a criminal act, nor are there any administrative sanctions imposed on medical institutions or healthcare professionals involved in surrogacy procedures. Furthermore, the practice does not appear to be sought after by Macanese citizens, whether in their own country or abroad.[44]

It is noteworthy that also the other Special Administrative Region of the PRC and part of Greater China, namely Hong Kong, has legislation in place that specifically regulates surrogacy, but in an opposite sense. In consideration of the profound influence of UK legislation on its legal system, Hong Kong adopts a permissive stance on surrogacy, subject to specific criteria. This approach may be regarded as an illustration of a 'tolerant approach' from an Eastern perspective. In particular, Part III (Prohibitions) of the Hong Kong Special Administrative Region's Human Reproductive Technology Ordinance (2000, last revised in 2021, hereinafter referred to as the HRTO) prohibits the provision of HART, including surrogacy, to individuals who are not married, and it also prevents the occurrence of posthumous children (art. 15 HRTO). Further-

41 Pedro Rute Teixeira, 'Portugal' in Claire Fenton-Glynn, Jens M Scherpe and Terry Kaan (eds), *Eastern and Western Perspectives on Surrogacy* (Intersentia 2019) <https://www.cambridge.org/core/books/eastern-and-western-perspectives-on-surrogacy/portugal/F4FA10B4799375F597239870C5373137> accessed 1 February 2025.

42 Vera Raposo and U Sio Wai, 'Surrogacy in Greater China: The Legal Framework in Taiwan, Hong Kong, Macao, and Mainland China' (2017) 34 UCLA Pacific Basin Law Journal 144 <https://escholarship.org/uc/item/41d104d5> accessed 1 February 2025.

43 Ibid.

44 Ibid.

more, the HRTO prohibits commercial dealings in prescribed substances (gametes, embryos, foetal ovarian tissue, etc.) (Art. 16) and surrogacy arrangements on a commercial basis (Art. 17 HRTO), 'whether in Hong Kong or elsewhere' (Art. 16 and 17, (a)).[45]

Conversely, in other 'Sinic societies,' such as Japan and South Korea, the topic is not regulated by state norms, but only governed by ethical guidelines internal to the medical profession. In particular, in Japan surrogacy is prohibited by the guidelines issued by Japan Society of Obstetrics and Gynecology (hereinafter, JSOG),[46] while in South Korea the Ethical Guidelines on Assisted Reproduction, issued in January 2011 by the Korean Society of Obstetrics and Gynaecology provide eligibility criteria for women acting as surrogate,[47] defining pregnancy through gestational surrogacy as 'the transplant of embryos from sperms and eggs of married couples into the womb of another person and attempting pregnancy.'[48] This makes only legally married couples who can produce embryos from their own eggs and sperms eligible for surrogacy agreements; nevertheless, all these norm are non-binding and enforceable.[49]

It is interesting to note that, since the end of the second decade of the twentieth century, the Eastern perspective on surrogacy no longer includes a free-market approach comparable to that typical of some US states. This approach was once adopted for example by Thailand and India, which use to be a privileged destinations for reproductive tourism, so much so that an Indian village, Anand, was called 'the cradle of the world.'[50] Following a series of scandals that exposed the exploitation of surrogate mothers and the commercialisation of children – such as the case of 'Baby Gammy' (2014), in which commissioning parents from Australia left Baby Gammy in Thailand with his surrogate mother due to his diagnosis with Down syndrome, and only took his

45 Daisy Cheung, 'Surrogacy in Hong Kong' in Jens M Scherpe, Claire Fenton-Glynn and Terry Kaan (eds), *Eastern and Western Perspectives on Surrogacy* (Intersentia Ltd, 2019).

46 Shinichiro Hayakawa, 'Japan' in Jens M Scherpe, Claire Fenton-Glynn and Terry Kaan (eds), *Eastern and Western Perspectives on Surrogacy* (Intersentia 2019) 441 <https://www.cambridge.org/core/books/eastern-and-western-perspectives-on-surrogacy/japan/64738C71422DC01C209203FF8156A906> accessed 20 July 2025.

47 Ock-Joo Kim and Byung-Hwa Lee, 'South Korea' in Jens M Scherpe, Claire Fenton-Glynn and Terry Kaan (eds), *Eastern and Western Perspectives on Surrogacy* (Intersentia 2019) 461–462 <https://www.cambridge.org/core/books/eastern-and-western-perspectives-on-surrogacy/south-korea/778B382D9190B8B380198D77BBC18AAD> accessed 20 July 2025.

48 Ibid 462.

49 Ibid.

50 Aditya Ghosh, 'Cradle of the World' (*Hindustan Times*, 24 December 2006) <https://www.hindustantimes.com/india/cradle-of-the-world/story-sPA9Q9b2r4MHrQ9R7dNJnK.html> accessed 29 July 2025.

twin sister home –[51] both states have amended their legislation. In Thailand, after the enactment of the Protection for Children Born through Assisted Reproductive Technologies Act, B.E. 2558 in 2015, only heterosexual married couples are eligible as intended parents, provided that at least one of the spouses is Thai; commercial surrogacy is prohibited, and surrogate mothers must be of Thai nationality and a relative of one spouse (section 24); parental rights are ensured by law to recognised intended parents at birth (section 30).[52] Similar rules are in force in India, where art. 38 of the 2021 Surrogacy Act (SA) prohibits commercial surrogacy, and the exploitation of surrogate mothers and children born through surrogacy.[53] In particular, art. 2 of SA only allows altruistic surrogacy to Indian married heterosexual couples and single women widowed or divorced, and aged 35–45. Moreover, according to its art. 7:

> The intending couple or intending woman shall not abandon the child, born out of a surrogacy procedure, whether within India or outside, for any reason whatsoever, including but not restricted to, any genetic defect, birth defect, any other medical condition, the defects developing subsequently, sex of the child or conception of more than one baby and the like.

Many empirical studies have shown that, as soon as a 'repronhub' ('less-known locations offering smalls scale, niche cross-border gestational surrogacy or surrogacy services for a regional market,' according to the definition given by Whittaker, Gerrits and Weis)[54] becomes unavailable, other countries

---

51 Andrea Whittaker, 'From "Mung Ming" to "Baby Gammy": A Local History of Assisted Reproduction in Thailand' (2016) 2 Reproductive Biomedicine & Society Online 71. About cross-border surrogacy, see also: Yingyi Luo, 'Unraveling Informality and Precarity: New Labor Law Strategies for the Global Reproduction Network of Cross-Border Surrogacy' (2023) 16 Asian Bioethics Review 185.

52 'Surrogacy In Thailand: A Comprehensive Analysis' (*Thai Law Online*, 4 April 2025) <https://thailawonline.com/surrogacy-in-thailand-comprehensive-analysis/> accessed 20 July 2025.

53 Gaurang Narayan and others, 'The Surrogacy Regulation Act of 2021: A Right Step Towards an Egalitarian and Inclusive Society?' 15 Cureus e37864; 'Surrogacy Law in India – New Era for Surrogacy in India (2025)' (*Dr. Rita Bakshi*) <https://drritabakshi.in/the-surrogacy-regulation-act-2021-a-new-era-for-surrogacy-in-india/> accessed 20 July 2025.

54 Andrea Whittaker, Trudie Gerrits and Christina Weis, 'Emerging "Repronubs" and "Repropreneurs": Transnational Surrogacy in Ghana, Kazakhstan, and Laos' (2022) 63 International Journal of Comparative Sociology 304.

assume its place.[55] Nevertheless, an increasing number of legal systems, even among destination jurisdictions, are responding to the growth of surrogacy on a global scale by enacting legislation that limits exploitation and abuse of women and children.[56] This happened in Cambodia, where many surrogacy agencies moved after the ban in India and Thailand,[57] and in Laos, which became their destination after the surrogacy ban in Cambodia.[58] It is worth mentioning that, commencing in 2023, even Laos has implemented a ban on commercial surrogacy, with a particular focus on foreign nationals engaging in such activities. According to Article 215 of the Lao Criminal Code, surrogacy is treated as a form of human trafficking, and those who hire, recruit, or promote such services face serious criminal charges, being punishable by up to nineteen years in jail.[59]

I referred to Laos not by chances, since it was precisely its proximity to the PRC's borders which made its fortune as 'repronhub.' In fact, many Chinese nationals (including, as we have seen, the plaintiffs of the Yixin cases) sought to get there the surrogacy services which are illegal in their country, at a cheaper price than in Western destinations.

2 Surrogacy in the PRC: Market, Tradition, and Ethics (but What about the Law?)

As in many other countries, the prohibition on surrogacy imposed on institutions and medical staff in the PRC since the beginning of the twenty-first century has not impeded Chinese infertile couples and individuals from realising their aspiration of becoming parents. In case of wealthy people, transnational surrogacy can be an option. In fact, despite the financial cost of surrogacy in

55 Ibid 319.

56 Scherpe and Fenton-Glynn (183*n*54) 5.

57 admin, 'Surrogacy Worldwide – Fertility in Laos – Surrogacy in Laos' (10 May 2017) <https://www.laosfertility.com/surrogacy-worldwide/> accessed 21 July 2025.

58 '"Wombs for Rent" Business Flourishes in Communist Laos | Reuters' <https://www.reuters.com/article/world/wombs-for-rent-business-flourishes-in-communist-laos-idUSKBN18Z0CW/> accessed 21 July 2025; Whittaker, Gerrits and Weis (228*n*54) 319.

59 '"Wombs for Rent" Business Flourishes in Communist Laos | Reuters' (229*n*58); Vientiane Times, 'Illegal Surrogacy Punishable by up to 19 Years in Jail, Lao Government Warns as Cases Reported' <https://asianews.network/illegal-surrogacy-punishable-by-up-to-19-years-in-jail-lao-government-warns-as-cases-reported/> accessed 21 July 2025; Phontham Visapra, 'Lao Government Warns Against Surrogacy Amid Rise in Illegal Cases' (*Laotian Times*, 30 May 2025) <https://laotiantimes.com/2025/05/30/lao-government-warns-against-surrogacy-amid-rise-in-illegal-cases/> accessed 21 July 2025.

the US, ranging from 180,000 to 250,000 US dollars for a surrogate child, two American surrogacy organisations interviewed by Lianhe Zaobao in 2024 confirmed that approximately half of their clients come from China, with this proportion exhibiting an upward trend.[60] However, due to the significant financial constraints, a considerable proportion of Chinese individuals or couples who aspire to become parents through surrogacy turn to the clandestine surrogacy industry within China. In this sector, the financial outlay required for surrogacy can range from 450,000 RMB (approximately 62,150 US dollars) to 800,000 RMB.[61] As demonstrated in the statistics published by the Chinese media outlet Caixin in 2017, there were approximately one thousand companies providing surrogacy services, with an estimated twenty thousand births per year. The headquarters of these companies are typically located in Chinese cities that have been identified as having the highest income levels. Examples of such cities include Beijing, Shanghai, Guangzhou, Wuhan, and Hangzhou. In these cities, the services offered by these companies are not overtly advertised. Instead, they use code words such as 'dy' for surrogacy (*daiyun* 代孕) and 'quL' for egg retrieval (*qu luan* 取卵) to refer discreetly to their services.[62] In contrast, surrogate mothers are typically drawn from rural communities in less economically developed regions of the country and often possess limited formal education. It is important to note that the improvement in China's economic conditions, in combination with the high demand for surrogacy, is resulting in a reduced pool of women willing to become surrogates.[63] This is exactly what happened in Qili (Hubei). This locality was formerly regarded as a 'surrogacy village' on account of the high ratio of surrogate mothers per female villagers (99%, according to an interview conducted in 2017 by Chinese media). However, already in the early 2020s it was impossible to find a local woman willing to be a surrogate mother.[64] The aforementioned circumstances compelled the underground surrogacy industry to relocate to less developed areas, such as Yunnan, Guizhou, and Guangxi.[65] They also demonstrate, if

60 Li kang 黎康, 'Zhongguo te gao: Yinni ai yu lunli zhi sheng xieyuan dai gong xuqiu yu chanye qiaoran fazhan fāzhǎn 中国特稿: 隐匿爱与伦理之争 血缘代工需求与产业悄然发展 (China Special Report: The Hidden Love and Ethical Debate: The Demand for Surrogacy and the Quiet Development of the Industry)' *Lianhe Zaobao* 联合早报 (10 November 2024) <https://www.zaobao.com.sg/news/china/story20241110-5295949> accessed 21 July 2025.

61 Ibid.

62 Ibid.

63 Ibid.

64 Ibid.

65 Ibid.

necessary, that the decision to be a surrogate mother is often due to financial hardship, rather than by choice.

The interviews with surrogacy agencies located within China and the United States conducted by Lianhe Zaobao has also substantiated insights regarding the profile of those seeking surrogacy services.[66] In certain cases, their clientele consists of affluent families who opt for surrogacy as a reproductive technique despite the absence of infertility issues, as well as singles aspiring to have a child. However, it is important to note that approximately 90% of these requests are from individuals who are unable to carry a pregnancy to term for physiological reasons.[67] This group includes infertile couples, elderly people who have lost their only child, and individuals who have passed their reproductive age but still wish to have a second or third child, as is now permitted by law. Other people which can be included in the latter group are same-sex couples, particularly male couples, for whom surrogacy represents the sole viable option for achieving a biological child.

The importance of continuing the bloodline in Chinese culture, already explored in previous chapters with reference to abortion and PAR, is certainly also relevant to surrogacy. However, do additional aspects of traditional ethics and law have any influence on how this particular biotechnology is regarded in China in the present day? How does the interplay between legislative, doctrinal, and jurisprudential formants manifest itself in this particular field?

In the ensuing pages, I will address the aforementioned questions. However, given the significance of public opinion in the formulation of Chinese legal rules, this investigation will be preceded by an analysis of the current state of public discourse on the subject.

2.1 *Surrogacy in the PRC: A Hot Topic*

In Chapter 6, upon the description of the epilogue of Yixin's case, observations have been made concerning the favourable disposition displayed by the Chinese press and commentators in regard to the four elders entrusted by the court with custody of the embryos. Following numerous vicissitudes, they successfully employed transnational surrogacy to realise their aspiration to assume the role of grandparents, four years after the demise of their respective offspring. In the same section, reference was also made to the opposition of the Chinese citizens to the introduction of a surrogacy ban in the PFPL, as well as their broad support for the potential opening up of this practice by the Chinese legislature.

66 Ibid.

67 Ibid.

It is important to acknowledge that the data presented should not be interpreted as indicative of a monolithic, clear-cut PRC's positive public attitude towards surrogacy. Conversely, Chinese public opinion on it varies a lot, depending on the parties involved in the practice, the underlying reasons for its performance, and the age and personal situation of individuals providing an opinion on the matter.

At the beginning of 2021, for example, a wide and heated debate on surrogacy was caused by the news that a popular Chinese actress, Zheng Shuang, have conducted transnational surrogacy and intended to abandon the surrogate babies. The scandal was extensively covered by Chinese and international media, with even the Central Political and Legal Affair Commission (hereinafter: CPLAC) – an institution directly under the control of the Central Committee of the Communist Party of China – stepping in, condemning Zheng's behaviour.[68] In a statement made on its official account, China Chang'an network, CPLAC remarked that:

> It is important to note that surrogacy is explicitly prohibited in our country. Treating women's uteruses as reproductive tools, buying and selling newborn lives as commodities, and even discarding them at will – this clandestine black market operates on the fringes of the law, not only harming women's health and objectifying them for exploitation but also trampling on citizens' rights and corrupting moral values. As Chinese citizens, those who exploit legal loopholes to go to the United States for surrogacy because it is prohibited in China are not adhering to the law.[69]

The CPLAC's opinion was widely reposted and commented on social media. A study of microblogs from the social media platform Weibo published in the Yale Journal of Biology and Medicine examined the public's response to Zheng's decision. The study found that 63% of respondents expressed a negative opinion of Zheng's choice, while only 7% expressed support.[70] Addition-

68 Zhongyang zhengfa wei chang'an jian 央政法委长安剑 (Central Political and Legal Affairs Commission Chang'an Network), 'Zheng Shuang Daiyun Qi Yang Fengbo: Zuan Falü Kongzi, Zhe Jue Bushi Wugu 郑爽代孕弃养风波: 钻法律空子, 这绝不是无辜! (Zheng Shuang Surrogacy and Abandonment Strom: Taking Advantage of Legal Loopholes, This Is by No Means Innocent!)' (20 January 2021) <https://www.thepaper.cn/newsDetail_forward_10866725> accessed 13 July 2025.

69 Ibid.

70 Yue Liu, Xuechang Xian and Li Du, 'Perspectives on Surrogacy in Chinese Social Media: A Content Analysis of Microblogs on Weibo' (2022) 95 The Yale Journal of Biology and Medicine 305, 310.

ally, the study revealed that 89.8% of respondents who expressed an attitude towards surrogacy in principle opposed the practice, while 1.6% supported it.[71] The main critical arguments were based on ethical and moral concerns, such as that surrogacy is unfair and risky to surrogate children and that surrogacy is morally inacceptable.[72] A further issue that was identified pertained to reproductive rights and the presence of inequality in the context of transnational surrogacy. The high cost associated with implementing surrogacy in foreign countries has been shown to effectively restrict access to this service to individuals with significant financial resources.[73] It is worth mentioning that Weibo's users generally belong to younger generations.[74] Thus, not only do the results of the study not represent the opinion of Chinese citizens as a whole.[75] The age of the blogger also provides a potential explanation for the absence of any reference to the needs of the groups generally mentioned by proponents of surrogacy in policy debates and scholarly literature in the social media posts included in the analysis. These individuals include members of the LGBTQ+ community, families who have experienced the loss of a child in their 50s or 60s, and couples struggling with infertility.[76] As previously stated, the aforementioned groups also represent the vast majority of Chinese citizens who resort to surrogacy.

Moreover, the reported criticisms about surrogacy in general and Zheng Shuang's behaviour in particular bear a strong resemblance to those expressed in 2011 in the wake of another surrogacy-related scandal, the so-called 'octuplets incident.'[77] In this case, a wealthy couple in Guangzhou was investigated for having eight babies, five of which were carried by two surrogate mothers.[78] The fact that the one-child policy was still in place at the time, in conjunction with the details concerning the amount of money spent by the intended parents in artificial reproductive procedures and the number of nannies hired to

71 Ibid.

72 Ibid 312.

73 Ibid 312–313.

74 Ibid 313.

75 Ibid.

76 Ibid 313–314.

77 Sina_mobile, 'Guangzhou Fushang Sheng 8 Baotai I 广州富商生 8 胞胎? (Guangzhou Businessman Gave Birth to Eight Babies?)' (*Zhongguo Jingji shibao* 中国果经济时报, 20 December 2011) <https://finance.sina.cn/sa/2011-12-20/detail-ikftpnnx8552037.d.html> accessed 12 July 2025.

78 'China Couple with Eight Babies Sparks Surrogacy Debate' *BBC News* (21 December 2011) <https://www.bbc.com/news/world-asia-china-16275624> accessed 12 July 2025.

take care of the babies released by Chinese media,[79] served to exacerbate the prevailing sentiment of social injustice. This in turn led to a significant increase in internet users voicing their discontent regarding what has been termed 'unfair births' (*bu gongping de chusheng* 不公平的出生):[80] the possibility for wealthy, childless people to circumvent the law and have babies by alternative means.[81]

A review of the published opinions on these cases reveals an almost complete absence of any reference to the (il)legality of surrogacy. The lack of awareness regarding the content of the regulations in force in the PRC, or conversely, the unconscious awareness of their ineffectiveness, was evident in 2020 with the release of a short film titled *Baobei'er* (宝贝儿, lit.: sweetheart, English title: Ten months with you) by renowned Chinese director Chen Kaige.[82] The short film, presented as the final test in a television contest, is described in the clip's official description as the 'complex and painful relationships among three people who are connected by a newborn.'[83] These are an intended mother, who turned to surrogacy after having lost her only child; a surrogate mother, who signed the surrogacy contract without informing her boyfriend, and develops such a strong emotional connection with the foetus during pregnancy that she does not want to hand it over to the intended parents after giving birth; the surrogate mother's boyfriend, who eventually convinces her that the baby is not meant to be with them and that she must let it go. The film does not take an explicit ethical stand on commercial gestational surrogacy; moreover, it contains remarks on the illegality of the procedure in China, and in closing credits reminds viewers that 'surrogacy in strictly forbidden by Chinese law and those who violate it will be severely punished.'[84] Notwithstanding this, it received harsh critiques by Weibo's users, for supposedly portraying surrogate motherhood in a relatively positive light, and for its

79 Sina_mobile (233*n*77).

80 Ibid.

81 'China Couple with Eight Babies Sparks Surrogacy Debate' (233*n*78).

82 '"Farewell My Concubine" Director Chen Kaige in Hot Water Over Surrogacy-Themed Short Film' (7 December 2020) <https://radii.co/article/chen-kaige-surrogacy> accessed 13 July 2025; Ji Yuqiao, 'Short Film from Renowned Chinese Director Chen Kaige Sparks Discussion about Surrogacy in China – Global Times' (*Global Times*, 7 December 2020) <https://www.globaltimes.cn/content/1209254.shtml> accessed 13 July 2025; 'Chen Kaige Short Blasted for "Glorifying" Surrogacy' (*MCLC Resource Center*, 15 December 2020) <https://u.osu.edu/mclc/2020/12/15/chen-kaige-short-blasted-for-glorifying-surrogacy/> accessed 21 July 2025.

83 'Chen Kaige Short Blasted for "Glorifying" Surrogacy' (234*n*82).

84 '"Farewell My Concubine" Director Chen Kaige in Hot Water Over Surrogacy-Themed Short Film' (234*n*82).

unrealistic 'happy ending.' In this case, as in the Zheng Shuang scandal, it was primarily the state-owned media – such as *China Court Daily*,[85] the newspaper published by the Supreme People's Court, or *Global Times* and *China Daily*,[86] the official newspaper of the Central Committee of the Chinese Communist Party – that focused their critiques on the illegality of surrogacy in China, exploiting the opportunity to reiterate that certain behaviours are banned in the Chinese legal system.

In conclusion, it is possible to synthesise the Chinese public's attitudes towards surrogacy into two categories. Firstly, there is a sense of empathy for ordinary people who, deprived of offspring for reasons beyond their control, wish to fulfil their dream of having a child to perpetuate their lineage, regardless of the means employed. This is counterbalanced by disapproval of those who take advantage of their status and means to achieve goals, including reproductive ones, that are denied to the majority of other people. The unifying factor underpinning these seemingly contradictory expressions of thought is an almost complete absence of awareness regarding the legitimacy of certain practices and the legal consequences that may ensue from them.

This raises the question of the provenance of these phenomena. Is it possible to identify, within the contradiction between the law in force in the country and the rules perceived by its citizens, the presence of some cryptotypes that have emerged over millennia of patriarchal and polygynous society? If this is indeed the case, what form do these cryptotypes take?

A brief analysis of some typical institutions of traditional Chinese family law can assist in clarifying these aspects.

3 Surrogacy in China: Traditional Legacy

> [Xu Yingkui] was Governor-general of Fujian in 1897 […]. Xu was born to a concubine of his father's, who died after he had just passed the imperial examination. Xu's request to let his natural mother's (*sheng mu* 生母) coffin pass through the main entrance of the house during the funeral

---

85 @ Renmin Fayuan bao de Weibo @人民法院报的微博 (People's Court Daily Weibo), '#热点说法#【别以身… – @人民法院报的微博' (*Weibo* 微博, 5 December 2020) <https://weibo.com/3268047813/Jx75MfH1q?ref=collection&ssl_rnd=1607379858.6485> accessed 13 July 2025.

86 Zhang Zhouxiang, 'Movie Should Have Made Clear Surrogacy a Crime' (*China Daily*) <https://www.chinadaily.com.cn/a/202012/09/WS5fd0181aa31024ad0ba9aaab.html> accessed 6 July 2025; Ji Yuqiao (234*n*82).

> procession was repeatedly denied by his formal mother (*di mu* 嫡母). [...] At last, Xu asked, 'Will my own coffin be allowed to pass through the main entrance after my death?'. The formal mother answered: 'Yes, of course it will. You were an embryonic dragon temporarily nurtured in the belly of a bitch (*er nai long tai gou du* 儿乃龙胎狗肚) [...].[87]

While interference of technology and science in reproduction is unprecedented, the dissociation between biological and social parenting can be traced in history, as the Late Imperial China dialogue between Xu Yingkui and his 'formal mother' shows, in a crude but rather effective way.

In fact, as Francesca Bray pointed out,[88] Late Imperial China was '*a patrilineal, polygynous society, with its own forms and practices of surrogacy or multiple parenthood.*' The principle of patrilineal descent was at the basis of the Chinese socio-political system at least since the Western Zhou's era (1100 BC–771 BC) and it became an imperial cornerstone under the Han dynasty (206 BC–8 AD) when Confucian thought was transposed into government ideology. As we have often recalled, man's greatest duty was to provide his lineage with offspring, and 'son and grandson pervaded the hall' (*zisun mantang* 子孙满堂) represented the traditional Chinese view of a perfect family life.[89] Moreover, regarding women, 'The rites of the Elder' (*Da Dai Liji* 大戴礼记) listed 'being childless' among the 'seven out' (*qi qu* 七去), i.e.: the seven reasons that allowed a man to legally repudiate his wife (Dadai Liji – Benming, 大戴礼记-本命 n. 13).

In this context, multiple parenthood, generally stemming from adoption or polygyny, often appeared as the only solution for childless couples eager to avoid the shame of infertility. Indeed, not only adoption, but even concubinage could benefit at the same time husbands and wives, as the law considered the father's principal wife as the biological mother of all the children recognised by him.[90] The principal wife would become, in all respects, the

87 Kiung Jai Koh Clan Association, 'Genealogical Records of the Koh Clan in Singapore' 63.

88 Bray (184*n*62) 182.

89 Shi Lei 石雷 and Zhan Luxia 占 泸霞, "Gongneng Jiegou' She Yu Xia Woguo Daiyun Zhidu de Goujian '功能结构' 视 域下我国代孕制度的构建 (The Construction of a Chinese System of Surrogacy from the Perspective of Structural Functionalism' (2019) 79 Haixia Faxue 海峡法学 74, 79.

90 Yang Haichao 杨海超, 'Woguo Minfadian Zhong de Qinzi Guanxi Queding Wendi – Yi Daiyun Shenyu We Shejiao 我国民法典中的亲子关系确定问题——以代孕生育为视角 - 中国政法大学研究生院 (Chinese Civil Code Problem in Defining Parent-Child Relationship – from the Perspective of Surrogacy)' (2020) 35 Yanjiusheng faxue 研究生法学, 12, 13.

only legal and ritual mother (*dimu* 嫡母) of the family,[91] and the children had to mourn and worship her as their full parent,[92] regardless of who (concubine *qie* 妾, or maid, *nüyong* 女佣) had given birth to them.[93] Hence, both concubinage and adoption served principal wives as socially (and legally) approved forms of 'surrogate motherhood' or 'surrogacy,' allowing them to appropriate the biological labour of less privileged women.

The reason why in Chinese imperial society such behaviour was accepted as perfectly 'natural' could be more easily understood considering the value attributed by Confucian orthodoxy to education and, on the other hand, the dual understanding of women's fertility. According to Confucius, education was, at the same time, a means of transformation and cultivation of the self, and a way to acquire the Dao.[94] It was only through learning and practice that people could differentiate themselves: 'By nature, men are alike. By study, men become far apart (*xing xiang jin ye, xi xiang yuan ye* 性相近也, 习相远也) (Kongzi 孔子, ch. 17 n. 2). That means that people could only develop their potential if and how they preserved their heart-and-mind and cultivated their character.[95] It is through education that one could grow into a noble man (*junzi* 君子), a person at the same time worthy and morally obligated to serve the people and the state.[96] Not surprisingly, therefore, during imperial times the quintessence of motherhood was not to give birth, but to provide a child a moral education that would encourage him to pursue honourable goals and achieve social success.

That is not to say that biological contribution was considered of little importance. On the contrary, according to Chinese traditional reproductive medicine, it was one of the two fundamental aspects of female fertility: the ability to reproduce life (*sheng* 生), or to give birth (*chan* 产), counterbalanced by the ability to nurture life and successfully bring up a child (*yang* 养).[97] In the case of multiple motherhood, this yin-yang (阴阳) duality was embodied in the different roles assigned to concubines and maids on the one hand and

91 Ibid.

92 Bray (184*n*62) 186.

93 Ibid 185.

94 Charlene Tan, 'Confucianism and Education,' *Oxford Research Encyclopedia of Education* (2017) 3 <https://oxfordre.com/education/display/10.1093/acrefore/9780190264093.001.0001/acrefore-9780190264093-e-226> accessed 1 February 2025.

95 Rita Mei-Ching Ng, 'College and Character: What Did Confucius Teach Us About The Importance of Integrating Ethics, Character, Learning, and Education?' (2009) 10 Journal of College and Character 8, 3.

96 Ibid.

97 Bray (184*n*62) 189.

to principal wives on the other. Being strong and fecund (*yang* 阳 characteristic), the former were fit to give birth but unsuitable to educate the master's heir because of their humble origins (*yin* 阴 characteristic). Principal wives were, instead, too weak to conceive and deliver a child (*yin* 阴 characteristic), but had the social status, authority and culture required to bring up and educate their husbands' offspring (*yang* 阳 characteristic).[98] In this sense, multiple motherhood not only allowed the master of the house to give continuity to his lineage; through the (harmonious?) combination of the yin-yang characteristics of the household women, multiple motherhood also secured him a healthy, properly cultivated progeny, that would bring honour to family and ancestors.

Besides concubinage and adoption, Ancient China knew at least one other kind of 'surrogacy' and multiple motherhood: the custom of 'renting out' (*chujie* 出借) wives, also referred to as 'borrow a woman's belly to produce offspring' (*jiefu shengzi* 借腹生子) or, more technically, 'pawning wife' (*dian qi* 典妻).

This practice – which comes from the even more ancient custom of 'selling a wife' (*jiaqi/maimai* 嫁妻/卖妻)[99] – is mentioned for the first time in the 'Book of Southern Qi: The Biography of Wang Jingze '(*Nanqi shu: Wang Jingze chuan* 南齐书 • 王敬则传), Northern and Southern Dynasties era (approx. second half of the sixth century).[100] It is worth remarking that as other forms of *dian*, in the first phases of its development the *dianqi* was a kind of mortgage, or a sale with redemption agreement.[101] In particular, it was a contract according to which a man (the original husband, *yuanfu* 原夫) could pledge an asset (his wife, who became the *dian* wife, *dianqi* 典妻) to another man (the *dian* husband, *dianfu* 典夫) for a certain amount of time (generally between three and five years).[102] The wife was a sort of collateral for a loan; thus, once the term expired and the loan was reimbursed, she was supposed to return to her husband's home. However, due to the 'ordinary depreciation' of the woman after the years spent in *dian*, few husbands were willing to redeem

98 Ibid.

99 Xu Haiyan 徐海燕, 'Lüe Lun Zhongguo Gudai Dianwi Hunsu Jiqi Chansheng Genyuan 略论中国古代典妻婚俗及其产生根源 (Brief Discuss.Ion on the Origin of the Custom of Pawning a Wife)' (2005) 92 Shenyang shifan daxue xue bao (shehui liaxue ban) 沈阳师范大学学报(社会科学版) 77, 77.

100 Ibid; Li Qun 李群, 'Dianqi Yu Biantong de Lifa Heyong 典妻与变通的礼法适用 (The "Pawning of a Wife" and the Flexible Application of Rites)' (2010) 140 Dandai faxue (shunyueli) 当代法学(双月刊) 42, 42.

101 Li Qun 李群 (238*n*101) 42.

102 Xu Haiyan 徐海燕 (238*n*100) 78.

their wives when the contract expired.[103] Due to the inherent risks for the *dian* husband, this type of contract was not very common. It was only later, approximately during the Tang dynasty (618–907), that the *dianqi* changed its social function, becoming more appealing and spreading throughout China. In practice, it was transformed into a kind of contract of employment or leasing,[104] the characteristics of which could be slightly changed according to the will of the parties or local customs.[105] In its basic structure, it was a contract pursuant to which a man could rent out his wife for a certain time (five, ten or fifteen years, generally depending on the wife's fertility) to a childless man in exchange for a certain amount of money. The main purpose of this agreement was to let the *dian* husband perpetuate the *qi* (气, vital energy) of his family, so the *dian* wife had to have sex with him and get pregnant. In order to avoid confusion, she could not live with the original husband and sometimes she was not even allowed to look after her original children.[106] The parties (i.e. the original husband and the *dian* husband) also specified whether the *dian* wife had to live in the *dian* husband's home, or to meet the *dian* husband in another place.[107] Moreover, they established the ownership of the children she would give birth to during the *dian*. In fact, the *dian* husband could decide to keep all the children or choose to retain only the boys. In the latter case, once the *dian* period expired, the girls would have to follow their mother, and go back to the original husband's house. In any case, the son born during the *dian* would take the dian husband's surname, inherit his estate and be included in his genealogy.[108]

This practice, which was always considered immoral and contrary to the Chinese rites (*li* 礼),[109] became illegal starting from the Yuan dynasty.[110] Nevertheless, and even though the Ming and the Qing Codes harshly punished the crime of 'Facilitating and tolerating the wife's or concubine's fornication' (see arts. 391, The Great Ming Code, and 367, The Great Qing Code) under which the case of *dianqi* fell,[111] the custom of 'pawning a wife' continued

103 Ibid.

104 Ibid.

105 Ibid 79.

106 Ibid 78.

107 Ibid.

108 Ibid.

109 Li Qun 李群 (238*n*101) 43.

110 Ibid 42.

111 Matthew H Sommer, *Sex, Law and Society in Late Imperial China* (Stanford University Press, 2000) 227; Li Qun 李群 (238*n*101) 42.

over the centuries.[112] This happened perhaps also because imperial magistrates often failed to follow the law when deciding on such cases, especially in times of famine, or when the wife was the very last asset of a family, and renting her out was the family's only hope of survival.

The above custom was finally wiped out as was any other 'feudal' residue after the foundation of the PRC. However, infertile couples have always continued to look for solutions, due to the pressure of traditional culture, and the sense of inferiority and social discredit caused by the lack of children.

4 Surrogacy in Chinese Law and Practice

4.1 *Surrogacy in Chinese Statute Law*

4.1.1 Surrogacy in Chinese Administrative (Departmental) Regulations

As stated in the preceding chapters, although the PRC is still one of the most populous countries worldwide, its population growth rate has decreased since the 2010s, due to the stringent implementation of a family planning policy that has been in effect for the three previous decades. According to the data published by the National Bureau of Statistics of the PRC, the Chinese net population growth in 2021 was only 480,000, with the natural growth rate being only 0.034%. This is the lowest result since 1962. Furthermore, in 2022, the PRC's population decreased by 850,000 individuals, marking the first negative growth in the past six decades. In addition to the declining birth rate, China is undergoing a process of demographic ageing. As of the close of 2021, the population over the age of 60 was approximately 267 million, constituting around 19% of China's total population. Furthermore, the infertility rate within the childbearing population in China has increased from approximately 12% in 2007 to approximately 18% in 2020. It is estimated that by 2025, approximately 33 million couples of childbearing age will be experiencing infertility,[113] while other calculations suggest that this number must be at least doubled.[114] Among the potential factors contributing to these elevated

112 Xu Haiyan 徐海燕 (238*n*100) 78.

113 Shanna Logan and others, 'Infertility in China: Culture, Society and a Need for Fertility Counselling' (2019) 8 Asian Pacific Journal of Reproduction 1, 1.

114 Wangyi 网易 (NetEase), 'Yinxing de Daiyun Shichang: 65 Wan Xuan Xingbie Zai Jia 10 Wan Xi Ti Longfeng Tai/Shengyu/Huaiyun/Wangli/Fuyang Quan 隐形的代孕市场:65万全包 85万选性别 再加10万喜提 (The Hidden Surrogacy Market: 650,000 Yuan for a Full Package, 850,000 Yuan to Select the Gender, and an Additional 100,000 Yuan to Welcome a Set of Twins)' (Wangyi 网易 (NetEase), 3 March 2019) <https://www.163.com/money/article/G0LK9GBL00258105.html> accessed 23 July 2025.

figures, the interplay among the institutions of marriage and family, economic development and public policies appears to be of particular significance. Aware the risk they pose to the healthy and sustainable development of Chinese society, culture, and economy, which could no longer be guaranteed in an old country with few human resources, the Chinese leadership has sought to implement corrective measures starting in the middle 2010s. These include the implementation of measures to promote fertility, especially among younger generations, which have already been mentioned in relation to abortion, as for example the relaxation of family planning restrictions. This process ultimately resulted in the replacement of the one-child policy with a two-child policy in 2015, and then with a three-child policy in 2021. Moreover, the provision of bonuses for late marriages was discontinued in 2016.[115] While there is no evidence to suggest that these initiatives have altered the demographic trend, it is conceivable that they have, at least to a certain extent, influenced the increase in demand for HART treatments. In fact, many couples are still reluctant to get married – not to mention to procreate – at a young age, due to career pressure, intense competition, and the rising costs of buying a house.[116] Unfortunately, the right time to conceive in a social and economic perspective does not always coincide with the most fertile phase of life. Thus, since the beginning of the new century, an increasing number of people have been turning to assisted reproduction, and – once all the other infertility treatments have proven to be ineffective – to surrogacy. Among these families, there are the tens of millions couples that meet the conditions provided for by 2021 LPFP to have a second or a third child but biologically too old to procreate,[117] and parents whose single child died.[118] For the last two groups, as noticed above, surrogacy could be the last chance to fulfil the desire to have a(nother) biological child.

Not surprisingly, then, in the last two decades in the People's Republic of China surrogacy has boomed, as shown by increasing numbers of surrogacy

115 'End to Late Marriage Holidays Upsets Young Couples – Global Times' (*Global Times* (*Xinhua*), 10 April 2015) <https://www.globaltimes.cn/content/964661.shtml> accessed 29 June 2025.

116 'Single or Late Marriage – Tales of China's Younger Generations – Chinadaily.Com.Cn' <https://www.chinadaily.com.cn/a/201806/29/WS5b359b8ea3103349141dfb10.html> accessed 1 February 2025.

117 'Er Hai Zhengze Yi Nian Zhuizong: Sheng Bu Chu Hai Zhen Fannao 二孩政策一年追踪: 生不出二孩真烦恼 (One-Year Follow-up of the Two-Child Policy: Not Being Able to Have a Second Child Is Really Annoying)' *Renmin Ribao* 人民日报 (3 February 2017) <http://zw.china.com.cn/2017-02/03/content_40212924.htm> accessed 24 July 2025.

118 Sui Suli 睢素利, Li Jingru 李京儒 and Liu Hang 刘欢 (161*n*6) 804.

agencies springing up in big cities,[119] and the huge number of advertisements offering surrogacy services available on the web or even written on the walls.[120] Despite this, and as noticed with reference to other kinds of HART, the regulatory framework on surrogacy is still the one established by the (former) MoH at the beginning of the twenty-first century, in a totally different social, economic and (most of all) demographic situation. I am referring, once again, to MAHART 2001, TSHART 2003, BSHSP 2003, and EPIHARTSB 2003. It is worth reminding that art. 3 of MAHART 2001 makes it clear that 'the application of HART should be conducted in medical institutions for medical purposes and in accordance with national family planning policies, ethical principles, and relevant laws and regulations' and 'medical institutions and medical personnel shall not perform any form of surrogacy technology.' Furthermore, Article 22 stipulates that medical institutions and medical personnel which violate these provisions will receive warnings and administrative sanctions, with a maximum amount of RMB 30,000. In the event that the violation also constitutes a criminal offence, criminal responsibility shall be pursued in accordance with the law. TSHART 2003 and the EPIHARTSB 2003 reiterate this prohibition,[121] together with the ban on other surrogacy-related HART, such as the stimulation of ovulation to achieve multiple births or the provision of oocytes for commercial purposes.[122]

The sectoral nature of these regulations can provide a rationale for the apparent lack of awareness among Chinese citizens regarding the illegality of this practice. The confusion surrounding surrogacy legal status is then further fuelled by the national policies aiming to raise the birth rate through the improvement of assisted reproduction services. An example of these attempts is the introduction, in Article 37 of the 2021 PFPL of a provision requiring medical and health institutions to 'carry out infertility diagnosis and treatment in a well-regulated manner.'[123] Similarly, both the '14th Five-Year Plan for National Health and the 'Outline for the Development of Chinese

119 Shi Lei 石雷 and Zhan Luxia 占泸霞 (185*n*63) 360.

120 Ding Chunyan 'Surrogacy Litigation in China and Beyond' (2015) 2 Journal of Law and the Biosciences 33, 34.

121 Weisheng bu 卫生部, 'Weisheng bu guanyu xiuding renlei fuzhu shengzhi jishu yu renlei jingzi ku xianguan jishu guifan, jiben biaozhun he luli yuanze de tongzhi 卫生部关于修订人类辅助生殖技术与人类精子库相关技术规范、基本标准和伦理原则的通知 (Notice of the Ministry of Health on the Revision of Technical Specifications, Basic Standards, and Ethical Principles Related to Human Assisted Reproductive Technology and Human Sperm Banks)' (167*n*29) apps 3, Part I (3) 5,6.

122 Ibid 3, Par I (1) 2.

123 Zhan Zhongle 湛中乐 (162*n*11) 30.

Women' (2021–2030) have put 'regulating the application of assisted human reproduction technology and providing good fertility diagnosis and treatment services' on the national agenda.[124]

Nevertheless, the most significant factor contributing to the misinterpretation of the legitimacy of surrogacy is the absence, in the Chinese legal system, of any prohibition regarding it that is valid *erga omnes*, that is to say, applicable to all individuals and entities. Indeed, and as it has been often remarked, the prohibition imposed by the aforementioned departmental rules does not apply to Chinese citizens as such, and in particular it does not apply to intentional parents, to surrogate mothers, and even to private surrogacy agencies.[125] Consequently, the latter have an easy task in assuring their clients that 'surrogacy is not a crime.'[126] But is it really the case?

4.1.2 Surrogacy in Chinese Criminal Law

The most concise response to the question above is an unequivocal affirmation. Indeed, contrary to statements made by state media and Chinese leaders, surrogacy in the PRC is not a crime. Despite the elapse of time since the adoption of Article 22 of the MAHART 2001 and the numerous revisions of the Criminal Law (*Xingfa* 刑法, enacted in 1979 and amended in 1997, 1998, 1999, three times in 2001, 2002, 2005, 2006, two times in 2009, 2011, 2015, 2017, 2020, and 2023, hereinafter: CL), the CL does not stipulate any provisions that would result in the criminalisation of surrogacy,[127] even in circumstances where it is conducted within the frameworks and by personnel that are subject to the provisions of the MAHART 2001. The only rule which could be used with reference to medical staff working in surrogacy clinics is its art. 336, but merely in the case that they fall within the scope of it, i.e.: they 'engage in medical practice without having the qualification for it.'[128] With reference to surrogacy industry, from time to time proposals have been put forward that would equate organising commercial surrogacy with other crimes provided for by the CL, in particular the ones of organising the sale of human organs (art.

124 Ibid.

125 Ibid.

126 Li kang 黎康 (230*n*60).

127 Liu Changqiu 刘长秋, 'Lun Shangye Xin Daiyun de Xingfa Guize 论商业性代孕的刑法规制 (On the Criminal Regulation of Commercial Surrogacy)' [2024] Dongfang Faxue 东方法学 175, 182.

128 Song Jian 宋建 and others, 'Quan Liantia Fangfan He Dai Daiyun Gongzuo Jizhi Yanjiu 全链条防范和打击代孕工作机制研究 (Reserch on the Working Mechanism of Preventing and Attacking Surrogacy)' (2024) 32 Weisheng Faxue 卫生法学 100, 102.

234 CL) or organising prostitution (art. 358 et seq. CL).[129] However, despite some similarities, the characteristics of commercial surrogation are not perfectly comparable to the constituent elements of these crimes. Selling human organs implies the removal of an organ from the donor's body for transfer to the recipient in exchange for remuneration, while prostitution, which is not defined in the CL, in administrative regulation is considered as 'the act of providing sexual services to another party following a monetary transaction to satisfy the sexual desire of that party.'[130] Commercial surrogacy is an activity of renting/leasing the womb to obtain children in exchange of remuneration, the target of which is the right to use of the uterus and even the body of the surrogate woman during pregnancy. This makes it different both from selling human organs, which does not imply implying in any way control over the donor's body, and from prostitution, the objective of which is the act or service of sexual intercourse, without the person practising it being fundamentally affected by it.[131] Another possibility that legal scholars have explored is to assimilate the act of running a surrogacy agency with running an illegal business, as set out in Art. 225 of CL.[132] Undoubtedly, underground surrogacy agencies operate without registering with the Industrial and Commercial Administration and obtaining a legal licence, and are therefore themselves illegal operation.[133] Nevertheless, it is evident that they do not comply with the stipulations outlined in Article 225,[134] thereby falling short of being designated as illegal businesses. This is primarily due to their failure to undertake 'acts of a natural person or unit that contravene state regulations (meaning provisions issued by national legislative and administrative organs), intentionally engage in illegal business activities, and cause disruption to the market order.'[135] Since, as stated before, surrogacy does not violate any state regulations, surrogacy industry does not even meet the prerequisite for the crime of illegal business operations.[136]

Conversely, surrogacy clinics are certainty include within the scope of paragraph 1, Article 99 of the Basic Healthcare and Medical Promotion Law (*Jiben yiliao weisheng yu jiankang cujin fa* 基本医疗卫生与健康促进法 enacted on

129 Liu Changqiu 刘长秋 (243*n*128) 182.

130 Jiang Su and Zhang Huimin, 'Criminalization of Commercial Surrogacy in China' (2024) 12 Peking University Law Journal 23, 26.

131 Ibid.

132 Ibid.

133 Ibid.

134 Ibid; Liu Changqiu 刘长秋 (243*n*128) 183.

135 Jiang and Zhang (244*n*131) 27.

136 Ibid.

28 December 2019 and in force since the 1 June 2020, hereinafter: BHCMPL), according to which:

> Where a medical institution that has not obtained a medical institution practicing license practices medicine without permission in violation of this Law the people's government the health department of the people's government at or above the county level shall order the violator to cease its practicing activities, confiscate any illegal proceeds, medicinal products, and medical devices, and impose a fine of not less than five nor more than 20 times the illegal proceeds on it; and if the amount of illegal proceeds is under 10,000 yuan, the fine shall be calculated based on illegal proceeds of 10,000 yuan.

Nevertheless, this provision can hardly be a deterrent. Compared to the a business in which a single performance can easily exceed one million RMB in revenue, the confiscation of medicine and medical devices, coupled with a maximum fine which, due to the difficulty in verifying the actual income of these underground institutions, is often limited to 200,000 RMB, represents a risk that the surrogacy business can take without too much concern.[137]

In any event, prior to the potential implementation of sanctions against entities engaging in commercial surrogacy, these entities should be found. This can prove to be a challenging task, which can be attributed in part to the system of supervision that incorporates multiple departments.[138] The latter characteristic, due to the necessity to involve diverse domains of expertise, is predicated on the intricacy of the issues associated with surrogacy. The endeavour to combat it necessitates the monitoring of websites, the regulation of intermediary agencies, the supervision of medical personnel, and the oversight of pharmaceuticals that may be employed in activities pertaining to its performance.[139] In order to enhance the system's efficiency, in September 2017, the National Health and Family Planning Commission (a body which, it should be recalled, in 2013 merged the functions of the MoH and the National Population and Family Planning Commission, and which since 2018 has been renamed the National Health Commission) issued, in conjunction with twelve other ministries and ministerial-level agencies directly under the State Council, the Notice on Issuing a Special Action Plan to Investigate and Punish Illegal and Irregular Applications of Human Assisted Reproductive

137 Song Jian 宋建 and others (243*n*129) 102.

138 Ibid.

139 Ibid.

Technology (*Guanyu yinfa kaizhan chachu weifa weigui renlei fuzhu shengzhi jishu zhanxiang xingdong gongzuo fang'an de tongzhi* 关于印发开展查处违法违规应用人类辅助生殖技术专项行动工作方案的通知).[140] A similar 'Notice,' this time involving 14 departments, was enacted on 13 June 2023.[141] Despite these efforts, and the nationwide campaigns against surrogacy cyclically launched by the government,[142] the hurdle in coordinating many actors whose responsibilities often overlaps, the inefficiencies in the implementation of directives at the grassroots level, and the weak comprehensive enforcement make sometimes difficult to create an effective supervisory synergy.[143] It is worth remarking that the struggle against the surrogacy industry sometimes

140 Ibid.

141 Guojia weisheg jiankang wei bangong ting 国家卫生健康委办公厅 General Office of the National Health Commission, 'Guojia Weisheg Jiankang Wei Bangong Ting, Zhongyang Zhengfa Wei Bangong Ting, Zhongyang Wang Xin Ban Mishu Ju, Zuigao Renmin Fayuan Bangong Ting, Zuigao Renmin Jianchayuan Bangong Ting, Jiaoyu Bu Bangong Ting, Gongye He Xinxi Hua Bu Bangong Ting, Jiàoyù Bù Bàngōng Tīng, Minzheng Bu Bangongting, Shichang Jianguan Zongjiu Bangong Ting, Guojia Yao Jian Ju Zonghe Si, Guojia Zhong Yiyao Ju Zonghe Si, Quanguo Fulian Bangong Ting, Zhongyang Junwei Houqin Baozhang Bu Weisheng Ju Guanyu Yinfa Kaizhan Yanli Dai Feifa Yingyong Renlei Fuzhu Shengzhi Jishu Zhanxiang Huodong Gonzuo Fang'an de Tongzhi 国家卫生健康委办公厅、中央政法委办公厅、中央网信办秘书局、最高人民法院办公厅、最高人民检察院办公厅、教育部办公厅、工业和信息化部办公厅、公安部办公厅、民政部办公厅、市场监管总局办公厅、国家药监局综合司、国家中医药局综合司、全国妇联办公厅、中央军委后勤保障部卫生局关于印发开展严厉打击非法应用人类辅助生殖技术专项活动工作方案的通知 (Notice by the General Office of the National Health Commission, the General Office of the Commission of Politics and Law of the CPC Central Committee, the Secretary Bureau of the Office of the Central Cyberspace Affairs Commission, the General Office of the Supreme People's Court, the General Office of the Supreme People's Procuratorate, the General Office of the Ministry of Education, the General Office of the Ministry of Industry and Information Technology, the General Office of the Ministry of Public Security, the General Office of the Ministry of Civil Affairs, the General Office of the State Administration for Market Regulation, the Department of Comprehensive Affairs of the National Medical Products Administration, the Department of Comprehensive Affairs of the National Administration of Traditional Chinese Medicine, the General Office of the All-China Women's Federation, and the Health Bureau of the Logistic Support Department of the Central Military Commission Health of Issuing the Work Plan for the Special Action of Severely Cracking Down on the Illegal Application of Human Assisted Reproductive Technology).'

142 Xinhua, 'China to Crack down on Surrogacy Industry' (*People's Daily Online*, 15 April 2015) <http://en.people.cn/n/2015/0410/c90785-8876190.html> accessed 1 February 2025.

143 Song Jian 宋建 and others (243*n*128) 102; Wu Zhihong 吴志红 and Dai Ruxin 戴汝馨, 'Woguo Zhengzhi Daiyun Luan Xiang de Xingzheng Zhili Kunjing Ji Kefu Lujing W 我国整治代孕乱象的行政治理困境及克服路径 (The Preidcament of Administrative Governance of Surrogacy in China and Paths to Overcome It)' [2025] 卫生软科学 1.

involves the implementation of facial recognition systems in strategic locations, such as maternity clinics, neonatal wards, and birth registration offices. The Songjiang district of Shanghai provides a noteworthy illustration of this phenomenon. There, twenty medical institutions have been equipped with face recognition devices with the objective of identifying surrogate mothers and preventing surrogacy-related (illegal?) behaviours.[144]

Given the significant investment of resources and efforts in combating this phenomenon, the legislator's hesitation in including surrogacy among the offences punishable under the Criminal Code, at least in its commercial form,, is even more difficult to comprehend. This is also in contrast to the speed with which the legislative gap has been filled in relation to other applications of biotechnology linked to the beginning of life, such as the genetic manipulation of embryos.[145] This behaviour was not considered a criminal act in 2018, when biophysicist He Jiankui announced the birth of twin girls with DNA that he had modified in a Chinese laboratory. In the absence of a more specific provision, in December 2019 Dr He was convicted under the aforementioned Article 336 CL, which punishes illegal medical practice.[146] However, in 2020, the CL was amended to include Article 336(1), which since then regulates the behaviour of 'Whoever implants any genetically edited or cloned human embryo into the body of a human being or animal or implants any genetically edited or cloned animal embryo into the body of a human being.'

In light of this, the repeated decision by the Chinese leadership not to legislate on surrogacy in either the PFPL or the CL is surprising and can only be justified by a desire to allow time for public opinion to stabilise on the matter. It may also be motivated by a wish to allow scientific developments that would enable gestation outside the human body to be pursued, given that references to the potential of 'artificial wombs' are common in academic articles on the subject.[147]

Notwithstanding the availability of the latter technology (which, in any case, could possibly give rise to more ethical questions than it resolves), it is interesting to note that many criminal law scholars express a position in line with that of the legislator regarding the (in)appropriateness of explicitly including surrogacy among the offences punishable by law. They justify this on the basis

---

144 Song Jian 宋建 and others (243*n*128) 104.

145 Liu Changqiu 刘长秋 (243*n*127) 183.

146 Dennis Normile, 'Chinese Scientist Who Produced Genetically Altered Babies Sentenced to 3 Years in Jail' (*Science*) <https://www.science.org/content/article/chinese-scientist-who-produced-genetically-altered-babies-sentenced-3-years-jail> accessed 24 July 2025.

147 Li kang 黎康 (230*n*60).

of the principle of 'moderation of criminal law' (*xingfa qian yi*, 刑法谦抑).[148] This rationale has been the subject of criticism from other parties. For instance, in an article published in 2024,[149] Liu Changqi emphasised that the 'moderation of criminal law' doctrine refers to the mitigation of punishments and does not imply a refraining from the creation of new types of offence should such a need arise, as in his view it is the case for commercial surrogacy. Consequently, he calls for an immediate introduction of relevant commercial surrogacy offences and corresponding legal liability into Chinese criminal law, temporarily refraining from criminalising altruistic/non-commercial surrogacy.[150]

While awaiting the legislator's position on the matter, thousand surrogate children are born in China annually.[151] It is therefore necessary to examine the provisions of the law with regard to parental rights in relation to them.

4.1.3 Surrogacy in Chinese Law: Parent–Child Relationship

Notwithstanding the legal status of surrogacy, the determination of custodial issues and maintenance fees pertaining to surrogate children is a matter that Chinese courts are obligated to address.[152] Even in this particular instance, Chinese statutes provide minimal assistance, as they do not stipulate legal parenthood at the time of birth.[153] The promulgation of the CC did not result in the elimination of this loophole, with the exception of two articles dealing (indirectly) with the matter. In accordance with the stipulations set out in 1071, the legal rights of illegitimate children are to be accorded the same status as those of legitimate children, while art. 1073 governs the right of standing in legal proceedings for the purpose of affirmation or denial of maternity or paternity.

However, no definition of a legitimate child can be found in the CC or in any other Chinese legal provisions. Therefore, PRC's judges can only follow the guidelines on the determination of parenthood issued by the Supreme Peo-

148 Liu Changqiu 刘长秋 (243*n*130) 183.

149 Liu Changqiu 刘长秋 (243*n*130).

150 Ibid 185.

151 Yue Zhao, 'Protection of Rights and Legal Remedies for Surrogate Mothers in China' (2023) 10 Humanities and Social Sciences Communications 823, 2.

152 Kong Huiyuan 孔慧媛 and Tang Min 汤敏, 'Daiyun Suo Sheng Zinü de Fuyang Quan Queding Ji Fuyang Fei Chengdan de Wenti Yanjiu 代孕所生子女的抚养权确定及抚养费承担的问题研究 (Research on the Determination of the Custody of the Children Born of Surrogacy and the Commitment of the Maintenance Fee)' (2025) 17 医学与法学 57, 57.

153 Ibid 58.

ple's Court (hereinafter SPC) from the 1950s onwards.[154] In essence, as articulated by Shi Lei, the fundamental principles that Chinese courts adhere to in their jurisprudence pertaining to the parent–child relationship can be encapsulated as follows: (a) couples in a marriage are the legal parents of children born in that marriage; (b) a child born out of marriage is an illegitimate child. The legal mother is the woman who gave birth to the child. The legal father is the man who acknowledges paternity or the one who is proved to be the genetic father by a DNA test; (c) a child born through HART agreed by both husband and wife is that couple's legal child.[155]

It is worth noticing that most of these principles were formed well before the spread of HART. Thus, they work perfectly in 'normal' circumstances, when a child's biological mother, gestational mother, and intended mother are the same person. However, they are difficult to apply to surrogacy cases, where intended mother and gestational mother are always two different women, and sometimes even the gestational mother and the biological mother are not the same person.

These issues would continue to be relevant even if the legislator decided to take a clear position on surrogacy and whatever that position might be, whether to authorise it totally or partially, or to ban it completely. Consequently, it is not surprising that parent–child relationship is amongst the most frequently discussed topic within the context of Chinese doctrine on surrogacy.

The following section will explore legal scholars' opinions on surrogacy in more detail.

4.2 *Surrogacy in Chinese Legal Theory*

As previously observed in the context of PAR, Chinese legal doctrine also demonstrates a notable interest in the legislative and jurisprudential solutions adopted by other countries regarding surrogacy. In the relevant articles, the description of the situation in the PRC and the proposals to Chinese legislators and legal practitioners for the efficient and ethically acceptable management of the issue are often preceded or followed by a long overview of international

154 Shi Lei, 'China' in Claire Fenton-Glynn, Jens M Scherpe and Terry Kaan (eds), *Eastern and Western Perspectives on Surrogacy* (Intersentia 2019) 363 <https://www.cambridge.org/core/books/eastern-and-western-perspectives-on-surrogacy/china/5FD0E8EFB707B7E60C2CF2C57E347CFD> accessed 25 July 2025.

155 Ibid.

and comparative approaches to the issue,[156] with particular reference to EctHR case law and the 'tolerant approach' adopted in the United Kingdom.[157] The latter inclination is evidently associated with a further distinguishing characteristic of these works: the prevailing position in favour of the legalisation of this practice, which (especially when there is no exchange of money between the parties) is predominantly interpreted as a means to implement the reproductive rights of the citizens of the PRC.[158] While the conclusion may appear similar, however, the reasoning employed by different authors can vary considerably.

4.2.1 Surrogacy and Its Public Regulation

According to Yang Suiquan and Zhong Kai, for example, the imposition of a universal ban on surrogacy would constitute a violation of the fundamental human right to reproduce especially in cases of individuals incapable of conceiving due to natural factors or man-made accidents. On the contrary, they consider that regulating of surrogacy would be useful in combating human trafficking and contribute to the maintenance of social stability. On this basis, they suggest that surrogacy be permitted to a certain extent in the PRC.[159] A similar opinion is expressed by Wang Guisong, who interestingly challenges the conventional legal argument, according to which surrogacy should be banned because it disrupts public order and morality and violate human dignity. The author contends that the opposite is true: it is its illegality which makes surrogacy dangerous. Recognising surrogacy's role to facilitate

156 Ning Nuohua 宁诺花, 'Daiyun Zinü Jianhuren de Queding He Biaozhun 代孕子女监护人的确定原则和标准 (Principles and Standards for Determining the Guardian of a Child Born Through Surrogacy)' (2025) 174 Heilongjiang sheng zhengfa guali ganbu xueyuan xuebao 黑龙江省政法管理干部学院学报 57, 59; Qiu Qianyi and Meng Fanzhuang, 'Challenges and Future Prospects of Surrogacy Legislation in China' (2024) 12 Peking University Law Journal 47, 52–54; Li Haonan 李浩南, 'Kuaguo Daiyun Ertong de Shenfen Quanyi Baohu de Kunjing Yu Pojie 跨国代孕儿童的身份权益保护之困境与破解 (Dilemma and Solution of Identity Rights and Interests Protection for Transnational Surrogate Children' (2024) 16 Yixue yu faxue 医学语法学 113–114; Yang Qianqian 杨茜茜, 'Daiyun Qinzi Guanzi Falü Shiyong de Kunjing Yu Chuly 伦代孕亲子关系法律适用的困境与出路 (The Dilemma and Solution of the Laa Application in Surrogacy Parent-Child Relationship: From the Perspective of the Best Interest of the Child)' (2023) 44 Yixue yu Zhexue 医学与哲学 54, 56–58.

157 He Yue 何悦 and Yu Fenglei 俞风雷 (223*n*29).

158 Qiu Qianyi and Meng Fanzhuang (250*n*156) 48.

159 Yang Suiquan 杨遂全 and Zhong Kai 钟凯, 'Cong Teshu Qunti Shéngyu Quan Kan Daiyun Bufen Hefahua 从特殊群体生育权看代孕部分合法化 (Partial Legalisation of Surrogacy from the Perspective of the Reproductive Rights of Special Groups)' [2012] Shehui kexue yanjiu 社会科学研究 77, 79.

the fulfilment of the desire of individuals to procreate would therefore avoid the exploitation and abuse connected with this technology.[160] Liu Bibo adds to the legal analysis a recognition of the subject from an ethical and cultural standpoint, ultimately determining that surrogacy holds a 'metaphysical significance' (*xing'er shangyue yiyi* 形而上学意义) for Chinese individuals. This significance is firmly embedded within the cultural tenets of ancestral veneration and the obligation to uphold the continuity of the family unit, making surrogacy a step in the path to pursue the dignity of procreation; as such, it should be recognised and protected by the State.[161] Conversely, the notion of 'renting one's own womb' has been understood by certain authors as a means of articulating bodily autonomy. This is, for example, the case of He Yue and Yu Feng Lei, and of Ren Ruping, who – in consideration of the fact that the right of individuals to use and dispose of their own body, as well as their right to defend it from other parties' damages, should not be subject to restriction by the state – contend that surrogacy should be recognised and protected in the PRC, at least to a certain extent.[162]

Moreover, the demographic crisis has then led some authors to consider surrogacy from a public interest perspective, as a means of alleviating the problem of population aging.[163] For instance, in an article published in 2024 Zhu Xiaofeng not only demonstrates that the right to reproduction provided for in Article 17 of the PFPL falls within the personal rights protected by Articles 109 and 990(2) of the Civil Code.[164] In order to 'establish a favourable legal environment that would facilitate the realisation of reproductive intentions,

160 Wang Guisong 王贵松, 'Zhongguo Daiyun Guizhi de Moshi Xuanze 中国代孕规制的模式选择 (Choice of Models for the Regulation of Surrogacy in China)' [2009] Fazhi yu shehui fazhan 法制与社会发展 118, 121.

161 Liu Bibo 刘碧波, 'Wo Guo Daiyun de Lifa Yu Sifa Wenti 我国代孕的立法与司法问题 (Legislative and Judicial Issues of Surrogacy)' Xueshu jiaoliu 学术交流 115, 117.

162 He Yue 何悦 and Yu Fenglei 俞风雷 (223*n*29) 48; Ren Ruping 任汝平, '"Daiyun" de Falü" Lunjing Ji Qi Pojue 代孕" 的法律困境及其破解 (The Legal Dilemma of "surrogacy" and Its Solution)' [2009] Fujian luntan (renwen shehui kexue ban) 福建 论坛(人文社会科学版) 161, 161.

163 Qi Xiangguan 齐湘泉 and An Shuo 安朔, 'Kua Jing Daiyun Falü Guizhi Yanjiu – Jianyi Kuajing Daiyun Chansheng de Qinzi Guanxi Rending 跨境代孕法律规制研究—兼议跨境代孕产生的亲子关系认定 (Research on the Legal Regulation of Cross-Border Surrogacy – and on the Determination of Parent-Child Relationship Caused by Cross-Border Surrogacy)' (2021) 安朔 Zhongguo Qingnian shehui kexue 中国青年社会科学 109, 110.

164 Zhu Xiaofeng 朱晓峰, 'Lun di shengyulü shidai de shengyuquan xingshi guize 论低生育率时代的生育权行使规则 (On the rule for the exercise of fertility rights in the era of low fertility)' (2024) Shehui kexue jikan 社会科学辑刊 59, 62.

while achieving an equilibrium between the protection of individual legal rights and the promotion of public interest, and providing institutional safeguards to address social problems caused by the rapid decline in fertility rate,'[165] she also proposes to entrust Chinese courts with the task of verifying, on a case-by-case basis, the legitimacy of surrogacy performed to implement these rights. According to her (and apparently regardless of the existence of formal provisions on the matter) in adjudicating a surrogacy-related case the court should undertake a systematic evaluation, examining the legitimacy of the purpose, the necessity, the appropriateness, and the proportionality of the process.[166] The examples provided for the judge's consideration are drawn from legal practice, making them of particular interest in understanding the variety and value attributed to the motivations that may lead a Chinese couple to use this HART. With reference to the first criterion, Zhu Xiaofeng submits that surrogacy undertaken with the intention of providing emotional support following the loss of a child should be a legitimate purpose, but only if it is conducted on an altruistic basis. Conversely, surrogacy commissioned at cost can never been deemed legitimate, as it treats the human body as an object, it is against the law, public order and good customs (protected by art. 8 CC) and violates personal dignity (protected by arts. 109 and 990 CC).[167] Similarly, but with reference to the second criterion, surrogacy carried out by a couple who have become infertile to create a 'saviour sibling' to their sick child will not pass the necessity test, since it is not sure that the surrogate child will be a match and save the sick child's life.[168] Conversely, the determination of the criterion of 'appropriateness' hinges on the assessment of harm incurred by the surrogate mother. Therefore, the performance of surrogacy will be 'appropriate' when harm to the surrogate mother's body does not exceed that typically associated with pregnancy and childbirth.[169] Finally, surrogacy is considered as 'proportionate' when costs and benefits are balanced, as in cases in which the objectification experienced by the altruistic surrogate mother is balanced by the fulfilment derived from the birth of a child for those who have experienced infertility. In such cases, the decision to proceed with surrogacy can be likened to that of the donation of 'human cells, human tissues, human organs, and remains' permitted under Article 1006 of the PRC's CC.[170]

165 Ibid 64.
166 Ibid 66.
167 Ibid.
168 Ibid.
169 Ibid.
170 Ibid 67.

All the authors cited so far consider it appropriate for the system to open up to surrogacy from the point of view of protecting the rights and interests of individuals or even the community. Other authors, however, take a more pragmatic stance, noticing that the ban on surrogacy has been demonstrated to be useless in terms of eliminating the demand for surrogate maternity services.[171] On the contrary, the prohibitive approach implemented by the PRC has had the unintended consequence of driving surrogacy activities underground, with procedures being carried out in unregulated clinics, thereby increasing exploitation and health risks for the most vulnerable members of society. Furthermore, no prohibition can prevent affluent individuals from pursuing surrogacy procedures in foreign countries. In this context, the most effective method of promoting the protection of citizens' rights within their own country would be to legalise surrogacy.[172]

It is important to note that, in general, Chinese authors' support to surrogacy is limited to altruistic surrogacy,[173] while commercial surrogacy is typically denounced as a grave infringement of ethical principles and a violation of human dignity. An interesting exception to this are Qiu Qianyi and Meng Fanzhuan, who, in a 2025 article on the future of surrogacy regulation in China, note that the social situation in China and the dynamics within family groups make it very difficult for women linked to the intended parents by family ties to volunteer as surrogate mothers.[174] Consequently, intended parents would be compelled to seek a surrogate mother from outside their immediate circle, among women with whom they have no prior relationship and who would therefore be unlikely to agree to act as surrogate mothers without receiving adequate compensation.[175] It is therefore proposed that surrogacy should be legalised in a commercial context, whilst simultaneously imposing limitations on remuneration, with a view to averting the moral risks concomitant with the liberalisation of the surrogacy market. All these goals would be achieved through a strict system of government licenses and qualification checks.[176]

Even if an increased control over citizens' activities, including in the reproductive sphere, is undoubtedly consistent with the prevailing perspective of

171 Qi Xiangguan 齐湘泉 and An Shuo 安朔 (251*n*164) 110.

172 Zhang Yanling 張燕玲, 'Lun Daiyun Mu de Hefahua Jichu 伦代孕母的合法化基础 (On the Basis of the Legalisation of Surrogacy)' 24 Hebei faxue 河北法学 137, 140.

173 Zhan Zhongle 湛中乐 (162*n*11).

174 Qiu Qianyi and Meng Fanzhuang (250*n*156) 58.

175 Ibid 59.

176 Ibid.

the Chinese leadership, the implementation of commercial surrogacy may appear to be a complex undertaking, at least in the short term. This does not imply that altruistic surrogacy could be more readily implemented, nor that the challenges it poses to the legal system are any less than those posed by commercial surrogacy. A salient point of congruence among these surrogacy modalities, both in case of traditional and gestational surrogacy, pertains to the tension they engender within the paradigm of conventional parenthood. As previously indicated, the matter of child custody in instances of surrogacy is a distinct concern that is not contingent upon the legal validity of the practice itself. Once surrogate children are born, it is imperative to ascertain the most suitable party to assume responsibility for their care, irrespective of the legality of the reproductive technique employed in their conception and delivery.

4.2.2 Determination of the Custody of the Children Born through Surrogacy

The determination of the party to whom custody of surrogate children should be entrusted is perhaps the most hotly debated issue among Chinese legal scholars dealing with surrogacy. Prior to elaborating on their stance on the matter, they typically provide a concise overview of the potential approaches to the subject.[177] These approaches are: the 'bloodline/genetic theory '(*xueyuan lun* 血缘伦), the 'birth theory '(*fenmian lun* 分娩伦), the '*contractual theory*'(*qiyue lun* 契约伦), also known as 'parties-intention theory' (*danshiren yise lun* 当事人意思伦),[178] and the theory of the 'best interests of the child' (*ertong zuida liyi lun* 儿童最大利益伦). The bloodline relationship theory implies that custody of the surrogate child should be entrusted to the party with whom he or she has a blood/genetic link. This approach is based on the biological bond that generally exists between parents and children, and there-

177 Li Haonan 李浩南 (250*n*157) 112–113; You Wenting and Feng Jun, 'Legal Regulation of Surrogacy Parentage Determination in China' (2024) 15 Frontiers in Psychology 5 <https://www.frontiersin.org/journals/psychology/articles/10.3389/fpsyg.2024.1363685/full> accessed 2 December 2024; Qiu Qianyi and Meng Fanzhuang (243*n*130) 55–56; Ning Nuohua 宁诺花 (243*n*130) 58–59; Kong Huiyuan 孔慧媛 and Tang Min 汤敏 (248*n*153) 59; Liu Guanhe 刘冠合, 'Daiyun Zinü Qinzi Guanxi Rending: Biaozhunjiangou Yu Guize Chonggou – Jiyu "Minfadian" Di 1073 Tiao de Guifan Kaocha 代孕子女亲子关系认定: 标准检讨与规则重构 – 基于 "民法典第 1073 条的规范考察 (Determination of Paretn-Child Relationships in Surrogacy Cases: Review of Standards and Reconstruction Rules – Normative Investigation Based on Article 1073 of the Civil Code of China' (2025) 45 Huebei Shifan Daxue xuebao (zhexue shehui kexueban) 湖北师范大促额促额包(这数额社会科学版) 46, 47.

178 Kong Huiyuan 孔慧媛 and Tang Min 汤敏 (248*n*152) 59–60.

fore, according to some, it would be less problematic from an ethical and moral point of view.[179] However, it is difficult to apply when the sperm and eggs are not provided by the intended couple but by anonymous donors, because in that case the child would have to be entrusted to strangers who have never wanted to take care of him or her.[180] The birth theory, on the other hand, follows the rule of Roman law currently adopted by many legal systems and, as discussed before, usually implemented by Chinese courts. According to this theory, the woman who gives birth to the child is the mother. This theory is generally the easiest to apply. On the one hand it does not require any genetic test, since the rule generally implies that the husband of the woman who gave birth is considered as the child's father; on the other it recognises the bond between the pregnant woman and the foetus which often develops during pregnancy. In the case of surrogacy, however, it leads to the unfortunate outcome of the child being entrusted to the surrogate mother, who generally has neither the means nor the will to take on this burden.[181] The 'contract theory' refers to the determination of the legal guardian of the surrogacy child in accordance with the agreement between the parties. This solution is clearly more in line with the will of the parties concerned, but its applicability depends on the validity of the surrogacy agreement, which is deemed null and void in the jurisdictions which adopt a 'prohibitive approach' towards this HART. The 'theory of the best interest of the child' refers to the identification of the party that is more conducive to protecting the interest of the surrogate children from the perspective of the surrogate children themselves, according to the provision of art. 3 of the UNCRC and art. 4 the PRC Minors' Protection Law. The most significant problem in applying this theory is identifying what is the 'best interest' of a child in general, and what constitute the 'best interest' for that child in particular. This can lead to legal uncertainty, and in the end harm the interest of the child who should be protected. In any case, most Chinese legal scholars support the implementation of this theory in the PRC's legal system. It is worth mentioning that, to make their arguments stronger, they usually quote foreign case law, particularly the abovementioned *Mennesson v. France* case, but also German and Swiss cases decided by the ECtHR or by national courts where the principle have been applied to decide on the custody of a child born through surrogacy.[182] These

179 Li Haonan 李浩南 (250*n*157) 112; Yang Qianqian 杨茜茜 (250*n*157) 55.

180 Li Haonan 李浩南 (250*n*157) 112.

181 Ibid.

182 Ibid 114; Yang Qianqian 杨茜茜 (250*n*156) 58; Ning Nuohua 宁诺花 (250*n*156) 62.

decisions are of particular interest in the Chinese perspective, as they are related to jurisdictions where surrogacy is explicitly prohibited by law.

As regards the content to be attributed to this principle, the authors are fairly unanimous in arguing that 'the best interest' should not be assessed solely on the basis of the genetic links between the child and the parties, nor solely in terms of economic power, in the sense of the wealth and well-being that the parties can guarantee to the child. They consider it necessary for the child to be regarded as a subject of rights rather than as an object to be protected, and to the judge to consider which of the parties requesting custody can best guarantee the child's psychological, emotional, and spiritual well-being.[183] In any event, the human dignity of the family must be preserved, bearing in mind that – although the interest of the state is paramount – it is surrogacy, and not the surrogate child, that is unlawful.[184] Consequently, it is imperative to ensure that surrogate children are not subjected to any repercussions arising from the illegality of the HART through which they came into being.[185]

A dissenting voice is that of Kong Huiyuan and Tang Min, who argue that, with rare exceptions, the best interests of the child require that he or she be entrusted to the intended parents. The authors cite studies according to which surrogate mothers develop almost no attachment to the foetus during pregnancy and are unlikely to be interested in caring for it.[186] Their function is merely to carry the child during its development, and for this reason it makes no sense to apply the 'birth theory' in decisions regarding custody in cases of surrogacy. The theory that judges should follow is instead that of 'bloodline,' and only if the child is not biologically related to the intended parents should the 'contractual theory' be applied.[187] This position is also endorsed by You Wenting and Feng Jun, although they do not discuss the surrogacy contract (which, as we will see in the following pages, is consistently considered as null and void by Chinese courts). The two authors take the bloodline theory as a point of reference and defend the right of intended parents to obtain custody of the surrogate child at birth.[188] Furthermore, they call for a change in legislation that would immediately recognise the intended

183 Yang (104*n*18) 57.

184 Yang Qianqian 杨茜茜 (250*n*156) 59; Liu Guanhe 刘冠合 (254*n*178) 48.

185 Yang Qianqian 杨茜茜 (250*n*156) 57; Liu Guanhe 刘冠合 (254*n*178) 49.

186 Kong Huiyuan 孔慧媛 and Tang Min 汤敏 (248*n*152) 59.

187 Ibid 60.

188 You and Feng (254*n*177) 10.

parents' parentage rights in cases of gestational surrogacy.[189] Conversely, in traditional surrogacy the implementation of the aforementioned theory leads to consider the surrogate mother as the biological mother. However, also in this case the authors deem of paramount importance for the child to reside with the intended couple. This approach is justified by them as being 'more beneficial for the child's holistic well-being and development.'[190]

However, the preponderance of authors demonstrates a predilection for the birth theory, a standpoint that, in addition to its superior alignment with prevailing Chinese case law on custody, also to a certain extent acknowledges the rights and interests of the surrogate mother. Nevertheless, it is important to note that the similarities among the authors are limited to this point. In determining the applicable rules and the reconciliation of the best interests of the child with the birth theory in practice, the authors' positions are divided into different proposals, the feasibility of which in the current regulatory context varies.

Li Haonan, for instance, in view of the objective impossibility of applying the birth theory to transnational surrogacy, proposes amending Article 25 of the Law of the People's Republic of China on Choice of Law for Foreign-related Civil Relationships (*Shewai minshi guanxi fa shiyong fa* 涉外民事关系法适用法), so that it includes the possibility of applying the law of the habitual residence or nationality of the surrogate mother, instead of that of the child, which is often much more difficult to establish at this stage.[191] Conversely, Yang Qianqian's position is indicative of a perspective that reflects her conceptualisation of surrogacy as a vestige of a patriarchal mentality, underpinned by the notions of blood ties and the right to perpetuate lineage.[192] In this sense, according to her, surrogacy should be deemed illegal both by civil and criminal law.[193] However, in order to combine respect for public order and morality on the one hand, and the best interests of the child, who cannot be left without nationality and family on the other, she imagines a system in which the surrogate mother is considered the biological mother of the child, and the title of biological father is assigned to the intended father. Consequently, the responsibility for the maintenance and care of the child will be

189 Ibid.

190 Ibid.

191 Li Haonan 李浩南 (250*n*156) 115.

192 Yang Qianqian 杨茜茜 (250*n*156) 57.

193 Ibid 59.

shared by both parties, thereby ensuring that the child is not adversely affected by an unlawful act which he did not commit.[194]

The position adopted by Liu Guanghe is of particular interest, given the practical nature of the solution proposed in the context of the current state of the law. Furthermore, the concept of multiple motherhood, to which reference is made, can be seen as a continuation of the Chinese tradition examined in paragraph 3. The author puts forward the suggestion of the implementation of a system based on the Article 1073 of the Civil Code, according to which 'Where an objection to maternity or paternity is justifiably raised, the father or mother may institute an action in the people's court for affirmation or denial of the maternity or paternity.' In this system, the surrogate is initially identified as the biological mother and has the option to disclaim maternity in favour of the intended parents. The author posits that this would engender a scenario of legal-constructed 'double motherhood,' culminating in the recognition and protection of the rights of both the surrogate mother and the intended mother, as well as the establishment of their respective duties towards the child. The author's position is consistent with the prevailing view that to address surrogacy in an efficient and optimal manner and align it with the best interests of the surrogate child, it is imperative to modify the conceptualisation of parenting. This modification should encompass social components, such as the propensity to nurture a child, the pertinent obligations that arise after birth, long-term responsibilities, and the establishment of a familial unit. This standpoint is also adopted by Yang Haichao, who posits that the aforementioned components should be integrated with the biological aspects of parenting through a change in mentality that implies the acceptance of a certain conception of 'multiple parenthood.'[195]

As legislators await the opportune moment to regulate surrogacy, and academics strive to reach consensus on the most ethical and efficient legal management of the phenomenon, Chinese courts are compelled to respond and offer concrete solutions to the surrogacy-related controversies that have been brought before them. In essence, the legal framework governing surrogacy in the People's Republic of China is determined by the decisions made by the judiciary. The following discussion will examine the structure of this framework, with the caveat that, for the same reasons given in relation to PAR cases, the analysis of court decisions on surrogacy will also be based mainly on secondary sources.

194 Ibid.

195 Yang Haichao 杨海超 (237*n*90) 22–23.

4.3 *Surrogacy in Chinese Legal Practice*

Given the scale of surrogacy market, it is not rare that dispute arise between the parties involved. In the absence of specific provisions on the matter, the courts often cannot help but rule on the basis of the general principles of the law, or according to provisions designed for circumstances other than the one under consideration. In this situation, a high level of discretion comes into play, with the risk of inconsistency in courts' decisions or, using a Chinese expression: '*lei'an bu tong pan*' (类案不同判, litt.: same case, different judgment).[196]

4.3.1 Surrogacy in Criminal Cases

Of course, the path described above is precluded in the criminal sphere, where the principle of legality laid down in Article 3 of the CL prevents anyone from being convicted or given punishment for 'any act that no explicit stipulations of law deem a crime.' Since, as discussed above, surrogacy is not criminalised in China, people involved in underground surrogacy could only be pursued by punishing the other crimes eventually committed as collateral of it. In the context of traditional surrogacy, the legal charge is generally bigamy, a concept encompassing both bigamy itself and *de facto* marriages, characterised by cohabitation without formal registration. In other instances of surrogacy, the applicable offences may vary considerably, contingent on the specific circumstances surrounding the act.[197] This was, for example, the case of a certain Mr Shi, who in 2020 organised the illegal border crossing of a foreign surrogate mother during the surrogacy process and was prosecuted by the People's Court of the District of Huadu district (Guangzhou, Guangdong) for the crime of illegal border crossing, provided for by art. 318 et seq. of the CL.[198] Conversely, in a case related to surrogacy decided by the Intermediate Court of Yongzhou (Hunan) in the same year, the defendants were prosecuted for the crime of forging, altering, and selling official documents, certificates, and seals of state organs due to their actions of forging and selling birth medical certifi-

196 Liu Guanhe 刘冠合 (254*n*177) 48.

197 Xiao Yongping, Li Jue and Zhu Lei, 'Surrogacy in China: A Dilemma Between Public Policy and the Best Interests of Children' (2020) 34 International Journal of Law, Policy and the Family 1, 4.

198 *Shi mou zuzhi touyue guojing* 石某组织偷越国境 (*A certain Shi organise illegal crossing borders*) [2020] Guangdong sheng Guangzhou shi Huadu qu renmin fayuan 广东省广州市花都区人民法院 (People's Court of huadu district, Guang zhou city, Guandong province) (2020) (2020) Yue 0114 Xingchu 429 hao 粤 0114 刑初 429 号.

cates during the organisation of surrogacy activities.[199] In another case happened in Guangdong in 2021, three people who restricted the personal freedom of six foreign women who had illegally entered the country during the organisation of illegal surrogacy activities were prosecuted by the Intermediate People's Court of Foshan for the crime of illegal detention.[200]

It is clear from these decisions that there is a contradiction between the government's campaigns against surrogacy and the lack of legal instruments to punish this activity, once the perpetrators are identified. Not only does the offence charged by the courts not fully correspond to the act committed; the unlawful act triggered by surrogacy is also the only reason why the persons involved in underground surrogacy organisation are indictable, showing the complete inability of the law to regulate surrogacy activities as such.[201]

The resolution of the latter issue is the sole responsibility of the legislature, should it deem it appropriate. In the meantime, civil law issues pertaining to surrogacy agreements continue to be adjudicated by the courts, which are compelled to rule on the validity of such agreements, and, most crucially, on the determination of family relationships and custody rights in relation to children born through surrogacy. In the absence of regulatory references, it is possible to assess the principles, whether of legal, ideological or cultural origin, and the local differences that characterise the approach of Chinese law-in-practice to the subject.

4.3.2 Surrogacy in Civil Cases

4.3.2.1 *Cases Regarding Surrogacy-Related Contract*

4.3.2.1.1 Traditional Surrogacy Agreements

As noticed before, under a traditional surrogacy agreement the surrogacy mother provides the egg and is inseminated through sexual intercourses or IVF procedure. She is both the biological mother and the birth mother; therefore, her status as the natural mother of the surrogate child is rarely put into

199 *Wang moujia, Tang moujia weizo, bianshi, maimai guojia jiguan gongwen, zhengjian, yinzhang an* 王某甲、唐某甲伪造、变造、买卖国家机关公文、证件、印章案 (*Wang Moujia and Tang Moujia Forgery, Alteration, and Sale of State Organ Documents, Certificates, and Seals Case*) [2020] Hunan sheng Yongzhou shi zhongji renmin fayuan 湖南省永州市中级人民法院 (Intermediate People's Court of Yongzhou city, Hubei Province) (2020) Hu 11 Xing zhong 305 hao (2020) 湘 11 刑终 305 号.

200 *Liu mou, Xie mou, Xiao mou feifa jujin an* 刘某、谢某、肖某非法拘禁案 (*Liu Mou, Xie Mou, and Xiao Mou Illegal Detention Case*) [2021] Guandong sheng Fushan shi Zhongji renmin fayuan 广东省佛山市中级人民法院 (Intermediate People's Court of Fushan city, Guangdong Province) ((2021) Yue 06 xing zhong 190 hao (2021) 粤 06 刑终 190 号.

201 Liu Changqiu 刘长秋 (243n127) 83.

question. However, from time to time, courts are called upon to rule on the validity of a traditional surrogacy contract. The very existence of these cases seems to me to prove, once again, how far removed from common thinking is the idea that surrogacy is unlawful. If this were not the case, it would be difficult to explain why, in 2018, Ms Yan Xiaoli and her husband, Mr Xu Liang, turned to a people's court to demand the enforcement of the traditional surrogacy agreement they had signed with Mr Zheng Maoqing. According to it, for a consideration of 350,000 RMB, and a living cost of 3,000 RMB per month, Ms Yan had agreed to conceive a child for Mr Zheng through IVF procedure. Three months after the conception of twin girls, however, the pregnancy was voluntarily terminated due to Mr Zheng's failure to pay, the reasons for which were not clarified during the proceedings. Ms Yan therefore turned to the court to receive the agreed payment. In its ruling, the court inferred from Article 3 of the MAHART 2001 that surrogacy is prohibited in China, including traditional surrogacy. Based on this, the court held that the surrogacy contract between the parties was contrary to public order and morality and was therefore null and void under Article 153 of the General Principles of Civil Law of 2017. Consequently, Ms Yan was ordered to refund Mr Zheng the sum of money already received for the surrogacy, minus compensation for physical damage resulting from the abortion and other reasonable costs incurred.

The relevance of Article 3 MAHART 2001 to the case in question is highly debatable. However, even more questionable is the reference to 'the public order and morality, and the spirit and letter of the law' on the basis of which, as reported by Xiao, Li, and Zhu in a 2020 article, other Chinese courts have considered traditional surrogacy contracts invalid. In the cases examined by the authors, all decided between 2017 and 2018, the court did not indicate any specific provisions, nor did it articulate the content of the public policy and morality the agreement allegedly violated.[202] It is worthy of note, however, that in certain cases, the husband's entry into a traditional surrogacy agreement, particularly when conducted through sexual relations and without informing his wife, was regarded as indicative of the deterioration of the couple's relationship. This was considered sufficient grounds for granting the wife a divorce.[203]

202 Zhu Xiaofeng 朱晓峰 (252*n*164) 9.

203 Xiao Yongping, Li Jue and Zhu Lei (259*n*197) 10.

4.3.2.1.2 Surrogacy Brokerage Agreement and Other Surrogacy-Related Contracts

Very often, couples who wish to enter a gestational surrogacy agreement do not contact the surrogate mother directly but entrust an intermediary with the task of finding and agreeing terms with her. Even in these situations, things may not go as planned, and the intended parents may sue the intermediary, demanding the return of the money paid up to that point. The Donkou District People's Court (Shaoyang City, Hunan Province) published a description of a similar case on WeChat Public Platform in 2021.[204] The facts of the case are as follows: In 2018, Mr Wang and his wife, Ms Zhang were introduced to the defendant, Mr Liu, who was engaged in surrogacy services. On 21 September of that year, the parties entered into an 'Assisted Reproduction Service Agreement Guaranteeing Success.' After the agreement was signed, Wang made multiple payments to Liu totalling 32,840 yuan for surrogacy services. In April 2021, due to disputes between the parties, Wang filed a lawsuit against Liu in court. The court held that the 'Assisted Reproduction Package Service Agreement' signed by the plaintiff and defendant was clearly a surrogacy contract and therefore invalid as it violated legal provisions. The court also remarked that, while Chinese law currently does not explicitly regulate surrogacy contracts, it does mention the ban on surrogacy in MAHART 2001, which permits 'only the use of HART through the wife's uterus for pregnancy.' The court stated that, 'in essence, a surrogacy contract involves renting out the surrogate's uterus as a thing and treating the child as an object of a commercial transaction.' According to it, these aspects reflect that surrogacy contracts violate public order, good customs and social morality, as well as being inconsistent with the basic principles of the CC. Therefore, they should be deemed invalid. On this basis, the court ruled that the defendant should return the fees collected under the contract to the plaintiff. Both parties signed an invalid 'Assisted Pregnancy Package Service Agreement,' for which both parties were at fault. Therefore, each party should bear the other expenses incurred. The court did not support the plaintiff's claim for compensation for losses. In its final comment of the post, the same court remarked

204 'Jiaoyu Zhengdun – Hua 24 Wan Daiyun Hou Zhao Zhongjie Suopei. Fayuan: "Daiyun Hetong" Yin Weifan Gongxuliangsu Er Wuxiao J 教育整顿 | 花 32 万代孕后找中介索赔, 法院: "代孕合同" 因违反公序良俗而无效 (Education and Rectification | After Spending 320,000 Yuan on a Surrogacy, They Sought Compensation from the Agency. The Court Declared the Surrogacy Contract Invalid Because It Violated Public Order and Good Morals)' (*Weixing gongzhong pingtai* 微信公众平台 (*WeChat public platform*), 15 May 2021) <https://mp.weixin.qq.com/s/cjAAOCtoEROsndnzzz_SpQ> accessed 31 July 2025.

that 'A woman's uterus is not a reproductive tool, and the birth of a child should not be treated as a commodity.' Therefore: 'The chaos surrounding surrogacy should be curbed under the supervision of the law and public opinion.'[205]

It is noteworthy that the same conclusion was reached in the cases on the validity of a surrogacy broker agreement analysed by Xiao, Li, and Zhu in 2020.[206] According to the results of authors' research, such contracts were unanimously considered by the courts as void and unenforceable.[207] Moreover, in most judgments the court referred to art. 8 of the General Rules of Civil Law (now art. 8 of the CC), which prohibits civil activities in violation of law or public order and morals, and to art. 153 of the same law (now article 153 of the CC), which declares such activities null and void. The authors consider problematic the courts' approach of referencing to general principles, which are 'empty vessel,' and as such often subject to value judgment and open to interpretation. Nevertheless, they admit that it is difficult to understand how these concepts are construed by the court, as Chinese judgments do not offer much reasoning. What it seems to be a key factor in these decisions is (again!) the illegality of surrogacy, that the courts explicitly or implicitly drawn from MAHART 2001.[208]

It is important to acknowledge the complexity of the situation in which Chinese courts find themselves when adjudicating such cases. Nevertheless, it can be argued that these decisions are, at the very least, questionable. It is challenging to comprehend how a sectoral regulation, promulgated by an executive body, can be regarded as a benchmark for delineating the content of public order and morality, particularly in the context of the People's Republic of China's (PRC) current social and demographic context, which is so divergent from that of the country at the advent of the twenty-first century, and given the outcome of NPC's 2015 deliberation, the sole on the subject that has hitherto taken place.

However, a review of Chinese case law reveals that People's courts consider null and void not only surrogacy brokerage contracts, but surrogacy-related contracts in general. Such contracts include those between a dealer and commercial intermediaries specialised in surrogacy services carried out in countries where surrogacy is legal, such as the US.[209] They also include contracts

---

205 Ibid.

206 Xiao Yongping, Li Jue and Zhu Lei (259*n*197) 10.

207 Ibid.

208 Ibid 11.

209 Ibid 12–13.

between surrogacy brokers and companies specialised in cross-border reproductive services.[210] Finally, contracts for the creation of a website relating to commercial surrogacy are also considered null and void. In this sense, it has been rightly said that Chinese courts have established a *de facto* prohibition of surrogacy in contract law.

The outcome described above can be regarded as favourable for the Chinese leadership, provided that the objective is indeed to render this category of contract uncertain and consequently unappealing. The subsequent step is to ascertain how the court will proceed in civil cases where, rather than determining the validity of a surrogacy contract, it is tasked with adjudicating its consequences, particularly with regard to family relationships and the legal rights of custody regarding the child born through this HART.

4.3.2.2 *Cases Regarding Parentage and Sole Care and Control of the Surrogate Child*

As previously remarked, in traditional surrogacy there is no separation between genetic mother and birth mother. In deciding about parenthood in such cases, therefore, people's courts could easily (and do consistently) apply traditional parenting model, declaring the surrogate mother as the natural mother, and considering the surrogate child as a child born out of wedlock. On the contrary, the rules on traditional parentage are of little or none help when a gestational surrogacy is at stake, since the surrogate children are not only genetically un- related to their birth mother, but sometimes they are even not genetically linked to their intended mother.

In these situations, at least until 2017, the absence of specific standards both in statute and case law has led to recurrent inconsistency in courts' decisions across different regions.[211] In 2008, for example, the People's Court of Jiangnan District (Nanning City, Guanxi Province) ruled that custody of the surrogate child should be granted to the commissioning couple based on the principle of the 'maximising the interests of the minor' (*wei chengren liyi zuidahua de yuanze* 未成人利益最大化的原则). In 2010, the People's Court of Dingcheng District Court (Changde City, Hunan Province) ruled that custody of the surrogate child should be granted to the commissioning couple based on the terms of the surrogacy agreement, which was considered as true and not violating laws and administrative regulations.[212] In 2012, the People's Court of Siming District (Xiamen City, Fujian Province) ruled that custody of the sur-

210 Ibid.

211 Ning Nuohua 宁诺花 (250*n*156) 60; Yang Haichao 杨海超 (237*n*90) 14.

212 Ning Nuohua 宁诺花 (250*n*156) 60; Yang Haichao 杨海超 (237*n*90) 14.

rogate child should be granted to the surrogate mother based on the 'birth theory,'[213] while the surrogacy agreement was declared null and void, because it 'violated public order and common decency.'[214]

As discussed above, the latter position towards surrogacy contracts has become increasingly common among Chinese courts, both in commercial surrogacy and traditional surrogacy cases.[215]

On the contrary, the issue of legal parenting is still quite controversial, even after the decision of the case *Chen Yin v. Luo Ronggeng and Xie Juanru*, decided by the First Intermediate Court of Shanghai on 17 June 2016.[216] Considered as the 'first case on custody of a surrogate child,' this lawsuit was published in the SPC's journal, *Renmin Sifa* (人民司法) as an 'example-case,'[217] and it was even mentioned in the SPC's annual report to the National People's Congress as a showcase for the protection of the 'best interest of the child.' The facts are as follows: on 28 April 2007, Ms Chen Yin and Mr Luo Xin registered their marriage, the second one for both of them. At the time of the wedding, Mr Luo already had a son and a daughter, while Ms Chen suffered from infertility. They decided to have children through surrogacy. The embryo(s) were created using Mr Luo's sperm and a third-party donor's oocytes and were eventually transplanted into the womb of a surrogate mother through IVF. On 13 February 2011, the surrogate mother gave birth to twins, who lived with Mr Luo and Ms Chen. Furthermore, Mr Luo and Ms Chen managed to put their names on the birth certificate, and had the babies registered and raised as their own. On 7 February 2014 Mr Luo died. On 29 December 2014, having learnt that the twins had no blood relationship with Ms Chen, Mr Luo's parents filed a lawsuit, claiming the sole care and control of the surrogate children. On 29 July 2015, Shanghai Minhang District People's Court fully accepted the plaintiffs' claims: according to the court, there was neither a natural nor a social parent–child relationship between Ms Chen and the twins. Since the twins'

213 Ning Nuohua 宁诺花 (250*n*156) 60.

214 Yang Haichao 杨海超 (237*n*90) 14.

215 Xiao Yongping, Li Jue and Zhu Lei (259*n*198) 8–14.

216 *Chen Ying su Luo Ronggeng jianhu quan jiufen yi an ershe minshi panjueshu* 陈莺诉罗荣耕监护权纠纷一案二审民事判决书 *Civil Judgement of the Second Instance in the Case of Chen Ying v Luo Ronggeng Custody Dispute* [2016] Shanghia diyi zhongji renmin fayuan 上海市第一中级人民法院 (Shanghai First Intermediate People's Court) (2015) hu yizhong minzhong zidi 56 hao(2015) 沪一中少民终字第 56 号.

217 Hou Weiqing 侯卫清, 'Yangyu Muqin Huode Daiyun Zinü Jianyuquan Zhi Falü Jichu 养育母亲获得代孕子女监护权之法律基础 (Legal Basis for the Adoptive Mother to Obtain Custody of the Surrogate Child)' [2017] Anli-benqi guanzhu – Renmin Sifa 案例- 本期关注 – 人民司法 4, 4–11.

biological father was dead, and their mother was unknown, their father's parents should have custody of them. On appeal, the Shanghai First Intermediate People's Court reversed the decision and awarded Ms Chen the custody of the surrogate children. The court held that Ms Chen had formed a stepparent–child relationship with the children, and therefore she should take precedence over her husband's parents. Besides, she could guarantee a more comfortable and peaceful life to the children. According to the judge: 'In the case of unclear legal provisions or loopholes [...] the judge has to apply the functionalist approach, taking the "best interest of the child" as reference.'[218] At the same time, the court made it clear that the decision should not be taken as a judicial legitimation of surrogacy. In fact, it was merely a recognition of the fact that Ms Chen's guardianship was more conducive to the healthy growth and development of the twins, and more consistent with the children's 'best interest.'[219]

On the issue of natural motherhood, the court rejected the 'bloodline theory,' focussing instead on the connections developed during pregnancy between the surrogate mother and the foetus. According to the birth theory, therefore, they recognised her status of natural mother of the surrogate child. Conversely, the issue of fatherhood was decided using genetics as a criterion: the intended father was considered as the natural father of the surrogate child, who consequently was compared to a child born out of wedlock. With regard to the intended mother's rights, the court excluded that the principle of party autonomy could be applied in the determination of parenthood, thus ruling out the possibility for her to having acquired parentage rights based on the surrogacy agreement. Moreover, not having gone through the formal adoption procedure required by the law, she could not even be regarded as an adoptive parent. Considering her relationship with the surrogate twins as a de facto adoption, on the other hand, 'would produce the practical effect that parentage has transferred from the surrogate to the intending mother,' an outcome which the court considered as 'incompatible with the express (?) prohibition of surrogacy currently in force in China.'[220]

The solution was found by the court drawing an analogy between the situation of the surrogate twins and that of children from a previous marriage and children born out of cohabitation, adultery etc. In these circumstances, if the 'social mother' (i.e. the genetic father's wife) accepts the child into the family and assume the responsibility as a caregiver, a stepparent and child relation is

218 Ibid 11.

219 Ibid.

220 Xiao Yongping, Li Jue and Zhu Lei (259*n*197) 16.

formed. Ms Chen had been looking after the twins for five years, so the court considered her as the twins' stepmother.[221]

Even if the court framed the latter decision as a way to protect innocent children, the very idea of splitting motherhood in natural motherhood and social motherhood cannot help but remind me of the traditional concept of double motherhood, and the view according to which a child's 'social mother' is the woman who acts as the 'de facto' caregiver.

Notwithstanding the endorsement this ruling received from the Supreme People's Court, it appears that children are not universally regarded as equal in the PRC. Furthermore, the concept of 'double motherhood' is not universally accepted, and the utilisation of birth theory and genetic connection to identify the natural parents of a child born through surrogacy is not a universal solution in cases involving the custody of such a child. Additionally, the concept of the 'best interests of the child' is not universally consistent.

This is, at least, impression one gets reading the judgment given by the People's Court of Huli district (Xiamen city, Fujian Province) in what has been considered as the 'first same-sex surrogacy case in China.'[222] To be precise, the case in question does not concern the sole care and custody of a child born through surrogacy, but through Reciprocal In Vitro Fertilisation (hereinafter: RIV). This is a reproductive technique often used by lesbian couples, whereby one party provides the egg, a donor provides the sperm, and the other party carries the pregnancy to term. However, both Chinese doctrine and case law consider RIV to be a type of surrogacy, and the title with which this decision is generally referred to demonstrates it.[223]

According to a report published on WeChat Public Platform by the same court which decided the case,[224] the facts are as follows: The plaintiff, Dati,

221 Ibid 16–17.

222 Liu Guanhe 刘冠合 (254*n*177) 46.

223 Yang Lixing 杨立新 and Li Yiwen 李怡雯[, 'Baozhang Rengong Fuzhu Shengzhi Jishu Suo Sheng Zinü de Sheng Dexunyan – Rending Rengong Fuzhu Shengzi Jishu Suo Sheng Zinü de Falü Diwei de Jizhun Dian 保障人工辅助生殖技术所生子女的生的尊严——认定人工辅助生殖技术所生子女的法律地位的基准点 (Guarantee the Dignity of Children Born of Artificial Assisted Reproductive Technology: A Reference Point for Determining the Legal Status of Children Born of Artificial Assisted Reproductive Technology)' [2021] Zhongguo yingyong faxue 中国应用法学 77; Hao Zheng, 'Shared Motherhood or Free Surrogacy?: Risks and Vulnerabilities in a Chinese Lesbian's Family-Making' (2022) 69 Journal of Homosexuality 1881.

224 Huli Fayuan 湖里法院, 'Tamen Dou Shuo Ziji Shi Haizi de Mama 她们都说自己是孩子的妈妈 (They All Say They Are the Child's Mothers)' (*Weixing gongzhong pingtai* 微信公众平台 (*WeChat public platform*)) <https://mp.weixin.qq.com/s/eaVO6cZj6W6sBGFAvp-N3A> accessed 1 August 2025.

alleges that she is a single woman who has always desired to have a child but is unable to do so due to health issues. In 2018, she met Xiaomei, who, after learning of her situation, offered to assist with surrogacy. In March 2019, Dati contacted a reproductive services agency, and the two underwent multiple preliminary examinations and treatments at a hospital to prepare for IVF. On 2 April 2019, Dati underwent medical procedures to retrieve her eggs, which were then fertilised with sperm purchased from a third party to create an embryo. Five days later, the embryo was implanted into Xiaomei's uterus, and she became pregnant. In December 2019, Xiaomei gave birth to a baby girl, Yaya, at a hospital in Xiamen. In February 2020, Xiaomei took the child away and registered her as her own daughter, stating that she would no longer allow Dati to have any contact with the child. Dati sued Xiaomei, claiming that the child has no biological relationship with Xiaomei and that she is the child's biological mother. She requested the court to confirm the parent–child relationship between her and the child and order the child to be placed under her custody.[225]

Both the plaintiff and the defendant confirmed that the egg that formed Yaya's embryo was provided by Dati, and the sperm was purchased; Yaya was conceived through assisted reproductive technology by combining the aforementioned egg and sperm and was carried to term and delivered by Xiaomei. From her birth until 26 February 2020, Yaya was cared for by both parties, after which she was taken away by Xiaomei and has lived with her ever since.

The Huli Court, after reviewing the case, ruled that as same-sex partners, purchasing sperm and using assisted reproductive technology to conceive a child are not permitted under Chinese law. Although both parties confirmed that Yaya was conceived using Dati's egg and purchased sperm, and was carried to term by Xiaomei, in the absence of explicit legal provisions, it cannot be concluded that a legal parent–child relationship exists solely based on their mutual acknowledgement or the fact that Yaya possesses Dati's genetic information. Furthermore, Yaya's birth certificate clearly states that her mother is Xiaomei. Therefore, Dati's claim to establish a parent–child relationship with Yaya is unreasonable and lacks legal basis, and the court does not support it. Furthermore, Yaya was conceived and given birth to by Xiaomei, has been cared for by Xiaomei since birth, and is currently under one year of age and still requires breastfeeding. Having Xiaomei continue to raise Yaya aligns with legal provisions and is in the best interests of Yaya's healthy development. The plaintiff has no evidence to prove that she is Yaya's mother. Her request for

225 Ibid.

Yaya to be raised by her lacks both factual and legal basis and is also detrimental to the protection of the minor's physical and mental health. Therefore, the trial court dismissed all Dati's claims.[226] The judgment was confirmed in appeal.[227]

This decision has been widely debated on several basis, including for not considering the relevant provisions of the CC, such as, for example, the already discussed art. 1073, on the confirmation and denial of paternity, and art. 1072(2), on constructive parenthood based on a stepparent–stepchild relationship.[228] Furthermore, it is difficult to understand how a court, faced with the fact – admitted even by the defendant and proven by documentary evidence – of the provenience of the fecundated egg from Dati, could have argued that there was no proof of a genetic link between the latter and the child. Even more astonishing is the court's approach to the defendant's refusal to appear in court and to submit the child to a genetic test. Far from viewing the party's lack of cooperation in a negative light, the court in practice rewarded it, considering it impossible to determine the genetic link between the child and the plaintiff and on this basis (sic!) ruling out its existence.

The exemplary decision provided by the 'first custody case' of 2015 seems to have been followed by the Huli People's Court only in part, and only from a formal point of view. The birth mother was, in fact, considered the natural mother of the child. However, no room was left for the possibility that a social mother existed, nor for the identification of the other natural parent through genetic links, while the reference to the best interests of the child seems to play a very little role here, and even in that case only as a mere formality. What is certainly apparent is a strong hostility towards surrogacy – as we have seen common in Chinese courts, which thus interpret the will of the leadership – going hand in hand with an equally strong closure towards same-sex relationships and the parenthood of LGBTQ+ couples. The phenomenon under discus-

---

226 Ibid.

227 Mingyue lüshi 明月律师, 'Qiang Haizi, Cang Haizi; Eyi Weifa Jing de Yi 1抢孩子、藏孩子: 恶意违法竟得益 (Snatching and Hiding Children; Malicious Illegal Activities Actually Benefited)' (12 December 2020) <http://www.51-lihun.com/h-nd-4063.html>.

228 Yang Lixin 楊立新, 'Tongxing tongju zhe yuqi suo sheng zinü de qingzi guanxi rending – yi zhao "Minfa dian" guiding de qinzi guanxi guize zhi jiedu 同性同居者与其所生子女的亲子关系认定- 依照《民法典》规定的亲子关系规则之解读 (Identification of Paternity Between Same-sex Cohabitants and Children-Interpretation in Accordance with the Rules of Parent-child Relations as Stipulated in the Civil Code) 文' (2021) 39 Hebei Faxue 河北法学 27; Chunyan Ding, 'Chinese Legal Response to the Shared Motherhood Model in Lesbians' Family-Making' (2023) 10 Journal of Law and the Biosciences lsad015, 3–4.

sion is evidently underpinned by a conception of the 'traditional family' in its Chinese sense, which evokes, in its forms, the kind of 'traditional family' invoked by European right-wing parties. It may also be construed as a cryptotype whereby bloodlines (or genetic lines) are only relevant in a patrilineal sense.

It is particularly interesting to compare this case with another custody case involving children born through RIVF, decided by the Fengtai Court (Beijing) in 2024. The plaintiff, Zhang Peiyi, and the defendant, her ex-wife (whose name is not known), were a lesbian couple and had been in a long and stable relationship.[229] In 2016, the couple travelled to the United States of America for the purpose of marriage and, concomitantly, conceiving two children by means of IVF, as stipulated in their shared motherhood agreement.[230] Both eggs were provided by the defendant and the sperm was provided by an anonymous donor. The plaintiff was the bearer and the birth mother of the girl, and the defendant was the bearer and the birth mother of the boy, both born in 2017. Subsequently, the family returned to China. The plaintiff was responsible for the majority of childcare duties within the domestic environment until the dissolution of the relationship in November 2019. Without the plaintiff's consent, the defendant took the children to Beijing, where they have been cared for by the defendant's parents ever since. The plaintiff was prevented from both living with and visiting the children. Therefore, she initiated legal proceedings against her former spouse, seeking the court's recognition of her parental rights.[231] During the trial proceedings, the defendant advanced the argument that both children were genetically related to her. Furthermore, she claimed to have assumed financial responsibility for all expenses related to the utilisation of HART overseas. Consequently, she asserted that the children should be considered as her legal offspring.[232] Four years after the first hearing, held in November 2020, the Beijing court, in an unprecedented decision, recognised the legal parentage of both women regarding the daughter, whose custody, following judicial mediation, was awarded to the defendant, entailing monthly visits by the plaintiff. However, no parental rights were recognised to the plaintiff in relation to the son, who had no biological connection to her.

The decision was celebrated as a victory for the Chinese LGBTQ+ movement, as for the first time a court explicitly recognise that a child can have

229 Ding (242*n*120) 4.
230 Ibid.
231 Ibid.
232 Ibid.

two mothers.[233] However, the court's recognition of Zhang as the baby girl's natural mother depends solely on the fact that she gave birth to her. Conversely, her role as 'social' mother is not considered in any way, even if she acted as the *de facto* 'caregiver' of the two kids (including the baby boy) for the two years following their births.

The fact that, unlike in the Huli case, value was given to the genetic link between the defendant and the baby girl, thus assessing the importance of the bloodline also in the maternal sense, was certainly a fundamental achievement, and should not be overlooked. Nevertheless – and although a more reliable appraisal of the judgment would require a reading of its full text, not available online – in considering the best interests of the children, the court seems to have only taken into account biological aspects, without recognising the social aspects and the relational bonds that have been developed between the plaintiff and both children before separation. In this sense, it can be considered as a step back, or at least a step aside, from the 'exemplary approach' taken by the Shanghai Intermediate court in the 2015 case.

It is also true that, in considering the step-motherhood bond, the court would have ventured into the slippery and politically sensitive terrain of recognising same-sex couples as *de facto* couples,[234] since same sex marriage is not legal in the PRC. It is therefore understandable that, to avoid missteps, the judges gave priority to the need to protect public order from unions not permitted by law, placing the best interests of the child as defined in the 2015 ruling in the background. However, this approach has the potential to compromise the rights of innocent children to adequate care and fair treatment, as in such circumstances they may face discrimination in comparison to other children born through surrogacy to heterosexual couples.

It is worth remembering that the tendency to give priority to public order and morality over the best interests of the child is not unique to China. It is worth remarking that it is precisely because of violations of the rights of surrogate children committed in the name of protecting the state's interest in enforcing its laws that, as we have seen, the ECtHR has found itself sanctioning several European countries that take a prohibitive approach to surrogacy.

---

233 Shahana Yasmin, 'Chinese Woman Fighting Landmark LGBTQ+ Custody Battle Wins Right to Visit Daughter|The Independent' (*The Independent*, 14 August 2024) <https://www.independent.co.uk/asia/china/china-woman-custody-lgbtq-ruling-b2596209.html> accessed 2 August 2025.

234 Jie Cheng, 'The Legal Status of LGBTQ+ in China: A Law and Politics Perspective' (2024) 32 Constitutional Forum/Forum constitutionnel 31.

It is evident that these are highly sensitive balances between public and private rights and interests, which necessitating extensive ethical and legal deliberation at both domestic and international levels. Nevertheless, as has been demonstrated by the preceding analyses and elucidated by numerous Chinese authors,[235] refraining from adopting a position due to apprehension regarding social stability may prove to be an even more perilous course of action with respect to the safeguarding of the rights of the most vulnerable parties in a surrogacy arrangement: namely, the surrogate mothers and, most significantly, the surrogate children. The issue could only be resolved through the implementation of a regulated approach, with the objective of ensuring certainty within the framework of Chinese law and (possibly) promoting harmony in what has been regarded from ancient times to the era of Xi Jinping as the 'basic unit of society' (*shehui de jiben xibao* 社会的基本细胞): the family,[236] whatever shape it can take.

---

235 Xiao Yongping, Li Jue and Zhu Lei (259*n*197) 19.

236 Maurice Freedman, 'The Family in China, Past and Present' (1961) 34 Pacific Affairs 323; Liu Zhongshi 刘忠世, 'Jiating de Shehui "Xibao" Yiyi Zai Xianzai de Sangshi 家庭 的社会 "细胞" 意义 在现代 的丧失 (The Loss of the Social "Cell" Meaning of the Family in Modern Times)' Tianfu Xinlun 天府新论 47; The State Council Information Office of the People's Republic of China, 'Family Binds Nation, Its People, President Xi Says|English.Scio.Gov.Cn' (22 February 2018) <http://english.scio.gov.cn/m/topnews/2018-02/22/content_50580337.htm> accessed 1 February 2025.

Conclusions

This study employed the analytical tools of comparative law to examine the relationship between biotechnology, ethics, and law within a context historically perceived as 'distant' and 'different' from that of Europe and North America – namely, the People's Republic of China.

Since the initial encounter between the so-called 'West' (principally Europe and North America) and Chinese civilisation following the Opium Wars, China has been characterised as the 'Oriental Other': without God or Law, according to Marcel Granet's celebrated 1934 assertion, and purportedly lacking morality, or possessing a questionable moral framework, as recent controversies and scandals concerning clinical practices and biotechnological applications in the life sciences within the PRC appear to substantiate.

This analysis, rendered urgent by China's achievement of global scientific primacy from the 2020s onwards, departed from these considerations – encapsulated in the conceptualisation of China as a bioethical 'Wild East.' It focused on biotechnologies related to the beginning of human life to examine: first, the existence of a 'bioethics with Chinese characteristics' and its foundations in both European-American and traditional Chinese thought; secondly, whether and how these characteristics influence the PRC's legal regulation of biotechnologies and clinical practices related to the biosciences. The objective was to identify the values and legal norms that shape contemporary Chinese legal approaches to these issues, and to determine whether such approaches align with, contradict, or provide novel perspectives compared to international legislation and regulations operative within Western legal traditions.

The research adopted both diachronic and synchronic methodological approaches, emphasising historical and cultural dimensions. This framework facilitated the acquisition of interpretative tools appropriate for comprehending a legal and social context – as well as philosophical and political framework – rooted in an ancient civilisation that evolved according to its own principles and precepts throughout most of its existence. The endeavour was to adopt a non-orientalist perspective and a 'neutral' analytical stance, capable of critical observation from a viewpoint free from preconceptions and axioms derived from cultures other than that under examination.

To this end, the first part of this study juxtaposed descriptions of principal Western moral and bioethical definitions and theories with the interpretations offered by Qiu Renzong in 1987, in the first work dedicated to bioethics published in the PRC. Qiu Renzong's interpretations, which remain accessible

 | DOI:10.1163/9789004754300_011

only in the original language, enabled the initial identification of certain 'Chinese characteristics' in the reception of such doctrines, which have now been fully integrated into Chinese bioethical discourse and constitute its primary theoretical foundation. Particularly significant from this perspective is the integration, within Beauchamp and Childress's Four Principles, of pre-existing values derived from traditional and socialist cultural frameworks. Thus, concepts of sacrifice, self-cultivation, responsibility, modesty, self-control, and devotion, together with the principle of the sanctity of life and, crucially, the notion that the public good must invariably supersede personal benefit in cases of conflict, have enriched the meaning attributed in China to concepts originally elaborated by American authors within an American context. This has produced the remarkable effect of modifying their internal hierarchy. Consequently, within the PRC, unlike in the United States, the principle of beneficence is accorded priority over respect for individual autonomy, even in regulations clearly inspired by Beauchamp and Childress's theory, as exemplified by the EPIHARTSB 2003 examined in Chapter 6.

With a view to providing a synthetic, yet comprehensive, framework of the multifaceted and complex Chinese philosophical-moral context – too often confined in interdisciplinary works to Confucianism alone – an account was provided of the indigenous and 'foreign' philosophies that have shaped Chinese thought over the centuries. This analysis, encompassing Confucianism, Daoism, Mohism, Buddhism, and Chinese Marxism, was conducted with the aim of highlighting those ethical aspects most directly connected to medical ethics and to the formation and birth of human beings.

In the same spirit, the second part of this study identified its specific analytical focus through examination of the most prominent case concerning biotechnologies related to the commencement of life adjudicated by a Chinese court: the Yixin frozen embryos case. Analysis of this judicial decision illuminated several critical themes within the Chinese context regarding the intersection of law, morality, and clinical practice in reproductive biotechnologies: family planning and abortion, posthumous fertilisation, and surrogate motherhood. These issues therefore formed the focus of the final three chapters, which were dedicated to their detailed examination.

Each chapter approaches its respective theme through initial analysis of its historical and social evolution, supplemented with representations found in Chinese literary and artistic works. This methodology was adopted to delineate accurately the contextual framework within which formal legal rules, jurisprudential theories, and judicial solutions must operate in contemporary China. This contextual foundation is followed by examination of local and national legislation, consistently conducted from both synchronic and diachronic perspectives, succeeded by analysis of legal doctrine and consideration of related case law.

Whilst this subject matter remains in continuous evolution, the results achieved thus far permit certain preliminary conclusions to be drawn.

The analysis has demonstrated the considerable attention Chinese bioethicists pay to doctrines developed within 'Western' contexts, which now form the foundation of principal international public law instruments. These doctrines have been incorporated into Chinese university curricula for decades and constitute both the methodological basis and starting point for all studies published in the PRC on this subject matter. From a comparative perspective, however, one cannot overlook how the transplantation of ethical or bioethical principles developed within different cultural and social contexts shares the fate commonly encountered by legal transplants during the transition from formal law to practical application.

The principle of 'autonomy' exemplifies this phenomenon. In Chinese bioethical interpretation, this principle has become so similar to the concepts of 'respect' or 'personal dignity' that it has been effectively replaced by the latter in analyses of posthumous fertilisation through Beauchamp and Childress's Four Principles. From the Chinese perspective, this transformation represents not a devaluation of the individual per se, but rather a distinctive approach that considers individuals within their 'relational' context. Individual interests and rights are invariably evaluated and balanced against those of their reference social groups: the family, Chinese society as a whole, and the State. This approach clarifies why the EPIHARTSB 2003 incorporated references to family interests – alongside those of the individual and future generations – as factors that medical institutions and their staff must consider when administering HART or managing sperm banks. The emphasis on the 'relational' aspect of individual interests and rights, perceived not as absolute but in relation to broader social groups, perhaps represents the most significant distinguishing feature of Chinese bioethical approaches compared to their Western, particularly Anglo-Saxon, counterparts.

This relational approach is clearly reflected in the regulation of abortion, posthumous fertilisation, and surrogacy, both in written law and law in action. The research demonstrates that from the perspectives of Chinese culture, traditional medicine, and law, human life commences at birth. Consequently, until 2017, the foetus was accorded no legal capacity whatsoever. This situation changed with the entry into force of Article 16 of the General Provisions of the Civil Code (now Article 16 CC), which protects foetal interests regarding matters such as inheritance or donations, but only when the foetus is born alive.

Regarding the foetus's moral status, the Chinese approach diverges significantly from contemporary understandings influenced by Christian thought. Rather than being considered a human being, the foetus is regarded as 'a special entity with human biological life' – merely one stage in personal development. An individual becomes a person only when all developmental stages are complete and ceases to be a person at death, when transformed into a corpse. Like a corpse, the foetus merits respect but possesses no intrinsic value, only external value that may be expanded or restricted according to society's overall interests. This approach illuminates the family planning policies pursued from 1980 to 2015 through the one-child policy, and from 2015 onwards with increasingly pronounced pronatalist and eugenic attitudes. The compression and expansion of foetal rights and interests – including obligations or disincentives to abort for young, educated Han women – remains directly connected to society's demographic and ageing needs.

Another significant finding is the considerable attention Chinese jurists pay to comparative law. This perhaps little-known phenomenon emerges clearly from doctrinal literature, particularly regarding posthumous fertilisation and surrogate motherhood. Chinese legal scholarship spans both Civil Law and Common Law systems whilst incorporating international jurisprudence, particularly that of the European Court of Human Rights. Studies focus predominantly on European legal systems – France, Germany, and the UK – and American state law, whilst not overlooking debates and legal rules developed on Taiwan. Interestingly, solutions from other Global South legal systems generate less interest, even those from other so-called 'Sinic societies' such as Vietnam and Korea. Proposals advanced to the PRC legislature primarily draw from continental European experience, particularly German law, whose compatibility with Chinese circumstances is invariably assessed before adaptation. These comparative efforts aim to address the legislature's normative inertia.

Legislative reluctance to adopt clear positions, particularly regarding posthumous fertilisation and surrogacy, represents a recurring theme throughout this analysis. This proves particularly disconcerting regarding practices like commercial surrogacy, against which enormous resources are deployed. The justification may lie in desires to await more mature circumstances, develop technological solutions more respectful of human dignity – particularly that of surrogate mothers – or achieve greater certainty regarding popular sentiment towards this specific HART. This impasse is shared with Taiwan, culturally the most similar region to the PRC within Greater China, albeit differing ideologically and politically. However, legislation authorising altruistic surrogacy in the RoC has long appeared imminent; should this occur, examining its effects on the PRC will prove interesting, particularly given majority Chinese doctrinal support for this solution.

Meanwhile, judges must decide without certain normative references in reproductive matters where fundamental human rights recognised internationally and by the PRC's Constitution and Civil Code are often at stake. Analysis of Chinese case law regarding posthumous fertilisation suggests this represents an acquired right, particularly when the surviving spouse is the wife and the couple had commenced assisted fertilisation before bereavement. The Supreme People's Court's inclusion in 2020 of a posthumous fertilisation case among 'typical cases' for judicial guidance provides striking evidence. Even more scientifically interesting is the 2023 'San Menxia case,' which first recognised the right of a child conceived after the father's workplace accident death to claim compensation. This initial application of Article 16 CC to frozen embryos outside the maternal uterus, applauded by Chinese academia as 'a practical application of the best interest of the child' and 'a vivid interpretation of the socialist judicial philosophy of the New Era,' may generate interesting developments worthy of future research.

Surrogacy presents different challenges. As Chapter 8 demonstrates, legal uncertainty in court decisions emerges differently depending on issues and actors involved. In criminal law, courts often judge subjects guilty of practices that constitute crimes only declaratorily, not juridically, resulting in the absurd situation of imposing penalties for behaviour accessory to the principal (non-)crime. Regarding civil courts, jurisprudence has established a *de facto* prohibition of surrogacy in contract law, albeit based on vague principles interpreted through departmental norms relating to different subject categories than those in question.

Concerning parental and custody rights of children born from surrogacy, legal uncertainty persists despite principles established in *Chen Yin v. Luo Ronggeng and Xie Juanru*, decided by Shanghai's First Intermediate Court on 17 June 2016 and considered exemplary by the Supreme People's Court. In that case, consideration of the 'best interest of the child' and recognition of bonds between surrogate children and their intended mother, who had served as *de facto* caregiver from birth, led the court to apply Article 1072(2) CC, recognising the woman's stepmother status and thus custody rights. Analysis of recent cases, particularly those involving lesbian couples reproducing through RIVF, reveals far greater uncertainty. Chinese courts utilise consolidated principles such as birth theory to avoid implicitly recognising the de facto existence of homosexual unions. From this perspective, the 2024 case recognising 'dual motherhood' for the first time regarding a girl born from RIVF within a lesbian couple and analised in the last section of Chapter 8 certainly represents progress whose developments merit continued attention.

From a broader perspective, the research revealed, across all areas examined, a particular attitude towards women's reproductive rights and, perhaps more generally, their role in society. Despite Article 32 (formerly 51) of the PWRIL stipulating that 'Women have the right to bear a child and also the freedom not to bear a child,' this right has never appeared to be entirely at Chinese women's disposal, nor does it seem to be so currently. This is particularly evident regarding abortion, which was often forcibly imposed until at least 2012 and, as demonstrated in Chapter 6, now appears not only discouraged through propaganda but has, in some instances, become more difficult to obtain at the local level, especially for young unmarried women (and non-Uyghur women). For married women, it remains advisable that the decision to abort be shared and 'approved' by the husband, even though the PRC, precisely by virtue of communist ideology, eliminated the requirement for spousal authorisation in the 1950s – a requirement still in force in other Sinic societies such as Taiwan and Japan. As evidenced by divorce jurisprudence, a wife's autonomous decision to abort may, in such cases, worsen the woman's position with negative economic consequences and, particularly, regarding child custody arrangements.

Women's reproductive autonomy also faces limitations when they wish simply to postpone motherhood, awaiting a more stable or satisfactory phase of life in terms of relationships, career, or work, which might coincide with a less biologically fertile period. The collection and storage of ova in appropriate banks remains precluded to unmarried women, with rare local exceptions. The case of posthumous fertilisation further expands the range of subjects involved in decisions regarding the exercise of female reproductive rights to include the husband's family. In many cases, approval for embryo implantation is sought from the deceased's parents, even when the husband's approval was given during his lifetime. These data may be interpreted as vestiges of Chinese cultural tradition linked to 'family continuity' in a patrilineal sense, which imposes upon wives the duty to perpetuate the husband's family lineage. Alternatively, they may be viewed as manifestations of new social requirements arising from the PRC's particular demographic situation – the same circumstances that in 2023, during the 13th National Women's Congress, prompted Chinese leaders to remind women of their duty to contribute to the 'new Chinese journey' not only through commitment to work and social activities, but also through 'the correct view on marriage, love, fertility, and family.' In any case, at least regarding outcomes concerning control over women's bodies and their reproductive rights, these 'Chinese characteristics' do not appear, unfortunately, to be the sole preserve of China.

This does not mean, obviously, that all countries and cultures face identical problems, nor that they recognise the same issues as problematic, and certainly not that they must employ identical instruments to resolve them. However, for now at least, we all inhabit the same planet, with boundaries rendered increasingly fluid by advances in technology and science. 'To say almost the same thing' in law, as in ethics and science, may lead to grave misunderstandings and create enormous problems which, in the case of biotechnologies, may potentially extend to all inhabitants of the globe. Knowledge and consideration of others' perspectives, from their viewpoint, appears to me if not the solution, at least the first step towards finding strategies that account for all perspectives and interests at stake. After all, as it is said in the Dao De Jing, 'A journey of a thousand *li* starts beneath one foot' (*qianli zhi xing shi yu zu xia* 千里之行始于足下). To serve as that initial foundation was, ultimately, the aim of this book.

Bibliography

Ahern EM, 'The Power and Pollution of Chinese Women' <https://ehrafworldcultures.yale.edu/cultures/ad05/documents/029> accessed 7 February 2024

Ahluwalia U and Arora M, 'Posthumous Reproduction and Its Legal Perspective' (2011) 2 International Journal of Infertility & Fetal Medicine 9

Ahmed K, 'China to Clamp down on Abortions for "Non-Medical Purposes"' *The Guardian* (27 September 2021) <https://www.theguardian.com/world/2021/sep/27/china-to-limit-abortions-for-non-medical-purposes> accessed 20 May 2022

Ajani G, Francavilla D, and Pasa B, *Diritto comparato. Lezioni e materiali* (Giappichelli 2018)

Allison KC and others, 'Historical Development and Current Status of Organ Procurement from Death-Row Prisoners in China' (2015) 16 BMC Medical Ethics 85

Alviggi C and others, 'Dalle tecniche di preservazione della fertilità all'utilizzo con finalità riproduttiva post mortem di embrioni e gameti crioconservati. L'esperienza giuridica italiana, francese e spagnola a confronto' (2024) 20 bis *Actualidad Jurídica Iberoamericana* 72

Ames RT, *Confucian Role Ethics: A Vocabulary* (Chinese University Press 2011)

Ames RT and Rosemont JrH, 'Were the Early Confucians Virtuous?' in Fraser C, Robins D, and O'Leary T (eds), *Ethics in Early China: An Anthology* (Hong Kong University Press 2011) <https://doi.org/10.5790/hongkong/9789888028931.003.0002> accessed 15 May 2023

Angle S and Slote M (eds), *Virtue Ethics and Confucianism* (1st edition, Routledge 2015)

Anscombe GEM, 'Modern Moral Philosophy' (1958) 33 Philosophy 1

Ascarelli T, *Studi di diritto comparato e in tema di interpretazione* (Giuffrè 1952)

Baier AC, *Moral Prejudices: Essays on Ethics* (Harvard University Press 1995)

Bailey P, 'Voltaire and Confucius: French Attitudes towards China in the Early Twentieth Century' (1992) 14 History of European Ideas 817

Bardhan P, 'The Chinese Governance System: Its Strengths and Weaknesses in a Comparative Development Perspective' (2020) 61 China Economic Review 101430

Barsotti V and Varano V, *La tradizione giuridica occidentale: Testo e materiali per un confronto civil law common law. Quinta edizione* (G Giappichelli Editore 2014)

Beauchamp TL and Childress JF, *Principles of Biomedical Ethics* (Oxford University Press 2009)

'Beijing's Message to the National Women's Congress: Gender Equality Is Out, Family and Childbirth Are In | Council on Foreign Relations' <https://www.cfr.org/blog/beijings-message-national-womens-congress-gender-equality-out-family-and-childbirth-are> accessed 2 November 2024

Bell DA and Wang P, *Just Hierarchy* (2020) <https://press.princeton.edu/books/hardcover/9780691200897/just-hierarchy> accessed 18 May 2023

Beltrán Tapia FJ and Marco-Gracia FJ, 'Death, Sex, and Fertility: Female Infanticide in Rural Spain, 1750–1950' (2022) 26 European Review of Economic History 234

Bender FL, 'Marxism East and West: Lenin's Revisions of Orthodox Marxism and Their Significance for Non-Western Revolution' (1973) 23 Philosophy East and West 299

Benoza K, 'Consent Issue Casts Shadow on Safe Abortion in Japan' (*The Japan Times*, 28 September 2023) <https://www.japantimes.co.jp/news/2023/09/28/japan/science-health/international-safe-abortion-day/> accessed 13 October 2023

Bentham J, *An Introduction to the Principles of Morals and Legislation* (Dover Publications 2007)

Bernhardt K and Huang PCC, *Civil Law in Qing and Republican China* (Stanford University Press 1994)

'Bibbia NT Greco | Nuovo Testamento | Vangeli | Giovanni | 1' <https://www.bibbiaedu.it/GRECO_NT/nt/Gv/1/> accessed 29 July 2022

'Bible Gateway Passage: Exodus 21:22-23 – New International Version' (*Bible Gateway*) <https://www.biblegateway.com/passage/?search=Exodus%2021%3A22-23&version=NIV> accessed 11 August 2023.

'Bible Gateway Passage: 約 翰 福 音 1 – Chinese Union Version (Traditional)' (*Bible Gateway*) <https://www.biblegateway.com/passage/?search=%E7%B4%84%20%E7%BF%B0%20%E7%A6%8F%20%E9%9F%B3%201&version=CUV> accessed 29 July 2022.

Billingham J, '2. European and Medieval Contexts of Infanticide', 2. *European and Medieval Contexts of Infanticide* (Amsterdam University Press 2019)

Blackledge P, *Marxism and Ethics: Freedom, Desire, and Revolution* (SUNY Press 2012)

Bodurtha M and others, 'Contesting and Controlling Abortion in China's Courts' (Social Science Research Network, 17 February 2024) <https://papers.ssrn.com/abstract=4730082> accessed 3 November 2024

Bohannan P, 'Ethnography and Comparison in Legal Anthropology' in Nader L (ed), *Law in Culture and Society* (1969th edn, University of California Press 1997) <https://www.degruyter.com/document/doi/10.1525/9780520341807-023/html> accessed 25 July 2022

Branigan T, 'Photograph of Woman with Aborted Foetus Sparks Fury in China' *The Guardian* (15 June 2012) <https://www.theguardian.com/world/2012/jun/14/china-forced-abortion-photograph> accessed 12 October 2023

Bray F, *Technology and Gender: Fabrics of Power in Late Imperial China* (0 edition, University of California Press 1997)

Bray F, 'Becoming a Mother in Late Imperial China: Maternal Doubles and the Ambiguities of Fertility', *Chinese Kinship* (Routledge 2008)

Brenkert GG, *Marx's Ethics of Freedom* (1° edizione, Routledge 2013)

Brophy Marcus M, 'Abortion in China | Think Global Health' (*Council on Foreign Relations*, 7 October 2021) <https://www.thinkglobalhealth.org/article/abortion-china> accessed 30 September 2024

Burg W van der, 'Law and Ethics: The Twin Disciplines' (2020) 10–02 Erasmus Working Paper Series on Jurisprudence and Socio-Legal Studies <https://www.academia.edu/32618045/Law_and_Ethics_The_Twin_Disciplines> accessed 2 May 2022

Burg WVD, 'Bioethics and Law: A Developmental Perspective' (1997) 11 Bioethics 91

Butow PN, Tattersall MHN, and Goldstein D, 'Communication with Cancer Patients in Culturally Diverse Societies' (1997) 809 Annals of the New York Academy of Sciences 317

Caballero SM, 'Gestational Surrogacy in California' in Sills ES (ed), *Handbook of Gestational Surrogacy: International Clinical Practice and Policy Issues* (Cambridge University Press 2016) <https://www.cambridge.org/core/books/handbook-of-gestational-surrogacy/gestational-surrogacy-in-california/7F41E998A6EF652ACCB9C7546DFB4F10> accessed 20 July 2025

Callahan DJ, *Abortion: Law, Choice, and Morality* (First Edition, Macmillan Pub Co 1970)

Callahan JC, *Reproduction, Ethics, and the Law: Feminist Perspectives* (Indiana Univ. Press 1995)

Cao D, *Chinese Law: A Language Perspective* (1° edizione, Routledge 2017)

Cao Weiwei, 'The Regulatory Model of Abortion in China through a Feminist Lens' [2013] Asian Women <http://www.e-asianwomen.org/_common/do.php?a=full&b=22&bidx=73&aidx=826> accessed 17 January 2024

Cao Weiwei, '"Glorious Mothers" and "Rational Women": A Comparative Analysis of the Chinese and English Regulatory Models of Abortion' (2019) 67 The American Journal of Comparative Law 745

Cao Weiwei, 'The Regulation of Reproduction in New China: Seven Decades On' (2022) 30 Feminist Legal Studies 97

Capron AM and Michel V, 'Law and Bioethics' 27 Loyola of Los Angeles Law Review 25

'Changes in Rhetoric to China's Women's Congress Push Patriarchal Values' (*IR Insider*) <https://www.irinsider.org/home/9kf4dzaqcoy6454vq316i07i7vir06> accessed 2 November 2024

'Chapter 7: Posthumous Insemination' (2007) 87 Fertility and Sterility S26

Chen Chao-Ju, 'Compulsory Motherhood Challenged and Remade in the Name of Choice: Framing the Right to Choose Under Old and New Maternalism' in Lo C-F, Li NNT, and Lin T-Y (eds), *Legal Thoughts between the East and the West in the Multilevel Legal Order: A Liber Amicorum in Honour of Professor Herbert Han-Pao*

Ma (Springer 2016) <https://doi.org/10.1007/978-981-10-1995-1_12> accessed 16 January 2024

Chen Jianfu, *Chinese Law: Context and Transformation* (Expanded, Revised edizione, Martinus Nijhoff 2015)

'Chen Kaige Short Blasted for "Glorifying" Surrogacy' (*MCLC Resource Center*, 15 December 2020) <https://u.osu.edu/mclc/2020/12/15/chen-kaige-short-blasted-for-glorifying-surrogacy/> accessed 21 July 2025

Chen Zhaoyang 陈兆阳 and Zhang Boyuan 张博源, 'Sang'ou nuxing lendong peitai yizhi de hefa xing zhi bian 丧偶女性冷冻胚胎移植的合法性之辩 (Debate on the Legality of Frozen Embryo Transfer for Widowed Women)' (2025) 46 Yixue yu Zhexue 医学与哲学 46

Cheng Jie, 'The Legal Status of LGBTQ+ in China: A Law and Politics Perspective' (2024) 32 Constitutional Forum / Forum constitutionnel 31

Cheung D, 'Surrogacy in Hong Kong' in Scherpe JM, Fenton-Glynn C, and Kaan T (eds), *Eastern and Western Perspectives on Surrogacy* (Intersentia Ltd, 2019)

Chia-Shin Hsu J, 'Human Dignity in the Jurisprudence of the Taiwan Constitutional Court' in Hsu JC-S (ed), *Human Dignity in Asia: Dialogue between Law and Culture* (Cambridge University Press 2022) <https://www.cambridge.org/core/books/human-dignity-in-asia/human-dignity-in-the-jurisprudence-of-the-taiwan-constitutional-court/13B4E1A4A534CDB8BFFD565FFCDE92AD> accessed 17 March 2024

Childress JF, 'A Principle-Based Approach', *A Companion to Bioethics* (John Wiley & Sons, Ltd 2009) <https://onlinelibrary.wiley.com/doi/abs/10.1002/9781444307818.ch7> accessed 22 August 2022

'China – Jiangxi Province Has Restricted Abortion after the 14th Week of Pregnancy Because of the Sex Ratio Imbalance' (*International Campaign for Women's Right to Safe Abortion*, 27 June 2018) <https://www.safeabortionwomensright.org/news/china-jiangxi-province-has-restricted-abortion-after-the-14th-week-of-pregnancy-because-of-the-sex-ratio-imbalance/> accessed 20 October 2024

'China Becomes Brightest Nature Index 2016 Rising Star | Study In China' <https://www.studyinchina.com.my/web/page/china-brightest-nature-index-2016-rising-star/> accessed 4 August 2025

'China Couple with Eight Babies Sparks Surrogacy Debate' *BBC News* (21 December 2011) <https://www.bbc.com/news/world-asia-china-16275624> accessed 12 July 2025

'China's Five-Year Plan Proposal Stresses Eugenics in Birth Policy, Says Expert' (13 November 2020) <https://angelusnews.com/news/world/chinas-five-year-plan-proposal-stresses-eugenics-in-birth-policy-says-expert/> accessed 29 October 2024

'Chinese Baby Born Four Years after Parents' Death' (12 April 2018) <https://www.bbc.com/news/world-asia-china-43724395> accessed 14 December 2024

Chang D T, 'Transformation of Women's Status in Taiwan, 1920–2020' (*Taiwan Insight*, 17 March 2023) <https://taiwaninsight.org/2023/03/17/transformation-of-womens-status-in-taiwan-1920-2020/> accessed 20 May 2024

Christie O, 'Couple Win Legal Fight to Take Their Dead Son's Sperm and Use It to Create a Grandchild' *Daily Mail Online* (9 Oct 2024) <https://www.dailymail.co.uk/health/article-13940647/couple-win-legal-fight-dead-sons-sperm-grandchild.html> accessed 28 June 2025

Chung YJ, 'Better Science and Better Race?: Social Darwinism and Chinese Eugenics' (2014) 105 Isis 793

'Church Concerned as Taiwan Moves to Legalize Surrogacy- UCA News' (*ucanews.com*, 6 May 2020) <https://www.ucanews.com/amp/church-concerned-as-taiwan-moves-to-legalize-surrogacy/87931> accessed 1 February 2025

Clarke, 'He Weifang versus China's Legal Establishment on the "Three Supremes"' (*Chinese Law Prof Blog*, 12 August 2009) <https://lawprofessors.typepad.com/china_law_prof_blog/2009/08/he-weifang-versus-chinas-legal-establishment-on-the-three-supremes.html> accessed 27 June 2025

Clarke D, 'Anti Anti-Orientalism, or Is Chinese Law Different?†'

'CNKI' <https://oversea-cnki-net.bibliopass.unito.it/index/> accessed 9 February 2022

CNN A by JY and NG, 'Analysis: China Says It's Restricting Abortions to Promote Gender Equality. Experts Are Skeptical' (*CNN*) <https://www.cnn.com/2021/10/01/china/non-medical-abortions-mic-intl-hnk/index.html> accessed 20 May 2022

'Code de La Santé Publique – Légifrance' <https://www.legifrance.gouv.fr/codes/texte_lc/LEGITEXT000006072665/> accessed 22 June 2025

Cole-Turner R, 'Embryo and Fetus. IV. Religious Perspectives', *Encyclopedia of Bioethics* (3rd edn, Macmillan Reference USA 2004) 604

Collier A, *Socialist Reasoning: An Inquiry in the Political Philosophy of Scientific Socialism* (Pluto Pr 1990)

Confucius, 'Analects of Confucius 論語' (A Charles Muller tr) <http://www.acmuller.net/con-dao/analects.html#div-14> accessed 18 May 2023

Confucius and Lau DC, *The Analects* (James Legge T, 1° edizione, Penguin Classics 1979)

'Cong "Jingzhi" daiyun dao "guifang" fatiaoboyi beihou de shi yu 从"禁止"代孕到"规范"法条博弈背后的是与非|青岛|半岛网 (From "prohibiting" surrogacy to "regulating" it: the pros and cons behind the legal battle)' (*Bandao wang – Bandao doushi bao* 半岛网-半岛都市报, 1 January 2016) <https://news.bandao.cn/news_html/201601/20160101/news_20160101_2598426.shtml> accessed 19 January 2025

Cong Yali, 'Bioethics in China', *Annals of Bioethics: Regional Perspectives in Bioethics* (Taylor & Francis 2003)

Congregation for the Doctrine of the Faith, 'Donum Vitae (Respect for Human Life)'

Council of Europe, 'Oviedo Convention and Its Protocols – Human Rights and Biomedicine – Www.Coe.Int' (*Human Rights and Biomedicine*) <https://www.coe.int/en/web/human-rights-and-biomedicine/oviedo-convention> accessed 30 April 2025

Csikszentmihalyi M, *Material Virtue: Ethics and the Body in Early China* (Brill 2021) <https://brill.com/view/title/11174> accessed 6 January 2022

Daniels N, *Am I My Parents' Keeper?: An Essay on Justice Between the Young and the Old* (Oxford University Press 1988)

'Daoism, Bioethics in | Encyclopedia.Com' <https://www.encyclopedia.com/science/encyclopedias-almanacs-transcripts-and-maps/daoism-bioethics> accessed 31 May 2023

Dasgupta S, 'China Reverses Planned Surrogacy Ban to Encourage More Births' (*Voice of America*, 1 January 2016) <https://www.voanews.com/a/china-reverses-planned-surrogacy-ban-to-encourage-more-births/3127177.html> accessed 18 January 2025

Davies M, 'Italy Surrogacy Ban: Couples Banned from Travelling Abroad to Seek Surrogate' (16 October 2024) <https://www.bbc.com/news/articles/c62rmv630690> accessed 20 July 2025

Deal WE, 'Buddhism (Bioethics In)', *Encyclopedia of Bioethics* (Macmillan Reference USA 2004) 334

'Death Control in the West 1500–1800: Sex Ratios at Baptism in Italy, France and England' (*Routledge & CRC Press*, 2023)

Deng Xiaoping 邓小平, 'Jiefan sixiang, shishi qiushi, tuanji yishi xian qiankan (1978 nian 12 yue 13 ri)) 解放思想, 实事求是, 团结一致向前看(1978 年 12 月 13 日) (Emancipate the mind, seek truth from facts, and unite as one to look forward) (13 December 1978)', *Deng Xiaoping wenxuan – Dier Juan* 邓小平文选 — 第二卷 (*Selected Works of Deng Xiaoping*), vol 2 (1983rd edn, Renmin chubanshe 人民出版社) <https://www.marxistphilosophy.org/Deng/Dengxiaowen2.pdf>

Derrida J, *Of Grammatology* (4th edn, John Hopkins University Press 2016)

Diamond N, 'Women under Kuomintang Rule Variations on the Feminine Mystique' (1975) 1 Modern China 3

Diana LY-H, 'Posthumous Assisted Reproduction in the East Asian Context: Towards a Comprehensive Framework of Regulation' (2013) 5 Asian Bioethics Review 93

Dickson D, 'Concern Grows over China's Plans to Reduce Number of "Inferior Births"' (1994) 367 Nature 3

Ding Chunyan, 'Surrogacy Litigation in China and Beyond' (2015) 2 Journal of Law and the Biosciences 33

Ding Chunyan, 'Chinese Legal Response to the Shared Motherhood Model in Lesbians' Family-Making' (2023) 10 Journal of Law and the Biosciences lsad 015

Doan HT, Doan DTP, and Duong NKT, 'Post-Mortem Reproduction from a Vietnamese Perspective – an Analysis and Commentary' (2020) 12 Asian Bioethics Review 257.

Dominus S, '"It's a Terrible Thing When a Grown Person Does Not Belong to Herself"' *The New York Times* (3 May 2022) <https://www.nytimes.com/2022/05/03/magazine/surrogates-ukraine.html> accessed 21 June 2022

Donagan A, *The Theory of Morality* (New edizione, University of Chicago Press 1979)

Döring O (ed), *Chinese Scientists and Responsibility: Ethical Issues of Human Genetics in Chinese and International Contexts* (Institut für Asienkunde 1999)

Döring O, *BIONET-Textbook "Life Sciences in Translation – A Sino-European Dialogue on Ethical Governance of the Life Sciences* (2009) <https://www.lse.ac.uk/researchAndExpertise/units/BIONET/pdfs/BIONET%20Textbook%20-%202nd%20Edition%20-%20Dec%2009.pdf>

Duhem P, 'Physical Theory and Experiment' in Harding SG (ed), *Can Theories be Refuted? Essays on the Duhem-Quine Thesis* (Springer Netherlands 1976) <https://doi.org/10.1007/978-94-010-1863-0_1> accessed 11 August 2023

Durant A and Leung JHC, 'Pragmatics in Legal Interpretation' in Barron A, Gu Y, and Steen G (eds), *The Routledge Handbook of Pragmatics* (1st edn, Routledge 2017) <https://www.taylorfrancis.com/books/9781317362579/chapters/10.4324/9781315668925-38> accessed 29 July 2022

Dworkin R, *Sovereign Virtue: The Theory and Practice of Equality* (Harvard Univ Pr 2002)

Eco U, *Dire quasi la stessa cosa: Esperienze di traduzione* (Bompiani 2013)

'End to Late Marriage Holidays Upsets Young Couples – Global Times' (*Global Times* (*Xinhua*), 10 April 2015) <https://www.globaltimes.cn/content/964661.shtml> accessed 29 June 2025

Engelhardt HT, *Bioethics and Secular Humanism: The Search for a Common Morality* (Wipf and Stock Publishers 2011)

Engels F, *Anti-Dühring* (Wellred Books 2020)

English J, 'What Do Grown Children Owe Their Parents?', *Aging And Ethics* (Humana Press, Totowa, NJ 1992) <https://link.springer.com/chapter/10.1007/978-1-4612-0423-7_6> accessed 10 June 2025

'Er Hai Zhengze Yi Nian Zhuizong: Sheng Bu Chu Hai Zhen Fannao 二孩政策一年追踪: 生不出二孩真烦恼 (One-Year Follow-up of the Two-Child Policy: Not Being Able to Have a Second Child Is Really Annoying)' *Renmin Ribao* 人民日报 (3 February 2017) <http://zw.china.com.cn/2017-02/03/content_40212924.htm> accessed 24 July 2025

'Ethical Considerations of the New Reproductive Technologies. Ethics Committee of The American Fertility Society' (1990) 53 Fertility and Sterility 1S

'Ethics | Definition, History, Examples, Types, Philosophy, & Facts | Britannica' <https://www.britannica.com/topic/ethics-philosophy> accessed 7 August 2022

Faden RR and Beauchamp TL, *A History and Theory of Informed Consent* (Oxford University Press 1986)

Fan Linlin 樊林林, 'Shengyu Quan Tanxi 生育权探析 (Analysis of Reproductive Rights)' [2009] Faxue 32

Fan Ruiping, 'Introduction: Towards a Confucian Bioethics', *Confucian Bioethics: 61* (1999th edition, Springer 1999)

Fan Ruiping and Li Benfu, 'Truth Telling in Medicine: The Confucian View' (2004) 29 The Journal of Medicine and Philosophy 179

Fan Ruiping, 'Three Levels of Problems in Cross-Cultural Explorations of Bioethics: A Methodological Approach' in Kazumasa H (ed), *Japanese and Western Bioethics: Studies in Moral Diversity* (Springer Netherlands 1997) <https://doi.org/10.1007/978-94-015-8895-9_17> accessed 4 January 2024

Fan Ruiping 范瑞平, *Dangdai Rujia shengming lunli xue* 当代儒家生命伦理学 (*Contemporary Confucian Bioethics* (Beijing daxue chubanshe 北京大学出版社 2011)

Fan Ruiping, *Confucian Bioethics* (2002nd edn, Springer).

Fang Yuanzheng方圆震, 'Guanyu "Sheng Haizi" de Naxie Zhengce Yanbian' Nianbian Shi – Zhongguo Renkouy Zhengci 关于“生孩子”的那些政策 —— 中国人口政策演变“编年史”(Policies on "Having Children": A Chronicle of the Evolution of China's Population Policy)' (*Xhonguan zhengfu menhuwangzhang* 中央政府门户网站 (*Central govermment Portal*, 9 February 2015) <https://www.gov.cn/zhengce/2015-02/09/content_2816919.htm> accessed 25 June 2024

'"Farewell My Concubine" Director Chen Kaige in Hot Water Over Surrogacy-Themed Short Film' (7 December 2020) <https://radii.co/article/chen-kaige-surrogacy> accessed 13 July 2025

Fei Lanfang and Zhou Peng, 'The Law Itself Is Not Above Human Beings: Comments on China's First Case on Frozen Embryos' (2015) 29 International Journal of Law, Policy and the Family 260

Fei Xiaotong, Hamilton GG, and Wang Zheng, *From the Soil: The Foundations of Chinese Society* (1° edizione, University of California Press 1992)

Fellows R, Liu AMM, and Zhang S, 'What Is Fair? Perceptions of Justice' (2011) 2 J. Quant. Surv. Constr. Bus. 20

Fenton-Glynn C, 'England and Wales' in Fenton-Glynn C, Scherpe JM, and Kaan T (eds), *Eastern and Western Perspectives on Surrogacy* (Intersentia 2019) <https://www.cambridge.org/core/books/eastern-and-western-perspectives-on-surrogacy/england-and-wales/F0AC144381E76538FDF44089207A92C0> accessed 27 July 2025

Ferrari EI, *La traduzione del diritto comunitario ed europeo: riflessioni metodologiche. Atti del Convegno* (Università degli Studi di Trento 2007)

Fincher LH, *Leftover Women: The Resurgence of Gender Inequality in China, 10th Anniversary Edition* (Bloomsbury Academic 2023)

Fletcher JF, *Morals and Medicine: The Moral Problems of the Patient's Right to Know the Truth, Contraception, Artificial Insemination, Sterilization, Euthanasia* (Princeton University Press 2015) <https://www.degruyter.com/document/doi/10.1515/9781400868377/html> accessed 7 August 2022

Foucault M, *The History of Sexuality: 1: The Will to Knowledge* (1° edizione, Penguin Classics 2020)

Fox RC and Swazey JP, 'Medical Morality Is Not Bioethics – Medical Ethics in China and the United States' (1984) 27 Perspectives in Biology and Medicine 336

Fraser C, *The Philosophy of the Mòzǐ: The First Consequentialists* (Columbia University Press 2016)

Fraser C, Robins D, and O'Leary T (eds), *Ethics in Early China: An Anthology* (Hong Kong University Press 2011) <https://hongkong.universitypressscholarship.com/10.5790/hongkong/9789888028931.001.0001/upso-9789888028931> accessed 6 January 2022

Freedman M, 'The Family in China, Past and Present' (1961) 34 Pacific Affairs 323

Freeman M, 'Does Surrogacy Have a Future after Brazier?' (1999) 7 Medical Law Review 1

Furgalska M and Londras F de, 'Rights, Lawfare and Reproduction: Reflections on the Polish Constitutional Tribunal's Abortion Decision' (2022) 55 Israel Law Review 285

Yi Fuxian, 'China's Abortion Problem Can't Be Regulated Away | by Yi Fuxian' (*Project Syndicate*, 14 April 2022) <https://www.project-syndicate.org/commentary/china-abortion-restrictions-demographic-crisis-by-yi-fuxian-2022-04> accessed 20 May 2022

Gao Xinmin, Zhang Yu, and He Guanqi, 'The Truth-Seeking Objective of Chinese Philosophy of Mind' (2023) 13 Open Journal of Philosophy 195

'Genetic Health Act – Article Content – Laws & Regulations Database of The Republic of China (Taiwan)' <https://law.moj.gov.tw/Eng/LawClass/LawAll.aspx?PCode=L0070001> accessed 9 September 2022

Gervasi M, 'The European Court of Human Rights and Technological Development: The Issue of the Continuity of the Family Status Established Abroad Through Recourse to Surrogate Motherhood' [2018] Diritti umani e diritto internazionale

'Gesetz Zum Scjitz von Embryonen (Embryonenschutzgesetz – ESchG)' <https://www.gesetze-im-internet.de/eschg/BJNR027460990.html>

Gewirtz DS, 'Toward A Quality Population: China's Eugenic Sterilization of the Mentally Retarded' (*134994*, 1994) <https://repository.library.georgetown.edu/handle/10822/526049?show=full> accessed 29 October 2024

Ghosh A, 'Cradle of the World' (*Hindustan Times*, 24 December 2006) <https://www.hindustantimes.com/india/cradle-of-the-world/story-sPA9Q9b2r4MHrQ9R7dNJnK.html> accessed 29 July 2025

Gilligan C, *In a Different Voice: Psychological Theory and Women's Development* (Reprint edizione, Harvard Univ Pr 2016)

Ginsburg R, 'Some Thoughts on Autonomy and Equality in Relation to Roe v. Wade' (1985) 63 North Carolina Law Review 375

Giuffrida A, 'Surrogate Parents Too Afraid to Return to Italy after "Procreative Tourism" Law' *The Guardian* (17 March 2025) <https://www.theguardian.com/world/2025/mar/17/surrogate-parents-too-afraid-to-return-to-italy-after-procreative-tourism-law> accessed 20 July 2025

Glenn HP, *Legal Traditions of the World: Sustainable Diversity in Law* (Oxford University Press 2014)

Gómez G, 'China's Eugenics Law as Grounds for Granting Asylum' (1996) 5 Washington International Law Journal 563

Goodman DSG, 'Revolutionary Women and Women in the Revolution: The Chinese Communist Party and Women in the War of Resistance to Japan, 1937–1945' [2000] The China Quarterly 915

Goswami L, Larmar SA, and Boddy J, 'The Impacts of the Covid-19 Pandemic on Surrogacy in India: The Role of Social Work' (2021) 20 Qualitative Social Work 472

Graham AC, *Disputers of the Tao: Philosophical Argument in Ancient China* (First Edition, Open Court 1989)

Granet M, *La pensée chinoise* (3rd edn, Albin Michel 1934)

Greenhalgh S, *Just One Child: Science and Policy in Deng's China* (2008)

Grene MG, *The Knower and the Known* (First Paperback edition, University of California Press 1974)

Griffin J, *Well-Being: Its Meaning, Measurement and Moral Importance* (1988) <https://academic.oup.com/book/3189> accessed 18 August 2022

Guo Chao and others, 'Risky Sexual Behaviors and Repeat Induced Abortion Among Unmarried Young Women in China: Results from a Large, Nationwide, Population-Based Sample' (2019) 28 Journal of Women's Health (2002) 1442

Guo Zili 郭自力, *Xiandai yiliao jishu zhong de sheng ming lunli he falü wenti yanjiu* 现代医疗技术中的生命伦理和法律问题研究 [*Research on Bioethics and Legal Issues in Modern Medical Technology*] (Zhongguo shehui kexue chubanshe 中国社会科学出版社 2021)

Guo Zili 郭自力, *Shengwu yixue de falü he lunli wenti* 生物医学的法律和伦理问题 [*The Legal and Ethical Issues on Biomedicine*] (Beijing daxue chubanshe 北京大学出版社 2002)

Guojia weisheg jiankang wei bangong ting 国家卫生健康委办公厅 General Office of the National Health Commission, 'Guojia Weisheg Jiankang Wei Bangong Ting, Zhongyang Zhengfa Wei Bangong Ting, Zhongyang Wang Xin Ban Mishu Ju, Zuigao Renmin Fayuan Bangong Ting, Zuigao Renmin Jianchayuan Bangong Ting, Jiaoyu Bu Bangong Ting, Gongye He Xinxi Hua Bu Bangong Ting, Jiàoyù Bù Bàngōng Tīng, Minzheng Bu Bangongting, Shichang Jianguan Zongjiu Bangong Ting, Guojia Yao Jian Ju Zonghe Si, Guojia Zhong Yiyao Ju Zonghe Si, Quanguo Fulian

Bangong Ting, Zhongyang Junwei Houqin Baozhang Bu Weisheng Ju Guanyu Yinfa Kaizhan Yanli Dai Feifa Yingyong Renlei Fuzhu Shengzhi Jishu Zhanxiang Huodong Gonzuo Fang'an de Tongzhi 国家卫生健康委办公厅、中央政法委办公厅、中央网信办秘书局、最高人民法院办公厅、最高人民检察院办公厅、教育部办公厅、工业和信息化部办公厅、公安部办公厅、民政部办公厅、市场监管总局办公厅、国家药监局综合司、国家中医药局综合司、全国妇联办公厅、中央军委后勤保障部卫生局关于印发开展严厉打击非法应用人类辅助生殖技术专项活动工作方案的通知 (Notice by the General Office of the National Health Commission, the General Office of the Commission of Politics and Law of the CPC Central Committee, the Secretary Bureau of the Office of the Central Cyberspace Affairs Commission, the General Office of the Supreme People's Court, the General Office of the Supreme People's Procuratorate, the General Office of the Ministry of Education, the General Office of the Ministry of Industry and Information Technology, the General Office of the Ministry of Public Security, the General Office of the Ministry of Civil Affairs, the General Office of the State Administration for Market Regulation, the Department of Comprehensive Affairs of the National Medical Products Administration, the Department of Comprehensive Affairs of the National Administration of Traditional Chinese Medicine, the General Office of the All-China Women's Federation, and the Health Bureau of the Logistic Support Department of the Central Military Commission Health of Issuing the Work Plan for the Special Action of Severely Cracking Down on the Illegal Application of Human Assisted Reproductive Technology)'

'Guowuyuan Yinfa Zhongguo Funǚ Fazhan Gangyao He Zhongguo Ertong Fazhan Gangyao 国务院印发中国妇女发展纲要和中国儿童发展纲要' (*Zhong xin wang* 中新网) <https://www.chinanews.com.cn/gn/2021/09-27/9574812.shtml> accessed 30 May 2022

'Guowuyuan Zhuanfa Weisheng Bù Junguan Kuai, Shangye Bu, Ranliao Huaxue Gongye Bu "Guanyu Zuo Hao Jihua Shengyu Gongzuo de Baogao" 国务院转发卫生部军管会、商业部、燃料化学工业部"关于做好计划生育工作的报告" (The State Council Forwarded to the Ministry of Health's Military Commission, the Ministry of Commerce and the Ministry of Fuel and Chemical Industry the "Report on Improving Family Planning")' <https://www.gov.cn/zhengce/content/2015-11/19/content_10304.htm> accessed 25 June 2024

Hakeda Yoshito S and Abé R, *The Awakening of Faith: Attributed to Asvaghosha* (Columbia University Press 2005)

Hans JD, 'Attitudes Toward Posthumous Harvesting and Reproduction' (2008) 32 Death Studies 837

Hardacre H, *Marketing the Menacing Fetus in Japan: 7* (University of California Press 1999)

Harper D, '23. Spellbinding', *23. Spellbinding* (Princeton University Press 2018) <https://www.degruyter.com/document/doi/10.1515/9780691188140-028/html> accessed 7 February 2024

Harper SJ, 'Ethics versus Morality: A Problematic Divide' (2009) 35 Philosophy & Social Criticism 1063

Harris N, *The Mandate of Heaven: Marx and Mao in Modern China* (Haymarket Books 2015)

Harvey P, *An Introduction to Buddhist Ethics: Foundations, Values and Issues* (1st edn, Cambridge University Press 2000) <https://www.cambridge.org/core/product/identifier/9780511800801/type/book> accessed 4 February 2024

Hashiloni-Dolev Y and Others Triger Z, 'The Invention of the Extended Family of Choice: The Rise and Fall (to Date) of Posthumous Grandparenthood in Israel' (2020) 39 New Genetics and Society 250

Hashiloni-Dolev Y and Schicktanz S, 'A Cross-Cultural Analysis of Posthumous Reproduction: The Significance of the Gender and Margins-of-Life Perspectives' (2017) 4 Reproductive Biomedicine & Society Online 21

Have H ten, 'The Universal Declaration on Bioethics and Human Rights as a Landmark in the Development of Global Bioethics', *International Biolaw and Shared Ethical Principles* (Routledge 2018)

Hayakawa Shinishiro, 'Japan' in Scherpe JM, Fenton-Glynn C, and Kaan T (eds), *Eastern and Western Perspectives on Surrogacy* (Intersentia 2019) <https://www.cambridge.org/core/books/eastern-and-western-perspectives-on-surrogacy/japan/64738C71422
DC01C209203FF8156A906> accessed 20 July 2025

He Yue 何悦 and Yu Fenglei 俞风雷, 'Wo Guo Dayun Shengshi Lifa Yanjiu – Yi Yinguo Daiyun Shengzhi Lifa Shijiao 我国代孕生殖立法研究 — 以英国代孕生殖立法为视角 (Research on China's Surrogate Reproduction Legislation – from the Perspective of UK Surrogate Reproduction Legislation)' (2017) 38 Faxue zazhi 法学杂志 46

Head JW and Wang Y, *Law Codes in Dynastic China. A Synopsis of Chinese Legal History in the Third Centuries from Zhou to Qing* (Carolina Academic Press 2005)

Health Ministry Proposes Making Taiwan First in Asia To Legalize Surrogacy | TaiwanPlus News (Directed by TaiwanPlus News, 2024) <https://www.youtube.com/watch?v=DOyi-NPOVY> accessed 3 August 2025

Hegel GWF, *The Philosophy of History* (Batoche Books 2001)

Hill A, 'Favouring Young over Old in Covid-19 Treatment Justifiable, Says Ethicist' *The Guardian* (22 April 2020) <https://www.theguardian.com/world/2020/apr/22/favouring-young-over-old-in-covid-19-treatment-justifiable-says-ethicist> accessed 25 May 2022

Ho Chih-Hsing, 'Taiwan' in Fenton-Glynn C, Scherpe JM, and Kaan T (eds), *Eastern and Western Perspectives on Surrogacy* (Intersentia 2019) <https://www.cambridge

.org/core/books/eastern-and-western-perspectives-on-surrogacy/taiwan/B21919D856E746A68B19E99159D14C78> accessed 1 February 2025

Hooker W, *Physician and Patient; Or, A Practical View of the Mutual Duties, Relations and Interests of the Medical Profession and the Community* (Baker and Scribner 1849)

Hou Weiqing 侯卫清, 'Yangyu Muqin Huode Daiyun Zinü Jianyuquan Zhi Falü Jichu 养育母亲获得代孕子女监护权之法律基础 (Legal Basis for the Adoptive Mother to Obtain Custody of the Surrogate Child)' [2017] Anli-benqi guanzhu – Renmin Sifa 案例-本期关注 — 人民司法 4

Hu Wenhao 胡文浩, 'Anlesi zhiyi 安乐死质疑 [Euthanasia Challenges]' [1988] Shije zi yixueyuan bao 石河子医学院学报 137

Huang Jiliang and others, 'Attitudes toward Posthumous Assisted Reproduction in China: A Multi-Dimensional Survey' (2022) 19 Reproductive Health 122

Huang Jinxing 黄进兴, *Cong lunxue dao lunli xue: Qing mo Min chu daode yishi de zhuanhua* 从理学到伦理学: 清末民初道德意识的转化 (*From Science to Ethics: The Transformation of Moral Consciousness in the Late Qing and Early Republican Periods*) (中华书局 2014) <https://item.jd.com/11436389.html> accessed 15 February 2022

Huang PCC, *Code, Custom, and Legal Practice in China: The Qing and the Republic Compared* (Stanford University Press 2001)

Huang Qi 黄祺, 'Shijie Shang Di Yi "Shiguan Ying'er" – Lu Yi Si 世界上第一个"试管婴儿"露易丝 (The World's First "Test-Tube Baby," Louise)' *Xin min zhoukang* 新民周刊 (19 October 2023) <https://m.xinminweekly.com.cn/content/19238.html> accessed 1 May 2025

Huli Fayuan 湖里法院, 'Tamen Dou Shuo Ziji Shi Haizi de Mama 她们都说自己是孩子的妈妈 (They All Say They Are the Child's Mothers)' (*Weixing gongzhong pingtai* 微信公众平台 (*WeChat public platform*)) <https://mp.weixin.qq.com/s/eaVO6cZj6W6sBGFAvp-N3A> accessed 1 August 2025

Institute GT, 'The "One-China Principle": China's "Norm" versus Global Realities' (*Global Taiwan Institute*, 21 February 2024) <https://globaltaiwan.org/2024/02/the-one-china-principle-chinas-norm-versus-global-realities/> accessed 5 August 2025

Ivanhoe PJ and Van Norden BW (eds), *Readings in Classical Chinese Philosophy* (Seven Bridges Press 2001)

Jervolino D, 'Translation as Paradig for Hermeneutics and Its Implication for an Ethics of Hospitality' in Zaccaria G (ed), *Translation in Law* (LIT Verlag Münster 2000)

Ji Yuqiao, 'Short Film from Renowned Chinese Director Chen Kaige Sparks Discussion about Surrogacy in China – Global Times' (*Global Times*, 7 December 2020) <https://www.globaltimes.cn/content/1209254.shtml> accessed 13 July 2025

Jiang Su and Zhang Huimin, 'Criminalization of Commercial Surrogacy in China' (2024) 12 Peking University Law Journal 23

'Jiangxi Abortion Rule Seeks Sex Ratio Balance' <https://www.ecns.cn/news/society/2018-06-25/detail-ifyvmiee7354538.shtml> accessed 20 October 2024

'Jiaoyu Zhengdun – Hua 24 Wan Daiyun Hou Zhao Zhongjie Suopei. Fayuan: "Daiyun Hetong" Yin Weifan Gongxuliangsu Er Wuxiao J教育整顿 | 花32万代孕后找中介索赔，法院："代孕合同"因违反公序良俗而无效 (Education and Rectification | After Spending 320,000 Yuan on a Surrogacy, They Sought Compensation from the Agency. The Court Declared the Surrogacy Contract Invalid Because It Violated Public Order and Good Morals)' (*Weixing gongzhong pingtai* 微信公众平台 (*WeChat public platform*), 15 May 2021) <https://mp.weixin.qq.com/s/cjAAOCtoEROsndnzzz_SpQ> accessed 31 July 2025

Jin Ruining, 'Eugenics in China through the Lens of Cultural Additivity'

Jin Yongai and Hu Wenbo, 'Diverging Destinies: Changing Trends of Induced Abortion in China' (2023) 7 China Population and Development Studies 63

'John 1:1 In the Beginning Was the Word, and the Word Was with God, and the Word Was God.' <https://biblehub.com/john/1-1.htm> accessed 29 July 2022

Jonsen AR, *The Birth of Bioethics* (Oxford University Press 2003)

Jonsen AR, 'The God Squad and the Origins of Transplantation Ethics and Policy' (2007) 35 The Journal of Law, Medicine & Ethics: A Journal of the American Society of Law, Medicine & Ethics 238

Kale S, 'Surrogates Left Holding the Baby as Coronavirus Rules Strand Parents' *The Guardian* (14 May 2020) <https://www.theguardian.com/lifeandstyle/2020/may/14/surrogates-baby-coronavirus-lockdown-parents-surrogacy> accessed 21 June 2022

Kamenka E, *Marxism and Ethics* (Palgrave Macmillan UK 1969) <http://link.springer.com/10.1007/978-1-349-00592-5> accessed 17 June 2023

Kant I, *Critique of Practical Reason* (Thomas Kingsmill Abbott tr, DigiCat 2022)

Kass LR, 'The Wisdom of Repugnance. Why We Should Ban the Cloning of Human' [1997] The New Republic 17

Kasulis TP, 'Cultural Differentiation in Buddhist Ethics', *Encyclopedia of Religious Ethics* (John Wiley & Sons, Ltd 2022) <https://onlinelibrary.wiley.com/doi/abs/10.1002/9781118499528.ch72> accessed 3 June 2023

Katz K, 'Parenthood from the Grave: Protocols for Retrieving and Utilizing Gametes from the Dead or Dying' (2015) 2006 University of Chicago Legal Forum <https://chicagounbound.uchicago.edu/uclf/vol2006/iss1/11>

Khazova OA, 'Russia' in Fenton-Glynn C, Scherpe JM, and Kaan T (eds), *Eastern and Western Perspectives on Surrogacy* (Intersentia 2019) <https://www.cambridge.org/core/books/eastern-and-western-perspectives-on-surrogacy/russia/FC418EC7D4D0C8DE608BBC2D817EFF98> accessed 19 July 2025

Khazova OA, 'Chapter 19: Recent Changes in Russian Law on Surrogacy in the Eastern European Context' (2024) <https://www.elgaronline.com/edcollchap/book/9781802207651/book-part-9781802207651-27.xml> accessed 19 July 2025

Kilday A-M, *A History of Infanticide in Britain, c. 1600 to the Present* (Palgrave Macmillan 2013)

Kim O-J and Lee B-H, 'South Korea' in Scherpe JM, Fenton-Glynn C, and Kaan T (eds), *Eastern and Western Perspectives on Surrogacy* (Intersentia 2019) <https://www.cambridge.org/core/books/eastern-and-western-perspectives-on-surrogacy/south-korea/778B382D9190B8B380198D77BBC18AAD> accessed 20 July 2025

Kirkegaard JF, 'China's Population Decline Is Getting Close to Irreversible | PIIE' (18 January 2024) <https://www.piie.com/research/piie-charts/2024/chinas-population-decline-getting-close-irreversible> accessed 2 September 2024

Kirkland JR, 'The Roots of Altruism in the Taoist Tradition' (1986) LIV Journal of the American Academy of Religion 59

Kirkland R, 'A World in Balance: Holistic Synthesis in the "T'ai-p'ing Kuang-Chi"' [1993] Journal of Song-Yuan Studies 43

Kiung Jai Koh Clan Association, 'Genealogical Records of the Koh Clan in Singapore'

Kleinman A, *The Illness Narratives: Suffering, Healing, And The Human Condition* (New edizione, Basic Books 2020)

Kong Huiyuan 孔慧媛 and Tang Min 汤敏, 'Daiyun Suo Sheng Zinü de Fuyang Quan Queding Ji Fuyang Fei Chengdan de Wenti Yanjiu 代孕所生子女的抚养权确定及抚养费承担的问题研究 (Research on the Determination of the Custody of the Children Born of Surrogacy and the Commitment of the Maintenance Fee)' (2025) 17 医学与法学 57

Korsgaard CM, M G, and Timmermann J, *Kant: Groundwork of the Metaphysics of Morals* (2° edizione, Cambridge University Press 2012)

Kroløkke CH and Adrian SW, 'Sperm on Ice: Fatherhood and Life after Death' (2013) 28 Australian Feminist Studies 263

Krüger M, 'The prohibition of post-mortem-fertilization, legal situation in Germany and European Convention on human rights' (2011) 82 Revue internationale de droit pénal 41

Kuhse H, 'Clinical Ethics and Nursing: "Yes" to Caring, but "No" to a Female Ethics of Care' (1995) 9 Bioethics 207

Kuhse H and Singer P, 'What Is Bioethics? A Historical Introduction', *A Companion to Bioethics* (John Wiley & Sons, Ltd 2009) <https://onlinelibrary.wiley.com/doi/abs/10.1002/9781444307818.ch1> accessed 3 May 2022

LaFleur WR, *Liquid Life: Abortion and Buddhism in Japan* (Princeton University Press 1994) <https://press.princeton.edu/books/paperback/9780691029658/liquid-life> accessed 7 June 2023

Lam STS, 'Abortion, Sterilization and Genetic Control – the Hong Kong Perspectives', *Chinese Scientists and Responsibility. Ethical Issues of Human Genetics in Chinese and International Context* (Mitteilungen Des Instituts Für Asienkunde Hamburg 1999)

Lee C-F, 'A Study on The Extraordinary Appeal Decisions of Dali Yuan in the beginning of Republic of China' (2017) 29 Dong Wu fa lü xue bao. Soochow law review 47

Lee Kyung-hee 이경희, 'A Study on the Decision-Making framework for Posthumous Reproduction' (2007) 21 Korean Journal of Family Law 207

Lee LM, 'A Bridge Back to the Future: Public Health Ethics, Bioethics, and Environmental Ethics' (2017) 17 The American Journal of Bioethics 5

Lewis S, *Full Surrogacy Now: Feminism Against Family* (Verso 2021)

Li En-Chang, 'Bioethics in China' (2008) 22 Bioethics 448

Li Haonan 李浩南, 'Kuaguo Daiyun Ertong de Shenfen Quanyi Baohu de Kunjing Yu Pojie 跨国代孕儿童的身份权益保护之困境与破解 (Dilemma and Solution of Identity Rights and Interests Protection for Transnational Surrogate Children' (2024) 16 Yixue yu faxue 医学语法学

Li Hongwen 李红文, *Daojia Wenming Lunli de Chuantong Shiyu Yu Xiandai Zhuanxing* 道家生命伦理的传统视域与现代转型 [*Taoist Bioethics: Traditional Perspectives and Modern Transformation*] (Zhongguo shehui kexue chubanshe 中国社会科学出版社 2020) <https://item.jd.com/12662791.html> accessed 15 February 2022

Li Jiang, *Regulating Human Embryonic Stem Cell in China. A Comparative Study on Human Embryonic Stem Cell's Patentability and Morality in US and EU* (Springer 2016)

Li JT, 'Fate, Reincarnation and Medicinal Cannibalism in Lillian Lee's Dumplings', *Fate and Prognostication in the Chinese Literary Imagination* (Brill 2019) <https://brill.com/display/book/edcoll/9789004427570/BP000005.xml> accessed 29 September 2023

Li Kang 黎康, 'Zhongguo te gao: Yinni ai yu lunli zhi sheng xieyuan dai gong xuqiu yu chanye qiaoran fazhan fāzhǎn中国特稿: 隐匿爱与伦理之争 血缘代工需求与产业悄然发展 (China Special Report: The Hidden Love and Ethical Debate: The Demand for Surrogacy and the Quiet Development of the Industry)' *Lianhe Zaobao* 联合早报 (10 November 2024) <https://www.zaobao.com.sg/news/china/story20241110-5295949> accessed 21 July 2025

Li Lei 李磊 and Shen Yanru 沈燕如, 'Sihou Renlei Shengzhi de Lunli Sikao 死后人工生殖的伦理思考 (Ethical Thinking of Post-Mortem Artificial Reproduction)' (2021) 42 Yixue yu zhexue 医学与哲学 34

Li Qun 李群, 'Dianqi Yu Biantong de Lifa Heyong 典妻与变通的礼法适用 (The "Pawning of a Wife" and the Flexible Application of Rites)' (2010) 140 Dandai faxue (shunyueli)当代法学(双月刊) 42

Li Yan 李 琰, Li Jun 李 军 and Lan Liji 兰礼吉, 'Sihou Shenzhi Wenti de Shengming Sikao 死后生殖问题的生命伦理学思考 (Thinking on Bioethics in the Reproduction after Death)' (2007) 28 Yixue yu zhexue 医学与哲学 32

Liang Hongxia 梁洪霞, 'Wo guo duo shengshi "xianzhi funü duotai" guiding de he xianxing tanjiu – jianyi shengyu quan de xianfa baohu 我国多省市 "限制妇女堕

胎” 规定的合宪性探究* — — — 兼议生育权的宪法保护 (Constitutionality Research on Restricting Abortion in the Local Legislations of China – With Discussion on the Constitutional Protection of Reproductive Right)' (2018) 12 Beifang faxue 北方法学 37

Liang Linjun 梁林军、 and Liu Tiantian 刘甜甜, 'Qisi Zhongzhi Rengsheng How Zhangfu Qisu Qinfan Shengyu Quan 妻子中止妊娠后丈夫起诉侵犯生育权, 法院这么判 (After His Wife Terminated Her Pregnancy, the Husband Sued for Infringement of Reproductive Rights. The Court Ruled as Follows)' *Hongxing xinwen* 红星新闻 (13 February 2023) <https://static.cdsb.com/micropub/Articles/202302/208b8ceb48836607f10f50cf91b2f46e.html> accessed 5 November 2024

Lieber KB, 'Selling the Womb: Can the Feminist Critique of Surrogacy Be Answered?' (1992) 68 Indiana Law Journale 205

Liebman B and others, 'Rolling Back Transparency in China's Courts' (2023) 123 Columbia Law Review 2407

Lih ED-R Kris, 'The Unusual Shape of the Debate Around Fertility Treatment in Taiwan' (*Domino Theory*, 3 May 2024) <https://dominotheory.com/the-unusual-shape-of-the-debate-around-fertility-treatment-in-taiwan/> accessed 13 May 2025

Lin JY, 'The Household Responsibility System in China's Agricultural Reform: A Theoretical and Empirical Study' (1988) 36 Economic Development and Cultural Change S199

Linyi shi Lanshan qu Renmin fayuan guanli yuan 临沂市兰山区人民法院管理员 (Administrator of the People's Court of Lanshan District, Linyi City), 'Yi Lingfa Cu Shangshi Quanmian Shenhua Minfa Dian Guanche Shishi – Zuigao Fa Fabu Di Er Pi Renminfayuan Guanche Shishi Mín Fǎ Diǎn Diǎnxíng Ànlì 以良法促善治, 全面深化民法典贯彻实施 — — 最高法发布第二批人民法院贯彻实施民法典典型案例 (Promoting Good Governance with Good Laws and Comprehensively Deepening the Implementation of the Civil Code – The Supreme People's Court Released the Second Batch of Typical Cases of the People's Courts Implementing the Civil Code)' (31 January 2023) <http://qdzy.sdcourt.gov.cn/lylsqfy/367109/367114/9171392/index.html>

Liu Bibo 刘碧波, 'Wo Guo Daiyun de Lifa Yu Sifa Wenti 我国代孕的立法与司法问题 (Legislative and Judicial Issues of Surrogacy)' Xueshu jiaoliu 学术交流 115

Liu Changqiu, 'Definition of Life Law and the Situation with Problems of China's Life Jurisprudence' (2008) 19 Journal International De Bioethique = International Journal of Bioethics 33

Liu Changqiu 刘长秋, 'Lun Shangye Xin Daiyun de Xingfa Guize 论商业性代孕的刑法规制 (On the Criminal Regulation of Commercial Surrogacy)' [2024] Dongfang Faxue东方法学 175

Liu Guanhe 刘冠合, 'Daiyun Zinü Qinzi Guanxi Rending: Biaozhunjiangou Yu Guize Chonggou – Jiyu "Minfadian" Di 1073 Tiao de Guifan Kaocha 代孕子女亲子关系认

定: 标准检讨与规则重构 — 基于“民法典第 1073 条的规范考察 (Determination of Paretn-Child Relationships in Surrogacy Cases: Review of Standards and Reconstruction Rules – Normative Investigation Based on Article 1073 of the Civil Code of China' (2025) 45 Huebei Shifan Daxue xuebao (zhexue shehui kexueban) 湖北师范大促额促额包 (这数额社会科学版) 46

Liu Jinlin and others, 'Is Repeat Abortion a Public Health Problem among Chinese Adolescents? A Cross-Sectional Survey in 30 Provinces' (2019) 16 International Journal of Environmental Research and Public Health 794

Liu Yinliang, 'The Development of the Human-Assisted Reproductive Technology and Its Regulation in China: A Historical Narrative' (2024) 12 Peking University Law Journal 1

Liu Yuxiu and others, 'Disclosure of Cancer Diagnosis in China: The Incidence, Patients' Situation, and Different Preferences between Patients and Their Family Members and Related Influence Factors' (2018) 10 Cancer Management and Research 2173

Liu Yue, Xian Xuechang, and Du Li, 'Perspectives on Surrogacy in Chinese Social Media: A Content Analysis of Microblogs on Weibo' (2022) 95 The Yale Journal of Biology and Medicine 305

Liu Yajing 刘雅静, 'Zhongguo zhe ming ying'er shi chuanqi! Ta zai fumu qushi si nian hou shusheng 中国这名婴儿是传奇!他在父母去世四年后出生 (This baby in China is legendary! He was born four years after his parents died)' (*Jinri huawen* 今日华闻, 12 April 2018) <https://ihuawen.com/article/index/id/50864> accessed 18 January 2025.

Liu Zhongshi 刘忠世, 'Jiating de Shehui "Xibao" Yiyi Zai Xianzai de Sangshi 家庭 的社会“细胞” 意义 在现代 的丧失 (The Loss of the Social "Cell" Meaning of the Family in Modern Times)' Tianfu Xinlun 天府新论 47.

'Liuchan Shoushu Zhangfu Qianzi Zhineng Guibi Shengyu Quan Jiufen Ma 流产手术丈夫签字真能规避生育权纠纷吗 (Can a Husband's Signature on a Miscarriage Procedure Really Avoid Disputes over Reproductive Rights?)' (*Xinhua wang* 新华网, 15 September 2003) <https://news.sina.cn/sa/2003-09-15/detail-ikknscsi1244828.d.html> accessed 5 November 2024

Logan S and others, 'Infertility in China: Culture, Society and a Need for Fertility Counselling' (2019) 8 Asian Pacific Journal of Reproduction 1

'Logos | Definition, History, & Facts | Britannica' <https://www.britannica.com/topic/logos> accessed 2 August 2022

Long J and Novaretti S, '"You Were an Embryonic Dragon, Nurtured in a Dog's Belly" v. "Children Are a Piece of Heart". Surrogacy in China and Italy among Tradition, Ideology, Gender, and the Law' (2022) 2 (Comparative Family Law Methodology) Ius Comparatum 71

Lowe DM, *The Function of China in Marx, Lenin, and Mao* (First Edition, Berkeley, University Of California Press 1966)

Lu Tonglin, 'Fruit Chan's "Dumplings" – New "Diary of a Madman" in Post-Mao Global Capitalism' (2010) 10 China Review 177

Luk BH, 'Abortion in Chinese Law' (1977) 25 The American Journal of Comparative Law 372

Luo Hao and others, 'Repeat Induced Abortion in 30 Chinese Provinces: A Cross-Sectional Study' (2021) 154 International Journal of Gynaecology and Obstetrics: The Official Organ of the International Federation of Gynaecology and Obstetrics 532

Luo Jiajun and Kellogg T, 'Verdicts from China's Courts Used to Be Accessible Online. Now They're Disappearing.' (*ChinaFile*, 1 February 2022) <https://www.chinafile.com/reporting-opinion/viewpoint/verdicts-chinas-courts-used-be-accessible-online-now-theyre-disappearing> accessed 24 June 2025

Luo Yingyi, 'Unraveling Informality and Precarity: New Labor Law Strategies for the Global Reproduction Network of Cross-Border Surrogacy' (2023) 16 Asian Bioethics Review 185

'M. Tullius Cicero, De Fato, Section 1' <http://www.perseus.tufts.edu/hopper/text?doc=Cic.%20Fat.%201.1&lang=original> accessed 8 August 2022

Ma Juan 马娟, 'Guowuyuan Guanyu Yinfa Zhongguo Funǚ Fazhan Gangyao He Zhongguo Ertong Fazhan Ganya de Tongzhi (2011 – 2020) 国务院关于印发中国妇女发展纲要和中国儿童发展纲要的通知 中国妇女发展纲要 (2011–2020年) (Notice on the State Council Programme for the Development of Chinese Women and Children 2011-2020)' (2011) 23 Guowuyuan Gongbao 国务院公报 (State Council Gazette) <https://www.gov.cn/gongbao/content/2011/content_1927200.htm> accessed 6 October 2024

Ma Juan 马娟 'Guowuyuan Guanyu Yinfa Zhongguo Funǚ Fazhan Gangyao He Zhongguo Ertong Fazhan Ganya de Tongzhi (2021-2030) 国务院关于印发中国妇女发展纲要和中国儿童发展纲要的通知 中国妇女发展纲要 (2021–2030 年) (Notice on the State Council Programme for the Development of Chinese Women and Children 2011–2020)' (2021) 16 Guowuyuan Gongbao 国务院公报 (State Council Gazette) <https://www.gov.cn/zhengce/content/2021-09/27/content_5639412.htm> accessed 6 October 2024

Ma Yinchu 马寅初, 'Zai di yi ju quanguo renmin daibiao dahui di si ci huiyishang de fayan "Xin koulun" Ma Yinchu de shumian fayan 在第一届全国人民代表大会第四次会议上的发言 新人口论 马寅初的书面发言 (Speech at the Fourth Session of the First National People's Congress: 'New Population Theory Written statement by Ma Yinchu' *Renmin Ribao* 人民日报 (Beijing 北京市, 5 July 1957Cn) <http://politics.people.com.cn/ywkx/n/2015/0728/c363762-27371444.html> accessed 25 July 2024

MacIntyre A, *A Short History of Ethics: A History of Moral Philosophy from the Homeric Age to the 20th Century* (1° edizione, Routledge 2002)

MacIntyre A, *After Virtue: A Study in Moral Theory, Third Edition* (3° edizione, New Publisher 2021)

Macpherson C, 'Global Bioethics: It's Past and Future' (2022) 33 Global Bioethics 45

Maddox N, 'Children of the Dead: Posthumous Conception, Critical Interests and Consent' (2020) 27 Journal of Law and Medicine 645

Manning RC, *Speaking from the Heart: A Feminist Perspective on Ethics* (Rowman & Littlefield Pub Inc 1992)

Manning RC, *'A Care Approach'*, A Companion to Bioethics (John Wiley & Sons, Ltd 2009) <http://onlinelibrary.wiley.com/doi/abs/10.1002/9781444307818.ch11> accessed 25 August 2022

Mao Xin, 'Chinese Eugenic Legislation' (1997) 349 The Lancet 139

Margalit A, *The Ethics of Memory* (Harvard Univ Pr 2004)

Marinelli S and others, 'The Newly Enacted Italian Surrogacy Law: Effects on Reproductive Tourism' [2025] Journal of Assisted Reproduction and Genetics 1

Marx K, '(Trade or Opium?)' *New York Daily Tribune* (New York, 20 September 1858) <https://moodle2.units.it/pluginfile.php/101065/mod_resource/content/2/Marx_Writings_on_China_NYDT_1853-60.pdf>

Matignon JJ, *Superstition, crime et misere en Chine* (*Souvenirs de biologie sociale*) (Lyon : A Storck et cie; Paris, Masson et cie 1899) <http://archive.org/details/superstitioncrimoomati> accessed 19 July 2024

McKnite BE and Twitchett DC, 'China | Events, People, Dates, Flag, Map, & Facts | Britannica', *Encyclopedia Britannica*, (2025) <https://www.britannica.com/place/China> accessed 5 August 2025

McNeill PM, *The Ethics and Politics of Human Experimentation* (CUP Archive 1993)

Menski WF, *Comparative Law in a Global Context: The Legal Systems of Asia and Africa* (2nd edn, Cambridge University Press 2006) <https://www.cambridge.org/core/books/comparative-law-in-a-global-context/4705C7C2B21A97742DA59ED690FD9534> accessed 2 August 2022

Mill JS, *Utilitarianism* (CDED 2018)

Mingyue lüshi 明月律师, 'Qiang Haizi, Cang Haizi; Eyi Weifa Jing de Yi 抢孩子、藏孩子: 恶意违法竟得益 (Snatching and Hiding Children; Malicious Illegal Activities Actually Benefited)' (12 December 2020) <http://www.51-lihun.com/h-nd-4063.html>

Monitor SPC, 'More on the Supreme People's Court and Typical Cases' (*Supreme People's Court Monitor*, 2 May 2014) <https://supremepeoplescourtmonitor.com/2014/05/02/more-on-the-supreme-peoples-court-and-typical-cases/> accessed 27 June 2025

Moreno JD, *Undue Risk: Secret State Experiments on Humans* (Routledge 2013)

Moskowitz ML, *The Haunting Fetus: Abortion, Sexuality, and the Spirit World in Taiwan* (University of Hawaii Press, 2001)

Naftali O, ‘Rights of Children and Youth in China: Protection, Provision, and Participation’, *Handbook on Human Rights in China* (Edward Elgar Publishing 2019)

Nagel T, ‘Personal Rights and Public Space’ (1995) 24 Philosophy <html_ent glyph=“@amp;” ascii=“&”/> Public Affairs 83

Narayan G and others, ‘The Surrogacy Regulation Act of 2021: A Right Step Towards an Egalitarian and Inclusive Society?’ 15 Cureus e37864

‘Nature Index 2025 Research Leaders: United States Losing Ground as China’s Lead Expands Rapidly’ (*Nature Index*, 11 June 2025) <https://www.nature.com/nature-index/news/nature-index-research-leaders-united-states-losing-ground-china-lead-expands-rapidly> accessed 4 August 2025

Ng RM-C, ‘College and Character: What Did Confucius Teach Us About The Importance of Integrating Ethics, Character, Learning, and Education?’ (2009) 10 Journal of College and Character 8

Ni Liangduan 倪良端, ‘Jihua shengyun yu Shao Lizi 计划生育与邵力子(Family Planning and Shao Lizi)’ (*Zhongguo gongchangdang xinwen wan* 中国共产党新闻网, 25 February 2013) <http://dangshi.people.com.cn/n/2013/0225/c85037-20590077.html> accessed 19 June 2024

Ni Peimin, ‘Confucian Virtues and Personal Health’ in Fan R (ed), *Confucian Bioethics* (Springer Netherlands 2002) <https://doi.org/10.1007/0-306-46867-0_2> accessed 19 May 2023

‘Nicomachean Ethics: Text – IntraText CT’ <http://www.intratext.com/IXT/ENG2244/_P1V.HTM> accessed 24 August 2022

Nie Jing-Bao, ‘The Problem of Coerced Abortion in China and Related Ethical Issues’ (1999) 8 Cambridge Quarterly of Healthcare Ethics 463

Nie Jing-Bao, ‘Non-Medical Sex-Selective Abortion in China: Ethical and Public Policy Issues in the Context of 40 Million Missing Females’ (2011) 98 British Medical Bulletin 7

Nie Jing-Bao, ‘The Plurality of Chinese and American Medical Moralities: Toward an Interpretive Cross-Cultural Bioethics’ (2000) 10 Kennedy Institute of Ethics Journal 239

Nie Jing-Bao, *Behind the Silence: Chinese Voices on Abortion* (Rowman & Littlefield Pub Inc 2005)

–, *Medical Ethics in China: A Transcultural Interpretation* <https://www.routledge.com/Medical-Ethics-in-China-A-Transcultural-Interpretation/Nie/p/book/9780415724562> accessed 9 February 2022

Ning Nuohua 宁诺花, ‘Daiyun Zinü Jianhuren de Queding He Biaozhun 代孕子女监护人的确定原则和标准 (Principles and Standards for Determining the Guardian of a

Child Born Through Surrogacy)' (2025) 174 Heilongjiang sheng zhengfa guali ganbu xueyuan xuebao黑龙江省政法管理干部学院学报 57

Noddings N, *Caring: A Feminine Approach to Ethics and Moral Education* (2° edizione, Univ of California Pr 2003)

Normile D, 'Chinese Scientist Who Produced Genetically Altered Babies Sentenced to 3 Years in Jail' (*Science*) <https://www.science.org/content/article/chinese-scientist-who-produced-genetically-altered-babies-sentenced-3-years-jail> accessed 24 July 2025

'Nuremberg Code' (*United States Holocaust Memorial Museum*) <https://www.ushmm.org/information/exhibitions/online-exhibitions/special-focus/doctors-trial/nuremberg-code#Permissible> accessed 22 August 2022

Nussbaum MC, 'Danger to Human Dignity: The Revival of Disgust and Shame in the Law' (*The Chronicle of Higher Education*, 6 August 2004) <https://www.chronicle.com/article/danger-to-human-dignity-the-revival-of-disgust-and-shame-in-the-law/> accessed 10 May 2025

Oakley J, 'A Virtue Ethics Approach', *A Companion to Bioethics: Second Edition* (2010)

Oakley/Cocking, *Virtue Ethics and Professional Roles* (1° edizione, Cambridge University Press 2008)

Pang SM, 'Protective Truthfulness: The Chinese Way of Safeguarding Patients in Informed Treatment Decisions' (1999) 25 Journal of Medical Ethics 247

Pang SM, *Nursing Ethics in Modern China: Conflicting Values and Competing Role Requirements* (Brill 2021) <https://brill.com/view/title/31161> accessed 8 March 2022

Pang-White AA, 'Reconstructing Modern Ethics: Confucian Care Ethics' (2009) 36 Journal of Chinese Philosophy 210

Paul NW and others, 'Human Rights Violations in Organ Procurement Practice in China' (2017) 18 BMC Medical Ethics 11

Peng Peiyun 彭珮云, *Zhongguo jihua shengyu quanshu* 中国计划生育全书 (*China Family Planning Compendium*) (Zhongguo renkou chubanshe 中国人口出版社 1997)

Poli L, 'La Grande Camera e l'ultima parola sul caso Paradiso e Campanelli' (*SIDIBlog*, 21 February 2017) <http://www.sidiblog.org/2017/02/21/la-grande-camera-e-lultima-parola-sul-caso-paradiso-e-campanelli/> accessed 13 July 2025

Post SG, *Encyclopedia of Bioethics*, vol 1 (Macmillan Reference USA 2004)

'Posthumous Reproduction Practice Is Regulated' (*WHO Data*) <https://platform.who.int/data/sexual-and-reproductive-health-and-rights/national-policies/srh/practices-that-are-regulated-posthumous-reproduction> accessed 5 June 2025

Potter VR, 'Bioethics, the Science of Survival' (1970) 14 Perspectives in Biology and Medicine 127

Qi Xiangguan 齐湘泉 and An Shuo 安朔, 'Kua Jing Daiyun Falü Guizhi Yanjiu – Jianyi Kuajing Daiyun Chansheng de Qinzi Guanxi Rending 跨境代孕法律规制研究 — 兼议跨境代孕产生的亲子关系认定 (Research on the Legal Regulation of Cross-Border Surrogacy – and on the Determination of Parent-Child Relationship Caused by Cross-Border Surrogacy)' (2021) 安朔 Zhongguo Qingnian shehui kexue 中国青年社会科学 109

Qin Qian and Zhang Jiali, 'Sex Education in China: Actors and Dynamics of China's Policies and Practices' (2023) 10 Cogent Education 2270289

Qin Yu and Fei Wang, 'Too Early or Too Late: What Have We Learned from the 30-Year Two-Child Policy Experiment in Yicheng, China?' (2017) 37 Demographic Research 929

Qingshaonian shengzhi jiankang bu 'liu' shi '青少年生殖健康不"流"失' (Adolescent reproductive health is not 'lost') <https://wsjkw.zjtz.gov.cn/art/2022/2/21/art_1229568733_58941170.html> accessed 28 August 2024

Qiu Qianyi and Meng Fanzhuang, 'Challenges and Future Prospects of Surrogacy Legislation in China' (2024) 12 Peking University Law Journal 47

Qiu Renzong, 'Medical Ethics in China', *Chinese Scientists and Responsibility. Ethical Issues of Human Genetics in Chinese and International Context* (Institut für Asienkunde 1999)

Qiu Renzong 邱仁宗, *Shengsi zhi jian – daode nanti yu shengming lunli* 生死之间 — — — 道德难题与生命伦理 [*Between Life and Death – Moral Difficulties and Bioethics*] (Zhonghua shuju 中华书局 1988)

Qiu Renzong 邱仁宗, *Shengming lunli xue* 生命伦理学 [*Bioethics*] (1st edition, Zhongguo renmin daxue chubanshe 中国人民大学出版社 2020)

Qiu Renzong 邱仁宗, *Shengming lunli xue* 生命伦理学(增订版)(精)/当代中国人文大系 [*Bioethics*] (中国人民大学出版社 2020)

'Quintilian, Institutio Oratoria, Book 6, Chapter 2, Section 8' <http://www.perseus.tufts.edu/hopper/text?doc=Quint.%20Inst.%206.2.8&lang=original> accessed 8 August 2022

'Quintilian, Institutio Oratoria, Book 12, Chapter 2, Section 10' <http://www.perseus.tufts.edu/hopper/text?doc=Quint.%20Inst.%2012.2.10&lang=original> accessed 8 August 2022

Raj P, 'Regulating Surrogacy in India: Legal Frameworks, Ethical Considerations and Lessons from Global Practices' (2024) 4 Nyaayshastra Law Review <https://papers.ssrn.com/abstract=5017308> accessed 28 June 2025

Raphals L, 'Embodied Virtue, Self-Cultivation, and Ethics' in Fraser C, Robins D, and O'Leary T (eds), *Ethics in Early China: An Anthology* (Hong Kong University Press 2011) <https://doi.org/10.5790/hongkong/9789888028931.003.0008> accessed 22 May 2023

Raposo V and Wai US, 'Surrogacy in Greater China: The Legal Framework in Taiwan, Hong Kong, Macao, and Mainland China' (2017) 34 UCLA Pacific Basin Law Journal <https://escholarship.org/uc/item/41d104d5> accessed 1 February 2025

Ravitsky V and Bokek-Cohen Y, '"Life after Death": The Israeli Approach to Posthumous Reproduction' in Filc D and others (eds), *Bioethics and Biopolitics in Israel: Socio-legal, Political, and Empirical Analysis* (Cambridge University Press 2018) <https://www.cambridge.org/core/books/bioethics-and-biopolitics-in-israel/life-after-death-the-israeli-approach-to-posthumous-reproduction/1D27B44F4BCFBAF95A46E10AC6999CD2> accessed 28 June 2025

Rawls J, *A Theory of Justice*: *Revised Edition* (Revised edizione, Belknap Pr 1999)

Ren Ruping 任汝平, '"Daiyun" de Falü" Lunjing Ji Qi Pojue 代孕" 的法律困境及其破解 (The Legal Dilemma of "surrogacy" and Its Solution)' [2009] Fujian luntan (renwen shehui kexue ban) 福建 论坛(人文社会科学版) 161

Ren Zeping 任泽平, 'Zhongguo Fuzhu Shengzhi Yanjiu Baogao 中国辅助生殖研究报告2023 (China Assisted Reproductive Technology Research Report 2023)' (28 February 2023) <https://finance.sina.com.cn/cj/2023-02-28/doc-imyieiem8146136.shtml> accessed 2 May 2025

'Renmin Fayuan Guanche Shishi Min Fa Dian Dianxing Anli (Di Er Pi) 人民法院贯彻实施民法典典型案例 (第二批)(Typical Cases of the People's Courts Implementing the Civil Code (Second Batch))' (1 September 2023) <http://jningyzfy.sdcourt.gov.cn/jningyzfy/547173/386111/386155/12579963/index.html>

Reverby SM, *Examining Tuskegee: The Infamous Syphilis Study and Its Legacy* (Univ of North Carolina Press 2009)

Rigdon SM, 'Abortion Law and Practice in China: An Overview with Comparisons to the United States' (1996) 42 Social Science & Medicine 543

Rocha da Cunha T and Lorenzo C, 'Global bioethics from the perspective of critical bioethics' (2014) 22(1) *Revista Bioética* 116

Rocha LA, 'Translation and Two "Chinese Sexologies" Double Plum and Sex Histories' in Bauer H (ed), *Sexology and Translation: Cultural and Scientific Encounters across the Modern World* (Temple University Press 2015)

Rodriguez SM, *Reproductive Realities in Modern China: Birth Control and Abortion, 1911–2021* (New edition, Cambridge University Press 2023)

Rosemont H, 'Against Relativism' in Deutsch E and Larson GJ (eds), *Interpreting Across Boundaries: New Essays in Comparative Philosophy* (Princeton University Press 1988)

Rosemont H, 'Rights-Bearing Individuals and Role-Bearing Persons', *Confucian Role Ethics: A Moral Vision for the 21st Century?* (V&R unipress)

Rosemont H and Ames R, 'On Translation & Interpretation (With Special Reference to Classical Chinese)', *Confucian Role Ethics* (V&R unipress GmbH 2016)

Rosemont H and Ames RT, 'Introduction' in Henry JR and Roger TA (eds), *The Chinese Classic of Family Reverence: A Philosophical Translation of the Xiaojing* (University of Hawai'i Press 2008) <https://doi.org/10.21313/hawaii/9780824832841.003.0019> accessed 17 May 2023

Rothman CM, 'A Method for Obtaining Viable Sperm in the Postmortem State' (1980) 34 Fertility and Sterility 512

Roy O, *Leibniz et la Chine* (Librairie Philosophique J Vrin 1972)

Ruddick S, *Maternal Thinking: Toward a Politics of Peace* (Reprint edizione, Beacon Press 1995)

Ruskola T, 'Law, Sexual Morality, and Gender Equality in Qing and Communist China' (1994) 103 The Yale Law Journal 2531

Ruskola T, 'Law Without Law, or Is "Chinese Law" an Oxymoron?' [2003] SSRN Electronic Journal <http://www.ssrn.com/abstract=412380> accessed 1 July 2022

Ruskola T, *Legal Orientalism. China, the United States, and Modern Law* (Harvard University Press 2013)

Ruskola T, 'Legal Orientalism' 101 Michigan Law Review 57

Rute Teixeira P, 'Portugal' in Fenton-Glynn C, Scherpe JM, and Kaan T (eds), *Eastern and Western Perspectives on Surrogacy* (Intersentia 2019) <https://www.cambridge.org/core/books/eastern-and-western-perspectives-on-surrogacy/portugal/F4FA10B4799375F597239870C5373137> accessed 1 February 2025

Sacco R, 'Legal Formants: A Dynamic Approach to Comparative Law (Installment I of II)' (1991) 39 The American Journal of Comparative Law 1

Sacco R, 'Il Contratto in Prospettiva Comparatistica' [2001] Europa e diritto privato 479

Sacco R, *Antropologia giuridica* (Il Mulino 2007)

Sacco R, *Anthropologie juridique: Apport à une macro-histoire du droit* (Editions Dalloz 2008)

Said EW, *Orientalism* (Pantheon Books 1978)

Said EW, 'Orientalism Reconsidered' [1985] Cultural Critique 89

Said EW, 'Orientalism: An Afterword' (1995) 3 Raritan 32

Samama E, 'Within Me, But Not Mine: Surrogacy in Israel' in Rainhorn J-D and Boudamoussi SE (eds), *New Cannibal Markets : Globalization and Commodification of the Human Body* (Éditions de la Maison des sciences de l'homme 2015) <https://books.openedition.org/editionsmsh/10755> accessed 28 June 2025

Savage M, 'The Law of Abortion in the Union of Soviet Socialist Republics and the People's Republic of China: Women's Rights in Two Socialist Countries' (1988) 40 Stanford Law Review 1027

Scharping T, *Birth Control in China 1949-2000: Population Policy and Demographic Development* (Routledge 2013)

Scherpe JM and Fenton-Glynn C, 'Introduction', *Eastern and Western Perspectives on Surrogacy* (Intersentia 2019) <https://www.cambridge.org/core/books/eastern-and-western-perspectives-on-surrogacy/introduction/4DD3D0AACB5896A81EE50CD3DBBE2780> accessed 20 July 2025

Scherpe JM, Fenton-Glynn C and Kaan T (eds), *Eastern and Western Perspectives on Surrogacy* (Intersentia 2019) <https://www.cambridge.org/core/books/eastern-and-western-perspectives-on-surrogacy/2E5076101F2AAD8C4F85DA40EB802E41> accessed 13 July 2025

Schmidt CW, 'The Yuck Factor When Disgust Meets Discovery' (2008) 116 Environmental Health Perspectives A524

Schopenhauer A, *The World As Will And Idea: 3 vols in 1* (CreateSpace Independent Publishing Platform 2016)

'Seneca, Ad Lucilium Epistulae Morales, Seneca Lucilio Suo Salutem, Section 9' <http://www.perseus.tufts.edu/hopper/text?doc=Sen.%20Ep.%2089.9&lang=original> accessed 8 August 2022

Shalev C, *Birth Power: The Case for Surrogacy* (Revised ed edition, Yale University Press, New Haven & London 2009)

Shangwu yin shuguan bianyi suo bian 商務印書館編譯所編 (ed), *Da Qing Guangxu Xin faling* 大清光緒新法令 (*New Decrees of the Qing Emperor Guangxu*) (Shanghai Shangwu yin shuguan 上海商務印書館 1909)

Shanxi sheng difangzhi bangongshi 陕西省地方志办公室 (Local records office of the Shaanxi Province, 'Renkou He Jihua Shengyu Shi – Disi Pian Renkou He Jihua Shengyu Gongzuo Diyicheng Gonzuo Lishi Di Yijie Yunniang Chuzhi Shijian 人口和计划生育志 — 第四篇 人口和计划生育工作 第一章 工作历程 第一节 酝酿初始时期 (1950~1970) Population and Family Planning, Title IV Population and Family Planning Work Chapter I. History of Work Section I. The Initial Period of Conception (1950-1970)' (22 September 2017) <http://dfz.shaanxi.gov.cn/sqzlk/xbsxsz/szdel/rkhjhsyz/201709/t20170922_934742.html> accessed 29 July 2024

Shelley M and Gordon C, *Frankenstein: The 1818 Text* (1st edition, Penguin Classics 2018)

Shen V, 'The Ethics of Generosity in Chinese Mahayana Buddhism: Theory and Practice' in Wang Y and Wawrytko SA (eds), *Dao Companion to Chinese Buddhist Philosophy* (Springer Netherlands 2018) <https://doi.org/10.1007/978-90-481-2939-3_3> accessed 4 June 2023

Shi Luyan 石璐言, 'Xi Jingpiing; Guanyu "Zhonggong Zhongyang Guanyu Zhiding Guomin Jingji He Shehui Fazhan Di Shisi Ge Wu Nian Guihua He Er Ling Sanwu Nian Yuanjing Mubiao Di Jianyi" de Shouming 习近平: 关于《中共中央关于制定国民经济和社会发展第十四个五年规划和二〇三五年远景目标的建议》的说明 (Xi Jinping: Explanation on the CPC Central Committee's Proposal on Formulating the 14th Five-Year Plan for National Economic and Social Development and the

Long-Term Goals for 2035)' *Xin hua shi* 新华社 (3 November 2020) <https://www.gov.cn/xinwen/2020-11/03/content_5556997.htm> accessed 27 June 2025

Shi Jiayou 石佳友 and Ceng Jia 曾 佳, 'Shou Renlei Fuzhu Shengzhi Shengyu Zinü de Quanyi Baohu 死后人类辅助生殖生育子女的权益保护 (The Protection of the Rights and Interests of Children Born through Human Assisted Reproduction after Death)' [2023] Falü shiyong 法律适用 35

Shi Lei, 'China' in Fenton-Glynn C, Scherpe JM, and Kaan T (eds), *Eastern and Western Perspectives on Surrogacy* (Intersentia 2019) <https://www.cambridge.org/core/books/eastern-and-western-perspectives-on-surrogacy/china/5FD0E8EFB707B7
E60C2CF2C57E347CFD> accessed 25 July 2025

Shi Lei 石雷 and Zhan Luxia 占 泸霞, '"Gongneng Jiegou" She Yu Xia Woguo Daiyun Zhidu de Goujian '功能结构' 视 域下我国代孕制度的构建 (The Construction of a Chinese System of Surrogacy from the Perspective of Structural Functionalism)' (2019) 79 Haixia Faxue 海峡法学 74

Si Jingjing 司静静, and Si Yangyu 司衍鲁, 'Si Hou Rengong Shengzhi Hefa Hua de Lifa Qishi 死后人工生殖合法化的立法启示 (Legislative Enlightenment about the Legalisation of Artificial Insemination After Death)' (2018) 26 Chengdu Ligond Daxue xuebao (Shehui kexue ban) 成都理工大学学报(社会科学版) 54

Sidgwick H, *Methods of Ethics* (7° edizione, Hackett Pub Co Inc 1981)

Sim M, *Remastering Morals with Aristotle and Confucius* (Cambridge University Press 2007) <https://www.cambridge.org/core/books/remastering-morals-with-aristotle-and-confucius/E6E818D81A1815878D3D3DC88DCD676B> accessed 6 January 2022

Simana S, 'Creating Life after Death: Should Posthumous Reproduction Be Legally Permissible without the Deceased's Prior Consent?' (2018) 5 Journal of Law and the Biosciences 329

Sina_mobile, 'Guangzhou Fushang Sheng 8 Baotai I 广州富商生 8 胞胎? (Guangzhou Businessman Gave Birth to Eight Babies?)' (*Zhongguo Jingji shibao* 中国果经济时报, 20 December 2011) <https://finance.sina.cn/sa/2011-12-20/detail-ikftpnnx8552037.d.html> accessed 12 July 2025

'Single or Late Marriage – Tales of China's Younger Generations – Chinadaily.Com.Cn' <https://www.chinadaily.com.cn/a/201806/29/WS5b359b8ea3103349141dfb10.html> accessed 1 February 2025

Slote M, *Morals from Motives* (Oxford University Press 2003)

Sommer MH, *Sex, Law and Society in Late Imperial China* (Stanford University Press, 2000)

Song Jian 宋建 and others, 'Quan Liantia Fangfan He Dai Daiyun Gongzuo Jizhi Yanjiu 全链条防范和打击代孕工作机制研究 (Reserch on the Working Mechanism of Preventing and Attacking Surrogacy)' (2024) 32 Weisheng Faxue 卫生法学 100

Spar DL, 'For Love and Money: The Political Economy of Commercial Surrogacy on JSTOR' (2005) 12 Review of International Political Economy, 287

Spivack C, 'The Law of Surrogate Motherhood in the United States' (2010) 58 The American Journal of Comparative Law 97

Stephanie, 'Taiwan To Legalize Surrogacy' (17 November 2023) <https://surrogacy-lawyer.com/zh/taiwan-to-legalize-surrogacy/> accessed 3 August 2025

Stephens TB, *Order and Discipline in China* (University of Washington Press 1992) <https://uwapress.uw.edu/book/9780295971230/order-and-discipline-in-china> accessed 25 July 2022

Strathern M, 'Introduction. A Question of Context', *Technologies of Procreation: Kinship in the Age of Assisted Conception* (Manchester University Press, 1993)

Sturgeon D, 'Dao De Jing – Chinese Text Project' <https://ctext.org/dao-de-jing> accessed 31 May 2023

Sturgeon D, 'Mozi : Book 4 – Chinese Text Project' <https://ctext.org/mozi/book-4> accessed 27 June 2023

Sturgeon D, 'Mozi : Book 6 – Chinese Text Project' <https://ctext.org/mozi/book-6> accessed 26 June 2023

Sturgeon D, 'Mozi : Book 9 : Anti-Fatalism I – Chinese Text Project' <https://ctext.org/mozi/anti-fatalism-i> accessed 26 June 2023

Su Qi 苏琦, Zhang Jing 张静, and Wang Ping 王萍, 'Sihou Rengong Shengzhi Suo Yu Zinü Liyi de Falü Baohu – Yi Guonei Shouli Fuqing Gongwang Hou Shiguan Ying'er Suopei Fuyang Fei an Wei Shijiao 死后人工生殖所育子女利益的法律保护——以国内首例父亲工亡后试管婴儿索赔抚养费案为视角 (Legal Protection of the Interests of Children Conceived through Posthumous Assisted Reproduction after the Death of the Parent – – from the Perspective of the First Case of Test Tube Baby's Claim for Alimony after the Father's Death at Work in China)' (2024) 38 Weisheng ruan kexue卫生软科学 32

Sui Suli 睢素利, Li Jingru 李京儒 and Liu Hang 刘欢, 'Guanyu daiyun wenti de falü he linlun bianxi 关于代孕问题的法律和伦理辨析 (Legal and theoretical analysis on the problem of surrogacy)' (2017) 25 Zhongguo ji hua shengyu xue zazhi 中国计划生育学杂志 804

Sun Jitao, 'Between Emotion and Reason: The Judicial Practice of Disputes Involving Frozen Embryos in China' (2024) 12 Peking University Law Journal 83

Sun Jitao, 'The Social and Legal Implications of Elective Egg Freezing in China' (2024) 12 Peking University Law Journal 61

Sun Zhongshan 孙中山, 'Sun Zhongshan Xuanji 孙中山选集 [Selected Works of Sun Zhongshan]' (百度百科) <https://baike.baidu.com/item/%E5%AD%99%E4%B8%AD%E5%B1%B1%E9%80%89%E9%9B%86/2051325> accessed 19 January 2022

'Surat Al-Mu'minun [23:12-14] – The Noble Qur'an – القرآن الكريم' <https://legacy.quran.com/23/12-14> accessed 11 August 2023

'Surrogacy In Thailand: A Comprehensive Analysis' (*Thai Law Online*, 4 April 2025) <https://thailawonline.com/surrogacy-in-thailand-comprehensive-analysis/> accessed 20 July 2025

'Surrogacy Law in India – New Era for Surrogacy in India (2025)' (*Dr. Rita Bakshi*) <https://drritabakshi.in/the-surrogacy-regulation-act-2021-a-new-era-for-surrogacy-in-india/> accessed 20 July 2025

Tai MC-T, 'Natural and Unnatural – A Taoist Perspective' (2004) 2 Etica & Politica/ Ethics & Politic <https://www2.units.it/etica/2004_2/CHENG-TEK_TAI.htm> accessed 22 May 2023

Tai MC-T, 'Natural or Unnatural – An Application of the Taoist Thought to Bioethics' (2009) 21 Tzu Chi Medical Journal 270

Tai Yuru 戴瑀如, 'Sihou Rengong Shengzhi Shi Jingzhi Yu Kaifang – Yi Deguo Ji Taiwan de Caipan Wei Zhongxin 死後人工生殖之禁制與開放—以德國及台灣的裁判為中心 (The Prohibition and Liberalisation of Post-Death Reproduction: A Study Focusing on Court Rulings in Germany and Taiwan)' [2015] Huadong Zhengfa Daxue xuebao 华东政法大学学报 26

Tan C, 'Confucianism and Education', *Oxford Research Encyclopedia of Education* (2017) <https://oxfordre.com/education/display/10.1093/acrefore/9780190264093.001.0001/acrefore-9780190264093-e-226> accessed 1 February 2025

Tang Siew Tzuh and others, 'Patient Awareness of Prognosis, Patient-Family Caregiver Congruence on the Preferred Place of Death, and Caregiving Burden of Families Contribute to the Quality of Life for Terminally Ill Cancer Patients in Taiwan' (2008) 17 Psycho-Oncology 1202

Tang Siew Tzuh and Lee Shiu-Yu C 'Cancer Diagnosis and Prognosis in Taiwan: Patient Preferences versus Experiences' (2004) 13 Psycho-Oncology 1

Teiser SF, 'Introduction: The Spirits of Chinese Religion', *Introduction: The Spirits of Chinese Religion* (Princeton University Press 2018) <https://www.degruyter.com/document/doi/10.1515/9780691188140-022/html> accessed 7 June 2023

ten Have HAMJ, 'Potter's Notion of Bioethics' (2012) 22 Kennedy Institute of Ethics Journal 59

Terrats N, 'Surrogacy and Feminist Movements' (*IDEES*, 29 January 2020) <https://revistaidees.cat/en/gestacio-subrogada-i-feminismes/> accessed 20 July 2025

Terrizzi JA, Shook NJ, and Ventis WL, 'Disgust: A Predictor of Social Conservatism and Prejudicial Attitudes toward Homosexuals' (2010) 49 Personality and Individual Differences 587

The State Council Information Office of the People's Republic of China, 'Family Binds Nation, Its People, President Xi Says | English.Scio.Gov.Cn' (22 February 2018) <http://english.scio.gov.cn/m/topnews/2018-02/22/content_50580337.htm> accessed 1 February 2025

The State Council Information Office of the People's Republic of China, 'Full Text: The Report on Human Rights Violations in the United States in 2022' (2023) <http://ge.china-embassy.gov.cn/eng/xwdt/202303/t20230328_11050361.htm> accessed 16 September 2024

'Thousands at Risk of Forced Sterilization in China' (*Amnesty International*, 22 April 2010) <https://www.amnesty.org/en/latest/news/2010/04/thousands-risk-forced-sterilization-china/> accessed 1 November 2024

Times G, 'China's Family Planning Roadmap Aimed at Protecting National Fertility, Not Banning Abortion: Experts – Global Times' <https://www.globaltimes.cn/page/202202/1252012.shtml> accessed 31 August 2024

Times V, 'Illegal Surrogacy Punishable by up to 19 Years in Jail, Lao Government Warns as Cases Reported' <https://asianews.network/illegal-surrogacy-punishable-by-up-to-19-years-in-jail-lao-government-warns-as-cases-reported/> accessed 21 July 2025

'Torture, Forced Abortions: Key Allegations in UN Report on Xinjiang' (*France 24*, 1 September 2022) <https://www.france24.com/en/asia-pacific/20220901-torture-forced-abortions-key-allegations-in-un-report-on-xinjiang> accessed 2 November 2024

Trawick E and others, 'Posthumous Assisted Reproduction Policies among a Cohort of United States' in Vitro Fertilization Clinics' (2020) 1 F&S Reports 66

Treaty Office, 'Details of Treaty No.164' (*Treaty Office*, 4 April 1997) <https://www.coe.int/en/web/conventions/full-list> accessed 30 April 2025

Tsai Yun-Chu, 'You Are Whom You Eat: Cannibalism in Contemporary Chinese Fiction and Film' (University of California 2016) <https://escholarship.org/uc/item/7nk4v18m>

Ueda Noriyuki and others, 'Study of Views on Posthumous Reproduction, Focusing on Its Relation with Views on Family and Religion in Modern Japan' (2008) 62 Acta Medica Okayama 285

'Uighurs Tell of Forced Abortions and Torture in China' (*The Independent*, 3 June 2021) <https://www.independent.co.uk/asia/east-asia/china-uighur-muslim-abortion-torture-b1859027.html> accessed 12 October 2023

'UK Surrogacy Law: History and Reform' (*NGA Law*) <https://www.ngalaw.co.uk/knowledge-centre/uk-surrogacy-law-history-reform/> accessed 27 July 2025

UNESCO, 'Universal Declaration on Bioethics and Human Rights |' <https://www.unesco.org/en/ethics-science-technology/bioethics-and-human-rights> accessed 30 April 2025

Unschuld PU, *Medical Ethics in Imperial China. A Study in Historical Anthropology* (University of California Press 1979)

van der Burg W, 'Law and Bioethics', *A Companion to Bioethics* (John Wiley & Sons, Ltd 2009) <https://onlinelibrary.wiley.com/doi/abs/10.1002/9781444307818.ch6> accessed 2 May 2022 van der Burg W, 'Law and Ethics: The Twin Disciplines' (14 July 2010) <https://papers.ssrn.com/abstract=1631720> accessed 15 August 2022

Veatch RM, *The Basics of Bioethics* (3rd edn, Routledge 2016)

Vertommen S, 'Surrogacy at the Fertility Frontier: Rethinking Surrogacy in Israel/Palestine as an (Anti)Colonial Episteme' (2024) 14 History of the Present 108

Visapra P, 'Lao Government Warns Against Surrogacy Amid Rise in Illegal Cases' (*Laotian Times*, 30 May 2025) <https://laotiantimes.com/2025/05/30/lao-government-warns-against-surrogacy-amid-rise-in-illegal-cases/> accessed 21 July 2025

Wahlberg A, 'The Birth and Routinization of IVF in China' (2016) 2 Reproductive Biomedicine & Society Online 97

Wanyi 网易, 'Guonei Shou Li! Fuqin Gong Wang Hou, Shiguan Ying'er Suoperi Fuyan Fei, Yishen Xuanpan 国内首例！父亲工亡后，试管婴儿索赔抚养费,一审宣判→(A First in China! After His Father Died in a Work Accident, a Child Conceived through IVF Sued for Child Support, and the First Instance Verdict Was Handed Down)' (19 April 2023) <https://www.163.com/dy/article/I2ML3IJT0514R9KQ.html> accessed 27 June 2025

Wang DD-W, *The Monster That Is History: History, Violence, and Fictional Writing in Twentieth-Century China* (2004)

Wang Guisong 王贵松, 'Zhongguo Daiyun Guizhi de Moshi Xuanze 中国代孕规制的模式选择 (Choice of Models for the Regulation of Surrogacy in China)' [2009] Fazhi yu shehui fazhan 法制与社会发展 118

Wang Hongchun and others, 'To Tell or Not: The Chinese Doctors' Dilemma on Disclosure of a Cancer Diagnosis to the Patient' (2018) 47 Iranian Journal of Public Health 1773

Wang Hongling 王鸿麟, 'Wo guo shou li anlesi anjian pagjue – Hanzhongshi fayuan xuangao liang beigao wu zui 我国首例安乐死案件判决——汉中市法院宣告两被告无罪 [Verdict in China's first euthanasia case – Hanzhong City Court acquits two defendants]' [1991] Zhongguo yinxue lunli 中国医学伦理学 27

Wang J, Griffiths N, and Fang S, 'China's Lack of Sex-Ed Putting Young People at Risk' (*CNN*, 30 November 2016) <https://www.cnn.com/2016/11/30/health/china-sex-education-world-aids-day/index.html> accessed 13 August 2024

Wang Linwei 王林卫, 'Lun Woguo Shengyu Quan Gongfa Tiaojie de Fanwei He Bianjie 论我国生育权公法调节的范围和边界 (On the Scope and Boundary of Public Law Regulation of Reproductive Rights in My Country)' [2020] Renmin luntan – Xuexu qianyan 人民论坛•学术前沿, 108

Wang Liqing 汪丽青, 'Lun Meiguo Fa Shang Sihou Shengzhi Haizi de Liyi Baohu Ji Qi Dui Woguo de Qishi 论美国法上死后生殖孩子的利益保护及其对我国的启示 (Study on the Protection of the Interests of the Children Born by Posthumously Reproduction in the U.S. and Its Enlightenment to China)' (2020) 33 Yixue yu shehui 医 学 与 社 会 130

Wang Liqing 汪丽青, 'Lendong Peitai Si Hou Shengzhi Yunyong de Falü Peitai Si Hou Shengzhi Yunyong de Falü Guizhi 冷冻胚胎死后生殖运用的法律规制 (Legal Regulation of Post-Mortem Reproductive Use of Frozen Embryos)' (2025) 42 中国卫生事业管理 182

Wang Qingjie, 'The Confucian Filial Obligation and Care for Aged Parents', *Confucian Bioethics* (Springer, Dordrecht 1999) <https://link.springer.com/chapter/10.1007/0-306-46867-0_10> accessed 8 June 2025

Wang Tian and Jiang Quanbao, 'Recent Trend and Correlates of Induced Abortion in China: Evidence from the 2017 China Fertility Survey' (2022) 22 BMC Women's Health 469

Wang V, 'So, Are You Pregnant Yet? China's In-Your-Face Push for More Babies.' *The New York Times* (8 October 2024) <https://www.nytimes.com/2024/10/08/world/asia/china-women-children-abortions.html> accessed 2 November 2024

Wang Youru, 'Introduction: Chinese Buddhist Philosophy and Its "Other"' in Wang Youru and Wawrytko SA (eds), *Dao Companion to Chinese Buddhist Philosophy* (Springer Netherlands 2018) <https://doi.org/10.1007/978-90-481-2939-3_1> accessed 4 June 2023

Wang Zeying 王泽应, 'Xin Zhongguo lunlixue de lilun tezhi, lishi diwei he weilai zhanwan 新中国伦理学的理论特质、历史地位和未来展望 (Theoretical Qualities, Historical Status and Future Prospects of New Chinese Ethics)' (2023) 52: Shanghai Shifan Daxue Xuebao 上海师范大学学报(哲学社会科学版) 35

Wangyi 网易 (NetEase), 'Fumu lishi sinian hou haizi cai chusheng? Shuangfang fumu ai ru zhenbao: qin sunzi父母离世四年后孩子才出生? 双方父母爱如珍宝: 亲孙子 (The child was born four years after the parents died? Both sets of parents loved him like a treasure: their own grandchildren)' (*Wangyi* 网易 (*NetEase*), 18 April 2024) <https://www.163.com/dy/article/J025P180054179DD.html> accessed 18 January 2025

Wawrytko SA, 'The Sinification of Buddhist Philosophy: The Cases of Zhi Dun and The Awakening of Faith in the Mahāyāna (Dasheng Qixin Lun)' in Wang Y and Wawrytko SA (eds), *Dao Companion to Chinese Buddhist Philosophy* (Springer Netherlands 2018) <https://doi.org/10.1007/978-90-481-2939-3_2> accessed 7 June 2023

Weber M, *The Religion of China: Confucianism and Taoism* (The Free Press 1968)

Weisheng bu 卫生部, 'Weisheng Bu Guanyu Yinfa Renlei Fushu Shengzhi Jishu Yu Renlei Jingziku Pingshen, Shenhe He Shenbi Guanli Chengxu de Tongzhi 卫生部关于印发人类辅助生殖技术与人类精子库评审、审核和审批管理程序的通知 (Notice of the Ministry of Health on the Issuance of the Review, Examination, and Approval Management Procedures for Human Assisted Reproductive Technology and Human Sperm Banks)' <http://www.nhc.gov.cn/bgt/pw10303/200708/6998a89f66c247469a179482dd9f930c.shtml> accessed 26 April 2025

Weisheng bu 卫生部, 'Weisheng bu guanyu xiuding renlei fuzhu shengzhi jishu yu renlei jingzi ku xiangguan jishu guifan, jiben biaozhun he luli yuanze de tongzhi 卫生部关于修订人类辅助生殖技术与人类精子库相关技术规范、基本标准和伦理原则的通知 (Notice of the Ministry of Health on the Revision of Technical Specifications, Basic Standards, and Ethical Principles Related to Human Assisted Reproductive Technology and Human Sperm Banks)'

Weisheng bu 卫生部, 'Weisheng Bu Guanyu Yinfa Renlei Fuzhu Shengzhi Jishu Yu Renlei Jingzi Ku Jiaoyan Shishi Xize de Tongzhi 卫生部关于印发人类辅助生殖技术与人类精子库校验实施细则的通知 (Notice of the Ministry of Health on the Issuance of the Implementation Rules for the Inspection and Verification of Human Assisted Reproductive Technology and Human Sperm Banks)' <http://www.nhc.gov.cn/bgt/pw10604/200606/9ce14a2958214ef5936153115707d827.shtml> accessed 26 April 2025

'Western Eyes on China's Eugenics Law' (1995) 346 The Lancet 131

'What's the Difference Between Morality and Ethics? | Britannica' <https://www.britannica.com/story/whats-the-difference-between-morality-and-ethics> accessed 15 August 2022

Whitehouse PJ, 'The Rebirth of Bioethics: A Tribute to Van Rensselaer Potter' (2001) 14 Global Bioethics 37

Whittaker A, 'From "Mung Ming" to "Baby Gammy": A Local History of Assisted Reproduction in Thailand' (2016) 2 Reproductive Biomedicine & Society Online 71

Whittaker A, Gerrits T, and Weis C, 'Emerging "Repronubs" and "Repropreneurs": Transnational Surrogacy in Ghana, Kazakhstan, and Laos' (2022) 63 International Journal of Comparative Sociology 304

'Why Delhi High Court Approved Parents' Request for Their Dead Son's Sperm' *The Times of India* (11 October 2024) <https://timesofindia.indiatimes.com/etimes/trending/why-delhi-high-court-approved-parents-request-for-their-dead-sons-sperm/articleshow/114153469.cms> accessed 28 June 2025

Whyte MK, Feng W, and Cai Y, 'Challenging Myths About China's One-Child Policy' (2015) 74 The China Journal 144

Wilde L, 'Introduction: Marx, Ethics and Ethical Marxism' in Wilde L (ed), *Ethical Marxism and its Radical Critics* (Palgrave Macmillan UK 1998) <https://doi.org/10.1007/978-1-349-26865-8_1> accessed 17 June 2023

Williams B, *Ethics and the Limits of Philosophy* (Collins and Fontana 1985)

'"Wombs for Rent" Business Flourishes in Communist Laos | Reuters' <https://www.reuters.com/article/world/wombs-for-rent-business-flourishes-in-communist-laos-idUSKBN18Z0CW/> accessed 21 July 2025

Wong D, Cultivating the Self in Concert with Others' in Amy Olberding (ed), *Dao Companion to the Analects* (Blackwell 2013)

Woolf V and Gualtieri E, *On Not Knowing Greek* (Hesperus Pr 2008)

Woolston C, 'Nature Index Annual Tables 2023: China Tops Natural-Science Table' [2023] Nature <https://www.nature.com/articles/d41586-023-01868-3> accessed 28 February 2024

Wu Guide 吴桂德, 'Deguo Fa Shang Renlei Tiwai Peitai de Falü Baohu Ji Qi Jiejian 德国法上人类体外胚胎的法律保护及其借鉴 Legal Protection of the Human Embryos In-Vitro-Fertilization in German Laws and Its Reference' [2020] Jiaoda Faxue 交大法学 86

Wu Zhaohua, 'Conflicts between Chinese Traditional Ethics and Bioethics' (1994) 3 Cambridge Quarterly of Healthcare Ethics 367

Wu Zhihong 吴志红 and Dai Ruxin 戴汝馨, 'Woguo Zhengzhi Daiyun Luan Xiang de Xingzheng Zhili Kunjing Ji Kefu Lujing W 我国整治代孕乱象的行政治理困境及克服路径 (The Preidcament of Administrative Governance of Surrogacy in China and Paths to Overcome It)' [2025] 卫生软科学 1

Xi Jinping 习近平, *Zai zhexue shehui kexue gongzuo zuotanhui shang de jianghua* 在哲学社会科学工作座谈会上的讲话 (*Speech at the Symposium on Philosophical and Social Science Work*) (Renmin chubanshe 人民出版社 2016)

Xi Jinping 习近平, 'Xi Jinping Zia Shenbuji Zhuyao Lingdao Ganbu Xuexi Guanche Dang de Shiba Jie Wu Zhong Quanhui Jingshen Zhuanti Yantao Ban Shang de Jianghua 习近平在省部级主要领导干部学习贯彻党的十八届五中全会精神专题研讨班上的讲话_共产党员网 (Xi Jinping's Speech at the Seminar for Provincial Level Leading Cadres to Study and Implement the Spirit of the Fifth Plenary Session of the 18th CPC Central Committee)' (*Gongchandang yuanwan* 共产党员网) <https://news.12371.cn/2016/05/10/ARTI1462820587609178.shtml> accessed 25 June 2024

Xiao Yongping, Li Jue and Zhu Lei, 'Surrogacy in China: A Dilemma Between Public Policy and the Best Interests of Children' (2020) 34 International Journal of Law, Policy and the Family 1

Xiao Hongen 萧 宏恩, 'You Moxue duanshi dangdai yiliao kejixia renzhi shenming zunyan 由墨学端视当代医疗科技下人之生命尊严 La dignità della vita umana nell'ambito della tecnologia medica contemporanea nella prospettiva del Mohismo' (2018) 20 Wuhan keji daxue xuebao 武汉科技大学学报 635

Xie Tingyu 谢廷玉, 'Makesi zhuyi lishi lilun yu lunli sixiang de rong tong – Yinguo xuezhe Bauluo Bulaike liqi jiaoshuo fangtan 马克思主义历史理论与伦理思想的融通 —— 英国学者保罗・布莱克里奇教授访谈 (The Connection between Marxist Theory of History and Ethical Thought: An Interview with Professor Paul Blackledge)' [2022] Makesi zhuyi ye xianshi 马克思主义与现实 95

Xinhua, 'China to Crack down on Surrogacy Industry' (*People's Daily Online*, 15 April 2015) <http://en.people.cn/n/2015/0410/c90785-8876190.html> accessed 1 February 2025

Xinhua she 新华社, 'Zhonggong Zhongjian Yinfa "Guanyu Jiakuai Goujian Zhongguo Tese Zhexue Shehuikexue de Yiijian" 中共中央印发《关于加快构建中国特色哲学

社会科学的意见》_最新政策_中国政府网 (Opinions on Accelerating the Construction of Philosophical and Social Sciences with Chinese Characteristics Issued by the Central Committee of the Communist Party of China)' <https://www.gov.cn/zhengce/2017-05/16/content_5194467.htm> accessed 17 June 2023

Xinhua wang 新华网, 'Guanyu "sheng haizi" de naxie zhengce — — zhongguo renkou zhengce yanbian "bian nianshi" 关于"生孩子"的那些政策 — — 中国人口政策演变"编年史"' (*Xinhua wang* 新华网, 9 February 2015) <http://www.xinhuanet.com/politics/2015-02/09/c_1114311252.htm> accessed 25 June 2024

Xiong Yuezhi, '"Liberty", "Democracy", "President": The Translation and Usage of Some Political Terms in Late Qing China', *NewNew Terms for New Ideas: Western Knowledge and Lexical Change in Late Imperial China* (Brill 2001) <https://brill.com/view/book/edcoll/9789004501669/B9789004501669_s008.xml> accessed 3 November 2022

Xu Chenggang, 'The Fundamental Institutions of China's Reforms and Development' (2011) 49 Journal of Economic Literature 1076

Xu Haiyan 徐海燕, 'Lüe Lun Zhongguo Gudai Dianwi Hunsu Jiqi Chansheng Genyuan 略论中国古代典妻婚俗及其产生根源 (Brief Discuss.Ion on the Origin of the Custom of Pawning a Wife)' (2005) 92 Shenyang shifan daxue xue bao (shehui liaxue ban) 沈阳师范大学学报(社会科学版) 77

Xu Ming 徐明, *Shengming keji wenti de falü guizhi yanjiu* 生命科技问题的法律规制研究 [*Research on the legal regulation of biotechnology*] (Beijing Book Co Inc 2016)

Yang Cheng 杨成, 'Renkou Ji Sheng Fa Xiugai: Weiyuan Jianyi Na Diao "jingzhi Daiyun" Tiaokuan 人口计生法修改: 委员建议拿掉"禁止代孕"条款 (Amendment to the Population and Family Planning Law: Committee Members Propose Removing the Clause Prohibiting Surrogacy)' (*Renda xinwen wang* 人大新闻网, 23 December 2015) <http://npc.people.com.cn/n1/2015/1223/c14576-27967873.html> accessed 19 January 2025

Yang Chia-Ling, 'Competition and Change in the Discourse on Abortion in Taiwan' in Selberg R, Kolankiewicz M, and Mulinari D (eds), *Struggles for Reproductive Justice in the Era of Anti-Genderism and Religious Fundamentalism* (Springer International Publishing 2023) <https://doi.org/10.1007/978-3-031-31260-1_6> accessed 27 May 2024

Yang Haichao 杨海超, 'Woguo Minfadian Zhong de Qinzi Guanxi Queding Wendi – Yi Daiyun Shenyu We Shejiao 我国民法典中的亲子关系确定问题 — — 以代孕生育为视角 -中国政法大学研究生院 (Chinese Civil Code Problem in Defining Parent-Child Relationship – from the Perspective of Surrogacy)' (2020) 35 Yanjiusheng faxue 研究生法学, 12

Yang Linping 阳林平, 'Shengyu Quan Zhi Gainian Fenxi 生育权之概念分析 (Conceptual Analysis of Reproductive Rights)' Falü shiyong 法律适用 32

Yang Lixin 杨立新, 'Yi Fen Biaozhi Renlun Yu Qingli Shengsu de Minshi Panjue – Ren de Tiwai Peitai Quan Shu Zhengyi an Ershen Panjue Shi Ping 一份标志人伦与情理胜诉的民事判决 —— 人的体外胚胎权属争议案二审判决释评 (A Civil Judgment That Marks the Victory of Human Ethics and Reason: Commentary on the Second-Instance Judgment in the Case of the Dispute over the Ownership of Human in Vitro Embryos)' (2014) 11 Falü shiyong 法律适用 48

Yang Lixin 楊立新, 'Tongxing tongju zhe yuqi suo sheng zinü de qingzi guanxi rending – yi zhao "Minfa dian" guiding de qinzi guanxi guize zhi jiedu 同性同居者与其所生子女的亲子关系认定 - 依照《民法典》规定的亲子关系规则之解读 (Identification of Paternity Between Same-sex Cohabitants and Children – Interpretation in Accordance with the Rules of Parent-child Relations as Stipulated in the Civil Code) 文' (2021) 39 Hebei Faxue 河北法学 27

Yang Lixing 杨立新 and Li Yiwen 李怡雯 , 'Baozhang Rengong Fuzhu Shengzhi Jishu Suo Sheng Zinü de Sheng Dexunyan – Rending Rengong Fuzhu Shengzi Jishu Suo Sheng Zinü de Falü Diwei de Jizhun Dian 保障人工辅助生殖技术所生子女的生的尊严 —— 认定人工辅助生殖技术所生子女的法律地位的基准点 (Guarantee the Dignity of Children Born of Artificial Assisted Reproductive Technology: A Reference Point for Determining the Legal Status of Children Born of Artificial Assisted Reproductive Technology)' [2021] Zhongguo yingyong faxue 中国应用法学 77

Yang Qianqian 杨茜茜, 'Daiyun Qinzi Guanzi Falü Shiyong de Kunjing Yu Chuly 伦代孕亲子关系法律适用的困境与出路 (The Dilemma and Solution of the Laa Application in Surrogacy Parent-Child Relationship: From the Perspective of the Best Interest of the Child)' (2023) 44 Yixue yu Zhexue 医学与哲学 54

Yang Suiquan 杨遂全 and Zhong Kai 钟凯, 'Cong Teshu Qunti Shengyu Quan Kan Daiyun Bufen Hefahua 从特殊群体生育权看代孕部分合法化 (Partial Legalisation of Surrogacy from the Perspective of the Reproductive Rights of Special Groups)' [2012] Shehui kexue yanjiu 社会科学研究 77

Yasmin S, 'Chinese Woman Fighting Landmark LGBTQ+ Custody Battle Wins Right to Visit Daughter | The Independent' (*The Independent*, 14 August 2024) <https://www.independent.co.uk/asia/china/china-woman-custody-lgbtq-ruling-b2596209.html> accessed 2 August 2025

Ye Mingyi 葉名怡, 'Faguo Fa Shang de Rengong Peitai 法国法上的人工胚胎' [2015] Huadong Zhengfa Daxue xuebao 华东政法大学学报 35

Yin Li 尹力, 'Liangfa shi yu xia Zhongguo ertong baohu falü zhidu de fa zhan 良法视域下中国儿童保护法律制度的发展 (Advances of legal framework for protecting Chinese children from fine law perspective)' (2015) 249 Beijing Shifan Daxue xuebao (shehui kexue ban) 北京师范大学学报 (社会科学版) 40

You Wenting and Feng Jun, 'Legal Regulation of Surrogacy Parentage Determination in China' (2024) 15 Frontiers in Psychology <https://www.frontiersin.org/journals/psychology/articles/10.3389/fpsyg.2024.1363685/full> accessed 2 December 2024

Yu Jiyuan, *The Ethics of Confucius and Aristotle: Mirrors of Virtue* (1st edition, Routledge 2007)

Yu Jiajia 于佳佳, 'Renlei fuzhu shengzhi jishu yinyong fanwei de falü tiaozheng lun 类辅助生殖技术应用范围的法律调整论 (A Discussion on the Legal Adjustments to the Scope of Application of Assisted Reproductive Technologies)' [2024] Jiao Da faxue 交大法学 94

Yuan Li, Chia R, and Gosling J, 'Confucian Virtue Ethics and Ethical Leadership in Modern China' (2023) 182 Journal of Business Ethics 119

Zeng Pingjie 曾品杰, 'Lun Rengong Peitai Zhi Falü Diwei 论人工胚胎之法律地位——从法国法谈起(The Legality of Artificial Insemination: From the Perspective of French Law)' [2016] Jiao Da faxue 交大法学 97

Zhai Zhengwu and Jin Guangzhao, 'China's Family Planning Policy and Fertility Transition' (2023) 9 Chinese Journal of Sociology 479

Zhan Zhongle 湛中乐, 'Lun Daiyun Ji Qi Xingwei de Gongfa Guizhi 论代孕及其行为的公法规制 (On Surrogacy and Its Public Regulation)' (2024) 16 Yixue yu faxue 医学与法学 27

Zhang I, 'In China, a Fight for Reproductive Rights' (*Asia Pacific Foundation of Canada*) <https://www.asiapacific.ca/publication/china-fight-reproductive-rights> accessed 13 November 2023

Zhang Jiakai and others, 'Current Status and Reflections on Fertility Preservation in China' (2022) 39 Journal of Assisted Reproduction and Genetics 2835

Zhang Longxi, 'Translating Cultures: China and the West' in Pohl K-H (ed), *Chinese Thought in a Global Context: A Dialogue Between Chinese and Western Philosophical Approaches* (Brill 1999) <https://brill.com/display/book/edcoll/9789004501676/B9789004501676_s005.xml> accessed 20 November 2022

Zhang Longxi, 'Cross-Cultural Translatability: Challenges and Prospects' (2015) 23 European Review 369

Zhang Qianfan, 'Equality and Universal Love: Human Dignity in Mohism', *Human Dignity in Classical Chinese Philosophy: Confucianism, Mohism, and Daoism* (Springer 2016)

Zhang Yan 张园, Diao Feiyang 刁飞扬 and Liu Jiayin 刘嘉茵, 'Renlei "luanzi ku" jianshe shuping人类"卵子库"建设述评 (Commentary on the construction of human "egg bank" in China)' (2022) 42 Zhonghua shengzhi yu biyun zazhi中华生殖与避孕杂志 219

Zhang Yanling 張燕玲, 'Lun Daiyun Mu de Hefahua Jichu伦代孕母的合法化基础 (On the Basis of the Legalisation of Surrogacy)' 24 Hebei faxue 河北法学 137

Zhang Zanhua and Min Xiaoyan, 'The Ethical Dilemma of Truth-Telling in Healthcare in China' (2020) 17 Journal of Bioethical Inquiry 337

Zhang Zhengjun 张正军, 'Guowuyuan Guanyu Yinfa Zhongguo Funǔ Fazhan Gangyao He Zhongguo Ertong Fazhan Ganya de Tongzhi 国务院关于印发中国妇女发展

纲要和中国儿童发展纲要的通知 Notice on the State Council Programme for the Development of Chinese Women and Children' (2001) 21 Guowuyuan Gongbao 国务院公报 (State Council Gazette) <https://www.gov.cn/gongbao/content/2001/content_60887.htm> accessed 6 October 2024

Zhang Zhouxiang, 'Movie Should Have Made Clear Surrogacy a Crime' (*China Daily*) <https://www.chinadaily.com.cn/a/202012/09/WS5fd0181aa31024ad0ba9aaab.html> accessed 6 July 2025

Zhao Peng 赵 鹏, 'Shengwu yixue yanjiu lunli guizhi de fazhihua 生物医学研究伦理规制的法治化 [The Legalization of Ethical Regulation in Biomedical Research]' [2019] *Zhongguo fafa* 中国法法 25

Zhao Yue, 'Protection of Rights and Legal Remedies for Surrogate Mothers in China' (2023) 10 Humanities and Social Sciences Communications 823

Zheng Ge 郑 戈, 'Mai xiang shengming xian zhi – Falü ruhe huiying jiyin bianji jishu yingyong de fengxian 迈向生命宪制 -法律如何回应基因编辑技术应用中的风险 [Moving Towards Bioconstitutionalism: How Should Law Respond to the Risks Brought by Genome Editing Technologies]' (2019) 190 *Fashan yanjiu* 法 商 研 究 3

Zheng H, 'Shared Motherhood or Free Surrogacy?: Risks and Vulnerabilities in a Chinese Lesbian's Family-Making' (2022) 69 Journal of Homosexuality 1881

'Zhongguo Yixue Lunlixue 中国医学伦理学 [Chinese Medical Ethics]' <https://oversea-cnki-net.bibliopass.unito.it/KNavi/JournalDetail?pcode=CJFD&pykm=XNLX&Year=&Issue=> accessed 9 February 2022

Zhonghua renmin gongheguo jiaoyubu zhengfu menhu wangzhan 华人民共和国教育部政府门户网站, 'Zhonggong Zhonjian Bangongting Guowuyuan Bangongting Yinfa "Guanyu Jiaqiang Xin de Daifa Jiaoyu He Faxue Lilun Yanjiu de Yijian" 中共中央办公厅 国务院办公厅印发《关于加强新时代法学教育和法学理论研究的意见》 [General Office of the Central Committee of the Communist Party of China General Office of the State Council Issued the Opinions on Strengthening Legal Education and Legal Theory Research in the New Era]' <http://www.moe.gov.cn/jyb_xxgk/moe_1777/moe_1778/202302/t20230227_1047943.html> accessed 17 June 2023

Zhongyang zhengfa wei chang'an jian 央政法委长安剑 (Central Political and Legal Affairs Commission Chang'an Network), 'Zheng Shuang Daiyun Qi Yang Fengbo: Zuan Falü Kongzi, Zhe Jue Bushi Wugu 郑爽代孕弃养风波: 钻法律空子, 这绝不是无辜! (Zheng Shuang Surrogacy and Abandonment Strom: Taking Advantage of Legal Loopholes, This Is by No Means Innocent!)' (20 January 2021) <https://www.thepaper.cn/newsDetail_forward_10866725> accessed 13 July 2025

Zhou Jianghong 周江洪, 'Fazhi Hua Tuzhong de Rengong Peitai Falü Diwei – Riben Fa Zhuangkuang Ji Qi Xueshuo Jian Ping 法制化途中的人工胚胎法律地位—日本法状况及其學說簡評 (Legal Status of Human Embryos in Legalization Process – A

Brief Review of Japanese Law and Doctrinal Positions)' [2015] Huadong Zhengfa Daxue xuebao 华东政法大学学报 50

Zhu Qin, 'Ethics, Society, and Technology: A Confucian Role Ethics Perspective' (2020) 63 Technology in Society 101424

Zhu Xiaofeng 朱晓峰, 'Lun Di Shengyu Lü Shidai de Shengyu Quan Xingshi Guize 论低生育率时代的生育权行使规则 (On the Rules for the Exercise of Reproductive Rights in an Era of Low Fertility' (2004) 273 shehui kexue jikan 社会科学辑刊 59

Zhu Xiaofeng 朱晓峰, 'Lun di shengyulü shidai de shengyuquan xingshi guize 论低生育率时代的生育权行使规则 (On the rule for the exercise of fertility rights in the era of low fertility)' (2024) 0 Shehui kexue jikan 社会科学辑刊 59

Zou Linbing and others, 'The Association between Previous Induced Abortion and in Vitro Fertilization Outcomes: A Retrospective Cohort Study in Hefei, China' (2021) 262 European Journal of Obstetrics & Gynecology and Reproductive Biology 124

Index of Names and Subjects

www.ingramcontent.com/pod-product-compliance
Lightning Source LLC
LaVergne TN
LVHW102105300926
849161LV00001B/26